Salt Water Sportsman

Gary Soucie produced an entertaining and definitive text on the subject of terminal tackle. The author's well-researched information is far more detailed than anything currently available. The common quote by book reviewers is that a volume is "the definitive text" or "comprehensive work." In the case of *Hook, Line, and Sinker*, both descriptions are applicable.

The Fisherman Magazines

An essential handbook for the beginner and expert alike, *Hook, Line, and Sinker* is the ultimate guide to selecting, buying, using, and maintaining terminal tackle.

Fishing World (Keith Gardner)

It's fascinating, an omnibus of considerable wit and charm. One picks it up thinking here is a useful reference work, and ends up reading, and reading. It makes a great bedside book — going into it at random works perfectly well. Highly recommended.

The Augusta Chronicle & Herald (Bill Baab)

At last, it's here.

Asbury Park Press (John Geiser)

Here, at last, is a thorough work on terminal tackle. The author has spent years collecting the material for the book and his effort provides useful material for the veteran angler and nearly everything the beginner is likely to need for a long time.

Fins and Feathers (Ed Ricciuti)

Probably destined to become a sporting classic. A thorough, even scholarly, investigation of the most neglected and yet important part of a fisherman's gear. When he describes the worth of a piece of equipment — or the lack of it — he pulls no punches. When reading this book I tried hard to select a single chapter that was more interesting and helpful than any other. I failed. They are all excellent.

Wilmington Sunday News Journal (Glenn Dill)

Hook, Line, and Sinker is not light reading; it's most definitely a one-chapter-per-night book. It is, on the other hand, interesting and entertaining. Most important, it's eminently useful — the most useful book of its type that's come to our attention.

Outdoors Unlimited, Outdoor Writers Association of America

This is a must for any serious angler's library.

American Reference Books Annual/1984 (Ralph L. Scott)

Gary Soucie has produced a highly accurate and readable study of terminal tackle. It seems unlikely that an author could hold the reader spellbound for over 400 pages of "leaders and lures," but Soucie has a chatty anecdotal style that makes it hard to stop reading. Few libraries or anglers will want to be without this unique, colorful, and comprehensive guide.

The Washington Times (C. Boyd Pfeiffer)

A highly enjoyable, lively treatise.... It's fun to read, and I even enjoyed it better the second time around. Unlike a lot of other books, *Hook, Line, and Sinker* can be picked up at any point for profit.

Norwich Bulletin (Bob Sampson, Jr.)

A very detailed and comprehensive work. It is the best work of this type I have seen and I think over time will prove to be a bible of sorts for the serious and learning angler alike.

The Oakland Press (Don Vogel)

Soucie dares tread in this world of terminal tackle that others avoid. This book, the first to cover the full range of terminal tackle, may have arrived at the right time. More anglers than ever before are studying all aspects of fishing. This book is made to order for them. By studying such material they will continue to stay a step or two ahead.

Baltimore News American (Ed Dentry)

If it can be tied to a line or leader and is old, new, strange, or ordinary, it's in this book. Sounds boring, but is absolutely fascinating, well-written, and even funny in parts. Choice in the practical line, good for beginning anglers and old hands alike.

International Marine Books

This is a well-written book with a huge amount of fish-catching information. Ted Williams says, "Drop everything and read it." Good advice.

Minneapolis Star and Tribune (Ron Schara)

Nobody will outdo Gary Soucie. In the arena of angling — where everything is stretchable — he has achieved the impossible. The man has written a book entitled *Hook, Line, and Sinker*. There's more about the subject of terminal tackle than most fishermen know but ought to know. The mere weight of Soucie's tome makes him an unchallengeable expert on what, until now, has been a ho-hum topic. The book is filled with drawings and diagrams, and you'll never imagine how much he found to write about wire leaders.

Sports Afield

Hook, Line, and Sinker by Gary Soucie is an up-to-date guide to terminal tackle that explains everything you need to know for fresh or salt water. Choosing the correct combination can make a decided difference in the quality and quantity of one's catch. Fully illustrated with beautiful line drawings.

Pennsylvania Angler (Art Michaels)

This book is a thorough source of practical information, and it specifies the latest research findings, discoveries, and technical advances. The author's writing is clear, which makes technical details easy to read. Furthermore, the author shows you how to apply the data to your fishing, the book's most salient feature. Terminal tackle is the one subject many othewise skilled anglers know so little about. All in all, this comprehensive work on an important fishing topic is an essential handbook for angling beginners and experts.

Angler's News (Bob Roberts)

Hook, Line, and Sinker supplies about all you'll ever need to know concerning the hardware and software that makes our rods and reels perform for us. One of the most useful aspects of the book is the many simple drawings that show you how to select the right tackle hardware and then put it to use properly. In fact, these drawings have already paid off for me. . . . I retied a couple of rigs, using the preferred swivels. As a result, I'm hooking more of those sheepsheads and grunts that were stealing my bait!

Tacoma News Tribune

Just about anything an angler might want to know about terminal gear can be found between the covers of Gary Soucie's *Hook, Line, and Sinker*. A handy reference for all anglers, freshwater and salt.

Providence Journal-Bulletin (Les Boyd)

Valuable to both freshwater and saltwater fishermen. There's a wealth of information here for beginners and for veteran fishermen.

Southeast Farm Press (Pete Laurie)

Interesting and very readable. Best of all, this book will help you catch more fish. Whether you fish in salt or fresh water, *Hook, Line, and Sinker* has information you can use. You will want to read it through and then put it on the shelf for future reference. A fine addition to your fishing library.

Alaska Magazine (Tom Gresham)

This is a most valuable reference work. If you want to catch more fish, and you're serious about fishing, this book may well give you more genuinely useful information than any "how-to" book you can find. And you won't have to wade through reams of deadly dull writing to find the information you're looking for. Soucie didn't let the mass of information crowd out the humor he obviously brings to his passion for fishing. Whether you chase kings, halibut, rainbows, or grayling, there's something in this heavily illustrated book to help you increase your catches. *Hook, Line, and Sinker* has earned a prominent place on my bookshelf filled with fishing books that promised more, but delivered much less.

Hook, Line, and Sinker

The Complete Angler's Guide to Terminal Tackle

by Gary Soucie

A FIRESIDE BOOK

Published by Simon & Schuster Inc.
New York   London   Toronto   Sydney   Tokyo

First Fireside Edition, 1988
Published by Simon & Schuster Inc.
Simon & Schuster Building
Rockefeller Center
1230 Avenue of the Americas
New York, New York 10020
Published by arrangement with Henry Holt and Company, Inc.
FIRESIDE and colophon are registered trademarks of Simon & Schuster Inc.
Designed by Irving Perkins and Assoc.
Manufactured in the United States of America
10 9 8 7 6 5 4 3 2 1 Pbk.
Library of Congress Cataloging in Publication Data
Soucie, Gary.
    Hook, line, and sinker : the complete angler's guide to terminal
tackle / by Gary Soucie.— 1st Fireside ed.
      p.   cm.
    "A Fireside Book."
    Bibliography: p.
    1. Fishing rigs.   I. Title.
SH452.9.R5S68 1988
799.1'2'028—dc19   87-35619
ISBN 0-671-66152-3 Pbk.   CIP

For Shenli, Pam, and Juliette

Contents

1. A PENETRATING LOOK AT HOOKS   31
ANATOMY AND PHYSIOLOGY OF A FISHHOOK:
Points and Barbs • Offset • Bend and Pattern • Bite and Gap •
Shank • Eye • Size • Metal Alloy • Temper • Wire Size • Forg-
ing • Platings and Finishes • Baitholders • Weedless Arrange-
ments • A FEW WORDS ABOUT WORM HOOKS •
SINGLES VS. DOUBLES VS. TREBLES • ONE, TWO, OR
MORE HOOKS? • SHARPENING HOOKS • HOOK
SAFETY AND FIRST AID • NOTES ON HOOK PAT-
TERNS: Sproat • O'Shaughnessy • Beak or Eagle Claw • Kirby
• Carlisle • Limerick • Model Perfect • Siwash or Salmon •
Aberdeen • Wide-Gap • Special-Purpose Patterns (PIKE HOOK;
TUNA-CIRCLE HOOK; CHESTERTOWN; KEEL-FLY HOOK; SALMON-
EGG HOOKS; JIG HOOKS) • Double and Treble Hooks (TREBLE
HOOKS; DOUBLE HOOKS; BAITHOLDER DOUBLES)

11. C-O-R-R-O-S-I-O-N SPELLS TROUBLE   413

"When all you've got is a hammer, everything looks like a nail."

—*Anonymous*, Adage

"Man is a tool-using animal. Nowhere do you find him without tools; without tools he is nothing, with tools he is all."

—*Thomas Carlyle*, Sartor Resartus

"Men have become tools of their tools."

—*Henry David Thoreau*, Walden

Preface
to the
Fireside Edition

A LOT OF WATER HAS PASSED over the gills since *Hook, Line, and Sinker* was first published. As I set about updating some of the information for this edition, I was struck by how little terminal tackle has changed over the past five years. Pheremone- and protein-based scents have come on strong, and photorealistic lure finishes have pretty much faded from the scene, but most of the recent angling advances have been in rods, reels, and electronics. I've reconfirmed my thoughts about some of the things I wrote five years ago and changed my mind about others; in some cases I've changed my mind back again. This edition reflects those convictions and confusions. I'd like to be consistent, but I'm glad that fishing remains an insoluble puzzle.

Being the author of fishing books, I am regarded by some as an expert. I prefer to think of myself as an amateur, a lover of the sport. I love fish and I love fishing, as much for their vagaries as for anything else. Each time I go fishing, I learn something. Sometimes I learn a lot of things. Some of the things I learn are so obvious, I wonder why I didn't learn them long ago. But I guess I'm glad I didn't. Once I really understand fish, and know everything about fishing, I hope I have the good sense to take up pinochle or politics or something else I don't understand. In the meantime, I have taken up the mysteries of fly-fishing and offshore trolling. Their reputations to the contrary, so far the former has turned out to be a lot more strenuous than the latter. Try to imagine a 15-kilometer hike, in chest waders and under the midnight sun, over the rugged terrain and through the alder forests of Swedish Lapland. I can't, and I did it.

Having tried most of the forms of fishing I have heard about, I have learned some useful things: first, that technology and cost have little to do with satisfaction in fishing; second, that each fish and each form of fishing has something very special going for it; and finally, that the bumper sticker is right: "Even a bad day of fishing is better than a good day at work."

New York City, alas
October 1987

Preface

*And in this Discourse I do not undertake to say all that is known, or may be said
of it, but I undertake to acquaint the Reader with many things that are not
usually known to every Angler; and I shall leave gleanings and observations
enough to be made out of the experience of all that love and practise this
recreation, to which I shall encourage them. For Angling may be said to be like
the* Mathematicks, *that it can ne'er be fully learnt; at least not so fully, but
that there will still be more new experiments left for the trial of other men that
succeed us.*

—IZAAK WALTON, *The Compleat Angler*

ORIGINALLY, I hadn't intended to write a book at all. All I was
trying to do was to get answers to some questions about fishing
tackle that had come to perplex me. Things like why swivels so
often won't swivel, whether carbon-steel hooks are inherently superior to those of stainless steel, and how to tie knots that will
actually hold terminal rigs together. But you know how it is when
you dig into things—especially when the digging is tough and the
answers are interesting: you just have to tell someone else about
it. First it was just a tackle tip here, then an article there. Before
long, I had launched into a book.

The entire process, from head-scratching to book-writing, was
so gradual that I can't recall just when I finally decided to write a
book. But I remember all too well how that decision's announce-
ment was received by my angling acquaintances. "You mean to tell
me," one of them asked in what I hoped was hyperbolic incredulity, "that you intend to write a whole book on terminal tackle?
That you actually propose to devote entire chapters to things like
sinkers and snaps? Sinkers, for crying out loud?" As he went on
in this vein, it became apparent that his incredulity was genuine.
Not all of my fishing friends were quite so strongly convinced that
I had finally taken total leave of my senses, but they were skepti-
cal about the book.

I guess I can't blame them. After all, fishing sages far more celebrated and blessed with greater credentials than I have seldom devoted more than a few paragraphs or pages to terminal tackle—a chapter at the very most. But, while the skepticism of my fishing buddies wasn't exactly encouraging, it wasn't entirely discouraging, either. I knew, for example, that there was plenty of information for a chapter on sinkers. And their doubts confirmed my conviction that such information wasn't well known. I also knew that some widely held information on terminal tackle was little more than fanciful folklore, and that there was record to be set straight as well as to be set forth.

Once I got well into the research and writing of this book, my angling friends started coming around. They became quite interested in what I was discovering, and some of them even came to think the book was a good idea.

In my innocence, I had set out to get to the very bottom of the subject—to write the last word on terminal tackle. It wasn't long before I was overwhelmed by the enormity of the project. The subject was bigger and more complicated than I had imagined: There is no solid bottom to it, and the last word will be a long time coming. In the end—thanks to some people in the terminal-tackle industry who took the time to pass on a lot of information and advice—I decided to take my sails in a little and follow Izaak Walton's lead merely "to acquaint the Reader with many things that are not usually known to every Angler." As you can see from the heft of this volume, it was a path well taken.

Many people have had a hand in the development of this book, and without their help I couldn't have written it. I must take full responsibility, though, for the information that finally made it to print. I hope that I translated their information faithfully and well, that I haven't garbled it too much.

Of all those who helped, one man deserves a full share of the credit for this book's existence. He is Bob Roberts, who until his retirement in 1977 was "Mr. Stren" to fishermen and fishing writers in Du Pont's public-affairs department. Back when I first took up surf-fishing and ran into all sorts of new problems with knots and lines, it was Bob Roberts who took the time to write a four-page, single-spaced letter in answer to a lot of ingenuous questions. What's more, Bob Roberts also invited me to attend one of the seminars for sales representatives and fishing writers at "Stren University," which is what Du Pont engineers call the fishing-line division's test laboratories. There I discovered how complicated some of my dumb questions were, and how interesting the answers, even partial answers. After two days of testing knots on the Instron tensile-strength tester, running abrasion tests, looking through a scanning electron microscope, and talking to all sorts of chemists, engineers, and technicians, I was hooked. There was a whole dimension to tackle that most fishermen never get to see—one that, properly understood and applied, might make a world of difference in their fishing.

After that short course in polymer chemistry, I got into metallurgy, corrosion electrochemistry, and tribology when Rip Cunningham gave me the green light to research and write an article on seawater corrosion of fishing tackle for *Salt Water Sportsman.* Next thing you know, I had fired off a long, detailed book proposal to my agent.

This whole book is barely long enough to acknowledge all my indebtedness and to express my gratitude to all those who furnished information, technical data, test samples, catalogs, and the like. Even listing and identifying them all would take too much space. But a few gave so much of their time and expertise, sat through so many a long telephone conversation, and answered so many a long letter, that I must single them out for special thanks. Fishing-tackle people are a peripatetic lot, so some of them may no longer be with the companies listed, but you have to stop updating sometime: Consulting metallurgist Frank J. Ansuini, formerly with Kennecott's now-defunct Ledgemont Laboratory; Pete Renkert of Bead Chain Tackle Co.; Rod Towsley, formerly with Berkley & Co., Inc., and Berkley's Bob Knopf and Paul Johnson; Paul F. Sautter of the Dragon Fly Co., Inc.; John Hansen, Jack McKearin, Charlie Booz, Frank Zumbro, and Sam Waltz of E. I. Du Pont de Nemours & Co., Inc.; Lloyd Paulsen of Lakeland Industries; Frank Johnson of Mold Craft, Inc.; Klaus J. Kjelstrup of O. Mustad & Son (USA) Inc.; T. Smedsland of O. Mustad & Sön A.S.; Jack Frohlich of Rome Manufacturing Co.; John E. Spriggs of Sampo, Inc.; Christophe Viellard of VMC Pêche (Hameçons); Tony Pierson and John M. Sweeney of Wright & McGill Co. They helped well beyond the bounds of corporate duty or common courtesy. As for the others—who are represented by more than a hundred file cards, numerous file folders of correspondence and information, a two-and-a-half-foot stack of catalogs, and several large cartons full of measured, weighed, tested, and finally tangled product samples—space prohibits my naming them all, but many are mentioned by name or by company in the text. They all know who they are, and my thanks go out to them.

And I am indebted, too, to a great many authors of books and articles on fishing and fishing tackle. First, for getting and keeping me interested in the finest of all pastimes; second, for furnishing information and piquing my curiosity. As for my fishing companions who had to put up with a lot of tackle-testing and jaw-flapping, their patience and good humor were indispensable to my own enjoyment of this project. As Izaak Walton himself said, "In writing of it I have made myself a *recreation* of a *recreation*." Of all things that fishing can or ought to be, fun is the first of them.

Introduction: Getting Down to the Business End

IT USED TO MYSTIFY ME, how often I would see two anglers fishing side by side, to all appearances using the same tackle, bait, and techniques, yet one of them was loading up a stringer and the other wasn't getting much more than a slow burn. I used to credit the difference to that great imponderable, luck, but I know better now. If I can't detect any differences in their topside approaches to the same angling situation, I will look underwater, to their terminal tackle. That usually is where I discover the difference, and the difference is often quite small. Sometimes it is a matter of only a fraction of an ounce in sinker weight, a single wire size in hooks, a few inches in leader length. It doesn't take much to turn a potential skunking into a limit of fish. In fishing, little things mean a lot.

In his fine book, *The Art of Angling,* published in Canada nearly two decades ago, the Outdoor Editor of the *Toronto Telegram* wrote, "I would say that 85 percent of the lack of success in angling is because terminal tackle is not properly understood." I don't know where Tiny Bennett got his percentage figure (I suspect he plucked it out of thin air), but I certainly can't find fault with the gist of his argument. Terminal tackle is the business end of the whole fishing rig, the only part that fish get a chance to look over. If a fish rejects or is repelled by your underwater offering, you might as well chuck the rest of your gear. A single swivel that doesn't swivel properly can render the rest of an outfit utterly ineffective, no matter how much money was laid out on it. And, because so few fishermen really know how to choose and use them well, swivels often don't swivel properly.

Most anglers take it upon themselves to learn a good bit about their rods and reels. They spend a fair amount of money on them and take pretty good care of them. But those same anglers spend precious little time or money on their terminal tackle. Yet I'll bet that for every fish lost to a bad rod or balky reel, several more— maybe even dozens more—are lost to ill-considered, improperly rigged, or poorly maintained terminal tackle. A knowledgeable angler hand-lining a proper terminal rig can, I'm convinced, outfish another who is using the finest reels and the fanciest rods but the wrong terminal gear, no matter whether they are fishing in some fabled fishing Eden like the Florida Keys or in some murky pond close to home. To my knowledge, no one yet has caught a fish on fancy rod wrappings or costly cork handles, but I have seen many a fish lost to bad snaps and cheap hooks. To get the biggest bang for your angling buck, you've got to mind how you spend your pennies, too.

Maybe it's because terminal tackle is relatively cheap and unglamorous that fishermen pay so little attention to it. Or maybe it's because the unseen fish that doesn't strike or the bite that doesn't become a hookup isn't as obvious an indicator of tackle failure as are backlashed reels or rods that won't cast well. Whatever the reasons, fishermen give short shrift to terminal tackle, and the angling results speak for themselves.

Finding out about terminal tackle isn't easy. Most of it must be discovered by trial and error and by word of mouth, two methods that are discouragingly time-consuming and inefficient. Some useful information can be gleaned from the better books on fishing, and the outdoor magazines do publish helpful articles on the subject. Mostly, though, the printed information on terminal tackle occurs as the odd chapter here or the pertinent paragraph there. It isn't that fishing writers are a lazy lot, or that they are withholding information so they can outfish their fellows; it's just that there truly is a dearth of solid information available. Even the manufacturers don't know as much as they should about the terminal tackle they make. And what little they know they seldom tell, because no one seems to care. It's a vicious circle.

The manufacture and sale of rods, reels, and other relatively expensive, brand-name tackle components is a highly competitive, highly profitable enterprise. Competing for the fishing public's attention and interest—to say nothing of its patronage and market allegiance—the makers of such tackle fall over themselves explaining their wares to the angling audience. Much of what they publish, of course, is mere puffery, the standard, unsubstantiated claims of more and better. But sometimes the heat of competition forces them to back their advertising claims, to explain the whys and hows of using their products to best piscatorial advantage. So they will sometimes run full-page ads and publish big, four-color catalogs that fairly bristle with tackle tips and angling hints. Some tackle companies even publish their own fishing annuals or informational booklets and brochures of tips, tactics, and techniques. It is a great boon to the angling public for, self-promotional as all that literature surely is, it usually is educational as well.

Alas, no such educational subindustry exists for most terminal tackle. Even promotional flack on the subject is fairly light. Only the manufacturers of lures, lines, and hooks do much promotion, and in many cases even their educational profile isn't very high. Our lures will catch more fish because they look and act more natural, they tell us; our lines are thinner, limper, stronger, tougher; our hooks are stronger, sharper, more reliable. Seldom do they explain in useful detail just how or why their products are better, or how we anglers might best employ them.

Mostly, though, the terminal-tackle "industry" isn't much of an industry at all, and the companies that make sinkers, snaps, swivels, and the rest tend to be quite small. In fact, it is almost a cottage industry, run without benefit of engineering, design, or test staffs. Many manufacturers don't even have their own promotion departments. They rely instead on outside advertising and public-relations firms that employ pinstriped people who aren't sure whether a safety snap is something that goes on a fishing line, a baby diaper, or a nuclear warhead. Judging by the high proportion of junk on the market, quality control is another department much of the terminal-tackle industry does without. A lot of the terminal tackle on the American market is made overseas—mostly Japan—and the American importers tend to know little about it except how to get it onto the shelves of discount department stores.

Very few manufacturers of terminal tackle can afford to advertise much, if at all. Most anglers buy terminal tackle generically rather than by brand anyway; whether that is a cause or a result of the nonadvertising I can't say. Because the makers don't advertise, few publishers of outdoor magazines or fishing newspapers feel compelled to devote many of their valuable pages to the subject. Still, you can't lay all the blame on the publishers; it's the old squeaky-wheel syndrome: There aren't many terminal-tackle advertisers pushing for editorial space on the subject, and seldom do angling readers write to complain about the paucity of coverage. The vicious circle again.

I wish I could promise that the information in the following pages is all there is to know about terminal tackle, or all that you need to know to become a great sportfisherman. It isn't. Nor will all the tips and hints work all the time. If fishing were that easy, it wouldn't be half so much fun. Mystery is one of fishing's great attractions, and angling is still more art than science. General principles are important, but there are no hard-and-fast rules. Weather conditions, water chemistry, and a lot of other factors outside your control affect the outcome. Sometimes the sensitive touch, the intuitive hunch, and even plain dumb luck come into play. But sensitivity, intuition, and luck are hard to come by; mostly, you either are born with them or not. And none can be counted upon to save the day. So knowledge isn't everything in fishing, but it is the first thing, the great equalizer. Everyone is born with the same amount of fishing savvy: none. It must all be learned.

Because terminal tackle is so important in fishing, it pays to learn as much about it as you can. Knowledge breeds confidence, and confidence breeds success. The angler who knows his gear will fish it with authority, and the authoritative angler is almost always a successful one. There are several psychological and mechanical reasons why this is so, but one reason stands out above all others. The confident, authoritative angler simply spends more time fishing and less time fiddling. He who lacks knowledge lacks confidence, and he who lacks confidence spends too much fishing time doing something else: wondering and worrying, changing baits and tackle, looking around to see what everyone else is using. Or just plain looking for excuses. No bait, no lure, no terminal rig can catch fish when it isn't in the water. And the wrong bait or rig won't catch fish if it's soaked all day long. So knowledge and confidence go hand in hand.

Everyone gets skunked now and then—even the single-species specialists and tournament pros. Still, those who know what they are doing get skunked less often. Catching fish may not be the most important thing about fishing, but it makes all the rest—the companionship, the fresh air, the scenery, the communion with nature—that much more satisfying. Show me an angler who says he doesn't care whether he catches any fish and I'll show you a liar or a fisherman who is using a hookless practice-casting outfit. Successfully attracting and hooking fish is what fishing is all about; successfully playing and landing them is part of the *métier*. Feasting one's eyes upon a fish's wild beauty is one of the great tonics in life; feasting on a fish's fresh-caught wild flesh also ranks pretty high in my book.

No matter why you go fishing—whether you eat or release the fish you catch—you will be more successful and have more fun at it if you learn to use terminal tackle wisely and well.

1

A Penetrating Look at Hooks

DON'T ASK ME how they do it, but the top hook manufacturers somehow manage to turn out a precision-quality product at a bargain-basement price. I suppose we are fortunate indeed that such good hooks are available at such low prices, but I can't help wondering whether we mightn't be better off if hooks cost a great deal more. Then we might appreciate them more and take better care of them.

Time was when hooks were so highly valued they figured prominently in the barter economies of many societies around the world. In fact, symbolic hooks were made specifically for use as currency. When the British took over the island of Ceylon (now Sri Lanka) in 1815, "hook silver" was legal tender and remained so for quite a few years afterward. Even during the early years of this century, a traveling man could fare pretty well over much of the globe as long as he had plenty of fishhooks to trade for the necessities of life.

Thanks to mass production and to great technical advances in metallurgy and manufacturing, to say nothing of the great leaps forward in international commerce, fine fishhooks are today readily available even in the farthest corners of the world, and the traveler would be advised to have something other than hooks jingling in his pocket. The modern hooks that we take so much for granted are vastly superior to those much-prized hooks of

31

yore in virtually every respect: stronger, sharper, more durable, more versatile.

Don't be misled by a fishhook's apparent simplicity. It may be nothing but a crooked piece of wire that is sharpened to a point on one end, but the modern fishhook is also an instrument of considerable sophistication and complexity, a true marvel of design and metallurgical genius. Still, some of today's tempered-steel hooks are based on ancient, primitive patterns. The Tuna-Circle hook is nothing but a modern adaptation of the ancient Ruvettus hooks that the South Pacific islanders fashioned out of wood, bone, tortoiseshell, whale ivory, and other materials, often in lashed-together combinations.

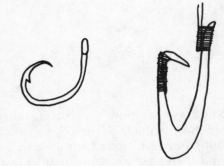

Tuna-Circle and Ruvettus Hooks

The catalog put out by O. Mustad & Sön of Gjøvik, Norway, the world's largest manufacturer of fishhooks, lists two steel hooks that more nearly resemble the Stone Age gorges that were designed to catch fish by getting caught crosswise in the throat.

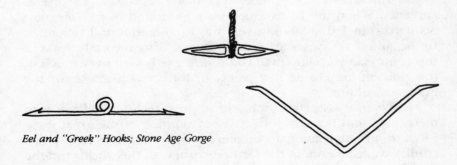

Eel and "Greek" Hooks; Stone Age Gorge

The one on the left is an eel "hook," and the one on the right is manufactured for sale exclusively in Greece, where its intended use is—dare I say it?—Greek to me.

In *The Compleat Angler,* Izaak Walton described how to make most items of tackle—even how to braid lines out of the long white hairs from the manes and tails of horses—but when it came to hooks he advised buying manufactured ones. In Walton's day the world's hook-making industry was pretty much centered in Great Britain, particularly in and around the English village of Redditch, in Warwickshire near the steel city of Birmingham. Things are very different now. Ten decades ago there were still dozens of hook-makers in and around Redditch. Some dozens more were located elsewhere throughout Britain, and perhaps a few dozen more were scattered across the European continent. Today the hook-making industry is more geographically diversified, but a majority of all the top-quality hooks made come from just a handful of manufacturers: Mustad in Norway and Singapore; Wright & McGill (the makers of Eagle Claw hooks) in Denver; VMC Pêche in Morvillars, France; Sealey and Partridge and a few holdovers in Redditch; and a very few others, less well known, in Belgium, Sweden, and elsewhere.

Not all of the hooks manufactured today are of high quality. Japanese hooks—at least the ones exported to the U.S.—are a pretty sad lot. That is an odd state of affairs, considering the Japanese appetite for fish, the technological superiority of the Japanese steel industry, and the proliferation of really fine rods and reels from such Japanese firms as Daiwa, Shimano, Ryobi, Fuji, and Kencor.

The problem isn't always low quality. For some reason, Japanese fishermen like very hard-tempered hooks. Such super-hard hooks tend to be brittle, but the Japanese fisherman would rather that a hook break than bend open. That brittle temper takes more than a little getting used to. French and British anglers also like their hooks a little harder than is really necessary, so you have to be on guard against overtempered hooks that are manufactured primarily for the Japanese, French, or British markets, no matter where they are made.

The world of hooks may no longer revolve about Redditch, but the British tradition persists. Most of the popular hook patterns were created during what I call the British Period: the Aberdeen, Carlisle, Dublin, Kendal, Kirby, Limerick, Sproat, and so on. Back when the sun never set upon the British Empire, and stubborn arrogance was not unknown in the British character, the English hook-makers went about numbering their hook sizes with utter disregard and even disdain for what anyone else was doing. Each maker had his own entirely arbitrary and irrational system, some increasing size numbers with physical size and others numbering in the opposite direction. When other companies began copying patterns, they had to retain the size-numbering system originally employed for each pattern, so to this day we are mired in a morass of hook-sizing that is an unfortunate legacy of British eccentricity.

Whether the proliferation and persistence of all the variant patterns, styles, and finishes of hooks is rational also is open to serious doubt. Fishermen are stubborn, individualistic, conservative traditionalists, and hook-makers have very little choice but to give fishermen the hooks they demand. On the other hand, experimentation and innovation also characterize many anglers, so new hook patterns and new variations of old ones are constantly being devised and developed.

Mustad manufactures more than fifty thousand different hooks—taking into account all the patterns, styles, sizes, finishes, and other variations. And there are still others listed in the catalogs of Eagle Claw, VMC, Sealey, and other makers. Making hooks isn't easy in any event. Wire of a certain size and drawn strength must be fed into a machine or series of machines that cuts the wire to length, forms the barb and point, bends the hook into shape, and forms the eye. Then the hook must be heat-treated or tempered. After that, the hooks are plated, bronzed, blued, lacquered, polished, epoxied, or otherwise finished. Then they have to be sorted, inspected, and packaged—all pretty much by hand. Some of the large big-game hooks are virtually handmade from start to finish; some makers—like A. E. Partridge & Sons—make nothing but handmade hooks.

If you are familiar with industrial processes, the above description might not sound too formidable. But let's say you had to set up Mustad's machinery to produce just one pattern of hooks, the O'Shaughnessy. Well, Mustad's English-language catalog lists nineteen different O'Shaughnessy hook styles, each with its own range of sizes, the extremes being 14/0 and 12. O'Shaughnessy hooks also come with two types of points: spear (Superior) and hollow or rolled. Some O'Shaughnessys are made of stainless steel, but those made of carbon steel may be bronzed, cadmium-plated and tinned, or plated in nickel or gold. Some of the hooks are forged and others are not. Wire sizes vary from normal to 2X strong and shank lengths from extra long to 3X short. Most of the Mustad O'Shaughnessys have straight shanks, but some are bent at forty-five or ninety degrees to form jig hooks, which have their eyes formed in a plane that is at right angles to the plane of the eyes of the regular hooks. The regular ringed eyes themselves come in two configurations, straight and bent down, and a few styles come with larger-than-normal eyes. One style, the 34091, comes with an open, soft (annealed) eye ring, and the big-game O'Shaughnessys have needle eyes. By my count, you would have to tool up to make 236 different O'Shaughnessy hooks for the American market alone.

I doubt that anyone really knows how many hooks are turned out by all the manufacturers around the globe. The Mustad people are very secretive about their production methods and sales volumes. At a recent fishing-tackle trade show, I heard someone make an educated guess that each day some fifty million fish-hooks are produced throughout the world. Several years ago a traveling salesman for Mustad received a single first order in Calcutta, India, for sixty million hooks. In 1968, the company received an order from Burma for ninety-three million hooks.

Whatever the actual figure, the number of hooks produced around the world is impressive. So is the quality of most of them. Such quality would be considered exceptional were it not standard. Substandard hooks, such as are found in most discount department stores and too many tackle shops, should be avoided because the decrease in quality and effectiveness is much greater than that in price. The differences between superior and inferior hooks can be, alas, as imperceptible as they are important. There is only so much you can tell about a hook by looking and feeling. You won't be able to discern much about the steel alloy that was used, or how it was drawn and tempered. And you would need more than a spring scale and desk ruler to detect crucial differences that are measured in thousandths of an inch or in tens of thousands of pounds per square inch.

You can play it safe and stick to the well-known and trusted brands. You won't go wrong that way, but you will miss out on the fine and sometimes unusual hooks offered by such companies as Tru-Turn, Grand Lake, Pequea, Lew Childre, Mister Twister, and other tackle companies. But before you can make an educated guess at what might be good, you need to know some more about hooks.

ANATOMY AND PHYSIOLOGY OF A FISHHOOK

Hook terminology isn't entirely standardized within the industry, so I had better label a typical hook according to the terms I have decided to use.

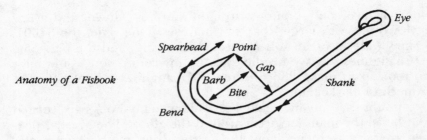

Anatomy of a Fishook

Besides these named parts and their unillustrated variations, there are a great many other things that should be taken into account when selecting a hook; among them are size, length, pattern, metal alloy and temper, wire thickness, and plating or finish.

Let's take a quick run-through the basic design variables and a brief look at how they affect hook performance.

Points and Barbs

This is the real business end of the hook—of the whole equipage of tackle, for that matter. A good, sharp point and well-designed barb can go a long way toward compensating for shortcomings elsewhere in your tackle or technique. We'll have more to say about sharpening hooks later.

Points and Barbs

Points may be formed by stamping and cutting, grinding, or a combination of these processes. Generally, ground points are sharper than cut points, and more expensive, too. Rolled or hollow points are quite effective in bait-fishing because they provide for almost coincidental lines (or vectors) of pull and penetration. A. D. "Drew" McGill's Eagle Claw hook, introduced in the 1930s, was the most impressively innovative of the early rolled-point hooks, and has been widely imitated, particularly by Mustad in its Beak pattern. Hooks with exaggeratedly curved-in points or spearheads work better on unattended lines, such as those used in commercial fishing, because you must have the patience of Job to let the biting fish get the hook point properly positioned in its mouth. Points that are parallel to the hook shank, or that are angled outward slightly, make fast contact with mouth tissue because of their raking action, but they have to be kept razor sharp and be set authoritatively.

Long, slender points penetrate faster than shorter, wedgier ones, but they are not as strong and must be set deeper to get the hook in past the barb. Initially sharper, such long, slender points become dulled rather quickly and should be touched up often. Some expert anglers claim to be able to set a short point more efficiently, but I have better luck with fairly long, supersharp, rapier-like points.

Most fishhooks have barbs, but some do not. Small barbless hooks usually are associated with no-kill or catch-and-release trout fishing, but some large tuna and mackerel hooks are made barbless so the commercial fishermen can shake their catches off the hooks and into the holds with a minimum of time and effort. Barbs are, of course, intended to keep a fish from working its way off the hook during a fight. Many anglers feel that the bigger and higher the barb, the better it will work, but this is seldom the case. It can be very difficult to drive even a very sharp point in past a big, high barb, particularly if the fish has a very tough or bony mouth. Setting such hooks isn't the big problem in soft-mouthed species; here the trouble is caused by the large hole such barbs tend to tear in tender tissues, which give the fish a pretty fair chance of throwing the hook. In general, it is a good idea to use hooks that have relatively low, small barbs. The best barbs are sliced into the hook's wire at a shallow, acute angle. Barbs that are sliced too deeply into the wire severely weaken the point.

The whole sharpened end of the hook, from the tip of the point to the beginning of the curved bend, is variously called the point, the spear, or the spearhead. I prefer the last term because the first is more properly restricted to the point section above the barb and the second confuses it with the spear point, the type of cut point called Superior point by Mustad and miscalled knife point by some. The knife, knife-edge, or filed point, commonly found in certain high-quality, big-game hooks, has a sharp edge ground or filed on the inside or outside edge of the point.

Offset

A hook's point, spearhead, and at least part of the bend may be offset to improve the chances of the point's striking flesh or bone when the hook is set on a biting fish. In an offset hook the bend is bent aside so that, when seen from above, the point is oriented at an angle to the shank. Usually half of the offset is to one side and half to the other, so that the tip of the point extends some distance beyond the plane that is perpendicular to the shank. If the offset is to the right, so that the point extends to the left, the hook is said to be kirbed, after Charles Kirby (whom Izaak Walton called "the most exact and best Hook-maker this nation affords," and whose Kirby hook was the first of the offset hooks). If the offset is to the left and the point extension to the right, then the hook is reversed.

Offsets

Kirbed   *Straight*   *Reversed*

It obviously makes no real difference whether the hook is offset one way or the other, but Mustad reports definite market biases. Commercial fishermen prefer kirbed hooks (when they use offset hooks), but sport anglers tend to select reversed hooks. In his history of fishhooks, Hans Jørgen Hurum reports that the commercial fishermen in the vicinity of a certain river's estuarine mouth on the west coast of Africa insist upon reversed hooks, but their colleagues to north and south stick with kirbed hooks. The angle of offset varies from pattern to pattern and here, too, market prejudices abound. English and French fishermen, according to Mustad and Hurum, like hooks that are only slightly offset, whereas Cuban fishermen want hooks that are somewhat more offset than the norm. The fish, I am certain, don't care.

Whether a hook should be offset or not is a debatable point. Most would agree that there isn't a single, universally applicable answer. It all depends. Clearly, if a fish has its mouth clenched over a baited hook and the angler snaps the rod to set the hook, the point is very likely to strike home if the hook is offset. If the hook is not offset, it could conceivably be pulled out without the point's making contact with the fish's mouth tissues. In the case of baited hooks still-fished on the bottom, it would be difficult for a fish to pick up the bait without taking an offset hook's point into its mouth. These will seem like unqualified assets until you look more deeply into the matter.

All other things being equal, most authorities who have taken positions on this point seem to agree that offset hooks work better on fast-biting fish, while flat hooks that are not offset seem to be better on the slow biters and bait-chewers. And, because of their unusual physiognomies, the flounders, halibuts, soles, and other flatfish are much more easily hooked on offset points.

When using strip baits, whole baitfish, and other baits in which you don't want to imbed the hook deeply, exposed offset points have a tendency to rotate so that the tip of the point is aimed at the bait. This, naturally, makes it more difficult to set the hook on a strike. With gobs of worms, salmon egg sacs, clams, mussels, and other really soft baits, though, offset hooks may be marginally better in holding the bait.

If you will be trolling, drifting, or retrieving baits or lures through the water, offset hooks will tend to revolve and spin. The same is true if you will be still-fishing off the bottom in a fast current or tidal rip. The spinning *may* be desirable—as in mooching cut spinnerbaits for salmon—but it usually isn't. For active fishing, flat hooks are the better choice most of the time. On leadhead jigs, spinners, flies, streamers, Texas-rigged plastic worms, and other small, light, single-hook lures, offset hooks are nearly always a bad idea.

Offset hooks may be quicker to strike flesh than flat hooks, but they are a lot harder to set, particularly in species that have bony, hard, muscular, or rubbery mouths. On crappies, weakfish, and other gossamer-mouthed species it makes no difference. The physics and geometry are difficult to explain briefly, but it takes more energy to set an offset hook, and the point must be moved farther to penetrate past the barb. If you have an engineer's grounding in vector analysis you will see this immediately; otherwise, trust me.

Hook strength is considerably affected by offsetting the point. The inherent strength of the bend shape is applicable only in the plane of the bend, and the offset gives a fish a head start on opening the hook sideways. Forging the hook—if it has any effect—probably further weakens an offset hook in this regard. Many offset hooks are made of heavier-than-normal wire to com-

pensate for this weakness, but others aren't. If you are fishing for
real brutes, or if you are going with small hooks on fairly heavy
tackle, your best bet might be flat hooks.

Bend and Pattern

I lump these together because the hook's pattern (Aberdeen, Siwash, Sproat, Faultless, whatever) is chiefly a matter of its bend
shape. However, some patterns are quite invariable as to shank
length, wire diameter, point type, and other features. The pattern
really is a package deal in hook design and performance. Many
anglers look to pattern first when selecting hooks, but until you
become intimately familiar with all the factors the patterns include, I'd advise selecting the individual design and performance
features first, then looking for the pattern that best incorporates
your individual selections.

The bend is the curved part of the hook from the bottom of
the spearhead to the beginning of the shank. More than any
other single feature, the shape of the bend influences the hook's
strength, penetration, and other performance characteristics.

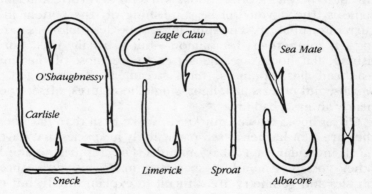

A Selection of Hook Patterns

Sharp angles in the bend tend to weaken a hook by making it
prone to breaking at those sharp angles. On the other hand, a
perfectly round bend is rather easily sprung open. Most hook
patterns have bends that are neither sharply curved nor perfectly
round. The parabolic bend was the first major improvement in
bend shape, but the more modern hook patterns have bend
curves that might be described as being asymmetrically asympto-

tic. All that mouthful of syllables means is that the bend is curved very gently on the side leading into the shank, and more sharply on the side approaching the spearhead.

Patterns like the Carlisle, Limerick, Kirby, O'Shaughnessy, Sproat, and Eagle Claw or Beak look virtually identical to the untrained eye, but a good engineer could give you more than an earful about important differences between them. Fortunately, all are good patterns, and it probably matters little whether the average angler selects one or another.

Bite and Gap

The bite—or, as Mustad prefers, the throat—of a hook is the distance from the bottom of the bend to the tip of the point, measured parallel to the shank. The gap, which some writers miscall the throat, is the straight-line distance from the shank to the tip of the point, measured at a right angle to the shank. Both of these dimensions are inextricably related to the bend shape, pattern, and hook size; however, each can and should be considered separately when selecting hooks. A hook that has a deep bite is more secure than one that has a shallow bite, because a fish can slide down away from the barb and point. A wide-gap hook can be useful in holding certain kinds of bait, in hooking long-snouted fish such as pike, pickerel, muskie, and barracuda, and in getting a barbed point set behind a thick jawbone. However, as the width of the gap increases beyond a certain point, the design begins to lose its inherent strength rather rapidly. Extremely wide-gapped hooks—such as the variously named Kahle Horizontal, wide gap, wide gape, or English Bait hook—are very weak indeed unless very close tolerances are used in manufacturing. Don't use off-brand hooks of such design.

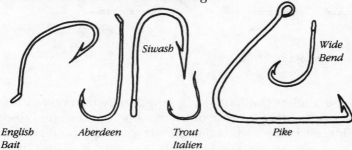

A Variety of Gaps and Bites

Shank

A hook's shank—the part between the eye and the bend—may be long or short, plain or adorned with bait-holder barbs, and straight, bent, curved, kinked, or twisted. Each variation has a different effect on a hook's performance.

Each hook pattern has a shank length that is considered normal or regular, although some patterns are much longer- or shorter-shanked than others. Many patterns are available in a variety of lengths. If the words "long" or "short" appear in a hook description, it means the shank length is the same as that of the next larger or smaller size hook in normal-length hooks of the same pattern. Add the word "extra" or the letter "X" and the variation in shank length is equivalent to that of a regular-length hook two sizes away. A "2X" or "2 extra" long or short hook is three sizes long or short, and so on. The 5X short hook is sometimes called a "half shank" hook because the shank length is about half the normal length for the pattern.

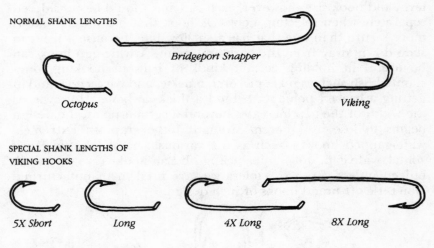

NORMAL SHANK LENGTHS

Bridgeport Snapper

Octopus

Viking

SPECIAL SHANK LENGTHS OF
VIKING HOOKS

5X Short   Long   4X Long   8X Long

Shank Lengths of Size 2 Hooks

Some anglers think of shank length only in terms of hook visibility, bait holding, or ease of unhooking, but the chief thing to be considered is strength. Long shanks provide the leverage that a fish can use to break a bend or to spring it open. In general, choose hooks that are regular length or shorter.

Most hook shanks are straight, but some are bent, tipped,

kinked, or otherwise angled to change the hook's bait-holding or penetration geometry. Such bends and kinks also weaken the shank somewhat, usually in proportion to the sharpness of the angle. To compensate, many angled-shank hooks are made of heavier wire. Simple curved-shank hooks are generally much more efficient in converting bites into hookups, particularly on unattended trot lines, jug lines, or commercial long lines. When a fish pokes at a baited, curved-shank hook from behind, the hook tends to rotate its point into play, whereas a straight-shank hook that is attacked from behind often will swing up and ahead, effectively taking the point out of play.

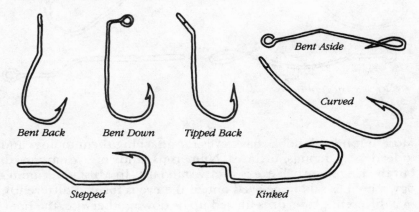

Shank Shapes

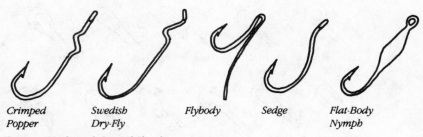

Fly-Tying Hooks with Special Shanks

Compound-curve or twisted shanks are designed to improve a hook's efficiency (the ratio of hookups to bites) by causing the hook to rotate the point and barb into play as the twisted shank is pulled through clenched jaws. But such corkscrew shanks are relatively weak, and the people at Wright & McGill candidly admit that their Messler rotating worm hook is, size for size, the weakest hook in the Eagle Claw line. Their other compound-curve hooks —the 45, 22, and 222 Automatics—are stronger. The side-stepped-shank Tru-Turn hook, which works in much the same way, is available in several patterns or styles, some of which employ thicker wire.

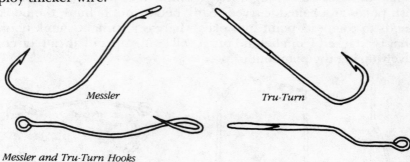

Messler   *Tru-Turn*

Messler and Tru-Turn Hooks

Eye

Most, but not all, hooks have eyes for attaching them to lines and to leaders, gangings, or lures. Numerous kinds of eyes are used, but the ringed or ball eye is pretty standard. In Mustad terminology, a hook is said to be eyed only if the eye is formed differently, in a different plane, or is turned up or down; otherwise, the hook is said to be ringed. Few other manufacturers make this distinction, and we won't either.

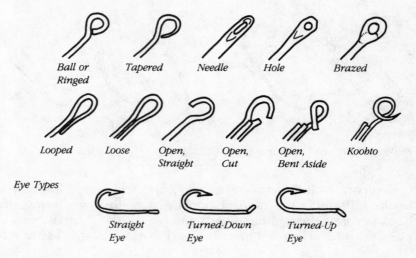

Ball or Ringed   *Tapered*   *Needle*   *Hole*   *Brazed*

Looped   *Loose*   *Open, Straight*   *Open, Cut*   *Open, Bent Aside*   *Koobto*

Eye Types

Straight Eye   *Turned-Down Eye*   *Turned-Up Eye*

Hook eyes are generally much stronger than bends and points, so strength isn't often mentioned in connection with eyes. In commercial and big-game fishing, though, eye strength can be an issue, and nothing beats the needle eye (which also permits neat and easy bait-rigging). Also popular among big-game and commercial fishermen are ringed-eye hooks whose eyes have been forged or brazed shut for extra strength.

Open eyes, which are made for easy changing of hooks on lures, wire leaders, and so on, are available in several varieties, and strength and security can be an issue. Open-shank double and treble hooks are the strongest and most secure. Most of the open-eye hooks with cut eyes are specially tempered so that you can close the eyes with fishing pliers. Usually the entire hook is specially tempered and made of slightly heavier wire. In such cases, the strength of the eye isn't worth worrying about. But don't try to reopen and reclose such eyes, because you will break them or weaken them severely. *Soft* open eyes are a different case altogether. Here, only the hook wire in the vicinity of the eye has been softened by a process called annealing; the rest of the hook is normally tempered. Such eyes are very easy to close and may be reopened and reclosed a couple or three times, but soft eye rings can be pulled open under the severe stresses of fighting trophy fish, particularly if you are using small hooks on fairly heavy tackle.

Looped-eye hooks, such as those used to tie salmon and steelhead streamer flies, are traditional rather than functional these days. Originally the open, looped eyes were used to enable fishermen to attach and detach hooks with looped leaders, but nowadays most steelheaders tie their streamers onto their tippets. The corkscrew or Koohto eye is a quick-change eye that looks less than really secure to me.

Eyeless hooks of several types are made by most of the major hook manufacturers, and a majority of the designs are intended to accommodate the manufacturing requirements of the tackle companies who use the hooks in their lures, rigs, and snells. Many

Eyeless Hook Shanks

Straight   Marked   Tapered   Marked   Spaded   Knobbed
                            Tapered

of these eyeless hooks are designed to be whip-snelled to a leader by machine, and can't be securely fastened by hand. However, the flatted, flattened, or spaded shanks are well suited to hand-snelling and are very popular in Europe, where knobbed shanks also have their adherents. Here, anglers seem to prefer hooks with turned-up or turned-down eyes for snelling. I like the spade-shanked hooks, when I can find them.

Size

Thanks to tradition and eccentricity, complete chaos reigns when it comes to hook sizes. To be perfectly accurate about a hook's size, you had better specify not only the size number but also the hook's pattern, its manufacturer, and its catalog number. Gertrude Stein's rose notwithstanding, a hook may be a size 4 in name only.

According to Mustad, a hook's size is a measure of its gap—the straight-line, perpendicular distance from hook shank to point tip. It isn't a unit measure, however, just an arbitrarily assigned number. Gaff hooks and some giant shark hooks are size-numbered according to the number of inches or millimeters of the gap, but the others are just numbered. A hook's gap, remember, is a function of its bend shape or pattern, and some hooks are naturally more wide-gapped than others, so you can't compare hook sizes just by comparing gap sizes alone.

There are some differences in size-numbering even of "identical" hooks among the manufacturers, so don't expect 7/0 Mustad and Eagle Claw Siwash hooks to be precisely the same size. Some of the shoddier manufacturers even vary the size of their hooks from batch to batch or year to year. Worse, within each pattern there are subgroups, which Mustad calls families, which may be sized a little differently. Within the Sproat pattern, for example, there are at least five or six such families. I tried—and failed—to devise some sort of rational method for measuring equivalency in hook sizes, so I could develop a nice, neat equivalent-size table. Now I know why the folks at Mustad and Wright & McGill seemed so amused when I announced my intention.

A majority of hook patterns are size-numbered so that the smallest hooks have the largest numbers; after size 1, the "aught numbers" are used, beginning with size 1/0 and continuing on up through 2/0, 3/0, and so on as the hook size increases. In the case of Mustad's odd-shaped Pike Hook, though, the system runs in reverse, with 1/0 being the smallest and size 12 the largest. Some hook patterns don't use aught numbers in their system, and the numbers may increase or decrease with actual size. In some cases, three-and four-digit size numbers are used. As I said, chaos is the rule.

However a hook is size-numbered, its size is important; sometimes it can be crucial to success or failure. Hook size should be matched to a number of things: the strength of the line and the power of the rod; the size, weight, feeding habits, and oral physi-

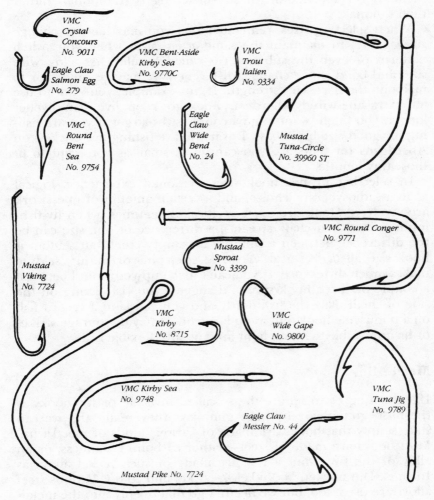

Size 4 Hooks, Compared

ognomy of the fish; the size, shape, texture, and nature of the bait. In the case of artificial lures, the hook or hooks must be of the proper weight to assure good lure action, and big enough so that a point will dig in if a fish's mouth slides off the lure. Trout fishermen often use exceptionally tiny hooks—Mustad makes them down to sizes 28 and 32—and saltwater anglers in California use hooks that New Englanders would consider downright diminutive. On the other hand, bass fishermen frequently use hooks that look awfully large for the fish, until you get used to them. A certain amount of size-matching is traditional, rather than rational.

When selecting sizes, remember that you may have to change size *numbers* to maintain the same *actual* sizes when you switch patterns or even the sub-patterns called families. As alloy, wire size, and bend shape change, different sizes may be called for to maintain the necessary strength. If, for example, you want to use an extra-fine-wired Aberdeen hook to keep live bait livelier longer, you might want to go a couple sizes larger if you are fishing for good-size black bass. But if you are fishing live crickets on Aberdeens for bluegills, you can go as small as you want to fit those tiny mouths.

In selecting proper hook sizes, seasoned experience, logical analysis, idiosyncratic choice, and a certain amount of guesswork are involved. Hook size can be critical. Sometimes, when fly-fishing heavily fished chalk streams, a difference of one size can be the difference between a full and an empty creel, but seldom is hook size all *that* critical. A single size, plus or minus, seldom makes much difference. If you can't make up your mind between a couple or three hook sizes, I'd suggest you risk erring on the side of small. Play the fish deftly and you can land a record fish on a minuscule hook, but a too-large hook may discourage strikes or be impossible to set on light lines or soft, flexible rods.

Metal Alloy

If we can agree to ignore the so-called invisible plastic hooks as the misbegotten novelty-store gimmicks they really are, we can state simply that hooks are made of various kinds of metal wire. Most hooks are made of steel—either carbon or stainless, or an alloy of the two—but a few are made of such nickel alloys as Inconel, Duranickel, M-Nikkel, Z-Nickel and so on. Various steel alloys are used, too, but we needn't go that deeply into the metallurgy.

Nickel-alloy hooks are relatively uncommon. The nickel alloys used are virtually immune to corrosion and are therefore favored by some saltwater fishermen, commercials and anglers alike. But the nickel-alloy hooks (*not* to be confused with nickel-plated steel hooks) have several disadvantages or liabilities. First, the alloys are relatively quite expensive, even compared to the finest grades of stainless steel. Second, they are a good bit more dense than steel, which makes them heavier (much heavier once the next point has been taken into account). Third, the virtually corrosion-proof nickel alloys can't be hardened by heat treatment after the hook has been shaped, and the wire can only be drawn so hard—that is, soft enough so it can still be bent and formed in the hook-making machines. A nickel-alloy wire suitable for making hooks is only about half as strong as a heat-treated steel wire of similar size, so to make the hooks strong enough the wire used must be extra thick. That makes the nickel-alloy hooks even heavier and more expensive. Some few nickel-based hooks are still made (some Siwash salmon hooks that are manufactured on the West Coast, for example), but Mustad discontinued its Z-Nickel and M-Nikkel hooks after only a few years, because of buyer resistance to the price and difficulties in making the hooks strong enough to meet Mustad standards.

Some anglers believe that stainless-steel hooks are softer (or harder) than carbon-steel hooks, that they are weaker (or stronger) and less sharp. Until a few years ago those things might have been true, because stainless steels are difficult to work with and exacting in their manufacturing tolerances. Now, all the well-known makers of high-quality hooks make stainless-steel hooks that are virtually indistinguishable from carbon-steel ones when it comes to things like strength, hardness, and sharpness. If anything, modern stainless-steel hooks have a slight edge over most carbon-steel hooks in all departments.

Once an appropriate steel alloy has been selected for its tensile strength, hardness, beam stiffness or modulus of elasticity, workability, corrosion resistance, and other physical and mechanical properties, wire is drawn to the desired diameter and degree of hardness, so that it can be bent, stamped, and otherwise worked by the hook-making machinery. Then the shaped hook is hardened by heat treatment to its ultimate strength and hardness. So far, the differences between carbon and stainless steel aren't worth an angler's worry, although industry metallurgists have to concern themselves with numerous important differences.

Good steel is better than so-so and poorer grades of steel in all respects—strength, hardness, flexibility, corrosion resistance, ability to take and hold a sharp point, you name it. Good hooks are made of good steel, not-so-good hooks are made of not-so-good steel, and so on down the line. Sometimes a shoddy manufacturer will use a good steel and ruin it by mishandling, but usually the finished hook is about as good or bad as the steel the maker began with. Much of the steel wire used to make fishhooks comes from Sweden, but some also comes from nations such as Japan and the United States. Back in Izaak Walton's day, fishhooks were made from steel sewing needles, and some hooks still are made from steel wire that is manufactured primarily for making industrial sewing-machine needles. Grand Lake Tackle's excellent Super Hook, for example, is made from such steel wire. But some other modern steel wires are as good for the making of hooks.

The stainless-steel alloys used by various hook manufacturers differ considerably from one another. The slipshod makers of cheapo hooks use really poor grades of stainless or they destroy better grades by mistreating them in the hardening. The standard marine grades of stainless steel—such as types 302, 304, and 316—are not suitable for hook-making because they can't be hardened sufficiently by heat-treating. So, special heat-treatable grades must be used. Wright & McGill freely admits that the alloys used to make stainless Eagle Claws aren't nearly so corrosion-resistant as the marine grades, and that their hooks will eventually rust away. (An advantage, W & M sometimes points out, in giving a fish that has broken off with a stainless-steel hook in its mouth a fighting chance of surviving the ordeal.) Mustad says it uses a special, heat-treatable alloy that has a high molybdenum content, which preserves corrosion resistance. Both companies make good stainless-steel hooks.

The good hook-makers, as I said before, use good steel alloys. The bad makers use steels that can be incredibly bad. Mustad, Wright & McGill, VMC, Sealey, Partridge, Tru-Turn, Grand Lake/Super, Pequea, Wilson-Allen, Mister Twister, Lew Childre, Lindy/Little Joe—I can't find enough good things to say about their hooks. As for the cheap off-brands you see in so many stores, avoid them altogether.

Temper

The final hardness and strength of a hook's steel wire—its temper—is achieved by heat treatment. A steel wire that is soft enough to be bent into shape by the manufacturing machinery is too soft to hold a scrapping fish. However, hardness in metals is a two-edged sword and there isn't anything like universal accord among anglers, angling experts, and hook manufacturers on just how hard a hook should be tempered. If it is too soft, it won't be stiff enough to resist being bent open. But if it is too hard, if it resists bending too much, it may break without much warning.

Many cheap, imported hooks are overtempered to the point of brittleness. The problem is compounded if the hook is made from a poor-grade wire that was mistreated during manufacture. Even the major-league hookmakers now and then let an under- or overtempered batch of hooks slip past their quality-control departments.

In hooks that have kinked or twisted shanks, exaggerated bend shapes, or extremely long, thin points, temper is especially important because those designs are inherently weaker than those of more "normal" hooks. For some sorts of bottom-fishing with bait I like to use those extremely wide-gapped hooks known as Kahle Horizontal or English Bait hooks, but I have learned not to use anything but relatively expensive, high-quality ones from such firms as Mustad, VMC, or Sealey. Then I know the temper will be acceptable. With off-brand versions I have run into hooks that could be snapped by tiny croakers or bent open by sunfish of quite modest weight.

Some few hooks are specially tempered soft, the Aberdeen being the best case in point. With its almost perfectly round bend (look closely enough and you will see that the curve actually is squared off a bit), the Aberdeen isn't likely to break, but its relatively thin wire (necessary for holding delicate live baits without puncturing lethal holes in them) isn't super strong. To make sure the fine wire doesn't break, Aberdeens are tempered softer than most hooks. This means you have to use a gentle touch when battling big fish on Aberdeen hooks, and it helps to use a fairly whippy rod, but it also means you can fish Aberdeens around thick weed beds or brush piles. If you get hung up, just pull steadily until the hook opens up and lets go of the offending hazard. You can bend the hook back into shape if you are in a hurry, short on hooks, or just plain tight, but the bending and rebending eventually weakens the wire by fatiguing it, and work-hardens it as well. I wouldn't worry about reshaping a soft-tempered Aberdeen a couple or three times, but after that I'd give serious consideration to tying on a new hook, particularly if there were large fish about. Most veteran 'toggers think I'm nuts, but the Aberdeen is one of my favorite tautog hooks. Sure, I lose a few of those rock-burrowing bulldogs to straightened hooks, but it is a price I am willing to pay for the high ratio of hookups to bites, a ratio that is depressingly low when I use the traditional, thick-wired, stubby-pointed Virginia hook.

Wire Size

The actual tensile strength of a hook's wire—which is a function of the alloy used, the way the wire is drawn, and how the hook is finally tempered—is expressed in so many pounds per square inches of cross-sectional area. It doesn't take an engineering wizard to figure out that, all other things being equal, a thick wire is stronger than a thin one.

As was the case with shank length, each hook pattern or style has a wire size that is normal to it, with some hooks ordinarily being made of thicker wire than others. Siwash and Aberdeen hooks are good cases in point. Both have round bends and fairly long points, yet you can't interchange the two patterns without making adjustments in size. In actual geometric dimensions, a 2/0 Aberdeen isn't much different in size from a 2/0 Siwash, but the former just can't handle the big, strong, acrobatic, sea-run salmon the latter was designed to subdue. Among the differences, the Siwash uses a wire that is quite thick for its size, whereas the Aberdeen is a fine-wired hook.

The wire-size-numbering system used in hooks is quite similar to that used in designating departures in shank length, only this time the operative words are "light," "fine," or "thin" on the one hand and "heavy," "stout," or "strong" on the other. The same numbering system with the letter "X" or the word "extra" applies, too.

Besides strength, wire diameter affects several other things about a hook's performance. Its visibility, for example. More important, its weight and action in the water. Consider, too, how large a hole a stout hook will poke in a bait. Finally, and perhaps most important, consider how wire size contributes to a hook's security in holding a fish. On tender-mouthed species like crappies and weakfish, thin-wire hooks can tear large, elongated holes in the mouth, giving the battling fish a much better opportunity to back the hook out or to throw it. On the other hand, a razor-sharp, thin-wired hook may be just the ticket for rubber-lipped species whose mouths aren't too bony. Such hooks penetrate easily and, once set, the fine wires aren't likely to tear any hook-freeing holes in the tough tissue. Be careful, though, about going too fine when the fish are big and heavy or their mouths too tough, hard, or bony; you will bend or break a lot of thin points before you can set them on such fish.

Forging

Some hooks are forged for extra strength; that is, the wire is stamped flat. This strengthens a hook because the forging makes the effective "diameter" of the wire thicker in that one dimension. Therefore, forging only strengthens a hook, increases its resistance to bending or breaking, in one plane. Because the wire "diameter" is effectively decreased in the perpendicular plane, a forged hook actually is weaker in that dimension.

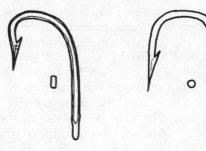

Forged and Unforged Hooks

Hooks are forged by stamping them on the side, which makes the wire thicker in the plane of the bend. (Some few hooks, particularly some VMC saltwater hooks, have forged eye rings as well.) This increases the forged hook's strength, *in the plane of the bend,* by about 20 percent, or the equivalent strength increase that could be obtained by using the next larger size hook. In the case of sidewise pressure, though, a forged hook isn't any stronger; in fact, it's a little weaker than an unforged hook of the same size and type.

Many big saltwater hooks, and particularly those designed for the big-game species, are forged for extra strength, but very few of them also have offset points. Forged wires and offset points both tend to weaken a hook, to make it easier to bend open, under sidewise pressure. Remember that. Many freshwater hooks and a lot of saltwater hooks that are intended for use on the smaller species are both forged and offset, but it is a combination that ought to be selected with care.

Like the fine-wire hook, the forged hook presents a fine edge on the inside of the bend, an edge which can rip large, hook-freeing holes in thin mouth tissues, particularly if the fish also are very strong or heavy or are energetic fighters. Except on heavy-mouthed or bony-mouthed fish, I wouldn't advise using forged hooks when fishing from bridges, piers, or other elevated platforms without benefit of bridge gaff or long-reach landing net.

Platings and Finishes

All hooks are polished by tumbling in an abrasive grit, to clean them, and some get no further finishing. Most stainless-steel hooks receive no finish coats. In one case, though, that of Mustad's 7691S knife-edge-point Southern and Tuna hook, electropolishing is used to finish a stainless-steel hook. The electropolishing does more than brighten the stainless steel; it also makes it incredibly smooth, filling in most of the microscopic surface pores that give corrosive salts a chance to pit the metal. As a result, this stainless-steel hook is about as corrosion-resistant as nickel-alloy hooks. It's expensive, though, so don't look for electropolishing to sweep the hook industry.

Some carbon-steel hooks, usually described as "bright," are not coated or plated. But most are given some sort of protective finish or plating because of carbon steel's susceptibility to rust and corrosion. Most of the common finish treatments—gold, nickel, bronze, blue—will provide adequate protection in fresh water, but if you fish in salt water you need more protection—tin, cadmium, or some other corrosion-protective finish. (See Chapter 11 for a more complete discussion of corrosion and hook platings and finishes.)

Besides corrosion protection, cosmetics is a major reason for giving a hook some sort of finish coat. Pin them down, and most hook-makers will admit that cosmetics probably plays the larger marketing role. A hook's look doesn't just catch fishermen, however—it sometimes can help to catch fish. The dark, dull finishes may be necessary to disguise the metal hooks when you are fishing for wary fish. At other times, the brightness of the hook's finish may help attract fish. Shad, kokanee salmon, yellow perch, white perch, and numerous other species may be taken on unbaited hooks with shiny gold or nickel platings, particularly if a few bright-colored beads are strung on the leader immediately ahead of the hook. Most of the time, though, it's a scientifically moot point whether a brightly plated, dull-finished, or colored hook will make any difference at all. Once you think you have it figured out, the next day the fish are likely to show the opposite preference. Experiment. Colored hooks haven't really caught on in a big way in America but, for other markets around the world, Mustad makes hooks that are finished in red, green, and copper as well as the finishes readily available here. Epoxy coatings show some signs of catching on, and I wouldn't be too surprised to see ceramic hook finishes hit the market.

Cadmium-plated hooks have long been standard in saltwater fishing, but some manufacturers would like to find a substitute, because of the hazards the metal poses to human health and environmental quality. So far, they haven't. Actually, several of the plating metals are toxic or troublesome, in the factory and in the environment.

In summary, gold and nickel platings are the ones to use if brightness is what's wanted in a hook finish. To camouflage a hook, look to the dull finishes: bronze, blue, black. To retard saltwater corrosion, use stainless-steel hooks or carbon-steel hooks that are plated with cadmium and/or tin, or use VMC's new, patented Perma Plate hooks.

Baitholders

Some hooks are supplied with a device to improve their bait-holding efficiency. The little barbs sliced into the shanks of many hooks are the best-known examples. Used with soft baits like worms, these barbs work fairly well. But they can make it hard to remove the hooks from a fish's mouth. When selecting hooks with sliced baitholder barbs, be careful not to use hooks that are sliced too deeply into the shank; such hooks will be considerably weakened. Bait must be placed carefully on baitholder hooks like these, or it won't look natural.

Less well known, but even more useful for fishing minnows and other baitfish, frogs, large strip baits, and similarly large baits, are the baitholder hooks known as Ryders. The Ryder is a second barbed crook affixed to the main hook somewhere up the shank. The Ryder barb may be brazed or wired in fixed place, or a tough plastic sleeve or some other gadget may be used to permit adjustment of the Ryder's position on the shank. Ryder hooks are relatively expensive, hard to find, and available in only a limited range of sizes, shank lengths, and patterns. You can make an acceptable Ryder out of almost any hook by whipping, soldering, or glueing (with waterproof cement, of course) a small second hook in place. Or you can use a small, short-shank hook with a turned-

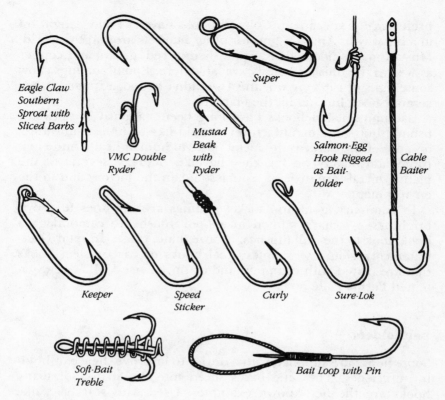

Eagle Claw
Southern
Sproat with
Sliced Barbs

VMC Double
Ryder

Mustad
Beak
with
Ryder

Super

Salmon-Egg
Hook Rigged
as Bait-
holder

Cable
Baiter

Keeper

Speed
Sticker

Curly

Sure-Lok

Soft-Bait
Treble

Bait Loop with Pin

Baitholder Hooks

up eye—the salmon-egg hooks used by trout and steelhead fishermen are perfect. Just thread the tiny hook onto your line or leader before tying on the main hook.

Various other baitholder gadgets and gimmicks have been applied to hooks, and some are quite useful. One of the most recent and clever additions to the field is Mister Twister's Keeper Hook. It is designed primarily for Texas-rigging plastic worms and other soft, fairly long plastic baits. The Keeper comes in two styles and also is incorporated into some of Mister Twister's leadhead jigs. It is nothing but a hook, to the eye of which is attached a tiny, free-swinging, barbed shank. The worm keeper looks like those barbed eyelets used by some fly-fishermen to make no-knot connections between fly line and leader. The Speed Sticker hook sold by Lew Childre & Sons is another clever design that makes Texas-rigging plastic worms easier, faster, and more certain. The Speed Sticker's eye is not a round, closed ring; instead, the tag end of the wire is bent back up again at an angle and the tip is pointed and barbed in a miniature version of the hook's other end. Similarly, the Sure-Lok hook, from Lindy/Little Joe, has its eye modified into a baitholder spade. Wilson-Allen's No-Knot Curly Hook, which comes in three sizes and two Sproat-patterned styles, has a small spiral of wire brazed to the shank at the eye for skewering the top end of the plastic worm. Various hook-makers turn out other spiral-wired hooks, both singles and trebles, that are intended for fishing doughballs, cheese, breadballs, and other soft baits. In such hooks, the coil of wire runs the entire length of the shank.

My favorite baitholder hook is both more versatile and more specialized than any of the above. More versatile, because it can be used in fresh or salt water and with a wide range of live and dead natural baits (minnows, crayfish, grass shrimp, worms, leeches, helgrammites, small frogs, grubs, grasshoppers, crickets, clams, mussels, and so on) as well as with a variety of other soft baits (doughballs, stinkbaits, bread, cheese, chicken livers, roe sacs, and so forth). More specialized, because it's a double hook that comes in just one pattern, two black finishes, and three small-ish sizes (2, 6, and 8). Jack Kenyon, president of Grand Lake Tackle Company in Colorado and inventor of the Super Hook (formerly and as aptly called the Magic Bait Hook), tells me that his wonderful little pieces of wire have caught some quite large fish; at this writing, the largest was a 100-pound sturgeon. In Chesapeake Bay, anglers have caught everything on them from spots and croakers to seatrout and even such notorious tackle-manglers as big bluefish. So far, the Super Hook is little known in salt water, perhaps because until recently it was available only in a black-lacquer finish of limited durability in the brine. Now that it comes in a special nylon-coated saltwater edition, that may change. It is just about the best flounder hook I have tried, maybe because it does such a good job of holding the mussel baits that flounders (and other fish) love, but that are difficult to keep on conventional hooks. Super Hooks do employ tiny sliced bait-holder barbs along the insides of the shanks, but it's the spring-loaded, "bowlegged" shape that really holds the bait so securely. And the hooks are particularly strong and sharp, being made of specially tempered industrial sewing-machine-needle steel.

Highly specialized hooks with all sorts of wires, pins, and harnesses are available in various parts of the country for fishing various kinds of baits. Some are so complicated, I guess they really shouldn't be called hooks, but terminal rigs. A couple of them are worth mention. Pequea Tackle sells something it calls a bait loop with pin, which is nothing more than a tapered-shank, eyeless hook that has whipped onto it a loop of braided cord. Strip baits and dead minnows can be skewered onto the pin and the loop used merely as a large, flexible eye, or the bait can be trussed up in the loop. And the looped hook can be fished internally, drawn up through a baitfish's anal vent and out its mouth with the aid of a bait needle. Similarly, and even more securely, the Cable Baiter can be used internally with whole baitfish. Used primarily in the Pacific Northwest by salmon fishermen, the Cable Baiter is made by crimping a short-shank salmon hook on one end of a piece of stainless-steel cable which has crimped onto its opposite end a pointed, flattened, and drilled piece of steel that acts both as hook eye and bait needle. Being flexible, the Cable Baiter gives a dead bait more lifelike action than do any of the long-shanked hooks, bait needles, and other rigs that are fished in this fashion. Cable Baiters come in lengths from 4 to 8 inches and in 6/0 and 7/0 hook sizes.

Weedless Arrangements

No hook is truly weedless. The hook hasn't yet been made that can be fished with complete impunity in heavy weed beds, brush piles, and other fearsome fish haunts. But some hooks come a lot closer than others.

Before we survey the weedless hooks, know that each type will, at least to some degree, cost you some fish—either because the weedless gadgetry scared the fish off or because it kept the strike from contacting the point. So don't use weedless hooks when you don't need them.

Most of the weedless hooks have some sort of wire guard attached to the upper end of the shank, near the eye, a guard that has to be spring-tempered just so. It must bounce an unweighted hook away from trouble, but let a wary fish unwittingly press it out of the way, exposing the barbed point. The single, Chicago, Wisconsin (or double), and horsecollar styles all have their advocates and detractors, but frankly I don't see much to choose between them. From time to time, all of the wire weedless guards will have to be re-formed so that their angle and aim are correct. You will see horsecollar types that contact the hook point fore and aft of the barb; those that strike the spearhead behind the barb are more prone to fouling.

Fiber and crimped-nylon weedless guards are used most often on leadhead jigs, and particularly on leadhead jigs that are employed by those patient Southern and Western anglers who practice the art of flippin', a sophisticated updating of the old cane-pole technique variously called jiggering, jigger-pole fishing, doodling, and doodle-socking. In all versions, the technique employs short flip casts to bankside cover and a patient, sensitive, bottom-hopping retrieve downslope until the jig is hanging straight down below. Why the fiber and crimped-nylon weedless guards should be so intimately associated with this sort of fishing is beyond me. I haven't used them often enough to know whether I think they are better or worse than wire guards.

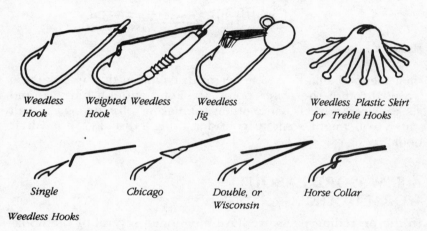

Weedless Hook

Weighted Weedless Hook

Weedless Jig

Weedless Plastic Skirt for Treble Hooks

Single

Chicago

Double, or Wisconsin

Horse Collar

Weedless Hooks

I have experimented, with varying degrees of success, with pieces of tubing to make hooks weedless. Thin, "spaghetti-type" surgical tubing and electrical-wire insulation will both work, but you have to rig the hooks carefully, to avoid making the hook "setless" as well. Texas-rigged plastic worms make a hook reasonably weedless, which, as much as anything else, I think, explains the phenomenal success of these baits on bass. M-F Manufacturing Co. makes and sells molds that enable the do-it-yourself angler to make his own weedless plastic baits called Weedless Tadpoles and Weedless Curly-Qs. Very clever.

On spinnerbaits, you can turn almost any hook into a weedless one just by securing a short, thin rubber band to the pull-loop at the wire form's axis via a girth hitch, and looping the other end of the elastic behind the barb of the hook. You can use the same technique on certain single hooks whose shanks or bends are sufficiently curved to put the eye of the hook in line with or above the point.

Eagle Claw's keel-fly hooks are virtually weedless as is, thanks to

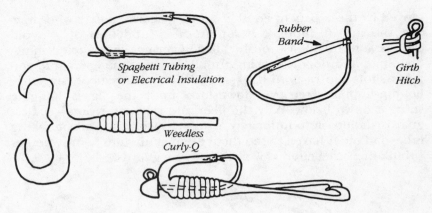

Spaghetti Tubing or Electrical Insulation

Rubber Band

Girth Hitch

Weedless Curly-Q

Weedless Riggings

their stepped shanks and a weight distribution that makes them travel through the water point up. For bottom-fishing around rocks, wrecks, reefs, and other submarine obstructions in salt water, you might want to consider using Mustad's Tuna-Circle hook.

A FEW WORDS ABOUT WORM HOOKS

In the preceding pages we have mentioned several of the hooks that are specially designed for fishing plastic worms: Keepers, Curly Hooks, Speed Stickers, Messlers, Tru-Turns. Virtually any hook of the proper size can be used to fish a plastic worm, but anglers and hook designers have discovered that certain hooks are particularly well suited to plastic worms, and especially to Texas-rigged plastic worms.

The Texas worm rig is nothing but a sliding slip sinker (often, but not always, bullet-shaped) on the line immediately ahead of a hook that is tied directly to the line without benefit of snap, swivel, or other hardware. A plastic worm is placed on the hook so that the head of the worm is slid right on up the shank and over the eye, but the rest of the worm trails away from the top of the shank at an angle so that the barbed point of the hook is imbedded it the body of the worm without protruding all the way

The Virtually Weedless Texas Worm Rig

through. Properly rigged, a plastic worm will trail through the water with a natural-looking, enticing wriggle, without hanging up on weeds, brush, stumps, or rocks. But the plastic is so soft that a proper setting of the hook will drive the point through the worm and into the fish's jaw. The old Sproat pattern provided just the proper blend of physical and mechanical properties, dimensions, and performance. In the beginning, plain Sproat hooks were used, but more recently special worm hooks have been devised, most of them based on the Sproat pattern.

Basically, worm hooks come in several shank configurations: straight and plain, straight with a baitholder barb or two sliced into the shank near the eye, tipped, bent back, kinked, side-stepped, or twisted. Some anglers also like to use keel fly hooks, and saltwater pioneers of the technique have employed a variety of other, stronger hook styles. The baitholder barbs obviously help to hold the head of the worm in place, and the altered shanks are favored by many Texas-riggers because they can get a

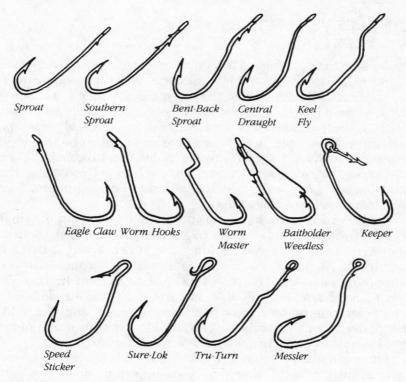

Sproat   Southern Sproat   Bent-Back Sproat   Central Draught   Keel Fly

Eagle Claw Worm Hooks   Worm Master   Baitholder Weedless   Keeper

Speed Sticker   Sure-Lok   Tru-Turn   Messler

A Sampling of Worm-Hook Patterns

worm better rigged to their satisfaction. Bass expert Tom Mann, inventor and maker of the famous Jelly Worm, favors the kinked-shank Eagle Claw Southern Sproat Worm Master, which is made with too heavy a wire (to compensate for the weakening of those right-angle bends) to suit some other largemouth gurus. They might prefer Mustad's Central Draught hook or a tipped-shank Sproat. Eagle Claw's Messler rotating worm hook has won a host of converts because of its efficiency in placing the point where it will take hold. The differently designed, but similarly intentioned Tru-Turn, which comes in a variety of patterns, including a Sproat worm hook, is so good the Defense Department rewrote the specifications for the hooks in the Army and Air Force survival kits, just so Tru-Turns could be used. Bass, which are the chief targets of Texas-rig worm fishermen, tend to attack so that they take the entire bait (and hook) inside their mouths, which makes the Messlers and Tru-Turns so effective.

SINGLES VS. DOUBLES VS. TREBLES

From time to time, anglers will fall to arguing over the merits and demerits of single and treble hooks, and some few will grind an ax in favor of double hooks. Various quasi-scientific tests of their relative hooking efficiencies have been conducted and, quite frankly, the published results have been considerably less than definitive. Philosophy, more than physics, seems to be the deciding factor with most anglers anyway. Some think treble hooks are the answer to an angler's prayer, while others are convinced that multibarbed gang hooks are antisporting. The argument, I am convinced, will never be settled.

Doubles and trebles have their places, to be sure, but the single hook is by far the best all-around, general-purpose hook. Because the single hook gives you just one shot at converting a strike or bite into a hookup, its size and pattern and sharpness are very important variables. That point has to be aimed at flesh, and it has to be sharp. With double and treble hooks, the odds of a point's striking home are considerably improved, and things like bend shape aren't nearly so crucial. That is why multipointed hooks come in so relatively few patterns and styles.

The treble hook or gang hook is the odds-on choice of lure manufacturers, and few anglers give the use of single hooks on artificial lures much thought, let alone much trial. It's no wonder that the manufacturers favor trebles, though. They want you to catch fish—so your bragging will help to sell their lures—and treble hooks can make up for a lot of ineptitude in hook-setting and fish-fighting techniques. The Helin Flatfish, for example, uses a multiplicity of tiny treble hooks, and during a long and strenuous fight is isn't unusual for a fish to keep hooking and unhooking itself on the various points and barbs that are flailing around. More than a few times I have landed a fish on a treble-hooked lure to discover that it was hooked, not *in* the mouth, but underneath the jaw or alongside the head. Once, in my youth, I caught a smallmouth bass that had missed the plug on its strike, but that had managed to snag one of the treble hooks on its caudal penduncle, the narrow part of the body just forward of the tail fin.

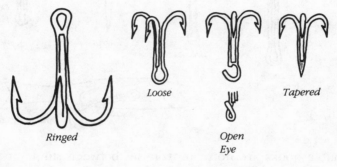

Ringed   Loose   Open Eye   Tapered

Treble Hooks

Because of the randomness of point penetration when fishing a multi-gang-hooked lure, some anglers feel that treble hooks are not sporting or that their use robs angling of at least some of its sport. IGFA won't entertain a world-record application if a treble hook was used with bait or with anything but "plugs and other artificial lures that are specifically designed for this use." As for using weighted treble hooks to snag fish, I don't care what your state's fish and game laws say about snagging salmon or shad or other food and game fish, it simply isn't sport in my book. Snag all the baitfish you want, but the snagging of game fish is just meat fishing, pure bush-league barbarism.

However much some single-hook purists look down their noses at the "sure" hooking of trebles, it is one of angling's finer ironies that some fishermen won't use trebles because they give fish too much opportunity to throw hooks. It's true, at times, that a treble hook can give a fish the leverage it needs to free itself from a hook.

Among the other disadvantages of treble hooks are the hazards they pose when unhooking a strong, *green* fish (also known as a fresh fish, one that hasn't been fought to utter exhaustion) that has been caught on a multigang-hooked lure or terminal rig. And treble hooks are particularly prone to fouling on weeds, sticks, rocks, and other hazards. They are more expensive than single hooks, too, and heavier. Nor do they work as well with pork rinds, strip baits, soft-plastic trailers, and other similar attractors.

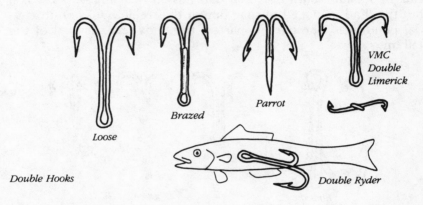

Loose

Brazed

Parrot

VMC
Double
Limerick

Double Hooks

Double Ryder

Double hooks are not compromises between single and treble hooks, although they can be used as such. For example, many a treble-hooked lure can be made more nearly weedless by removing the treble hooks and substituting double hooks whose barbs and points are oriented upward. (Or you can just snip the bottom barb, close to the shank, with side-cutting pliers.) But double hooks have their own particular uses and advantages, chief among them the fishing of whole minnows and baitfish. Various rigs and methods have been devised for using double hooks with whole baitfish, and one of the best is the so-called bait-needle rig, but the chief advantage of all of them is that the double shank of the hook can be pulled up inside the bait at the anal vent, leaving only the two bends and points exposed. In open, clear waters you might want to fish the points down, but in weeds and around brush piles or submerged timber it is better to fish the hook with the points oriented upward, snugged in alongside the bait.

Most double hooks look like trebles with one barb missing (and treble hooks are made by brazing a third barb to the shanks of a double hook), but VMC's no. 9506 double Limerick is unusual in that the offset points are diametrically opposed, which gives the hook yet another geometry when fished with a whole, dead bait-fish as described above. As for VMC's no. 9402 double Ryder hook, the eye and shanks are pulled into the baitfish as with conventional doubles, but the smaller of the two hooks is imbedded directly in the baitfish, holding it in place, and the larger barb is exposed directly beneath the bait. This hook and method of bait-rigging are popular among European pike fishermen.

I seldom use treble hooks when fishing bait, although I sometimes like to use them with doughballs, cheese baits, mussels, and other soft baits. And on trolley-line rigs for king mackerel, they are virtually *de rigueur*. In recent years I find myself more and more often converting lures—particularly spoons and spinners—to single hooks.

Homemade Hook Balance

When substituting single hooks for trebles on lures, take care that the singles are not very much lighter than the trebles you remove. Some lures, and particularly swimming plugs, are very carefully and delicately balanced to give them just the right action in the water. Lighter hooks may throw them off completely, or make their wriggles more frenetic. Generally, when substituting singles for trebles on lures, you should be using a larger size hook, and that takes care of part of the problem. You probably don't have a scale that is sensitive enough to weigh hooks, but a postage scale can be used to determine how many hooks it takes to make an ounce. Or you can build an accurate balance scale very easily, simply by twisting a piece of stiff wire. Just make sure that the hook-holding crooks at the ends of the wire are precisely the same distance from the center of the middle loop.

ONE, TWO, OR MORE HOOKS?

Heated as the argument over the number of a hook's points can be, it pales before the controversies that sometimes rage over the number of hooks there ought to be on a lure or in a terminal rig. And some of the same arguments are offered vis-à-vis sportsmanship, hooking efficiency, and so on. Removing a hook from a delicately balanced plug nearly always fouls up its action and requires the addition of a little ballast. However, because I mostly tie my own bottom rigs, I virtually never go bait-fishing with more than two hooks. It isn't a superior sense of sportsmanship (although I like to think that is part of it); it's a matter of practical efficiency. The time spent tying and baiting a multihooked rig is rarely worth the extra effort. Sometimes, when fishing for schooling species, the multiplicity of baits or lures will enhance the efficacy of the rig, but when I am fishing with a mackerel tree I know that I am fishing more for the freezer than for sport. And, effective as the multihooked umbrella rig might be for trolling bluefish, I simply won't use one. That is tackle more appropriately used by rod-and-reel commercial fishermen, not sport anglers.

In freshwater or light-tackle saltwater rigs, I much prefer to use a single, well-sharpened hook. It's safer and less apt to become fouled. But offshore I'll go with the flow, which is toward the use of two-hook rigs, the planes of the hook bends rigged at 90 degrees to each other. That way, a powerful fish isn't likely to crush the bait without encountering the hook. On the East Coast, Frank Johnson's Soft Head Pro Rigs have done much to popularize the use of heavy-monofilament two-hook rigs; on the West Coast, Allen Comstock and his Cable-Stiff Ultra Pro Rigs have led the charge of the cable-rigged two-hook brigade. Both men are among the most gifted tackle innovators I know.

SHARPENING HOOKS

Very few hooks come truly sharp from the factory. Some are better than others, but four-leaf clovers are easier to find than factory-sharp hooks. By sharp, I mean really sharp, not just pointy. A hook that is sharp enough for fishing ought to be at least a little hazardous to handle. If you don't draw your own blood now and then, your hooks aren't sharp enough.

It only takes a few seconds with a file or whetstone to make a hook truly sharp, but the cost of doing so keeps the manufacturers from taking that extra little step at the factory. Also, hooks are plated or finished after all the shaping, stamping, cutting, and grinding operations, and that finish coat dulls any point. The hook manufacturer doesn't want to remove any of that plating or finish and expose the hook to corrosion during shipment and storage. So it is best for everyone if the angler gives the hook its final sharpening. It doesn't take long, and certainly no special skills are involved.

There is a bit of a knack, though. The best way to sharpen a hook is to triangulate its point. Don't bother with those pencil-sharpener-type hook hones or those cheap little whetstones with the notch cut into them. Neither will do the job nearly so well as a small file or even a paint scraper.

A thin, sharp-edged blade penetrates more readily than a pointed object that is round in cross section. It does so because it offers less frontal-area resistance and because its sharpened edges cut their way in, whereas the conical point penetrates by puncturing. A blade-type hook point is impractical, because such a thin point would be extremely prone to breaking or bending under sidewise pressure. The best compromise between the strong (but dull) conical point and the sharp (but weak) blade point is the triangular point, a cross-sectional design that still finds its way into some swords and bayonets.

Before we get into the technique of triangulation, let's take a look at hook-sharpening tools. Many are available on the market, from small, soft, coarse whetstones and hones to expensive ceramic and diamond-studded tools. Any will do the job, but some will do it much better than others. For tiny hooks, such as those used in trout fishing, a hone is about as good as anything. But I mean a *good* hone, one that has fine pores and a hard, sharp grain

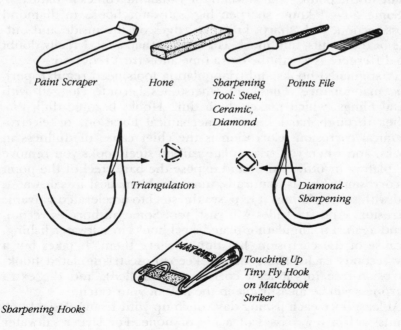

Paint Scraper   Hone   Sharpening Tool: Steel, Ceramic, Diamond   Points File

Triangulation

Diamond-Sharpening

Touching Up Tiny Fly Hook on Matchbook Striker

Sharpening Hooks

structure. But for larger hooks, like those used in saltwater fishing, and particularly stainless-steel hooks, nothing short of a power tool beats a good file. Almost any sort of file could be used, but my favorite is an ignition-points file such as can be purchased for a dollar or less at any automobile-parts store, hardware store, or most five-and-dimes. Points files are not only cheap, they are also very small. If you use a lot of rolled or hollow-ground points, like those employed on Eagle Claw hooks, you might also want to carry a round rattail file.

The properly triangulated hook should be filed flat across the inside or barbed side of the point and the other two sides of the triangle tapered away to meet on the outside of the point in a sharp angle—the sharper the better. If you can triangulate the entire length of the point, from tip to bottom of barb, better still. Begin by flattening the inside of the point, and then go to work on the sloped sides. Depending upon the size and the hardness of the hooks involved, and the "sharpness" of the file or hone, it will take anywhere from several seconds to a couple of minutes to sharpen a hook.

On really tiny hooks, triangulation isn't feasible. In such cases, just "strop" them with the file until the points feel lethally sharp. On rolled-point hooks, it makes no sense to flatten out the curved inside of the point. That is when the rattail file comes in handy.

Some guys I know sharpen big, saltwater hooks in diamond cross section, with sharp, knifelike edges on the inside and outside of the points, but, much as I admire their zeal, I really doubt the difference is worth the extra time and effort required.

Triangulated hooks and triangulating tools need regular, periodic maintenance. Files and whetstones become clogged with metal filings, which makes them dull. Hooks become dull, too, either through hard knocks, mechanical abrasion, or electrochemical corrosion. Corrosion is the chief cause of dullness in hooks, and when you triangulate carbon-steel hooks you remove the plating or other finish and expose the bare steel of the point to corrosion. This is, naturally, more problematical in salt water, and with some platings it exposes the steel to accelerated galvanic corrosion. And steel files will rust, too. Some authorities recommend against triangulating plated steel hooks in saltwater fishing, because of the corrosion, but don't believe them! It takes but a few seconds each fishing day to keep those triangulated hooks corrosion-free (or at least corrosion-controlled), and the extra sharpness will be measurable in the heft of your catch.

At least once each fishing day, touch up your triangulated hook points with a few passes of a file or hone. For larger saltwater hooks, and especially the hard stainless-steel ones, I like to use a Red Devil no. 3040 paint scraper. See your hardware or paint dealer, not your tackle-shop proprietor. The sharper you make your hooks in the first place, the less time it will take to touch them up.

Let your hooks air-dry before storing them away inside a dank tackle box. If you have been fishing in salt or brackish waters, rinse your hooks first in lots of running fresh water. You can keep steel files from rusting very badly by cleaning them regularly and by storing them in an airtight container (such as a plastic cigar tube) or in an oil-saturated rag. To clean the metal filings and accumulated corrosion from a file, use one of those gadgets called file cards, which resemble miniature dog-currying wire brushes. As for hones and whetstones with clogged pores, I've never had much luck restoring them. They're cheap; replace them.

I'm a real hook-sharpening nut, but I rarely can bring myself to sharpen all nine points on a three-treble-hooked surf plug once I hit the beach. It is much easier to spend those few minutes the night before. (Those plastic hook bonnets are a nice idea for treble hooks in your tackle box. They not only prevent tangles and cuts, they also protect those sharpened points from dulling corrosion and collisions.)

You have probably read somewhere or heard that stainless-steel hooks won't hold a sharpened point (or that stainless-steel knives won't hold an edge). That is pure metallurgical nonsense. Assuming you are using first-quality stainless-steel hooks, you won't have trouble keeping them sharp. Getting them sharp in the first place may be another story, though, because stainless-steel hooks can be quite a bit harder than those made of carbon steel, and more difficult to sharpen. Be patient, though, it only takes a few seconds longer—a few minutes more at the outside—and once you get them truly sharp they will stay sharp at least as well and as long, and probably longer and better than carbon-steel hooks. After all, corrosion, not abrasion, is the main cause of dulled hooks, and stainless steel is corrosion-resistant if not corrosion-proof. Most anglers who use stainless-steel hooks don't take the time and trouble to get them sharp enough in the first place. But with Texas Tackle's Point Maker, it takes little time and is no trouble at all to sharpen even the biggest stainless-steel hooks. Inventor Darrell Lehmann says you can even use it to sharpen flying gaffs! There is *no* excuse for fishing with dull hooks.

How sharp is sharp enough? Sharp enough so that you must be very careful in handling your hooks. There are several ways to test hook sharpness, all of which are potentially hazardous. The one I like best, because it is the least likely to send you to the emergency room, also is the simplest. Holding the sharpened hook gently by the eye (or by the leader, snell, or lure just above the hook), drag the hook—slowly, carefully, and without any downward pressure!—across your calloused palm, with the point section or spearhead lying flat against and parallel to your skin. If the hook is truly sharp, it will try to dig in. If it only factory-sharp, it will slide easily across your palm without catching or scratching. Take it slow and easy in any event, because even some factory-fresh hooks will be sharp enough to take a bite.

HOOK SAFETY AND FIRST AID

If your hooks are sharp enough to use, you will draw your own blood from time to time. The little nicks and scratches should cause no grief, if you keep your tetanus booster shots current; it's the nasty wounds you want to avoid at all costs. Routine caution and common sense will prevent most problems. When tying hooks on, and particularly when pulling those terminal knots up tight, I like to use parallel-jaw fishing pliers like Sargent Sportmates to hold the hooks perfectly still and secure.

For all the caution, though, from time to time you may wind up with a sharpened hook imbedded past the barb in your own or a fishing partner's flesh. If it is a very large hook, sunk deep, you probably will need the immediate assistance of a surgeon. Don't panic, just get to a doctor's office or emergency room. If the hook is of manageable size, and imbedded in an extremity (finger, hand, arm, leg), you can probably remove it and administer the necessary postoperative first aid yourself. It's still not a bad idea to see a doctor, because puncture wounds that have been sullied by fish and bait slime can be troublesome.

For years the standard operating procedure for removing a deeply imbedded hook involved driving the point on through, using the curve of the bend to force the point and barb back up through the skin in a second place, then snipping off the spearhead with side-cutting pliers and backing the barbless hook out. That drill is now recognized as the sadomasochistic barbarism it is. Medics now advise using the following technique:

1. If the hook is attached to a lure or terminal rig, cut it free. If it can be done without tearing the flesh or causing too much pain, orient the hook so that the plane of the bend is perpendicular to the surface of the skin.

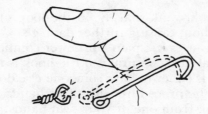

2. Take 2 feet of a 25- or 30-pound-test line (or two or more strands of 15-pound-test or three or more strands of 10-pound-test) and tie a knot in the loose ends, forming a circle of line. Place the knotted line around the back of your hand and hold the other end between thumb and forefinger, forming a small loop.

3. Place the small loop over the eye and shank of the hook and center it in the hook's bend.

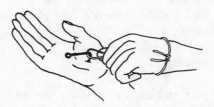

4. With the thumb of your other hand (if it's available), press down on the hook, causing the puncture to become more slitlike. (This should disengage the barb from the flesh; if necessary, apply slight backing-out pressure on the hook or pinch the wound gently together.) At the same time as you are pressing

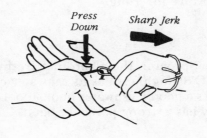

Press Down   Sharp Jerk

down on the hook, yank sharply on the loop of line. The hook will pull free without causing further damage.

This method causes less pain and fewer complications than the old hook-removal drill. Naturally, if the hook is imbedded in one of your hands it is easier to have someone else do the removing. I have illustrated the procedure with three hands, but it is possible to remove a hook from one of your own hands; it just requires a little patience and dexterity. It is better, though, to seek assistance.

After removing the hook, let the blood flow a bit to help cleanse the interior of the puncture. Then treat the wound to prevent infection. Alcohol or another disinfectant belongs in every first-aid kit, and a first-aid kit belongs in every boat and tackle box. Loosely cover the wound, to prevent its becoming dirty, with a Band-Aid or other small dressing, and keep an eye peeled for festering, undue swelling, red streaking, or other signs of infection. Because blood poisoning, tetanus, and gangrene are very serious, visit a doctor as soon as possible.

NOTES ON HOOK PATTERNS

At this point, it is probably a good idea to make a few observations about some of the hook patterns commonly encountered in tackle shops and tackle boxes, even a few of the more interesting but less common ones.

Sproat

This old standby with the asymmetrically parabolic bend is one of the best and strongest patterns made. It is also one of the most difficult to form properly. The Sproat is about the closest thing there is to a do-everything hook in freshwater fishing, and a lot of saltwater anglers like to use it as well. Most of the special hooks that have come along in recent years for fishing plastic worms are based on the Sproat pattern. When in doubt, reach for a Sproat and you probably won't go wrong.

O'Shaughnessy

Having picked the Sproat as the all-around freshwater hook, let me nominate the O'Shaughnessy as its saltwater counterpart. In the smaller sizes, it's a good freshwater hook, too. Like the Sproat, the O'Shaughnessy has a strong parabolic bend. It often is forged for extra strength, and its flat (nonoffset) point is raked slightly outward for sure contact. (Sometimes, but rarely, O'Shaughnessy pattern hooks are made with offset points.) The very best single hook for saltwater fish of small to moderate size, when still-fishing with bait, the O'Shaughnessy works best on heavy-mouthed, slow-biting species.

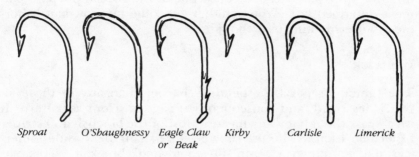

| *Sproat* | *O'Shaughnessy* | *Eagle Claw or Beak* | *Kirby* | *Carlisle* | *Limerick* |

Parabolic-Bend Hooks

Beak or Eagle Claw

Mustad's Beak and Wright & McGill's Eagle Claw patterns are not truly identical, but they are close enough. Considering freshwater *and* saltwater fishing together, I suppose the Beak/Eagle Claw pattern comes as close as any other to being a universal favorite. The offset hollow or rolled point makes this pattern a sure sticker, but it takes a little muscle to set the point past the barb, something worth remembering when fishing for hard-mouthed fish. Many anglers and lure manufacturers, especially on the West Coast, use this pattern for trolling and cast-and-retrieve fishing, but I recommend it more for bait-fishing or still-fishing. It isn't as strong as the Sproat or O'Shaughnessy, but it is a good one. Most Octopus hooks and VMC's Faultless pattern are closely enough related to the Beak/Eagle Claw to be considered interchangeable.

Kirby

The first of the offset hooks, and Izaak Walton's personal choice, the Kirby still enjoys a lot of favor among fishermen, but I think one of the three patterns listed above would be a better choice. Large Kirby Sea hooks are quite popular among commercial fishermen.

Carlisle

Another parabolic-bend pattern that is superficially similar to all the above patterns, the Carlisle is mostly used in long-shanked configurations when bait-fishing for toothy freshwater species. It is a good pattern, but I seldom use it anymore, preferring one of the first three patterns named, or one of the special-purpose patterns described later. You couldn't get some minnow-bait fishermen to use anything else, though.

Limerick

The Limerick's parabolic bend is sharper than any of those already described, and consequently it isn't as strong a pattern. It isn't weak, though, by any means. Most of the bluefish and striper fishermen I know who use tube eels use shank-bent-aside Limericks, and no one ever complains about hook breakage. This pattern is, however, most popular among fly-fishermen. Limericks are available in straight-, kirbed-, and reversed-point versions.

Model Perfect

Another fly-tyer's favorite, the perfectly round-bend Model Perfect is known by a variety of names: Round, National Round, and so on. Not a particularly strong hook, it is favored among some who stalk smaller fish because of its wide gap.

Siwash or Salmon

The round-bend, long-point, short-shank, heavy-wire Siwash is a great favorite among salmon and steelhead fishermen on the West Coast, and it is beginning to make inroads among the

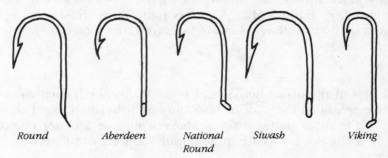

Round   Aberdeen   National   Siwash   Viking
Round

Round-Bend Hooks

striped-bass, bluefish, cod, and weakfish anglers in the East. The Siwash or salmon hook is very strong, and especially secure, with its deep bite, on leaping species.

Aberdeen

The Aberdeen's round bend actually has slightly squared corners, for extra strength against opening under pressure. With longish shanks and fine-diameter wires, Aberdeens are very popular among freshwater panfishermen and bass fishermen who fish weedy and brushy waters. Most are specially tempered so they can be bent and unbent several times. Many, perhaps most, freshwater jig hooks employ the Aberdeen pattern, but the stronger O'Shaughnessy is virtually standard on saltwater jigs.

Wide-Gap

Only a few years ago, wide-gap hooks would have been considered special-purpose hooks, but now their use is becoming widespread. Wide-gapped hooks run quite a gamut of exaggeration, from Eagle Claw's moderately shaped Wide Bend to the so-called Kahle Horizontal or English Bait hook. No really wide-gapped hook can be as strong as a parabolic-bend hook, but the name-brand wide-gap hooks are strong enough for their purposes, which are mostly bait-fishing and ice-fishing. Mai-Tai's Musketball jig uses wide-gap hooks, which is unusual.

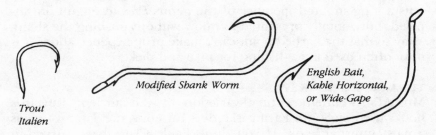

Trout
Italien

Modified Shank Worm

English Bait,
Kahle Horizontal,
or Wide-Gape

Wide-Gap Hooks

Special-Purpose Patterns

Among the dozens, perhaps even hundreds, of special-purpose patterns, a handful merit consideration here because their applicability is wider than their application, or because they are so darned good for their special purposes.

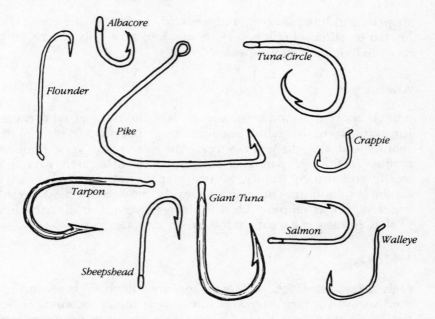

Hooks Patterned to Fit the Mouths
of Specific Fish

PIKE HOOK

Mustad's Pike hook is an especially wide-gap hook with an almost triangular shape and a very short point. Its unusual shape permits a long-snouted member of the genus *Esox* to engulf an impaled, horizontally presented minnow without pushing the shank away so that the barbed point can't make proper penetration. It is most often used in ice-fishing for pike and pickerel.

TUNA-CIRCLE HOOK

Mustad's twentieth-century variation of the ancient Ruvettus hooks used by South Pacific islanders for eons, the Tuna-Circle is a most unusual hook. If you think Eagle Claws have curved-in points, wait until you see a Tuna-Circle. It is hard to believe that a tuna can become lip-hooked on such a hook, but it isn't difficult to believe that, once hooked, tunas rarely escape from untended long lines. Recent research has shown that these circle hooks are especially effective on cod and their relatives (pollock, the hakes, burbot, and so on) and on certain of the small to medium sharks. Intended for fishing on untended long lines, Tuna-Circle hooks

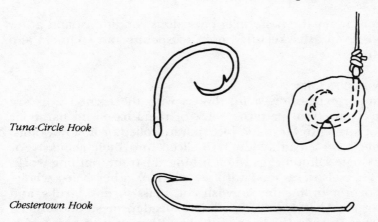

Tuna-Circle Hook

Chestertown Hook

can be still-fished by *patient* bait fishermen; you must give a fish lots of time to hook itself. This is not a hook for anglers with happy trigger fingers.

CHESTERTOWN
Northeastern flounder fishermen will think it strange that I list the Chestertown among the Tuna-Circle and other oddities. But this is a section on special-purpose hooks, and the extra-long-shank, offset, angular-bend Chestertown certainly is that. Its odd shape makes it perfectly suited to the odd mouth arrangement of the winter flounder, and I suspect it could be used as effectively on other small flatfish and eels. Watch out for the cheap, low-quality hooks in some packages of snelled flounder hooks, though.

KEEL-FLY HOOK
This stepped-shank hook, popularized by Wright & McGill, is best known to fly-fishermen, who use it to tie flies that ride with their points up in weedy waters. But it also is used by canny bait

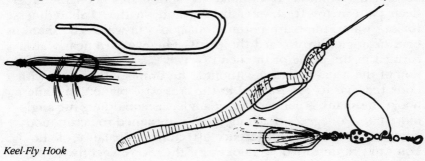

Keel-Fly Hook

fishermen under the same snag-hazardous conditions, and a few whiz kids even affix keel-fly hooks to spoons and spinners and other lures.

SALMON-EGG HOOKS

These super-extra-short-shank hooks with the turned eyes are made in a variety of patterns, most of them based on parabolic bends for strength. Most also incorporate rolled or hollow points, and some have a baitholder barb sliced into their shanks. For holding single salmon eggs when fishing for trout, nothing works better. They also are good with a variety of other baits: whole-kernel corn, nymphs, tiny crayfish and grass shrimp, grubs, and small worms. Always snelled to line or leader, these hooks need turned eyes to keep the lines of pull and penetration reasonably close together. Alas, on such short-shanked hooks, turned-down eyes encroach into what is already a small "available hooking area," but turned-up eyes can cause the point to swing out of play when you try to set the hook. I also use these hooks in salt water; I string one on the leader before tying on the main hook, so I can use it as a baitholder hook for strip baits, sand eels, and the like.

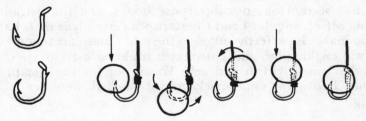

Salmon-Egg Hooks

JIG HOOKS

Most hook manufacturers make jig hooks. Based on the Aberdeen pattern for freshwater fishing and on the O'Shaughnessy for salt water, these are nothing but hooks in which the shank is bent or angled up toward the point. The eyes are nearly always formed in the plane of the bend (which is a 90-degree modification of the usual practice), although the Bomber Jig comes with a hook that has its eye formed in the crosswise plane. On some jig hooks the shank is bent at a right angle, and on others the angle is more like 45 degrees. Each jig mold is designed to accommodate one or the other, the difference affecting the balance of the jig. You can use unleaded jig hooks as if they were keel fly hooks, or

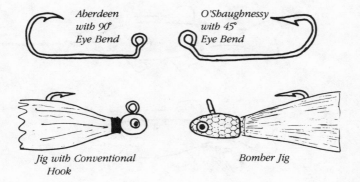

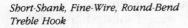

Jig Hooks

you can use them in Texas-rigging plastic worms. Special barbless tuna jig hooks are made by Mustad, VMC, and others, but they are almost never seen in the U.S.

Double and Treble Hooks

Almost as much attention should be paid to shank length, wire size, finish, and eye construction when fishing treble hooks as singles. But there aren't as many variations available in these and other features. Double hooks can be quite varied, though, thanks to the various baitholder types on the market.

TREBLE HOOKS
Most trebles are made with parabolic bends and straight spear points, but quite a few employ rolled or hollow points, and those made for the French and certain other European markets have round bends and wide gaps. The last type is commonly furnished on such imported lures as Mepps and Panther Martin spinners.

Short-Shank, Fine-Wire, Round-Bend Treble Hook

DOUBLE HOOKS
The "normal" double hook is formed of one piece of wire so that the eye is open. This makes the double a favorite hook of many anglers who fish dead minnows and whole baitfish. A double hook is especially effective on such baits when used in conjunc-

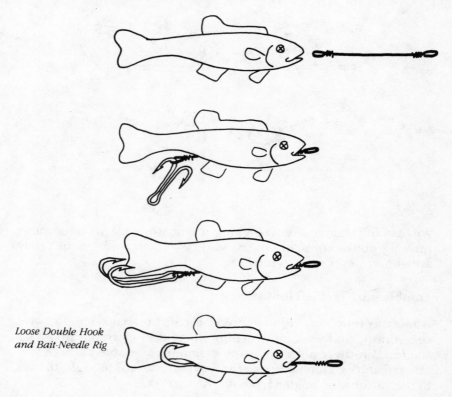

*Loose Double Hook
and Bait-Needle Rig*

tion with a wire "bait-needle" rig. For extra security, some anglers and lure manufacturers prefer double hooks whose shanks have been brazed together.

BAITHOLDER DOUBLES

A plethora of types is available, but perhaps we can single out a few of the better ones. Mustad and several others make a safety-pin double hook that has a third shank and bend formed into a long baitholder needle; this, in turn, is secured, ladies'-pin fashion, near the eye of the hook by a hasp. What Mustad calls a Universal Double Bait hook is actually two hooks. The main hook, a long-shanked double, has a brazed-solid shank and a spear-pointed upper end which has a hole drilled through it. A second hook, which Mustad calls a rod, goes through this drilled hole, enabling the main hook to be removed for easy bait-rigging. The second hook holds the bait in place so that it can't slip down the shank and become unattractively bunched over the barbs and points. VMC's Ryder hook looks like a treble hook with two normal and one terribly deformed point, but it is actually a double hook. The third shank, the Ryder, is simply bent up away from the shank at a barely acute angle, and its point is barbed on the outside. This Ryder point is used to secure plastic or natural baits, mostly minnows and baitfish. These Ryders are seen in the U.S. only in imported lures, such as the Mepps Minno. The VMC double Ryder, which is very popular in Europe for fishing dead baitfish for pike, looks like a double hook with one long shank and one short shank. It actually is fished as a single hook, the short-shanked point being nothing but a baitholder or Ryder.

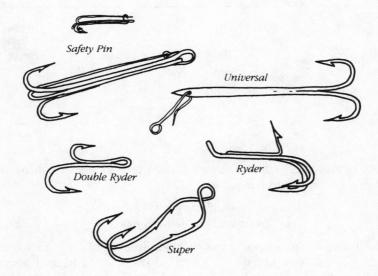

Safety Pin

Universal

Double Ryder

Ryder

Super

Baitholder Double Hooks

Grand Lake's Super Hook used to be called the Magic Bait Hook. Either name is fair enough. It is a spring-loaded, bow-legged double hook with a semi-closed eye. It can be used to hold any sort of small bait, dead or alive, concocted or natural. Known mostly among the freshwater ranks, the Super Hook can be used as effectively on the smaller saltwater species as well. As for using the other kinds of double hooks in salt water, both VMC and Mustad make very large, very strong double hooks that are used mostly in commercial fishing. VMC even sells its Tuna Double equipped with a heavy-duty swivel for long-lining.

2
Sinkers and Other Weighty Matters

Here is the first commandment, the golden rule of fishing with sinkers; commit it to memory:

Use only as much weight as you actually must, as little as you possibly can.

I can't stress the importance of that little aphorism too much. Violate it and you sacrifice a lot of your fishing fun and angling effectiveness. Overweighted terminal rigs discourage a lot of fish from striking, especially those that nibble at the bait before really chomping down on it. As soon as they feel the resistance of that weight they look for greener pastures. Less wary soft-strikers that chew the bait before swallowing will get away with it because heavy sinkers give them good leverage for their larceny and dampen the vibrations so much you won't know what's going on down there. And you will miss some of the strikes you do feel because so much of the energy you put into your hook-setting jab will be absorbed in moving the sinker rather than the hook.

Heavy sinkers require heavy tackle, and heavy tackle is more tiring, less sporting, and less fun to use. Small fish can't provide much excitement on heavy tackle. Even big ones tire soon if they have to battle heavy sinkers, which can turn a battle with a trophy fish into an exercise as scintillating as reeling in a log. Ironically, heavy sinkers often result in fish lost during these leaden fights, either because the hook hadn't been set securely or because the sinker helped the hook to tear a large hole in the mouth tissue and then gave the fish the leverage it needed to throw or simply drop the hook.

Sinker weight and sinker design go hand in glove. Contrary to what many anglers think, a sinker is much more than a mere gobbet of lead. Choose the proper design for the fishing you will be doing, and you can get by with less weight. Choose a poor design and it will take more weight to force the balky sinker into doing what you want it to.

Before you can select the proper sinker design, and therefore the minimum weight necessary, you must consider the demands you will be making on your sinker. This requires some understanding of the sinker's several different functions, the physical properties that affect those functions, and the physical forces at work on the sinker.

Weight is a function of the volume and density of a material. Virtually all sinkers are made of lead, which has a specific gravity of about eleven; that means it is eleven times heavier than the same volume of water. Lead is the heaviest or most dense of the common elements, which explains its almost universal dominance as the sinker material of choice. Lead is relatively abundant around the world, is easily reduced, has a low melting point, and is easily recycled—factors that keep its cost down and make it easy to work with. The first sinkers used by primitive fishermen doubtless were of stone, but lead sinkers have been used since before the dawn of recorded history.

There are dozens, perhaps even hundreds, of types of lead sinkers available, and each has its unique set of physical properties. Whether these properties are angling assets or liabilities depends upon how the sinkers are used. The variety complicates the making of a proper choice, but it does give the thoughtful fisherman a good shot at selecting a sinker that verges on the ideal for any angling chore. There is probably a very best sinker for each angling situation, but there usually are several types that will serve almost as well.

Being an incurable experimenter, I stock my tackle shelves with a rather large array of sinker types and sizes. Yet I probably do nearly half of my bait-fishing with a single type: the venerable bank sinker. There is no such things as perfection, but the bank sinker is the closest thing to a do-everything, all-purpose sinker. Call it the king of sinkers. Unless someone repeals the laws of physics, it isn't likely ever to be dethroned.

If you tried to carry all the sinker types and sizes that would enable you to use the very best sinker for each angling situation you might conceivably encounter, you wouldn't be able to lift your tackle box. A reasonable selection of weights and styles that will adequately cover the conditions you are likely to encounter should suffice. Stock a few more special-purpose types back home, which you can carry when you think you will really need them. But before you can make these choices intelligently, you have to consider the principles, properties, and functions of sinkers.

SINKER PRINCIPLES, PROPERTIES, AND FUNCTIONS

Fishing sinkers are used to cast, sink, anchor, drift, and troll baits or lures. Placing the baits on target and presenting them at the proper level—these are the objectives that sinkers can help or hinder. Since fishermen care more about functions than principles and properties, what follows is organized around those practical functions.

Casting

Assuming the sinker's weight is within the recommended casting-weight range of your rod, and that the strength of the line also is in balance, the sinker that casts best—easily, accurately, and far— will be one that is compact, streamlined, and bottom-heavy. Besides gravity, about which we can do nothing, the forces that interfere with a sinker's flight include air resistance, aerodynamic drag, and line drag. If your tackle is properly balanced, we can consider line drag to be a constant. So that leaves us coping with air resistance and aerodynamic drag.

All things considered, the best-casting sinkers are teardrop-shaped. Bulkier sinkers offer too much frontal area and create turbulent drag. Thin, flat sinkers may slip through the air with little resistance, but they tend to sail off course. Sinkers with a weight distribution other than bottom-heavy tend to flop, tumble, and wobble in flight. These motions absorb some of the kinetic energy you put into the cast and actually expose the sinker to as many as ten additional aerodynamic factors. All these unnecessary forces can cause a sinker to fall wide or short of the mark. If you are casting to structure—a reef, rocks, a wreck, pilings, a weed bed, whatever—a few feet can mean the difference between success and failure.

Sinking

Hydrodynamics and aerodynamics are simply different aspects of the same branch of physics called fluid mechanics, so many of the same considerations listed above apply here. The major difference is that, in sinking, gravity is working for rather than against the angler. So, for superior sinking, choose sinkers that are compact, streamlined, and bottom-heavy.

Water currents compound the sinking problem because they tend to push a sinker away from a vertical course through the water. Even if a sinker hits the water on target (regardless of whether it was cast or lowered), it can be drifted away from the intended bottom target by currents. The faster a sinker descends, the less time currents have to work on it and its trailing line. You can increase the sink rate by increasing weight, but it's better to go with the same compact, streamlined, bottom-heavy shape that helped to speed the sinker on its way in casting.

Anchoring

Once a sinker hits the bottom, it's a new ball game. Whole new sets of considerations apply. A sinker that casts and sinks well may or may not be a good anchor. If the water is perfectly still, the teardrop-shaped sinker will work as well as any. But if there are strong currents flowing, or energetic waves slapping against the line, you have to look at your sinker the way a sailor looks at an anchor. Whether you are anchoring a boat or a bait in moving water, you have to consider whether the bottom is soft or hard, clean or broken. To simplify things for the sake of space, we'll consider all sand, mud, and gravel bottoms as soft and clean. Rocky bottoms and those complicated by reefs, wrecks, heavy weeds, stumps, brush, and other submerged obstructions we'll call broken.

On soft, clean bottoms you want a sinker that will dig in and resist the forces of moving water acting against the sinker and, especially, against the line. A teardrop-shaped sinker is easily rolled or dragged across the bottom, so angular, more complicated shapes are better when currents are strong. Flat sinkers and those with an open design (such as the triangle surf sinker discussed later) tend to bury themselves in soft bottoms in response to the current-induced line drag that is trying to move them. Angular sinkers with wide shoulders or spurs really dig their heels in against such forces.

On broken bottoms, you don't want your sinker to really dig in, you just want it to lie still. Alas, you will probably have to fish a heavier sinker on bad bottoms. Really angular sinkers wedge themselves irretrievably among the obstructions. Rounded sinkers can be rolled under rocks, into crevices, and around sticks and stems. Bottom-heavy sinkers are slightly less likely to become fouled than others, all other things being equal. You can't avoid losing a few sinkers on broken bottoms; all you can hope for is to cut your losses to the practical minimum, without sacrificing the anchoring that is necessary in still-fishing the bottom.

Drifting

For our discussion purposes, this term will include moving baits across the bottom more or less continuously, whether from a drifting or moving boat, fishing from an anchored boat or shore while letting the bait drift along the bottom with the current, or simply reeling the bait along the bottom. Again, it makes a big difference whether the bottom is clean or broken. On clean bottoms, most sinkers could be used, but some are clearly better than others. For practical purposes, it is better to select drift sinkers as if the bottom were broken. That way you won't run into many nasty surprises, and you will get a much smoother, more trouble-free drift.

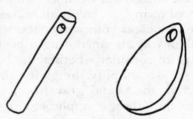

Drift Sinkers

Good drift sinkers tend to be either cylindrical or more or less flat. The best drift sinkers in the latter category are at least somewhat bottom-heavy, and are thus wedge- or spoon-shaped. What you want to avoid are sinkers that are easily snagged, that twist the line, or that lurch and catapult about, tangling the terminal rig or giving the bait an action that doesn't entice fish. Drift sinkers must be able to maintain contact with the bottom during the drift, which isn't exactly easy, since most of the forces imparted by the motion will be trying to lift the line, sinker, and bait up off the bottom.

Trolling

Bottom-trolling is simply an energy-consumptive version of drifting, so here we are restricting the term to mean dragging an artificial or natural bait through the water at a specified depth. In trolling, entirely different demands are made on sinkers. There are two principal objectives: The bait must be held at the desired level, and the sinker should not twist the line or impart any undesirable action to the bait. Good trolling sinkers are streamlined to minimize the interference of hydraulic forces or designed to dive deeper than their weight alone would carry the line. They must also be stabilized in some fashion to prevent spinning, twisting, or unwanted wobbling.

The best trolling sinkers are designed so that the bulk of their weight hangs below the line. As for shape, they may resemble airplanes, sailboat keels, bananas, ocarinas, or kites. All good trolling sinkers are shaped and balanced to be down-weighted, no matter how unlike each other they look. Many also incorporate swivels, as insurance against unthinking anglers who forgot that a trolling sinker must be swiveled in the rig.

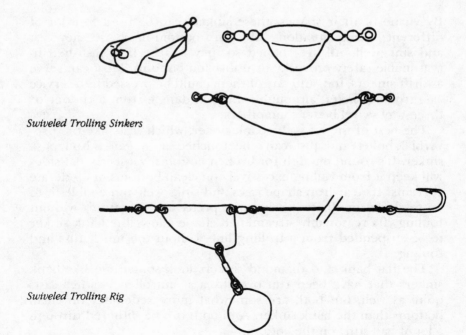

Swiveled Trolling Sinkers

Swiveled Trolling Rig

In a pinch, a great many sinker types may be used in trolling, so long as they are swiveled at their attachment point and they hang below the line without much hydrodynamic struggling. In such cases, it is often a good idea to attach the sinker to the bottom edge of a plastic or metal trolling rudder that is attached to the line with swivels. But you can use a wire trolling triangle, or just a three-way or crossline swivel. I realize that many swiveled, torpedo-shaped sinkers are sold as trolling sinkers, and that those who sell and use them are earnest. However, I advise that you avoid these sinkers. Stick to the stabilized, down-weighted, swiveled trolling sinkers and you won't go wrong.

SURVEY OF SINKER TYPES

In this survey of relatively common sinker types, I intend to keep my comments on each fairly brief, because this section ends with a report card.

General-Purpose Casting and Bottom-Fishing Sinkers

By virtue of their shapes, these sinkers can be used in a lot of different fishing situations. Most are bottom-heavy, so they cast and sink well. All are shaped so they can be bottom-fished in reasonable safety on rocky or unbroken bottoms. Most can serve as drift sinkers, too, and any of them could be pressed into service as a trolling sinker, although some will dangle from a rudder or three-way swivel better than others.

The best of the lot is the bank sinker, which casts like the proverbial bullet and just can't be touched as a general-purpose sinker. It's round enough for broken bottoms, yet its six flat sides will keep it from rolling excessively on clean bottoms in moderate currents. Its teardrop shape casts and sinks well and enables it to be retrieved or drifted over some pretty awful bottoms without fouling. Its reasonably streamlined shape allows the bank sinker to be suspended from a trolling line without too much fuss and fouling.

The flat bank and diamond sinkers look something like bank sinkers that have been run over by a steamroller. Neither casts quite as well, but both are somewhat more sedentary on clean bottoms than the bank sinker. And both can be slithered through a lot of bad stuff on the bottom.

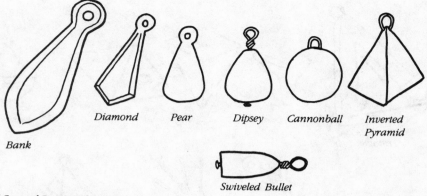

Bank Diamond Pear Dipsey Cannonball Inverted Pyramid

Swiveled Bullet

General-Purpose Casting and Bottom-Fishing Sinkers

The more rounded Dipsey, bass-casting, pear, bell, and swiveled bullet sinkers cast well but are prone to roll around in a current. The swiveled sinkers are particularly good for drifting or bottom-trolling. Ball sinkers, also known as sport cannonballs or minie balls, roll around a lot, but they cast reasonably well and are very good when bottom and current conditions aren't severe.

Slab-sided inverted pyramid sinkers aren't very popular anymore, but they are still good sinkers for casting to rocky bottoms in strong currents. If you mold your own sinkers, cast them with eyes on both ends and you can fish them either way, as bottom conditions dictate.

Soft-Bottom and Surf Sinkers

Tradition puts the surfman on a sandy beach, and the term "surf sinker" nearly always applies to a sinker intended for use on soft, sandy bottoms. However, surf fishermen are not the only ones who must contend with strong currents and clean bottoms and who need specially designed sinkers that dig into sand or mud to resist being dragged around. None of these sinkers should be used on broken bottoms because they are easily fouled.

Pyramid sinkers are almost as well known and popular as bank sinkers. They are good anchors—their wide, angular shoulders really dig in against line-drag forces. But they aren't the best soft-bottom sinkers, their reputation and popularity notwithstanding. Being top-heavy, they don't cast particularly well, and distance

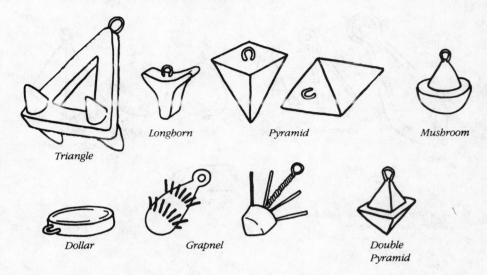

Triangle   Longhorn   Pyramid   Mushroom

Dollar   Grapnel   Double
Pyramid

Soft-Bottom and Surf Sinkers

can be critical on a windy and sandy beachfront. The less popular three-sided pyramid is a more effective anchor than the more common four-sided or true pyramid.

The best surf sinkers I've ever seen or used are endemic to Southern California. The farther you get from Los Angeles, the less likely you will be to find them. There are two types. The so-called surf sinker (also known as the triangle sinker) is the best sand-bottom sinker you can use. Thanks to their weight distribution and open design, these triangles cast very well, sink fast and true, and begin burying themselves in the sand as soon as they hit bottom. They are a little too "sticky" for drifting, but when being retrieved across the bottom they won't flip, flop, and tangle the way pyramids do. The other Southern California winner is known as the longhorn, bulldog, or bulldozer sinker. It seems to be popular in lighter weights and for fishing bays rather than the open surf. It isn't quite as effective as the triangle sinker on hard-packed mud or sand, and flops around more when being retrieved across the bottom, but it is a real burrower in soft bottoms.

Some West Coast surfmen dote on flat, round sinkers variously called dollar, bar, disk, or surf sinkers, but the triangles and longhorns are much better. Although dollar sinkers bury themselves in the sand fairly well and can be dragged across the bottom without too many acrobatics, they tend to sail off-target on a long cast into the wind.

The mushroom "sinker" actually is a decoy anchor. But it is a good, heavy-tackle choice for surfcasting over sand bottoms or for fishing moderately rough bottoms of hard-packed sand and patch rock from a boat. An angular, double-pyramid version sometimes seen is better because it won't roll around. There are two grapnel sinkers. One is a British innovation that enables anglers to cast upcurrent with very light tackle for maximum sport with mackerel, flounder, and similar saltwater panfish. The other is popular among Texas surf fishermen. Neither is easy to find in most tackle stores.

Drift Sinkers

Sinkers that are drifted, trolled, dragged, or retrieved across the bottom should be designed to stay on the bottom without fouling it. You don't want a drift sinker to anchor itself, nor do you want it to gyrate and somersault so much that it tangles the terminal rig. Several of the general-purpose sinkers, such as the bank and Dipsey, are quite good drift sinkers. Drift sinkers may be rigged to slide along the line, or they may be tied fast to the rig, either on a dropper or directly to a three-way swivel.

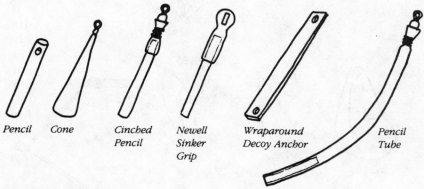

Pencil   Cone   Cinched Pencil   Newell Sinker Grip   Wraparound Decoy Anchor   Pencil Tube

Pencil-Type Drift Sinkers

The various pencil types are extremely popular among steelhead anglers in the Northwest. Some pencil sinkers are cast in molds, but most are fashioned from coils of lead wire in diameters of less than ⅛ inch to more than ¼ inch.

The cinched pencil leads are especially good in treacherous bottoms because the fouled lead is easily pulled out of its cinch tub-

LENGTH/WEIGHT RATIOS FOR PENCIL LEAD WIRE

WIRE DIAMETER	APPROXIMATE LENGTH-TO-WEIGHT RATIOS
$\frac{1}{16}$ in	50 in/oz or $\frac{1}{50}$ oz/in
$\frac{1}{8}$ in	$12\frac{1}{2}$ in/oz or $\frac{1}{12}$ oz/in
$\frac{3}{16}$ in	$5\frac{1}{2}$ in/oz or $\frac{1}{5}$ oz/in
$\frac{1}{4}$ in	3 in/oz or $\frac{1}{3}$ oz/in
$\frac{5}{16}$ or $\frac{3}{8}$ in	$1\frac{1}{3}$ in/oz or $\frac{3}{4}$ oz/in

ing or holder. The long pencil tube doesn't cast well, but it is an excellent if expensive sinker for trolling a bait just above the bottom. Cone sinkers cast better than the pencils but they are almost prohibitively expensive. Note the angling use of yet another decoy anchor, the wraparound.

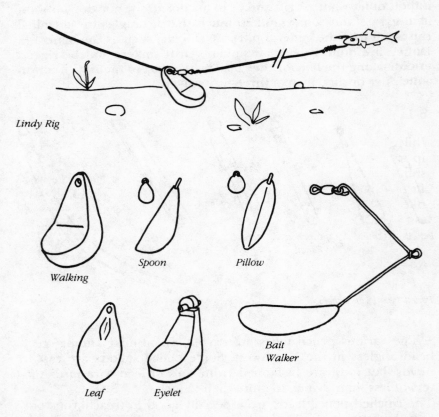

Lindy Rig

Walking

Spoon

Pillow

Bait Walker

Leaf

Eyelet

Walking-Type Drift Sinkers

Ever since the invention of the Lindy rig, which has almost revolutionized walleye fishing, walking-type sinkers have become very popular. There are many varieties, and the names given them are very confusing. The names I have used to label the illustrations aren't all in common use, but at least they are rational. Many leaf sinkers are called spoon sinkers, but I think the West Coast spoon deserves that name all to itself, being a much better casting sinker than the thinner types. The pillow or cushion sinker is sort of a cross between a drift sinker and a general-purpose sinker.

Two recent developments deserve special mention. Mister Twister's eyelet drift sinker is a quick-change version of Lindy's walking sinker, a nifty idea for those who fish streams that have fast channels, eddies, and backwaters or for those who fish in tidal waters with their ever-changing currents. At first glance, Gapen's Bait Walker looks like an expensive and fancy variation of a drift sinker hung on a dropper from a three-way swivel, but it isn't. Once you have tried a Bait Walker and discovered its snaglessness, sensitivity, and balance, you won't balk at paying the price. It's a great way to tow a floating surface plug just above a bottom that would snag a diving or bottom-bumping plug.

In-Line Slip Sinkers

While a great many (perhaps nearly all) sinkers can be fished as slip sinkers—either sliding directly on the line or attached to a fishfinder or other sliding clip—these sinkers are designed specifically for that purpose. In fresh water, the bullet-shaped worm sinker is well known among bass anglers who fish for largemouth bass with Texas-rigged plastic worms. However, other species can be fished the same way, and so can other baits.

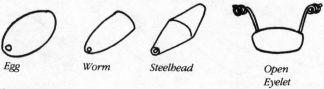

Egg   Worm   Steelhead   Open
Eyelet

In-Line Slip Sinkers

Egg sinkers are reasonably popular throughout the country in fresh water and, on the Gulf Coast, in the salt. In fact, a slip-rigged egg sinker is frequently called a Gulf fishfinder rig. On the West Coast, the ball slip sinker is sometimes used similarly.

Open-eyelet sinkers are quite uncommon these days, but they are worth mentioning because they can be wound onto and off the line without retying the terminal rig and because, hanging below the line as they do, they can be used for trolling.

I haven't been out in steelhead country for a while, but I suspect the old steelhead drift sinker has pretty much gone the way of the great auk, its former function having been usurped by the better-suited pencil lead and its physical type by the bullet or worm sinker.

In-Line Fixed Sinkers

I am not particularly fond of the sinkers in this category. I'm happy to report that the granddaddy of the family—the torpedo or cigar sinker—has almost disappeared from the freshwater scene.

I don't like in-line fixed sinkers because they permit—and sometimes cause—line twist, get caught in all sorts of crevices and crannies, expose the line to needless abrasion, and roll around when still-fished.

Rubbercore sinkers and the clasp-on types they replaced can be handy to add a little weight here and there or to provide just enough weight to coax a live-lined baitfish below the surface, but I don't care much for them as primary weights. But both are better than the torpedoes they replaced, because they are handier and because few anglers are tempted to use them as primary trolling weights. Thanks to Milt Rosko for showing the way, a rubbercore sinker is very handy for supplemental weighting of a three-hook flounder rig, which could be adapted for many other species as well (see p. 249–250).

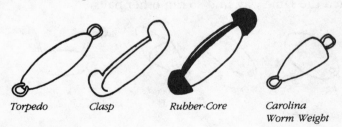

Torpedo   Clasp   Rubber-Core   Carolina
                                                     Worm Weight

In-Line Fixed Sinkers

The Carolina worm weight, which Arbogast calls the Super-Pro Worm Weight, is sometimes used instead of toothpicking a slip sinker in place when you want to fish a plastic worm some precise distance above the bottom. It is less prone to snag weeds, but I'd still rather use a small Dipsey sinker on a dropper, or a walking sinker in some variation of the Lindy rig.

"Tuning" Sinkers

I like to call the weights in this category tuning sinkers because they are excellent for fine-tuning bait rigs, lures, or what have you. Split shot are the best known of the lot. British anglers, who have raised the use of split shot to a fine art called ledgering, don't think much of North American split shot because they tend to be very hard, the lead alloyed with antimony or some other metal. They are right. Shop around for the softest split-shot sinkers you can find. I am especially fond of the ones that have ears so you can reopen them without the use of teeth, pliers, knife blade, or other tool. And the ones with rippled or toothed slots stay put better on slippery monofilament.

Split Shot

Let me suggest two ways to rig split shot. Both are superior to the usual method of simply clamping them onto the main line. If you want to fish them fixed on the line, make a loop in the line and clamp them onto both strands of the loop and they will stay put. Better still, fish them on a dropper, particularly around weeds, brush, and bad bottoms. Clamp them less than completely tight and you will have rigged a strip shot dropper, one that will allow the shot to be stripped off if they get snagged. Make the dropper out of a doubled piece of monofilament looped over the

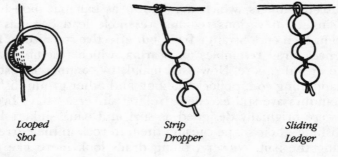

Looped Shot   *Strip Dropper*   *Sliding Ledger*

Rigging Split Shot

main line and you have a sliding shot dropper, what the British call a sliding ledger, sort of an ultralight fishfinder rig.

Wraparound sinkers come in two types, wire and ribbon. The wire usually comes spooled like thread and the strips in little, matchbook-type packages. Both are very good for setting an imbalanced lure right. If you can't find either type, use tin-lead solder, which weighs about three-fourths as much as lead (the 50–50 solder is heavier than the 60–40). Soft, moldable sinker putty is hard to find, but it's terrific for fine-tuning.

Wraparound Sinkers

Trolling Sinkers

My definition of trolling sinkers does not permit inclusion of center-weighted, in-line weights like the torpedo. If it isn't stabilized by its weight balance or geometrical design, then it isn't a trolling sinker, no matter what the label says.

Lead rudders are nice because they combine the stabilizing design of the trolling rudder and the weight of a sinker. Old-fashioned heart-shaped folding keels are handy, if you can still find them. Be sure to tie in swivels fore and aft. Keel sinkers are nothing but torpedo sinkers that have a small keel added, but that little vane of lead makes all the difference. These are good trolling sinkers, particularly the ones that are molded around a Bead Chain swivel.

Crescent sinkers, which are known as banana, mooching, or spin sinkers in various regions, resemble lead bananas with a swivel in each end. Strange fruit, but effective stabilizers. The old gooseneck drail resembles an ocarina, which resembles a sweet potato or little goose. Now used mainly by commercial fishermen for handlining cod, pollock, halibut, and other groundfish, these old standbys are still excellent trolling sinkers. I have been told they were originally designed as surf and bank sinkers for bottom-fishing, their shape causing them to rock in the current, undulating the bait. Newer trolling drails look more like the tail ends of lead airplanes.

Huge, heavy cannonball sinkers are used by some Pacific

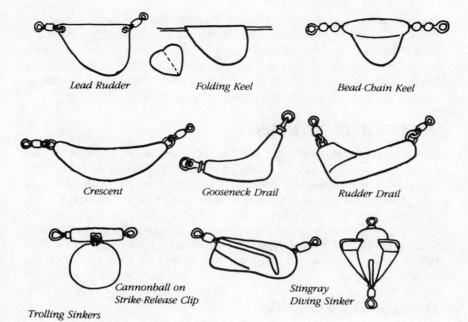

Lead Rudder   Folding Keel   Bead-Chain Keel

Crescent   Gooseneck Drail   Rudder Drail

Cannonball on
Strike-Release Clip

Stingray
Diving Sinker

Trolling Sinkers

salmon trollers; they are rigged on strike-release clips so the sinker will be jettisoned and the fish can give the fisherman the full benefit of its fight. Because of the one-way use, most big cannonballs are made of cast iron, which is cheaper than lead.

Diving weights are of two general types: weighted diving planers and delta-winged diving sinkers like the Stingray trolling sinker. Both will take a trolling line much deeper than their weights suggest. In virtually all cases, the divers are balanced so

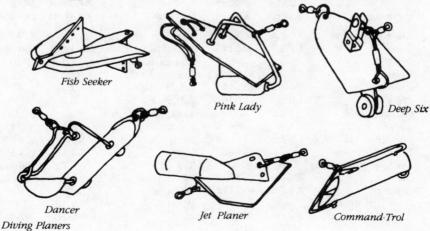

Fish Seeker

Pink Lady

Deep Six

Dancer

Jet Planer

Command-Trol

Diving Planers

that the weight of a striking fish will cause the sinker or planer to climb toward the surface. The relatively small Stingray sinkers also may be used for drift-fishing or surfcasting. The planers range in complexity from the simple, one-piece, plastic Fish Seeker, through the metal Pink Ladies and Deep Sixes, to magnetic-trip types and sliding-weight Oregon Divers.

RATING THE SINKERS

In the report card on page 99 I have tried to be as objective as possible—but let's face it, fishing is a very personal, subjective thing, and my biases are no doubt reflected in the grades. Don't accept at face value the grades I have assigned. If you have a lot of experience with a sinker and disagree strongly with the grades I have given and don't change your mind after analytical reflection, then pencil in your own grade. I defer to experience and personal preference, so long as they aren't founded simply on habit.

MAKESHIFT SINKERS

Many a youngster has gone fishing with old nuts, bolts, or chunks of waste material of one sort or another as sinkers. If ever you are caught in need of weight, with nary a sinker in the tackle box, you might be able to jury-rig an acceptable substitute. When using a material other than lead, be aware that it isn't going to sink as fast or cast as well because of the decreased density. Here are some specific gravities and densities to keep in mind when scuffling around for makeshift sinkers:

MATERIAL	SPECIFIC GRAVITY	DENSITY LB/CU FT	MATERIAL	SPECIFIC GRAVITY	DENSITY LB/CU FT
Aluminum alloys	2.6-2.8	166-176	Lead	10.7-11.4	677-708
Bone	1.7-2.0	102-125	Nickel alloys	8.1-8.9	506-555
Brick	1.4-2.2	87-137	Plastics, hard	1.1-1.3	66-92
Brass	8.2-8.8	511-546	Rubber, hard	1.2	75
Bronze	7.4-8.9	463-553	Rubber, soft	1.1	69
Clay	1.8-2.6	112-161	Salt, rock	2.2	136
Concrete	2.3	145	Sand, dry, compact	—	110
Copper	8.9	556	Sand, damp, loose	—	94
Copper-nickel alloys	8.2-8.9	511-558	Solder	8.5-8.9	529-555
Earth, dry, loose	—	65-88	Steel	7.7-8.0	484-501
Earth, moist, compact	—	95-135	Tin	5.7-7.3	360-455
Glass	2.4-5.9	150-370	Water, fresh	1.0	62.4
Granite	2.5-2.8	165-172	Water, sea	1.025	63.99
Gravel, damp, loose	—	82-125	Wood	0.1-1.3	7-83
Gravel, dry, compact	—	90-145	Zinc	6.9-7.1	192-446
Iron	7.0-7.9	441-491			

SINKER "REPORT CARD"

SINKER TYPE	CASTING	SINKING	ANCHORING ON SOFT BOTTOMS	ANCHORING ON BROKEN BOTTOMS	DRIFTING OVER CLEAR BOTTOMS	DRIFTING OVER BROKEN BOTTOMS	TROLLING
Ball, eyed	B+	B+	D	C+	C+	D	C−
Ball, slip	B	B	D	C	C	D−	D−
Bank	A	A	B−	B	B	B	C
Bar	D	D	B	D	C+	D+	F
Bell	A	A	C−	C	B	C	D
Bulldozer or Longhorn	A	A	A	F	F	F	F
Cannonball	B	B+	D	C+	C	D	C+
Carolina Worm Weight	B+	B+	D+	B	B+	A	D
Clasp-On	C−	C−	D	D+	D+	D−	F
Cone	A	A	D−	C+	A	A	C
Crescent or Banana	D	C	C−	D−	B+	C−	A
Decoy Anchor, wraparound	C	C	C−	B−	A	A	D−
Diamond	C+	B	B	C+	B	B	F
Dipsey or Bass Casting	A	A	D	B−	B+	B	C−
Diving Sinker	C	A	B+	F	B+	D	A
Egg	B	A−	D	C	C	D−	D
Flat Bank	B−	B	C+	B−	B	B	F
Folding Keel	F	B	F	F	C−	F	A−
Gooseneck Drail	B	B+	C+	C−	B−	D	A
Grapnel	A−	A	A	F	F	F	F
Inverted Pyramid	A−	A−	B−	B+	B−	C	F
Keel	B−	B	C−	D	C	C−	A+
Lead Rudder	F	B−	D	F	C−	D	A
Leaf or Snagless	D+	C−	D+	D	A	A	F
Sinker Putty	C−	C	C	C	D	D+	D
Mushroom	B−	B+	A−	D−	F	F	F
Pencil	B	B+	D	C	A	A	C−
Pencil Tube	C−	C	D−	C−	A	A	C−
Pillow or Cushion	B	B+	C−	C+	B	C	F
Planer, diving	F	A	F	F	D+	F	A
Pyramid, 3-sided	C	C	A	F	F	F	F
Pyramid, 4-sided	C	C	B	F	F	F	F
Rubbercore	C−	C−	C	C−	D+	D−	F
Split Shot	C	C	C	B−	B+	B	C−
Spoon	B−	B−	C−	C	A	A−	F
Swivel	A−	A−	D	A	A−	A	D
Torpedo or Cigar	D+	C−	D	C−	D+	D	D−
Triangle Surf	A	A	A	F	D−	F	F
Walking	B+	C	D	D+	A	A	D
Worm or Bullet	B+	B+	D	B+	A	A	D
Wraparound	C−	C	D	B	B	C	D

Here's an idea from the West Coast, where surf fishermen often cast live and dead baits out into the high surf over really terrible bottoms. To get the bait out, but to keep it off the rocky bottom, they fill a plastic sandwich bag with water or a rag with packed sand, squeeze out all the air, and tie the neck closed with a piece of fishing line. It doesn't cast as well as a bank sinker, but the price is right. The plastic bags tear free of rocky snags very easily and may be used with water or sand.

An even cheaper and simpler casting weight is the plain ball of mud packed around the baited hook, lure, or light sinker. As soon as the rig hits the water the mud will fall off, so this method won't affect the action of a bait or a lure. For automatic chumming, mix a little chopped bait in the mud ball.

Old wheel-balance weights make excellent sinkers. You might be able to talk your neighborhood garage into giving you the balance weights they remove when changing tires. Remove the metal clips, drill a hole near one end, and you have an excellent drift sinker, similar to a pencil lead. Drill holes in both ends and install snap swivels, and the bent, off-weighted tire weight becomes a passable trolling sinker.

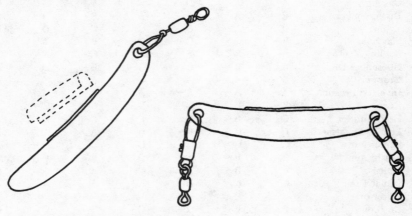

Makeshift Sinkers from Automobile
Wheel-Balance Weights

Most anglers who collect wheel-balance weights melt them down and cast their own sinkers. This is very easy to do and really saves a lot of money. And it's a great way to while away those long, dull nights of the off-season. I figured that if you paid top dollar for a precision mold and had to buy lead from a scrap-metal dealer at 25¢ a pound, you would come out ahead once you had cast your first $5 worth of lead into sinkers. Instructions come with the mold and vary somewhat according to the mold's material and the way it is made.

Makeshift Grapnel Sinkers

The only tackle shops I've seen that carried grapnel sinkers were in England and on the coast of Texas. I live in New York, so I had to figure out how to make my own. The Carolina pier fishermen I have watched trolleyline-fishing for king mackerel tie big treble hooks onto their sinkers. It's a good way to use up old, rusted trebles when you remove them from plugs. I clip off the points and barbs, so they aren't as likely to become permanently attached to the bottom. In one of his books, the old tipster Vlad Evanoff recommends driving four or six common nails into a bank sinker to increase its holding power. It's a good idea, but it isn't quite as easy as it first seems. After spending several precious and frustrating minutes on a sandy beach, trying to drive nails into a hard lead bank sinker with a whelk shell for a hammer, I decided one ought to drill some pilot holes into the sinker.

It was during one of these pilot-hole-drilling sessions that I got the idea for my makeshift grapnel sinkers. First, get some fairly soft brass or copper wire. I use the brass wire that is used to make spreaders and other saltwater terminal hardware. It is .064 inch in diameter and goes by such names as spreader wire, fun wire, gimmick wire, trick wire, and so on. Using a drill of approximately the same size, drill three holes, each at a slightly different position, through a bank sinker. Run a piece of wire through each hole, so that about 2 inches of wire stick out of each side. Bend those wire legs into J shapes. If you want to stop the legs from

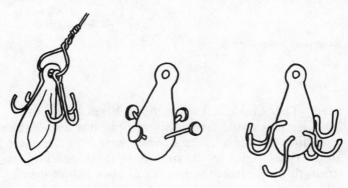

Makeshift
Grapnel Sinkers

clattering against and fouling one another, use a rubber band or tie them with string. It really isn't necessary.

The grapnel sinker you have just made will hold bottom much better than its weight would suggest, enabling you to fish lighter-than-standard tackle for the water and current conditions at hand. It isn't as fancy as a British or a grapnel sinker, but it works. With line testing 10 pounds or more, you should be able to free a fouled sinker by pulling until the crooked legs straighten out. Pull gingerly and you might unstick a grapnel on 6-pound line.

RIGGING SINKERS

Unless your sinker is sliding on or directly affixed to your line, it is a good idea to insure yourself against snags by rigging the sinker on some sort of breakaway dropper. Most of the time, when your bottom rig gets snagged, the sinker is the offending

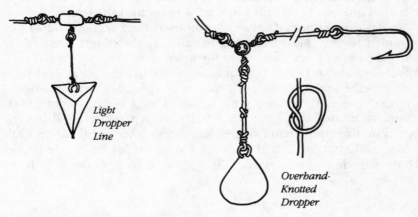

Light Dropper Line

Overhand-Knotted Dropper

Breakaway Sinker Riggings

party. The simplest way to rig a breakaway sinker is to use a dropper line made from fishing line that tests lighter than your main line. You can use a separate length of the same line and tie an overhand knot in the middle of it. Depending upon the knot strength of the line, the overhand knot should weaken it by 20 to 60 percent.

There are various kinds of sinker-release snaps and wires you can buy or make. Here is the easiest to make:

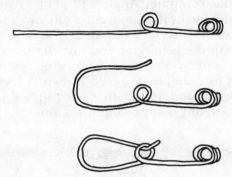

Sinker-Release Snap

An egg sinker can be attached directly to a line in breakaway fashion by wrapping it to the line with soft copper wire (usually in the vicinity of a swivel or other piece of hardware that will keep it from sliding). So-called ballyhoo wire or rigging wire is ideal, but you can strip the insulation from standard household electrical wiring and use single strands of the wire. Wrap loosely, so the sinker will cut loose easily.

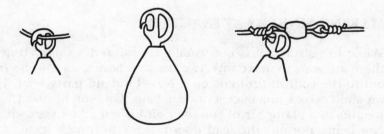

Snap-Loc Dipsey Sinker

If you want to fish a sliding sinker, most sinker eyes require that the sinker be slipped onto the line before the rest of the rig is tied. Mister Twister's detachable eyelet drift sinker has been mentioned already. Water Gremlin's Snap-Loc Dipsey sinker has an ingenious, patented, plastic eye that allows three methods of attachment. A conventional fishfinder rig must be threaded onto the line before the terminal rig is tied, but Claude Rogers and other members of the Tidewater Anglers Club of coastal Virginia have pioneered in the use of the connecting link or slide-link connector between the line and the fishfinder. Unless you need the swivel, you could skip the fishfinder and just clip the connecting link directly to the sinker. Sliding sinkers offer one very large advantage: When a fish samples the bait, it doesn't feel the resistance of the lead weight and its pickup is telegraphed up the line to your rod tip without any dampening by the sinker.

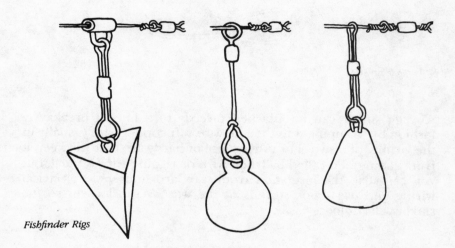

Fishfinder Rigs

MAKING SINKERS ATTRACTIVE

While fish-attraction is not usually considered a sinker function, there are ways to make sinkers attractive. Sometimes, while riding out to the codfish grounds on a New England party boat, I'll let my sinkers soak in a bucket of clam baits. Or I might soak the lead weights in a plastic jar of cod-liver oil I often take to sea with me. Not being porous, the lead doesn't soak up much scent, so the effect is short-lived, but I figure that when I am fishing in a shoulder-to-shoulder crowd I can use every little bit of help.

That is why I sometimes paint my sinkers. It is an old flounder-fishing trick, and you will see a lot of southern flounder anglers using egg sinkers that are painted red. I prefer to paint mine yellow, chartreuse, and phosphorescent. Sometimes I'll cover the flat sides of pyramid sinkers with prism tape.

Before you paint or tape, it is necessary to remove the oxide film from the lead—unless the sinkers are fresh out of the mold. It takes an acid bath to do it, either a commercial metal cleaner, acetone (which must be used with caution because it rivals gasoline in volatility), or plain white vinegar. Then I use a white primer coat because I think white improves the brilliance of the finish coats. After trying a lot of types, I have settled on Rust-Oleum. Painted sinkers get battered and beaten in use, so paint durability can be a problem. Several thin coats are much more durable than one or two thick ones. Oven-baked automobile touch-up paint is fairly durable. Frankly, though, no paint can compete with coral, granite, acorn barnacles, and gritty sand. The toughest final coat is just clear epoxy cement—not very pretty, but serviceable.

Many bass fishermen like to use painted slip sinkers with their Texas-rigged plastic worms. Most select a color that is similar to the worm's, apparently opting for a camouflaging of the lead. But bass strike moving targets at the head end, and painted slip sinkers just might help a bass home in on your concealed hook. Tests have shown that bass are most responsive to bright red.

Strader Tackle in Florida encases its lead slip sinkers in colored shells of hard plastic, so the sinker rattles in its shell. I like to use Strader's Rattleworm Heads on surgical-tubing eels in salt water as well as with plastic worms for freshwater bass. Clicking sounds definitely appeal to fish, as can be guessed from the recent explosion of lures with built-in rattle chambers. Any sliding-sinker rig can be turned into a rattler by slipping a couple of glass or hard plastic beads on either side of the sinker. Choose the beads for the sound they make when you rattle them in your hand, not for their looks.

Rattleworm Head

Finally, don't overlook using leadhead or diamond jigs in lieu of sinkers when you are fishing over fairly clean bottoms. In the Northeast where I live, this is standard operating procedure among cod, pollock, mackerel, and ling (red hake) anglers.

3

Snap
Decisions

SNAPS ARE A CONVENIENCE rather than a necessity in fishing, and they have their good points and their limitations. For the convenience of the quick-change connections that snaps make possible, there are offsetting penalties or prices.

Like all other pieces of terminal hardware, snaps add weight, bulk, drag, visibility, cost, and the opportunity for trouble to a fishing rig. Anywhere a snap can be used, a properly selected, properly tied knot will serve as well if not so conveniently. As angling hardware goes, snaps are pretty weak sisters, typically the weakest pieces of hardware in a terminal rig. In the run-of-the-mill combination snap-swivel, the snap usually is very much the weaker of the two components.

For all these drawbacks, snaps are handy and useful. In a many-parted terminal rig in which component changes will have to be made frequently, the snap's convenience may considerably outweigh its liabilities. If the fishing is fast and furious, and time is of the essence, using a snap or two can make the difference between a so-so catch and one you will remember to your grave. This is particularly true when you are after schooling fish and run into one of those blitzes you spend your life reading and dreaming about. In such a situation, every second counts.

Let's say you have lucked out and run across a school of feeding bluefish. If they are feeding on the surface, your opportunity to cast to them may be limited to a few minutes, before they move off or go down deep. Because of their size, savagery, and dental armament, bluefish must be subdued with a fish billy before you can unhook them safely. In the midst of a hit-and-run feeding frenzy the last thing I want to do is spend time wrestling with chopper blues. A good, strong snap on the end of your leader and a bunch of hooks snelled to short, looped wire leaders can really save the day. It is the same in fresh water, but for different reasons. Bullheads sometimes congregate in schools or at least feeding swarms, and they often swallow a bait and hook themselves in the throat. You can spend a lot of time struggling with a slimy, spiny bullhead, trying to get a deeply imbedded hook out of that tough throat tissue, or you can just unsnap the snelled hook and snap on a new one. You can recover your hooks at cleaning time.

In function, one snap is pretty much like another. All will permit quick, easy, convenient changes of tackle. But in performance there is a world of difference between them. Before we compare the different choices available, let's take a quick look at some of the things that affect a snap's performance.

MATERIALS

Even the best snap will bend, break, or pop open when the going gets too tough, and that usually means when you have a fish on the line that is much bigger and tougher than you had anticipated. (In other words, a once-in-a-lifetime trophy.) So buy the best snaps you can afford. Within each type that probably means the most expensive, but snaps are considerably cheaper than most other tackle. Many of the snaps you will see on the shelves and pegboard racks are junk.

Metals

Most of the one-piece snaps are made of steel wire, either a plated carbon steel or stainless steel. Most of the two-piece snaps have a steel wire in a brass body. (Exceptions are noted in the type descriptions that follow.) Because of the platings and finishes used,

One-Piece vs.
Two-Piece Snaps

it can be difficult to tell which metals were used to make a given snap. Typical platings include nickel, chrome, and copper. Non-plated finishes—usually applied by oxide-conversion processing, burnishing, or "painting"—include black, brown, bronze, and blue.

Plating and finishes are applied to snaps for several reasons: to make the metal more resistant to corrosion, to make the snap less visible, to make it shiny (shininess seems to be the "sizzle" that sells metal fishing tackle), or to camouflage the lousy metal underneath. Shiny snaps can be used to enhance the attraction of an already flashy spoon or spinner, but most experienced anglers prefer the darker, duller finishes. As for corrosion protection, see Chapter 11.

"Brass" can mean almost anything in fishing tackle. Brasses are copper alloys that contain zinc, but the word "brass" often is applied to other copper alloys, particularly the bronzes that are alloyed with tin, aluminum, or silicon. The suitability of brasses and bronzes varies considerably, and not all snap-makers choose wisely. Those which contain more than 16 percent zinc are totally unsuitable for water that is salty, alkaline, or very acid. Most brass wires are too soft—too flexible, and not springy enough—for security in a snap. Unfortunately, some cheap snaps use those soft brass wires.

Brasses and bronzes are about 12 percent more dense than steel alloys, so brass snaps will be at least that much heavier than steel snaps. In reality they will be much heavier, because correspondingly more brass must be used to produce a snap as strong as a steel snap. With few exceptions, brass snaps are inferior to those of steel or of brass and steel.

Spring-tempered carbon steel is good, but only if it is protected by a rust-resistant finish or plating. Stainless steel is better in terms of corrosion resistance, particularly in salt water, but not all wire manufacturers have got the hang of tempering stainless steel for maximum strength and uniform quality. A snap with a stainless-steel wire and brass body will corrode galvanically in salt water, the severity of the corrosion being dependent upon the brass alloy used.

Snap Wires

I single out snap wires for separate mention because the wire, much more than the body, gives a snap its strength and security. If a snap is going to perform badly, you can bet it will be the wire that acts up.

In general, avoid snaps with brass wires. They are too heavy, too easily deformed, too susceptible to spontaneous opening. A major exception is the all-brass McMahon snap, which is one of the strongest and most secure of all the snaps.

Steel snap wires must be hardened and spring-tempered properly. If the wire isn't springy enough, it won't close securely and will come open when you least expect it. If the tempering is overdone, the wire will be brittle. All wire pieces of tackle represent compromises between hardness and malleability, and I don't know of an easy way to assess this balance accurately. Open and close a snap a few times and see how it feels. Check to be sure the wire locks precisely into place each time you close it; a soft wire won't. Open it just a wee bit farther than you might expect to in normal fishing use and see whether the wire bends out of shape when you close it again. A really brittle wire will break during these tests, which won't make you a hero in many tackle shops. Even if you must buy that broken snap it is a very small price to pay for valuable information.

DESIGN FACTORS

We'll be going more deeply into design when we assess each type, but there are a couple of general design factors that greatly contribute to or detract from a snap's performance.

Size

Snap sizes are not standardized, which makes a discussion of size rather difficult. Size is important because it affects water drag and visibility and because it is inextricably tied into considerations of strength, weight, and shape.

Some snap designs are inherently larger than others, but even within design types there can be significant differences. An 80-pound-test Sampo lock snap and a 120-pound Bead Chain lock snap have the same size stainless-steel clasp body. Which is "bigger"? That's hard to figure, and it depends what you mean. The Sampo uses thinner wire and is shaped so that it is longer and wider. The shorter and narrower Bead Chain uses much thicker wire, so is heavier and bulkier. Both are strong, dependable, high-quality snaps. And there is more difference between them than their rated test strengths (to say nothing of the swivels to which they are usually attached). For light weight, ease of opening, and the free swing its wide bend affords a lure, the Sampo would be my choice. For brute strength and slimness of profile, a factor when fishing snaggy bottoms, Bead Chain gets the nod. Compare either of these snaps to a cheap, off-brand, brass-and-steel lock snap and you will discover worlds of difference in strength, dependability, and quality.

Sampo vs. Bead Chain
Lock Snap Sizes

Because of design differences like the one above, it is almost impossible to rate snaps by size and strength. I wish it weren't so, but it is.

Shape

Shape is inherent in the very design of each type of snap, but there is a shape consideration worth mentioning. I alluded to it above when I mentioned the greater lure action afforded by the Sampo lock snap's wider bend shape, and the Bead Chain's greater strength. In Chapter 1 we discussed bend shape and strength in hooks, and the same principles apply in snap-wire shapes. The very strongest snaps—the Coastlock, Pompanette, Cross-Lok, and stainless-steel corkscrews—all have asymmetrical bends. (So does the much weaker safety snap, but it isn't a one-piece snap and it is always made of thinner wire.)

A round and symmetrical snap's bend isn't without its pluses, however. The wider, rounder, and more open a snap's bend is, the more freedom of action the snap will give to a lure, bait, or other piece of tackle. An asymmetrical bend not only restricts a lure's action, but causes it to swing, wobble, or move more to one side than the other. If you are going to use a snap to attach a lure, you will have to go a little large or a little weak to get the proper action out of the lure. I wouldn't worry about going too weak, if you are fishing a properly adjusted drag. That assumes, of course, the snap is of good quality. A large snap will inhibit a lure's action because of its weight. If you are having trouble com-promising between a snap's size, weight, strength, and bend shape, better use a good, strong loop knot instead.

SURVEY OF SNAP TYPES

Safety Snap

The safety snap is the granddaddy of the safety-pin-type connectors (many old-timers refer to all snaps as safety pins or safety snaps). Because of its sharp, asymmetrical bend, the safety snap is never a very good choice for attaching a lure. Even elsewhere in a terminal rig the safety snap is only so-so, being somewhat marginal in strength and security. Seldom used in salt water, but still quite popular among freshwater anglers, the venerable old safety snap probably deserves a well-earned retirement after generations of honorable service.

Safety Snap

Most safety snaps are made with steel (carbon or stainless) wire and a brass body, but some are all stainless steel. If the wire is properly spring-tempered, the safety snap is not very prone to spontaneous opening, but it can rather easily be pulled open when heavily stressed. The working end of the wire (the end that does the opening and closing) lies in a channel of the snap's body and can be dragged straight out under heavy stress.

Lock Snap

Also called the locking or Interlock snap, the lock snap is a real problem to discuss in general terms. It is perhaps the most popular snap in current use, and there are so many manufacturers—and such a variance in quality and design—that you almost have to have a lock snap in hand before you can analyze it.

The lock snap's wide, round bend makes it an obvious choice for attaching lures that can handle a snap. The working end of the wire has a tang, which is secured behind a gap in the body channel and makes the lock snap less prone than the safety snap to pulling open under stress. So far so good, but there are many different varieties of lock snaps. We've already discussed the design differences between the Sampos and Bead Chains, but the more important differences are in quality.

Lock Snap

Chief among the problems plaguing the cheaper lock snaps are the tempering, drawing, and alloy selection of the wire. Some are too soft and deform rather easily, making the snaps subject to spontaneous opening. It doesn't take many openings and closings to bend these wires out of shape so that they won't close securely. Choose lock snaps with care.

Duolock Snap

This one-piece snap, made from a single piece of spring-tempered steel wire (usually stainless), is one of my favorites. Like the other all-wire snaps that will be discussed below, the Duolock uses a crook in the working end of the wire for security. Actually, there are two working ends, because you can open a Duolock from either end, a really handy feature that enables you to join two pieces of tackle that have closed eye rings.

Duolock Snap

The round, wide bend, light weight, security, and good strength of the Duolock make it my first choice for direct attachment to a lure. Under extreme pressure the Duolock should deform without opening, closing against itself, and I have never had any problems with them, but I have heard some grumbling about the smaller sizes opening as they deform.

Duolock snaps are available in plain-finish stainless steel and flat black. Most are sold separately, in six sizes testing from 20 to 150 pounds of breaking strength, but a few are sold as part of a snap-swivel combination. Because of the double-ended design, the Duolock can be joined by the angler to almost any swivel or other piece of fishing hardware.

Lockfast Snap

Lockfast snaps seldom are sold separately; most of them are manufactured as an integral part of a snap swivel, the Lockfast snap replacing one of the eyes on a brass barrel swivel. Like other single-wire snaps, the Lockfast is supposed to deform onto itself without opening under stress, but it is one of the least secure of all snap designs.

Most of the Lockfast snaps you will see—and this is particularly

true of the integral snap swivels—are made of brass wire, and brass is simply too soft to be reliable in a snap. As release-type sinker snaps they are fine; otherwise forget them. Even in stainless steel, the Lockfast snap leaves something to be desired. I had one rated at 75-pound breaking strain open one day while fishing 30-pound-test Micron line, with a drag setting of about 8 pounds, on a 15-pound bluefish.

Coastlock Snap

The Coastlock is probably the most popular of all snap designs among saltwater anglers, and is the odds-on choice of surfcasters in the northeastern states. It is a strong, secure, dependable snap, virtually always manufactured of high-quality stainless-steel wire. When the Coastlock is over-stressed and the wire begins to bend, its design causes the loop that closes the snap to slide along the straight shank, deforming without opening. In the smallest sizes, the thin wires are very hard-tempered to achieve the necessary stiffness and springiness, so they are somewhat prone to breaking if you try to open them too far.

Part of the Coastlock's strength comes from its asymmetrical bend. This shape causes it to partially restrict the action of a lure and to exert a line of pull that is not precisely along the center axis of the lure. For this reason alone, I think the Coastlock as a direct attachment for lures is somewhat overdone among surf and other saltwater anglers. It is a super snap, though.

Coastlock or Pompanette Snap

Pompanette Snap

Virtually everything I have said about the Coastlock snap applies to the almost identical Pompanette, which is formed with a slightly sharper bend, giving it a narrower shape and making it less acceptable than the Coastlock as a direct attachment for lures. It is more popular than the Coastlock among offshore trollers, perhaps because of its narrower profile, and perhaps because Pompanette, Inc., is almost synonymous with bluewater tackle.

In the large sizes (75-pound test and above), Pompanette snaps are often made so that the eye is formed with a double circle of wire. When a Pompanette snap is made for incorporation in a snap swivel, however, even the big ones have their eyes formed the same way as a Coastlock's, as a normal barrel-turn or twisted eye. Pompanette swivels are sized by name rather than by number; the sizes are spin, heavy-duty spin, casting, dolphin, sail, marlin, and tuna.

Cross-Lok Snap

The Cross-Lok snap, which was introduced by Berkley and Company for the 1979 fishing season, is a clever addition to the field, superficially resembling a cross between the duolock and the coastlock or Pompanette. It is a double-ended snap like the former, which gives it great versatility in rigging, and it is just about equivalent in strength to the latter. The Cross-Lok snap is available in four sizes (testing 40, 75, 125, and 200 pounds), and two finishes (stainless steel or flat black) and is sold separately or attached to barrel swivels or to Berkley's new ball-bearing swivels.

Cross-Lok Snap

Slim and quite snag-resistant, the Cross-Lok has an asymmetrical bend, which helps to give it superior strength but makes it somewhat restrictive of lure action. On balance, though, it rates very high in my book.

McMahon Snap

On the West Coast, those who troll offshore for tuna and black marlin and who jig deep reefs for giant seabass favor the McMahon snap, a strong, secure snap that superficially resembles old-fashioned ice tongs. Secure as it is, though, the McMahon isn't as strong as the Coastlock, Pompanette, or Cross-Lok. The McMahon is a chrome-plated brass snap (in bright or black finish), and brass is both softer and heavier than stainless steel. It is good, high-quality brass, however, plenty strong and hard.

McMahon Snap

The McMahon is a relatively short, reasonably narrow snap, but it is a bit heavy for its size and fairly thick in the crosswire dimension, thanks to the density and tensile strength of brass. I am told that the McMahon's popularity on the West Coast is beginning to wane in the face of competition from Coastlocks, Pompanettes, and corkscrews, but it seems to be gaining ground in the East.

Corkscrew Snap

The corkscrew really shouldn't be called a snap because nothing on it snaps. But it's a great connector. The corkscrew ranks right alongside the Coastlock, Pompanette, and Cross-Lok in strength and security, and beats them all for ease of attachment and detachment. It isn't as versatile as the other super-strength snaps, however; the corkscrew is designed for making quick-change replacements of looped leaders. It has been popular for years among those who troll the offshore tuna and billfish grounds around Hawaii, and in recent years the smaller sizes have become quite popular among salmon trollers in the Pacific Northwest.

Corkscrew Snap

As its name implies, the corkscrew snap is a spiral design, which makes it handy for changing looped, pretied, and usually pre-baited trolling leaders. Thread the wire on the open end of the spiral into a leader loop, twirl a couple or three times, and voilà! After a few false starts and weird-looking results, I have taught myself how to make lightweight corkscrew snaps out of heavy stainless-steel leader wire (sizes 15 to 19) using two pairs of pliers, one roundnose and the other parallel-jaw Sargent Sportmates. My home-builts aren't nearly as strong, secure, or streamlined as the factory jobs, but you can't easily buy corkscrew snaps in the East.

The Sampo Company of Barneveld, New York, has a ball-bearing snap-swivel that features stainless-steel corkscrew snaps made by the Rome Specialty Company in Rome, New York, but they are sold mostly in Hawaii and on the West Coast. The Rome corkscrews are super-duty heavyweights. They are available only in two large sizes that probably test considerably in excess of the 165 and 200 pounds conservatively listed in the Sampo catalog. Virtually all other corkscrew snaps are made of plated brass. Those made by the Evans Manufacturing Company of Camano Island, Washington, are nearly as strong as Rome's stainless ones. Evans corkscrews are sometimes sold separately, but they are seen more often incorporated into flashers, dodgers, and other tackle made by Luhr Jensen, and some other West Coast tackle companies. The softer brass corkscrews imported from Japan by Martin Tackle and a few other companies aren't nearly as strong, but they are strong enough for salmon sport fishing. The people at Martin tell me their corkscrews are about half to three-fourths as strong as McMahon snaps of similar size.

If you can find them, try corkscrew snaps; I am confident you will like them and will join me in wondering why they haven't caught on east of the Rockies.

Fly Clips

The smallest and lightest snaps I know are the tiny spring clips used by lazy fly-fishermen who like to change flies but who don't like to tie knots. Several companies make these clips and market them under various names; the Wilson-Allen No-Knot Fas-Snap and the Kwik Klip by Al's Goldfish Lure Co. are among the better known brands or trademarks. These little snaps are made in three sizes, the smallest of which supposedly will not sink a dry fly. All are reasonably strong for their size, being made of nickel-plated, spring-tempered carbon steel. The larger sizes are often used by ultralight- and light-tackle spinfishermen. The well-known and extraordinarily effective Frisky Fly comes with a fly clip more or less permanently attached to the eye of its hook. Just why it is better to tie the line to a fly clip rather than to the hook eye (via a loop knot, of course) I do not know, but the Frisky Fly works so well I'm not tempted to experiment with adaptations.

Fly Clip

Anyone who has used fly clips on the end of a line or leader already knows that they are secure only when the size of the fly clip is appropriate to the wire diameter of the lure's ringed eye. If you snap a fly clip onto an eye of fairly large-diameter wire, the thicker wire may spring open the fly clip. And a sprung fly-clip is anything but secure, especially if you switch back to lures with finer-gauge wire eyes.

The Lindy/Little Joe swivel clip, a barrel swivel in which one of the wire swiveling shafts is formed as a clip-type snap instead of a looped or twisted eye, employs a smilar but more secure clip. Unlike the standard fly clip, these are not easy to unspring and so can be used safely with a variety of gear.

Swivel Clip

Ampersand Snap

These little devils, slightly larger cousins of fly clips, go by dozens of trade names and I don't know what their proper generic name is. Some people call them figure-eight snaps, which confuses them with several other snaps and connectors that go by that name. I call them ampersand snaps because that is what they most closely resemble: the ampersand, that strange symbol (&) that means "and."

Ampersand Snap

By whatever name, ampersand snaps are used for much the same purposes as the smaller fly clips, but are less popular among flycasters and more popular among spinfishermen. They come in two or three sizes, all of which are larger, heavier, and a little more secure than fly clips. Actually, there are two variations or configurations. One uses a little tang or loop to hold the snap shut, and the other doesn't. The one with the tang is more secure.

Butterfly Snap

A few years ago butterfly snaps were extremely popular offshore trolling accessories. Essentially a single piece of wire bent so that a Pompanette or Coastlock-type snap is formed in each end, the butterfly snap is used to make quick-change connections between looped leaders, terminal hardware, and other components of a complex trolling rig. In recent years, the butterfly snap has been

Butterfly Snap

losing out to connecting links, Abe 'n' Al hookups, and to Pompanette's own swiveled double snaps. This last is simply a barrel swivel with a Pompanette snap attached to each end. Butterfly snaps are very easy to make (in light-tackle sizes) from stiff stainless-steel leader wire.

Connecting Link

I grew up calling these slide-link connectors, a name that describes them well, but connecting link has become the standard monicker. Unfortunately, the various little pieces of hardware that often come attached to the eye of lures are also known collectively as connecting links. At any rate, the connecting link I mean is the one in which the bent wire forms the outline of an old-fashioned barbell or long dumbbell, with a folded sleeve that slides along the connecting shafts.

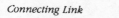 *Connecting Link*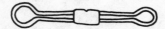

These double-ended connectors are very handy for constructing special-purpose terminal rigs. They are often incorporated in, or used as, fish-finder rigs with sliding sinkers, and some anglers use them as sinker snaps in standard, fixed-sinker terminal rigs. In either case, connecting links are too strong to be considered sinker-release clips.

Considering the ease with which they may be opened and closed, connecting links are surprisingly strong and secure. I suppose it is possible to open one accidentally by knocking it against a rock or other bottom obstruction, but its long arms usually will prevent its dropping the attached tackle. Connecting links are made of nickel-plated brass, and the brass wire is almost as strong and stiff as that used to make McMahon snaps.

Sinker-Release Snaps

When bottom-fishing, particularly on rocky, broken bottoms, around wrecks and reefs, or anywhere the subsurface environment offers a lot of snags and hazards, it is a good idea to rig your sinker so that you can leave it behind when it becomes irretrievably fouled, without having to break off the rest of your terminal rig. The simplest way to do this is to make sinker dropper lines that test a good bit lighter than your main fishing line, or to tie a simple overhand knot in the weight's dropper line. But if you will be changing weights frequently to cope with tidal flow, water depth, countercurrents, and other variables, you might want to use a sinker snap instead.

Sinker-Release Snap

On sinkers that have wire eyes, almost any lightweight snap can be used, as long as it is weaker than your fishing line. But with bank sinkers and other weights that have thick eye rings molded into the lead, larger sinker snaps will have to be used. Many configurations are used in sinker-release snaps, but the most common is the one I have illustrated. They are commercially available in most tackle shops, but are also very easy to make. How readily the snap will drop a sinker depends upon the type, temper, and diameter of the wire used, the shape of the snap's bend, and the distance the release leg extends past the securing loop. Soft brass wire is your best bet, but I sometimes use wire leader material (either stainless-steel or piano wire), and I've even used sections of coat hanger.

Other designs are less common, but one you can make very easily out of wire is a jumbo version of the ampersand snap. If you have nothing handy but soft, flexible wire trolling line or bait-rigging wire, just attach the sinker however you can, making several loose wraps with the soft wire. It will unravel under stress. Don't be afraid to use twine, cotton string, rubber bands, or anything else that will withstand the stresses of the cast or retrieve but will break before your line will.

Miscellaneous Connectors

Numerous other pieces of connecting hardware find their way into most terminal rigs or the components thereof. Unless you are a real tackle tinkerer you probably don't buy these little bits of metal separately. Most of them—S-connectors, figure eight links, spring-screw eyes, and so on—usually come more or less permanently attached to plugs, spinners, and other lures and gadgets. Their shapes and designs do not affect their strength and security nearly as much as the wires from which they are made. You won't be able to get test strengths or any other data on most of these pieces, but they often are stronger than you might otherwise imagine. Still, I don't think you should use any piece of hardware in which you lack confidence. If it looks or feels suspiciously weak, replace it. Confidence counts a lot in fishing.

SPLIT RINGS

Split rings deserve special mention because they are used on so many pieces of tackle, are regularly replaced by anglers in routine tackle maintenance, and are used instead of snaps by a small minority of anglers with exemplary patience and tough thumbnails. Split rings, I am sorry to say, are not as strong as many anglers and tackle companies believe. When replacing the treble hooks on plugs and other lures intended to take muskies, salmon, lunker largemouths, a few other freshwater gamesters, and most saltwater species, I much prefer to use hooks with open eye rings.

Split Rings

It isn't always easy to tell what kind of metal was used to make the wire in a split ring, nor how hard the wire was drawn or tempered. Unfortunately, the strength, security, and corrosion resistance of split rings is heavily dependent upon those three, usually unknown, variables. Split rings may be made of brass, carbon steel, or stainless steel, and the metals may be plain, plated with nickel or chrome, blackened, or otherwise finished. Because I fish so often in salt water I prefer to use stainless-steel rings for their superior strength and durability. But they are more expensive and aren't always easy to find.

Rosco split rings are quite strong, as split rings go, so don't try to apply the following Rosco size-strength relationships to split rings made by other manufacturers:

SIZE	STRENGTH	SIZE	STRENGTH	SIZE	STRENGTH
2/0	10 lb	3	30 lb	7	60 lb
1/0	15 lb	4	30 lb	8	80 lb
1	20 lb	5	40 lb	9	100 lb
2	25 lb	6	50 lb	10	170 lb

As is obvious in the above chart, split-ring size numbers reverse the procedure used in size-numbering hooks; that is, the aught numbers are used for the smallest sizes.

O. Mustad has introduced oval split rings, which are particularly nice for attaching hooks to plugs and other lures. The sharp-ended oval shape prevents some of the hook tangling that can plague the angler who casts multi-gang-hooked lures.

JUMP RINGS

A jump ring is nothing but an open ring of fairly hard, heavy-gauge wire which is butted together without any overlapping of the ends. Jump rings are often soldered, brazed, or welded shut.

 Jump or Butt Ring

Some manufacturers prefer to call them butt rings; still others like the term cut rings. Sampo and a good many other tackle companies that use welded jump rings usually call them solid rings. No matter what the name, those that have been closed by one of the means described are stronger than those that are simply butted together, and much stronger than split rings of the same overall ring diameter. The rated breaking strengths of three different ball-bearing swivels will give you some idea just how much stronger, because the rings are the weakest components.

	SIZE:	1	2	3	4	5	6	8
Size & Breaking Strength (lb)								
Sampo w/ Split Rings		10	12	15	30	50	70	—
"Cheapos" w/ Silver-Soldered Split Rings		25	45	60	80	100	200	—
Sampo w/ Welded Jump Rings		—	—	100	150	200	300	500

All of the rings rated above are made of reasonably high-quality stainless steel, with the Sampos having an edge in the alloy department. The size numbers used above are those assigned by Sampo and one seller of the cheap import to their ball-bearing swivels, the bodies of which are closely equivalent in size. However, there are some differences in size among the rings themselves—which are size-numbered differently anyway—so don't try to draw too many specific conclusions from the comparisons just made.

COMPARING SNAP SIZES AND STRENGTHS

There are major differences in strength between the various types of snaps, and I would love to be able to give you a simple chart that tells the whole story in just a few words and numbers. However, as is so often the case in fishing tackle, snap sizes are not standardized, either among types or among manufacturers.

Although it is difficult to rank or compare them in a universally meaningful or scientifically precise way, we are going to give it a shot anyway.

Besides the actual size and configuration or design of the snap itself, variations in the alloy, temper, and diameter of the wire used to form the snap affect its strength. Snaps of a single type made by the same manufacturer will vary somewhat from batch to batch because of variations in raw materials and tolerances in manufacturing. These variations explain, at least in part, the often imponderable differences in listed test strengths from catalog to catalog. That some makers have better quality control—and therefore more uniform products—goes without saying.

Having said all that, let me throw caution, and perhaps common sense as well, to the winds and try listing size-strength relationships for the major types of snaps. Several caveats are in order:

Pay no attention to the size *numbers* listed here, because they are arbitrary numbers assigned by me. (In my table, a size 1 safety snap is about 7/16 inches long, and a size 6, about 1⅜ inches.) Different size-numbering systems are used for the different types of snaps, and not all manufacturers of the same type use the same system. Nor are the sizes listed in the column and assigned the same number necessarily strictly equivalent in actual physical size. Within some types the size step-ups are orderly and uniform, but in others some of the leaps are a bit large. Subjective though it may be, I have skipped a size number here and there, if eyeball logic seemed to dictate doing so. Alas, there isn't an entirely logical and objective way to bring order to this chaotic situation.

I have had to omit listing certain types, principally because there are too many differences from manufacturer to manufacturer, and from batch to batch by the same manufacturer. I haven't been able to obtain, either by inquiry or bench testing, even reasonably reliable "average" strengths for fly clips, ampersand snaps, or Lockfast snaps, for example. There simply is too much variation. In the case of Lockfasts, the ones made of brass wire are quite erratic in performancae, but *all* the variations fall on the weak side of acceptable strength. Those made of stainless steel by the Bead Chain Tackle Company are another story. I haven't listed them in the chart below for fear you might expect the brass ones to perform as well. They won't. Bead Chain's Lockfast snaps are available only as integral parts of their various swivels, leaders, and rigs; they aren't sold as loose snaps. The three sizes Bead Chain makes are rated at 25, 75, and 150 pounds. While we are on the subject of Bead Chain snaps, I ought to warn you that the company seems to have a go-it-alone attitude on terminology, listing their Lockfast snaps as "lock type snaps" and their Interlocks as "safety snaps."

One more thing. The test strengths listed below were supplied by manufacturers of high-quality examples of each type. Because of my limited access to proper test equipment, I have not tried to verify the ratings. But my crude bench tests seem to show that the manufacturers of the high-quality snaps are pretty accurate, maybe even a little conservative. Now and then, however, nearly everyone seems to get hold of some poorly tempered wire and turns out a batch of snaps that are a bit weak, so if a snap wire feels softer than usual, pass it by. As for cheap, shoddy examples of the types listed, don't expect them to perform as well. And take with a grain of salt any test or breaking-strength figures you might see listed for them. Manufacturing tolerances of the cheapies are so great that variances in their strengths make average figures meaningless.

With all those caveats in mind, then, let us take the icy plunge:

		Size and Breaking Strength (lb)							
SNAP TYPE	NOMINAL SIZE:	1	2	3	4	5	6	7	8
Safety		15	25	40	50	55	60	75	NA
Interlock		15	25	40	50	55	60	75	120
Duolock		20	25	40	NA	50	NA	85	150
Coastlock		NA	40	75	NA	125	200	250	450
Pompanette		18	22	50	NA	75	95	160	300
Cross-Lok		NA	40	NA	NA	75	125	200	NA
McMahon		NA	18	40	80	80	110	150	NA

It wasn't possible to include corkscrew snaps in the above table because none of the manufacturers could furnish the breaking strengths. And the corkscrews are too strong to test on the jerry-built rigs I have been using in my study. My best guess is that the corkscrews that are manufactured in this country by Rome Specialty Company (of stainless steel) and Evans Manufacturing Company (plated brass) are at least as strong as Coastlocks and Pompanettes of similar size. The cheap plated-brass ones from Japan probably are about as strong as the same-size McMahons, maybe a little weaker.

USING SNAPS

The proper and effective employment of snaps is very simple. It is, in fact, a snap. When used in the middle of a long, complicated trolling rig, snaps can be fairly large because strength and security are more important here than weight, drag, or visibility. At the terminal end of a casting or spinning rig, though, the smaller and lighter the snap, the better. If the snap will be attached directly to a lure, the shape of its bend also becomes important.

Any high-quality snap of appropriate size is strong enough for midrig trolling application, but the strongest, most secure designs generally are best: Coastlock, Pompanette, Cross-Lok, corkscrew, McMahon. If weight and drag are critical, forget the last two.

Light weight is usually important when a snap is tied onto the terminal end of a line or leader, and the one-piece wire snaps are generally lighter than the snaps that have sheet-metal bodies. Corkscrew and McMahon snaps, while one-piece designs, are fairly heavy and probably should be used only when a long leader will separate the snap from the hook or lure. If a lure is being attached directly to a snap, make sure the snap has a wide, round, symmetrical bend. Taking all things into consideration—shape, size, weight, and strength—the Duolock snap is generally my choice for direct attachment of a lure. But if I need super strength and think the lure can tolerate the slightly off-center pull and the relative constriction of the narrower bend, I won't hesitate to use a Coastlock, Pompanette, or Cross-Lok. As for the one-piece round-bend, symmetrical Lockfast snap, it's strictly *caveat emptor*. Avoid those made of soft brass wire, and test the steel ones for strength and security before depending on them in a tough fight with a big fish.

So far I haven't even mentioned safety and Interlock snaps, which are the most popular ones in use today. It isn't that I think they are bad snaps, or that I never use them, because I do. It's just that they are never my first choice. I often use both types in freshwater angling, because they are so readily available and because they come built into so many rigs and tackle items. Anyway, they usually are acceptably strong and secure for freshwater angling. In salt water, though, I almost never use safety snaps and I use interlock snaps only when I haven't anything else handy or when I don't anticipate really heavy stress loads.

I use connecting links (slide-link connectors) for all sorts of things: to make fishfinder rigs for surf-fishing; in a lot of my bench testing; and almost any time I need a double-ended, reliable, reasonably strong connector. Connecting links are not very good as terminal connectors, however, because of their size and weight.

As for split and jump rings, there isn't much I can add to what I have already said. Split rings are so variable in quality that it isn't possible to be very dogmatic about their strength, security, corrosion resistance, or anything else. If you can get strong split rings, they can be more secure than snaps whenever you want to join two pieces of tackle that don't have to be unsnapped very often. For tackle tinkering at home, I have found that a two-dollar pair of split-ring pliers comes in very handy. My tackle boxes are already so cluttered I don't often take those special-purpose pliers fishing, though.

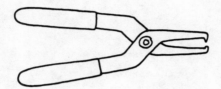

Split-Ring Pliers

4

Swivel Tips

WE MIGHT AS WELL get one thing straight right at the outset: Contrary to popular usage, combination snap-swivels should almost never be used to attach lures to line or leader and never to attach hooks. In fact, as handy a combination as snap-swivels are, they ought to be used sparingly and cautiously anywhere in a terminal rig.

I don't know why, but a lot of fishermen seem to think that snaps and swivels go together like shoes and socks. Snaps and swivels are separate pieces of tackle with altogether different functions and purposes. Swivels prevent or remove line twist, and snaps permit quick-change connections. They must be considered apart from one another in making terminal-tackle selections and decisions, and much of the time they should be tied into terminal rigs separately. When used appropriately, snap-swivels are useful and handy, even terrific. But when used inappropriately, they are terrible. When in doubt, don't use them—go with separate snaps and swivels.

Combination Snap-Swivel

Why so wary of the combination? Because most anglers reach for the combination hardware when only a snap or a swivel is

126

wanted, and because our goal should be to minimize our use of terminal hardware. Extra hardware in a terminal rig adds weight and bulk, which dampen the lure action and the vibrations that a nibbling fish sends up the line; cause the terminal-rig geometry to sag; pull surface lures too low in the water or even beneath the surface; increase water drag and visibility; and cause other hydrodynamic complications. A snap-swivel adds the weight and bulk of two pieces of hardware in the same place, thus exaggerating all these problems. Every little bump and angle in your terminal rig increases its chances of fouling in weeds, rocks, brush, or whatever else lurks down below. And a piece of hardware superfluously employed is needlessly exposed to the hazards of damage, corrosion, and outright loss. In the case of swivels, corrosion exposure is the greatest of these hazards. All swivels corrode, and corrosion fouls up swivels. Use swivels only when you need them and they will be more likely to work when they must.

When tying a terminal rig, give each component due consideration: If a piece of tackle won't help to entice, hook, battle, or land a fish, leave it in the box. If you need a swivel, use a swivel. If you need or want a snap, use a snap. If you need both, think twice before settling on a combination snap-swivel. Don't feel guilty if you finally decide to use the combo. It's the habit that's wrong, not the hardware. Base your decision on conscious reflection, not unconscious reflex.

In trolling, snap-swivels are a godsend. The average trolling rig usually needs to be swiveled in several different places and during the course of a day's trolling an angler might make dozens of changes in the components of the rig: bait, lure, keel, dodger or flasher, leader, sinker, and so on. Snap-swivels facilitate these changes without adding appreciably to the already considerable weight, bulk, water resistance, and visibility of the trolling rig.

Trollers who use wobbling spoons, and perhaps even some other lures that are wont to revolve, may be justified in using a snap-swivel at the end of the rig. For such lures, the terminal *swivel* is probably necessary or at least desirable; as for the *snap,* a loop knot would suffice. But some wobbling spoons, I confess, are not hampered in their action by snaps and a very few might even work better when snapped rather than loop-knotted to the leader.

Ordinarily, though, a snap-swivel right at the lure is about as effective as using a dirty sock for bait. The weight nearly always dampens the lure's action, turning well-designed wriggles into uncertain quivers and lurches. Some lures use torque or rotational force against the line or leader to produce their action. A swivel at the lure will certainly destroy the action; as for a swivel located a foot or so up the line, follow the instructions that came with the lure, or experiment. In the case of very small lures that don't use metallic flash in their attractive repertoire, a shiny snap-swivel attached to the nose may frighten wary fish. If you had a dime for every time you actually *needed* to use a snap-swivel on the end of your line or leader, you probably would still be working on the price of a decent lure. (If you troll a lot with spoons, make that the price of a decent reel.) If you had a dime for every time it were even permissible to use a snap-swivel to attach a hook, I doubt you would yet have even the price of a local pay-phone call.

Visibility is a real problem if you attach a baited hook to a snap-swivel. At best, smashing strikes will be turned into tentative nibbles. In addition, snap-swivels at the hook introduce all sorts of unwanted and unpredictable angles and rotational motions into the geometry and physics of hook-setting, not to mention the odd actions and visual aspects they can give a bait.

So much for the sermon. Now for a sinner's testimony. I grew up using snap-swivels on everything—plugs, spoons, spinners, jigs, hooks, snells, leaders, you name it. I don't remember just why, but I did. I had become so set in my ways that, once I discovered the error of them, it took years to break the bad habit. Long after I knew better, it just didn't *feel* right to tie a terminal rig that didn't have a snap-swivel down at its nether end. I tried tapering off gradually and I tried going cold turkey, but I couldn't get the monkey off my back. Finally I took the most drastic step I could think of.

I removed all of the inexpensive brass snap-swivels from my tackle boxes and replaced them with top-drawer, top-dollar, stainless-steel Sampo ball-bearing snap-swivels. Now, Sampos are worth every penny they cost, but it takes quite a few pennies to purchase one. The smallest Sampo ball-bearing snap-swivels cost at least half a buck, the ones I use for surf-fishing go for around a buck, and the really big, heavy-duty ones used in offshore big-game fishing can cost considerably upward of $3 or $4 apiece!

Each time I caught myself using a snap-swivel on the end of my line, I cut it off and threw it away. (You should have seen some of the looks I got, tossing those bright, shiny, expensive Sampos into the drink. Mindful of the waste, I once tried giving one of them to a fellow who was fishing next to me on a party boat, but he wouldn't accept it. Instead, he moved to the other side of the boat, apparently figuring me for a degenerate or a crazy.) This approach to the problem shot hell out of my fishing budget for a while, but it finally cured me of the habit. Poorer but wiser, as the saying goes.

TO SWIVEL OR NOT TO SWIVEL

The question of whether and when to use a swivel can be a vexatious one. It is also a question of considerable controversy among angling experts. Over the years I have been exposed to the whole gamut of opinion and I have tried it all, from swiveling everything to swiveling nothing. As you might guess, I have decided that the extremists of both camps are misguided and that the truth sprawls rather awkwardly across the gray places in the middle. *Whether* to use a swivel in a particular rig is ultimately a personal decision, and I'm not sure there are a lot of objective truths that can be turned into guidelines. But *how* to swivel a rig is something else again, a matter of pure and applied physics, and specifically that branch called *tribology,* the study of friction.

Those who hold the extreme positions in the range of opinion on swivels can marshal a lot of logic but not much hard data in defense of their positions. If you ever read fishing articles in the outdoor magazines, or books on fishing, you are probably familiar with the arguments. Even if you aren't, I don't intend to trot them out, line them up, and present the pros and cons. Instead, I'll give you my own biased, middle-ground position on the subject, and I'll try to marshal as much scientific support as I can.

Swivels are primarily for preventing or removing twist in the line or leader and secondarily for permitting or promoting baits, lures, spinners, or other parts of a terminal rig to revolve. Your mental picture of a swivel should be a *motion* picture. Swivels should not be used when other pieces of tackle or a simple knot will do. In the United States, for example, most anglers use swivels as stops when fishing with sliding-sinker rigs. In Australia and New Zealand, small brass rings are used for this purpose. In Canada and Great Britain, split-shot sinkers are more common. All three pieces of hardware will do the job, but of the three, the swivel is the largest and most expensive and the most "overqualified." Why soak a swivel in corrosive water if you don't need its swiveling capacity?

The almost inherent unreliability of most swivels—they won't always turn when you want them to—coupled with the uncertain strength of some inexpensive ones, had me edging toward the no-swivel end of the spectrum, until I switched almost entirely to fixed-spool spinning tackle. Spinfishermen and spincasters know that line twist is a serious and perennial problem, and it will get the best of you if you don't learn how best to select and rig swivels.

HOW SWIVELS WORK AND WHY THEY OFTEN DON'T

What we anglers call a *swivel,* a mechanical engineer would call a *thrust bearing* (and a primitive one at that). The great advances made in recent years in bearing design and construction and in lubrication are of little consequence when it comes to swivels. No angler is going to pay the going price of a modern, efficient industrial bearing, which would be too heavy besides. When we go fishing we subject the thrust bearings we call swivels to all sorts of horrendous conditions that would cause an industrial engineer to go prematurely gray. No wonder swivels are so generally undependable.

Two forces are chiefly at work on and in a swivel: line pull or tensile stress (which bearing engineers call *load*) and rotational or torsional stress (*torque* for short). Torque is both the reason we need to use swivels (to prevent the torque from twisting the line) and that which makes a swivel work. Load or tensile stress is what keeps a swivel from working, by pulling the two bearing surfaces together tightly so they resist moving against one another. That resistance to motion we call *friction,* and it is measured as the equal and opposite force that is required to overcome the resistance. That *frictional force* is a function of the torque or rotational force. So long as the torque exceeds the frictional force, the swivel will twirl as intended. If the torque is less than the frictional force, the bearing surfaces won't move against one another and the whole swivel will revolve as a single unit, passing the torque up the line as twist.

Forces at Work on a Swivel   Torque   Load

Frictional force is not constant in a swivel or bearing. It is directly proportional to the load or tensile stress. This means that a doubling of the load will result in a doubling of the required frictional force, and so on. Because the relationship between load and frictional force is constant, it can be expressed as a fraction or ratio called the *coefficient of friction,* usually listed as a decimal figure. For brass-to-brass slider-bearing swivels, the coefficient of friction in water is roughly 0.173; it is about 0.0008 for stainless-steel ball-bearing swivels. Unfortunately the angler has very little control over these forces—load, torque, or friction—so he has to choose and rig his swivels to make the most of what little control he does have.

Before we get into the merits and demerits of the different types of swivels, let us consider a few more principles.

Quality

Manufacturing quality is all-important in swivels because thrust bearings are extremely dependent for their efficiency on the smoothness and mating of the bearing surfaces. Industries spend hundreds and even thousands of dollars on a single thrust bearing to get the necessary quality, and in fishing swivels we are talking pennies. It is no surprise, then, that swivels are sometimes woefully inefficient. It makes no sense whatsoever to try stretching the angling budget by pinching on swivels. Buy better swivels and skip one can of beer or cup of coffee. The best swivels for a given job aren't necessarily the most expensive, but they are never the cheapest ones available. Your best guide to quality is the good reputation of certain brand names. When in doubt, rely on close visual inspection and on the bench tests described later.

In the ideal swivel, the bearing surfaces would be perfectly smooth, perfectly matched, and made of a hard, noncorroding metal that had a very low coefficient of friction. In addition, the swivel would be designed so that the load or tensile force pulled the bearing surfaces together in a direction perpendicular to the plane of their perfectly matched surfaces. For many practical reasons, the ideal swivel does not exist. But some come a lot closer than others.

Size

The second law of friction states that friction is independent of the surface areas of the bearing surfaces involved. This is tricky to explain, but try to imagine two apparently smooth metal plates magnified several thousand times. One expert in tribology said that pressing two polished metal surfaces together is a little like turning Austria upside down on top of Switzerland. There are rather dramatic peaks and valleys among the surface grain structures of all metals, and when two metal surfaces are pressed together the peaks are crushed and flattened until the actual contact area will *bear* the force that is being applied. That is why they are called "bearings."

Nevertheless, for complicated reasons small swivels are generally more efficient than larger swivels of the same type, material, and quality. By more efficient, I mean they turn more easily or exhibit less frictional resistance.

Strength

All swivels except the very shoddiest are relatively strong. Without even knowing the breaking strength of a swivel, you probably won't be tempted to choose one so small that it would break before your line does. Most swivels tend to pull apart when they finally give up the ghost. In the case of ball-bearing swivels, the rings will break before any part of the swivel's body even approaches its breaking point. Offshore swivels are the strongest of all swivels. I have never seen one break.

Because of vast differences in size-numbering systems among the various types of swivels, it isn't possible to provide a simple size-strength chart that covers all the different types. And there are differences between different manufacturers of the same type of swivel—differences in numbering systems and differences in breaking strengths. I wish I could boil the accompanying wilderness of tables down to one, but it simply isn't possible.

SIZE-STRENGTH TABLE FOR OFFSHORE SWIVELS

SIZE	BREAKING STRENGTH (LB)
4	243
5	243
6	397
7	529
8	617
9	794
10.5	992
12	1653
14	1940

SIZE-STRENGTH TABLE FOR BARREL AND BOX SWIVELS

Breaking Strength (lb)

SIZE	IMPORTED "CRANE"	BERKLEY	POMPANETTE	ROSCO	ONO BOX
12	NA	NA	50	20	20
11	NA	NA	NA	NA	22
10	NA	75	NA	30	24
9	NA	NA	NA	NA	26
8	NA	NA	NA	NA	29
7	NA	75	75	75	33
6	40	NA	NA	NA	37
5	56	100	100	90	42
4	64	NA	NA	NA	49
3	101	100	NA	100	60
2	125	NA	NA	NA	73
1	163	150	150	150	88
1/0	214	200	200	NA	104
2/0	295	250	NA	225	121
3/0	390	300	300	NA	141
4/0	460	350	NA	350	163
5/0	496	400	NA	NA	214
6/0	NA	500	NA	600	298
7/0	NA	NA	NA	NA	408
8/0	NA	1000	NA	900	639
9/0	NA	1000	NA	1000	728
10/0	NA	1500	1500	NA	NA
11/0	NA	1500	NA	NA	NA
12/0	NA	NA	NA	1500	NA

NOTE: *The breaking strengths listed in the first four columns are for various brands of modern, split-head-type barrel swivels, often called Crane swivels. Caution is advised in using the figures in the first column. These figures, supplied by Lakeland Industries, are for a single, high-quality brand of swivel imported from Asia, and the size numbers are those of the manufacturer. These size numbers are not directly equivalent to the sizes used by and listed for the three prominent American brands following. (The breaking strengths listed for the American brands tend to be on the conservative side.) The various importers, distributors, and retailers of imported Crane swivels often use their own size-numbering systems, further confusing the situation.*

The breaking strengths listed in the last column—again supplied by Lakeland Industries—are for the high-quality Ono brand of box swivels, which are just about the only ones available in the U.S. The same strengths may be attributed with some confidence to old-fashioned, twisted-eye (or single-head) barrel swivels of the same size and quality; the same relatively soft brass wire is used to make the twisted eyes in both cases. However, test strengths for twisted-eye swivels are extremely dependent upon overall manufacturing quality.

SIZE-STRENGTH TABLE FOR BEAD-CHAIN SWIVELS

SIZE	BREAKING STRENGTH (LB)
20 series	25
30 series	30
60 series	35
100 series	75
130 series	175

NOTE: *The sizes and breaking strengths listed above are for swivels manufactured by the Bead Chain Tackle Company, and may or may not be applicable to bead-chain swivels made by other companies. Rosco's bead-chain swivels, for example, come in three sizes rated by the manufacturer at 30, 100, and 150 pounds.*

SIZE-STRENGTH TABLE FOR BALL-BEARING SWIVELS

Breaking Strength (lb)

SIZE	SAMPO W/SPLIT RINGS	SAMPO W/SOLID RINGS	BERKLEY	IMPORTS
1	10	NA	50	25
2	12	NA	75	45
3	15	100	135	60
4	30	150	175	80
5	50	200	260	100
6	70	300	290	200
7	NA	NA	310	NA
8	NA	500	NA	NA

NOTE: *Sampo's top-quality ball-bearing swivels are supplied with various snaps and with split rings or "solid" rings (actually, welded stainless-steel jump rings). The breaking strengths of Sampo swivels depend upon the hardware attached to the swivel itself, which is extremely strong.*

Imported ball-bearing swivels sold in this country under a variety of brand names come from various sources. The sizes and strengths listed here are typical.

Berkley's new ball-bearing swivels are supplied with soldered split rings in sizes 1 through 3 and with welded or "solid" rings in sizes 4 through 7.

In selecting a certain size swivel, keep in mind not only its breaking strength, but also its size, weight, and efficiency. Small swivels are more efficient than large ones, but most swivels (box, barrel, bead-chain, and so-called Crane swivels, for example) will stop swiveling when the load or tensile stress is a little short of half the swivel's rated breaking strength. So if you want the swivel to work under fairly high stress loads, you may have to use a slightly larger swivel—or a small one of a more efficient type. Offshore and ball-bearing swivels are much more efficient than the others.

COMPARING SWIVEL TYPES

All swivels are thrust bearings, but there are two major types of thrust bearings among the swivels: slider bearings and ball bearings. Within the slider-bearing category there are many different types, each with its peculiar set of assets and liabilities. In reading the paragraphs that follow, keep in mind that differences in manufacturing quality can be so great as to more than offset the described design differences among the types. And some types are more quality-dependent than others.

Slider-Bearing Swivels

Most fishing swivels are slider-type thrust bearings. That is, the bearing surfaces slide against one another when the swivel is operating. There are four major types of slider-bearing swivels: barrel, box, bead-chain, and offshore swivels. (We'll discuss three-way and crossline swivels separately.) Actually there are two subtypes of barrel swivels: the old-fashioned, single-head kind with twisted wire eyes, and the more modern, split-head kind often identified as "Crane" swivels. Most domestic manufacturers of "Crane-type" swivels simply call them barrel swivels and say the name "Crane" should be restricted to Oriental imports of the same design. Semantics aside, there are enough differences between the two kinds of barrel swivels to justify treating them as distinct types.

BARREL SWIVEL, SINGLE-HEAD TYPE

Twisted-eye barrel swivels have not been made in the United States for about two decades and all those you see on the market are imported, mostly from Asia. Their quality ranges from pretty fair to utterly worthless. I'm not being a flag-waving, buy-American jingoist, either. Domestic tackle entrepreneurs make a fair share of angling junk, and some truly superior tackle hails from Japan. The very design of the single-head barrel swivel incorporates several disadvantages, which are tolerated because of its low cost of manufacture. (Ironically, American manufacturers gave

Barrel Swivel, Single-Head Type

up on the type because of cost. It doesn't lend itself to mechanized or automated methods, so is cheap to make only where labor is cheap.)

Like the majority of swivels, barrel types are of all-brass construction. There are many different alloys of brass, and they vary considerably in strength, corrosion resistance, and hardness, but it is impossible to determine which alloys are used to make which swivels. This observation applies to all swivels, not just twisted-eye barrel swivels. Sometimes the brass is blackened or darkened or plated with nickel or other metals, but it's brass underneath.

The body of the barrel swivel begins life as a brass tube, which is cut to appropriate length and then crimped or swaged around the bearing heads of the previously formed swiveling eyes. The barrel-shaped body is quite strong, but it does have the disadvantage of a curved bearing surface.

The eyes of a barrel swivel are made of brass, too, but it is always a softer brass, one that lends itself to bending and twisting. After the eye has been twisted, the other end of the wire is inserted through a tight-fitting, doughnut-shaped brass collar. A spinning cup is then jammed up against the collared end of the wire and spun at speeds high enough to cause the wire and collar to become fused. If all these manufacturing steps are taken with extreme care, a good swivel is produced. Any shortcuts always result in little defects, deformities, or mismatches in the bearing surfaces of the swivel body or beaded wire, which increase friction and promote binding.

Because of the soft wire used to make the eyes, these old-fashioned barrel swivels are not particularly strong. They are, typically, the weakest of all swivels, size for size. Because of the curvature of the bearing surfaces, barrel swivels (and bead-chain swivels as well) are subject to compression seizure. If the curved surfaces were perfectly matched, then compresson seizure wouldn't be a problem. What happens is that, under pressure, a relatively small mating area actually bears most of the pressure, a concentration which really mashes down those "alpine peaks." In addition, the soft wire shank of the swiveling eye is easily bent, resulting in off-center loading of the bearing surfaces and consequent binding.

I have seen barrel swivels of this old-fashioned type so poorly made you could pull them apart in your hands because the bearing bead or collar was too small for the opening in the barrel body. More than once I have had such swivels come apart when I was tightening knots.

BARREL SWIVEL, SPLIT-HEAD TYPE
The split-head barrel swivel is a marked improvement over the twisted-eye or single-head type. The body is made the same way and the curved bearing surfaces are still subject to compression seizure, but the swivels are shorter, stronger, and less prone to binding under off-center loads, and often are more efficient. The wire eyes are made of stronger, heavier wire, and the bearing heads are made by forging or stamping the ends of the wires. Prior to forging, the ends of the wires are forced slightly apart, which helps to increase the apparent area of the bearing surfaces.

Barrel Swivel, Split-Head Type

Because of the double shanks, split-head barrel swivels are not nearly as subject to off-center loading and consequent binding. The quality ranges from excellent to mediocre, with domestic and imported brands occupying all positions of the spectrum. Stick with the brands you know; Berkley, Rosco, and Pompanette are among the best. Because of marketing methods, it is difficult to keep track of the imported brands.

BEAD-CHAIN SWIVELS
Bead Chain is both a brand and a type of swivel, which can be confusing. These swivels look very much like the beaded pull chains on lighting fixtures, because that is precisely what they are. They are stronger than lamp chains because the first bead chains produced during a manufacturing run, when the dies are new and the product more precisely fabricated, are diverted to tackle use. After the dies wear in a little, the bead chains they stamp out aren't so strong or precise, so they go into lamps and lighting fixtures.

Bead-Chain Swivel

Bead chains resemble tiny barrel swivels strung together, but there are several differences. I don't know about the other, lesser brands, but those made by the Bead Chain Tackle Company of

Bridgeport, Connecticut (which also makes the famous Bridgeport diamond jigs), use nothing but stainless steel. They used to make them of Monel, a nickel-copper alloy, and you might find some Monel bead chains on the market still. Both metals are harder, stronger, and more corrosion-resistant than brass and have lower coefficients of friction. The one-piece, forged end rings are very strong and will not break before the swivel pulls apart, nor will their shanks bend very readily.

The bead-chain swivel is longer, thinner, and of course more flexible than a barrel swivel of equal strength. The thinness and flexibility make bead-chain swivels among the least likely to hang up on submerged snags. Like barrel swivels, bead chains are subject to compression seizure under extreme pressure, but they are much less subject to off-center binding. The flexibility of the chain tends to reduce the off-center angle of pull from bead to bead. Bead chains are more reliable and much more efficient than barrel swivels, because of the multiplicity and careful mating of the bearing surfaces. If a manufacturing defect, grain of sand, speck of corrosion, or anything else increases the friction in one bead, the others are available for handling the torque. Because stainless steel is so subject to crevice corrosion, bead-chain swivels that have been fished in salt water *must* be rinsed in fresh water.

Flexibility vs. Binding

BOX SWIVELS

Box swivels look like open-sided barrel swivels, and that is pretty much what they are. You don't see many box swivels on the American market anymore, but they are still quite popular in Australia, New Zealand, and the Orient. The body of the box swivel is made of a single piece of cast brass, rather than swaged brass tubing, and is stronger. However, because of the soft-wire eyes, which are made the same way as those of the old-fashioned, twisted-eye barrel swivels, the overall strength is not great.

Box Swivel

The major advantage of the box swivel, one which gives it an edge in efficiency over barrel swivels, is that the bearing surfaces of the cast body are flat. So are the bearing surfaces of the bearing beads on the eye wires. With its flat bearing surfaces, the box swivel is not very subject to compression seizure. It is, however, prone to binding under off-center loading because of those soft wire eyes.

Its open-sided construction can be a plus or a minus. It is, of course, more subject to fouling and snagging, but that open body provides a convenient way to suspend a sinker, a dropper fly, or a leader, without having to use a three-way or crossline swivel. It also permits inspection of the bearing surfaces for corrosion or manufacturing precision and allows lubrication (with a drop of reel oil, never grease).

OFFSHORE SWIVELS

Also known as big-game, torpedo, heavy-duty, and giant-tuna swivels, these are the biggest, heaviest, strongest, most efficient, and most dependable of the slider-bearing swivels. They aren't general-purpose swivels, however, and the smallest of them has a breaking strength of 243 pounds.

Offshore swivels are made of solid, machined brass, and are made with much more precision than other slider-bearing swivels. As a result, the bearing surfaces are very flat, very smooth, and very closely mated. Only ball-bearing swivels are more efficient. All of the offshore swivels I have seen and used came from Japan, but I have been told some are imported from France and some are made in a San Diego machine shop. I understand all are of the same precision and exceptionally high quality.

 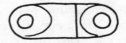

Offshore Swivel

The size numbers assigned represent the diameter of the swivel in millimeters. In price they are about midway between good barrel and ball-bearing swivels, and are an excellent value.

Offshore swivels are not very subject to fouling or binding under off-center loads, and I doubt that their flat bearing surfaces ever seize up under compression. I've never seen one stressed to its breaking point, nor have I ever seen one fail to swivel in response to torque.

Ball-Bearing Swivels

Ball-bearing swivels are much more expensive than slider-bearing swivels, which deters a lot of anglers from using them. But they are so much more effective and efficient that they really are worth the price premium—if you stick to high-quality ones, which are the most expensive of all.

Slider bearings use sliding friction, and ball bearings use free-rolling friction. People have known for at least twenty-four centuries that rolling friction is easier to overcome than sliding friction. Ball bearings are more efficient than slider bearings for a lot of reasons, but the big one is that in slider bearings the friction is overcome by shearing the two surfaces, whereas in a ball bearing the surfaces are peeled apart.

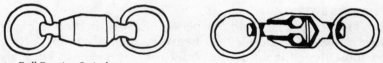

Sampo Ball-Bearing Swivel

A Sampo brand ball-bearing swivel costs about ten to fifteen times as much as a high-quality barrel swivel of similar size and strength, but is more than two hundred times more efficient. If the efficiency factor isn't immediately impressive, think of it this way: Under the 10-pound tensile load of a big fish, a good brass barrel swivel would require close to 2 pounds of torque to function; a lesser amount of torque would be passed up the line as twist. Under the same conditions, it would take just ⅛ ounce of torque to make a Sampo ball-bearing swivel operate.

Nowhere in fishing does the great difference in swiveling efficiency show up as much as in removing the line twist that is caused on each cast or retrieve by fixed-spool spinning, spincast, or sidecast reels. It takes very little torque to twist a monofilament spinning line, but considerably more torque to make a swivel turn. The smallest practical ball-bearing swivel, properly tied into the rig, can handle the twist; a slider-bearing swivel must let the twist build up until there is enough torque to turn the swivel, and even then only at the end of a cast, before you begin the retrieve or tighten the line for bottom-fishing.

Not all ball-bearing swivels are alike, however, and I can tell you from experience that none of the moderately priced, cheaply made, imported ball-bearing swivels—not even Berkley's new ball-bearing swivels, which are made in Taiwan—can hold a candle to Sampos. The imports cost a good bit more than barrel and bead-chain swivels, and aren't much better than the former and are worse than the latter. They may be Sampo look-alikes, but they certainly aren't work-alikes.

A few years ago, after I had convinced myself of the superiority of ball-bearing swivels, I thought I had achieved a real coup, discovering a source of ball-bearing swivels that cost a lot less than Sampos. So I stocked up rather heavily. What I discovered very early was that there is a world of difference between cheapos and Sampos. The ball-bearing swivels I bought weren't nearly as smoothly efficient, they would jam and balk under all sorts of conditions, and they were horribly prone to crevice corrosion. In several instances, they would virtually seize up (under normal angling pressure) after a single exposure to salt water. Most of the important differences between Sampos and cheapos aren't outwardly apparent—nickel-plating the bearings and raceways prior to assembly, for example. The preassembly nickel-plating of the ball bearings and raceways is absolutely necessary to prevent crevice corrosion, to which stainless steel is particularly prone. Stainless steel is a lot harder than brass, and the nickel-plating of the raceways also keeps the bearings from digging ruts into them. Tapered raceways aren't as subject to jamming as square-shouldered raceways are. Finally, the hourglass-shaped holes to which the rings are attached make them self-centering, preventing binding.

Besides the type illustrated above, there is another kind of ball-bearing swivel, but I don't think it is sold in America. I discovered it in the Hardy Brothers catalog, where it is listed as an Anti-Kink Ball Bearing Swivel. I was able to get a couple of samples direct from marketing director James L. Hardy in Alnwick, England.

In outward appearance the anti-kink ball-bearing swivel could pass for a twisted-eye barrel swivel, but this is what it looks like inside:

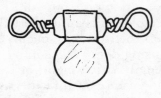 

*Anti-Kink Ball-Bearing Swivel
with Plastic Vane*

The Hardy catalog listed just one size, rated at 25 pounds breaking strength, and my bench tests show its efficiency to be less than the Sampo's, but greater than that of the offshore swivel. Considering its limitations and practical unavailability, why mention it? Because of a unique innovation—a removable plastic vane or keel. This helps to stabilize the swivel, to keep the body from turning. It doesn't do any good in air, as my tests showed, but water is about a thousand times more dense than air and the vane really does help make up for any deficiencies in design or imprecision in manufacture. When we get into swivel rigging, we shall see that swivels must be stabilized by location next to weights or keels if they are to deliver their optimum efficiency. If such plastic vanes were generally available for swivels, rigging would be a whole lot simpler and swivels would be more dependable.

Superior as good ball-bearing swivels are, you needn't use them all the time. Whenever considerable torque will be generated, a properly rigged Bead Chain or other top-quality slider-bearing swivel will suffice. But if you are a light-tackle spinfisherman, better spend the money to stock up on a lot of ball-bearing Sampos.

TESTING SWIVELS

Having tested and used a lot of different swivels, I would rate the types in this order for swiveling efficiency:

1. Ball Bearing
2. Offshore
3. Bead Chain
4. Box
5. Split-Head Barrel
6. Single-Head Barrel (twisted eye)

These efficiency rankings apply only to swivels of the same general size and of similar quality. A cheap, poorly designed, and haphazardly assembled specimen of any type might slip two or three places, maybe more. For example, a cheap, imported ball-bearing swivel would probably rank between top-quality Bead Chain and box swivels. And this ranking doesn't take into consideration such angling factors as strength, size, weight, or cost. In assigning the ratings, I have tried to balance such factors as general reliability, coefficient of friction, and susceptibility to compression seizure and binding under off-center loads.

Quality is so important in swivels it pays to use nothing but the best representatives of a given type. If you have a tackle box fully stocked with swivels of uncertain quality and forgotten brands, you had better test them and discard the ones that won't pass muster.

First, give your swivels a careful visual inspection. Toss out all swivels that show signs of corrosion, worn rings, cracked swivel bodies, badly bent eye shanks, and so on. Watch, too, for barrel swivels with holes that seem unduly large for the wire shanks; they are especially subject to compression binding or breakage. Having eyeballed the whole lot, you are ready to begin the actual testing.

You needn't test every swivel you own. Begin by separating your swivels into look-alike piles (not just by type; consider overall appearance, so you can get various brands or quality ranges separated). Once you have your swiveling hardward sorted, spot-test a few samples from each pile.

Twirling a swivel in your fingers is about as useful a test as playing swordsman with a barebacked fishing rod in a store aisle or kicking tires in a used-car lot. If you can't resist, go ahead, but such a "test" won't mean anything. Holding a tiny swivel in your fingertips, you won't be able to exert much tensile stress or load; yet hands that can open a pickle jar can generate enough torque to overpower even the balkiest swivel.

Without access to very sophisticated test equipment, you are limited to crude tests, but it doesn't matter. You aren't interested in producing a lot of data for a technical paper, just in getting a better feel for how easily or poorly the swivels work and which ones work better than others. Of all the bench tests I have tried, the following three seem to be the most revealing.

A cautionary note: Accidents aren't very likely in these tests, but you will be working with metal under stress—so you really should wear safety glasses, even if they are nothing but shatterproof sunglasses or corrective lenses.

Load Test

You will need some fishing line, a small spring scale, a short piece of stiff wire such as a bait needle or section of coat hanger, and, of course, swivels. Take a 6- to 8-inch piece of fishing line and tie loop knots in each end. The line should be strong enough, when knotted, to withstand approximately 10 pounds of tension. (See Chapter 10, if you don't already know how to tie a surgeon's loop.) Attach one loop to one eye of a swivel via a girth hitch.

Anchor the other swivel eye in a bench vise or over a securely fastened nail or cup hook. The second loop in the line attaches to the hook of the spring scale. To minimize the chances of the line's being cut by the scale's hook, you might use a split ring, snap, or similar smooth metal connection.

Now insert the stiff wire perpendicularly through the eye of the swivel that is nearer the spring scale. Holding the spring scale in one hand, apply a little tension, just a pound or two. Use the other hand to twist the swivel with the stiff wire. It ought to turn very easily. Now increase the tension by another pound or two and twist again. Keep increasing the tension by increments and notice how rapidly the swivel's resistance to turning builds up. In swivels of the same type and size, this resistance will build up more rapidly in lower-quality swivels because of irregularities in, or mismatches of, the bearing surfaces. If you have any ball-bearing swivels to test, notice how much more easily they turn at all loads.

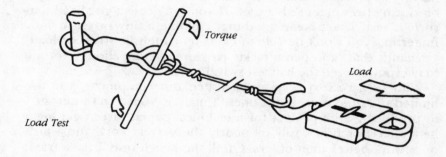

Don't pay much attention to the numbers you see on the spring scale. This test isn't precise enough to make any numerical comparisons, and your swivels ought to turn two or three times as easily when they are under water.

Twist Test

The load test will give you a pretty good idea of how well your swivels will work when you have a fish on, but it can't tell you much about how a swivel will perform under the light loads and torsional stresses experienced while trolling, drift-fishing, retrieving a lure, or still-fishing in a current. And it can't tell you anything about removing reel-caused line twist in spinning.

All you need for the twist test is some line and a spring scale.

Make end loops in a piece of line about a foot long. Attach one loop to one eye of a swivel, whose other eye is anchored (to a vise, nail, hook, etc.). Attach the other loop to the scale and subject the line and swivel to about a quarter of the line's test strength, which would be a normal drag setting. Without letting up on that tension, rotate the scale until you have twisted the line ten times. Now ease up on the tension gradually, keeping an eye on the swivel. As soon as the swivel's lower eye spins, note the scale setting. You probably will have had to release all of the tension before the swivel would turn.

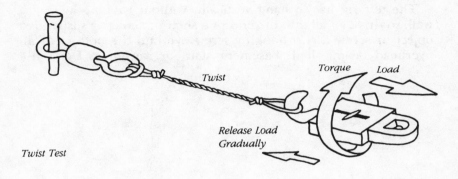

Twist

Torque   *Load*

*Release Load
Gradually*

Twist Test

Repeat the test with fifteen, twenty, twenty-five, and thirty twists in the line. A foot of line twisted twenty or thirty times is so severely twisted you would have great difficulty fishing with it. I think you will be surprised how much tension you have to release before even such a severely twisted line will twirl the swivel. On the other hand, if you are testing a Sampo ball-bearing swivel, chances are good the swivel will start turning before you can put thirty twists in the line.

No matter how carefully you load line onto a spinning or spincast reel, you will get line twist while fishing. The only way you can remove that twist is to tie the smallest, most efficient swivel you have at the upper end of your terminal rig, above any sinkers, droppers, or other pieces of tackle. Unless your line is very severely twisted, a slider-bearing swivel won't be able to remove that twist under normal fishing loads. A metallurgical engineer suggested to me that line twist is probably removed by a swivel only at the end of a cast, when the line suddenly and momentarily goes slack.

Head-to-Head Test

The previous tests will demonstrate the superiority of ball-bearing swivels, but you might not be able to distinguish much difference between the various types of slider-bearing swivels. To pit them head-to-head you will need some sinkers and three double-opening snaps. Connecting links, also called slide-link connectors, are ideal. What you are going to do is connect two swivels in tandem with one connector, using a second connector to attach a sinker to the bottom swivel, and the third connector to suspend the whole rig from a securely anchored nail or cup hook.

The test rig has to hang vertically, without rubbing against a wall, so drive a nail into the end of a shelf or similarly suspended object or screw a cup hook or screw eye into the bottom of an overhead beam, shelf, basement stair, or sawhorse. Don't use

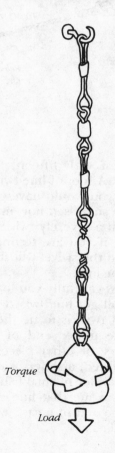

Head-to-Head Test

Torque

Load

swiveled sinkers. And the more compact the sinker the better. The smaller cannonballs are perfect, but you can get by with bank or bell sinkers.

Before pitting the various types against one another, test two swivels of identical size, type, and quality. Spin the sinker and notice that (if the swivels are truly identical) the lower eye of the lower swivel does all or most of the rotating. This is an important point to remember, not only in these tests but in tying together your terminal rigs. *The swiveling component nearest the source of torque will turn most readily.*

Now use two swivels that are identical in all respects but size. This time the smaller one should do the work, whether it is rigged above or below the larger swivel. If you want to run some interesting tests, compare different sizes of different types until the apparent difference in efficiency disappears or reverses. This will give you a size-efficiency rating you can put to good advantage in assembling your terminal rigs.

Now have at it, pitting any pair of swivels against one another. There is almost no end to the variations you can test. For example, you can rig a huge, 500-pound-test Sampo ball-bearing swivel above a tiny, 20-pound-test Rosco barrel swivel. You will discover that the ball-bearing swivel does all the work. Once you have established some sort of pecking order, try increasing the weight. If you were using a 1-ounce sinker, go to 3 or 4 ounces. And test again with 8 ounces. If you are testing large swivels, you probably will want to go to at least 16 to 20 ounces.

I have spent many pleasant, eye-opening hours running these tests, testing the swivels after various periods of immersion in salt water, even using 16-pound sash weights. The rankings with which I began this section on testing are the result of all my tests. You might come up with a slightly different ranking, but I am confident it won't be too different. Of this I am certain: Sampo ball-bearing swivels are going to stand out head and shoulders above all the rest; among the slider-bearing types, offshore swivels will show themselves clearly superior under stress, but bead-chain swivels will surpass them when the load is very light.

THREE-WAY AND CROSSLINE SWIVELS

We have saved three-way and crossline swivels for last because of the special purposes for which they are used. Several different types are available, but all are slider-bearing swivels. All are used to attach dropper lines, leaders, snells, sinkers, and the like in branched terminal rigs. They are almost indispensable in trolling and drift-fishing but are perhaps overused in bottom-fishing. Their uses are identical, but their performances are not.

Bead Chain's "three-ways" (which look more like crossline swivels to me) are the most versatile and efficient of them all. The ordinary three-way swivel is the least efficient.

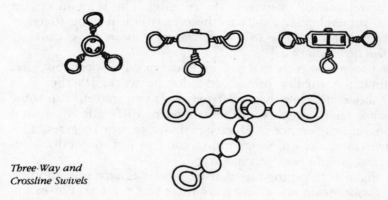

*Three-Way and
Crossline Swivels*

Because the eyes of the common three-way swivel are spaced evenly about the open circle of the swivel's body, the geometry is symmetrical and the physics is awkward. In most applications, the result is off-center loading and consequent binding. The three-way swivel is fine for making a single, low-hook terminal rig for bottom- or drift-fishing—in which the sinker is attached directly or on a short dropper to one eye and a long-leadered hook is attached to another—but for most purposes the crossline swivel is

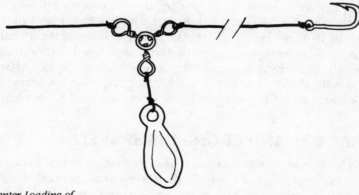

*Off-Center Loading of
Three-Way Swivel*

better. The center swiveling eye is subject to off-center loading in crossline swivels, which is why the flexible Bead Chains are better still. In typical usage, three-way swivels bind in two or three eyes; the crossline in one, and the Bead Chains in none. Between the crossline swivels, the barrels are stronger and the boxes are more efficient.

Three-way swivels are seldom well made, so they are not particularly strong or efficient. Crossline swivels are usually of the same quality as barrel or box swivels from the same manufacturer. Bead Chain's swivels are of uniform high quality and strength, no matter what their configuration (in fact, the only really high-quality crossline or three-way swivels I have seen were made by the Bead Chain Tackle Company).

The Abe 'n' Al rigs used by West Coast salmon trollers are difficult to classify, so I might as well mention them here. They are nothing but three swivels or snap-swivels strung on a single split or jump ring, which is then welded or brazed for greater strength and security. For trolling, you just can't beat them. Because the three swivels slide freely on the ring, they are self-centering and are almost immune to binding. One, two, or even three snap-swivels instead of plain swivels can be used to increase their versatility. I especially like the corkscrew snaps that are used on the A/A rigs sold by Martin Tackle Company in Seattle. To make your own Abe 'n' Al rig, begin with a fairly heavy-duty (preferably stainless-steel) split ring, slide on the three swivels or snap-swivels of your choice, and you will have a versatile, self-centering, three-way swivel that will be as mechanically efficient as the swivels you have selected—even ball-bearing swivels. The split ring will be the weakest link in the thing. If you are an accomplished welder, perhaps you can home-build really strong ones.

Abe 'n' Al Trolling Swivel

SWIVEL RIGGING

With the principles of swivel functioning in hand, I can safely boil this section down to general guidelines:

1. Use swivels only when you need them. Most bottom rigs need not be swiveled for still-fishing, unless currents are particularly strong or you are using very active live bait. Most drift rigs and virtually all trolling rigs should be swiveled. Those who use spinning, spincast, or side-cast reels should use swivels most but not all of the time. Casting rigs may or may not need swiveling, depending upon the tendency of the bait or lure to rotate. Spoons, spinners, and certain bait rigs are more likely to spin than plugs and jigs. Swivels are necessary in all wire-line fishing.

2. Small swivels work better than large swivels of the same type, but don't stress barrel and most other slider-bearing swivels past half their rated breaking strengths.

3. Two swivels are more reliable than one, so if you really need a swivel you might need two or more. When rigging multiple swivels, remember the relative efficiencies of the types and sizes. A rig that incorporates both ball-bearing and barrel swivels is just soaking the barrels, because they won't get a chance to turn. Multi-swiveled rigs should employ swivels that are identical in size, type, and material—unless you have determined otherwise by a torsional-stress analysis of your rig.

4. Under the light torsional loads normally encountered in angling, swivels must be stablized to function well. It is the water adhering to the line within a few feet of the swivel that enables it to work at all. It will work better and more efficiently if you stablize it as much as possible in your rig. (See the next several points.)

5. When trolling with flashers, cowbells, lake trolls, big spinners, or other whirling dervishes, you will need three swivels. Locate one immediately ahead of the sinker to handle line twist, another between the sinker and the rotator to permit free spinning, and the third immediately aft of the rotor to remove leader twist.

Swiveling a Rotating Trolling Rig

6. All trolling sinkers, whether in-line or suspended from the line, must be swiveled fore and aft. A crossline swivel or Abe 'n' Al rig is the appropriate way to swivel a suspended sinker.

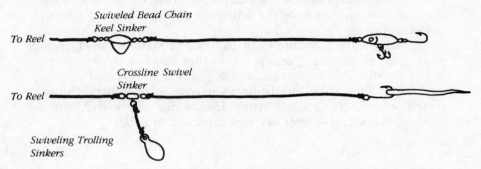

Swiveled Bead Chain Keel Sinker

To Reel

Crossline Swivel Sinker

To Reel

Swiveling Trolling Sinkers

7. Never rig a keel, rudder, or other stabilizer (such as a droppered jig or sinker, an off-weighted trolling sinker, a diving planer, or anything else) above the topmost swivel when trolling or when fishing with a fixed-spool reel. A swivel should always be the topmost component in any terminal rig used in spinning or trolling.

8. When using ball-bearing swivels on spinning or other fixed-spool tackle, tie the uppermost swivel into the rig with the small, swivel-pin end aimed up the line toward the reel. The swivel pin turns more easily than the whole body and should always be aimed at the source of torque.

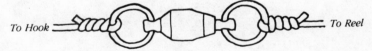

To Hook   To Reel

Ball-Bearing Swivel in Spinning Rig

9. Swivels turn easier on the end that isn't stabilized, so rig swivels *ahead of* sinkers, keels, or other stabilizers to take care of line twist, and *behind* them to remove leader twist or to permit baits or lures to spin freely. Don't be afraid to use swivels in both places if you need them.

10. Swivels work efficiently only when stress is applied directly along the bearing or swiveling axis, perpendicular to the mating surfaces of the bearings. For this reason, do not use loop knots to tie swivels into a rig, and check frequently to make sure that your knots are centered on the eyes, unless you are using swivels with self-centering rings.

11. Snap-swivels should be used sparingly in any terminal rig, and should rarely be used at the end of the rig to attach a lure. *Never* use a snap-swivel to attach a hook. Trollers have better reason for using snap-swivels than other fishermen, and trollers who use wobbling spoons have the only *good* excuse for using a terminal snap-swivel.

12. Swivels are available in plain brass or stainless steel, nickel plate, gold plate, black, and several other finishes. As a rule, the duller finishes are preferred, unless flashiness is part of the rig's attraction. Even then, bright-finish hardware may attract misdirected strikes, particularly when fishing for aggressive, sharp-toothed, schooling species like mackerel and bluefish.

5

Floating Sensations

COMPARED WITH our British and European counterparts, American anglers are bobber barbarians. Nevertheless, I'll bet most of us got our fishing starts by dangling worms or other bait beneath bobbers. Fishing fathers know what they are doing, using bobbers to initiate their smallfry into the pleasant mysteries of sportfishing, for fishing floats are easy to use and are wonderfully effective besides. So easy and effective, in fact, that bobbers enjoy a curiously Jekyll-and-Hyde reputation among American anglers.

On the one hand, there is a sizable minority—perhaps even a majority in the freshwater ranks—who use bobbers virtually all the time. On the other hand there is a smaller but more vocal minority of fishing snobs who disdain floats as being fit only for small children, doddering octogenarians, rank amateurs, and lazy cane-pole proletarians. Both extremist camps are wrong. Caught in the middle is another minority of anglers—perhaps the smallest of the three groups, but surely the smartest—who have the proper perspective. These anglers know that floats are neither panaceas nor the angling equivalent of training wheels. They know that floats are extremely useful fishing tools when used properly and with precision at the right time and in the right places.

In America, only a handful of panfish specialists and Gulf Coast seatrout anglers have developed much sophistication in their approach to fishing with floats. In Europe and the British Isles, fishing with floats has been refined into an angling art of the highest order. Virtually every knowledgeable British and Continental angler carries an impressive array of fishing floats and the knowledge of how to use them. The red-and-white plastic spheres that account for the majority of bobber sales in America are all but unknown on the other side of the Atlantic, and it isn't because Old World anglers are falling behind. *Au contraire*, the popularity of the plastic globe bobber is virtual proof of just how backward *we* are.

The Abominable
Plastic Globe

Floats, bobbers, corks, drifters—call them what you will, these buoyant bits of tackle are great angling tools and should be a part of every fisherman's armory. Even more indispensable than the floats themselves is the knowledge of how to choose, rig, and fish them properly.

Britons, who are perhaps the most advanced users of fishing floats, call fishing with a bobber "float-fishing," a term used here in America to describe the fishing of flowing streams from canoes, jonboats, inflatables, and other small craft drifting along in the current. Throughout this chapter I'll be using float-fishing in the British sense and hoping I don't confuse my fellow Yankees.

Before getting into the details, let me say a few words about float-fishing fun. As outdoor writer Byron W. Dalrymple said in one of his books, bobber-fishing is among the most *dramatic* of the angling arts. Once that bobber starts to bounce, you can feel the tension building up in your solar plexus and the short hairs on the back of your neck begin to tingle as you try to decide when to set the hook. Each gust of wind, each rippling of the water's surface, gives that bobber a tilt that stops conversation short and tugs on the heartstrings. Much as I enjoy plug-casting, I don't believe it matches float-fishing for continuous drama.

Having said all that about bobbers, let me caution against overestimating the importance of the float's visual role. More important than its ability to signal bites or strikes, a float allows you to control your fishing depth, to suspend a bait at the proper level, anywhere from top to bottom. There won't be many bites to signal if your float is presenting bait at the wrong depth.

The first fishing float was surely just a chunk of buoyant wood wound into a vine or a rawhide line by some clever caveman who figured the fish were biting best at a certain depth. Wood is still used in the manufacture of floats—particularly balsa and some of the more buoyant softwoods—but many other materials have been and are used as well: cork, porcupine and peacock quills, fish bladders, and plastic. Several kinds of plastic are used, including hard, hollow plastics and solid, closed-cell foam plastics. In the upper Midwest, ice fishermen use small floats made of soft sponge rubber. All you have to do is squeeze them to get rid of the water and prevent freezing.

Of all the variables in fishing, none may be as important as depth, and that is why the bobber is such an effective fishing

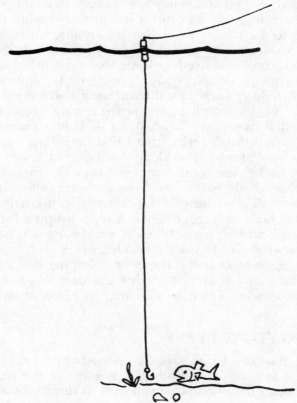

*Bottom-Fishing
with a Float*

instrument. Fish seek water temperatures, currents, cover, and light conditions that make them comfortable. Each species has its own set of favored environmental conditions, and when it comes time to eat, the predators will go where the forage species are hanging out. (See chart on page 451.) The fisherman who isn't using modern electronic gadgets to find or measure all these things keeps trying different depths until he finds the winning one. And the float is the easiest way to control your fishing depth.

If currents aren't too strong, even bottom fishermen can use floats effectively to present bait right on or just above the bottom in depths up to 20 feet. Deeper than that, or in strong currents, it is better to use a submerged "float" in your terminal rig. Trollers or casters can work a lure just above the bottom or just above a weed bed using a floating lure and a sinker tied in an appropriate number of feet up the line.

A properly rigged and manipulated float can enable you to fish bait right on the surface or just a few inches beneath it. When I was going to the University of North Carolina, I used to take an awful lot of sunfish and a few bass out of farm ponds by fishing a tiny popping bug on a five-foot leader behind a Jitterbug or Hula Popper. I couldn't cast the popping bug with the spincast outfit I had and I couldn't keep it on the surface if I added even a single split shot. The floating plug gave me the casting weight and buoyancy I needed, as well as a little extra action and commotion.

At the time, I didn't realize that I had rigged up a pretty good approximation of what speckled-trout (spotted seatrout) fishermen even farther south call a popping-cork rig. Even later I discovered that Rhode Island surf-fishermen use something similar (which they call a broomstick rig) on early spring striped bass. I suspect that both such rigs originated from dropper flies and jigs tethered to a floating plug. When it was discovered that most of the strikes were directed at the smaller, droppered lure, it made economic sense to abandon the expensive plug and substitute a more rudimentary float. Never curse the fates that you forgot to pack a bobber when you have a floating plug in your box.

FISHING FLOAT TYPES

A fishing float can be as basic as a wine-bottle cork tied onto a cane pole's line, or as sophisticated as some of the really clever patented floats that incorporate all sorts of design innovations. It doesn't matter much whether a float is made of wood, balsa, cork, rigid or foam plastic, quill, or any other material, as long as its buoyancy and design are right. Material costs vary considerably, which may affect your choice, and so do aesthetics, which shouldn't. Good Portuguese cork has become so expensive and difficult to obtain that the cheaper grades that were once used to make bobbers are now being diverted to rod grips. Some materials are naturally more buoyant than others, and some are more durable, but the ultimate buoyancy, sensitivity, and durability of the finished product are often more dependent upon the care with which the float is made than the material is it made of. Plastics already dominate the float field, and I wouldn't be surprised to see that trend continue.

Float Shapes and Sizes

Fishing floats seem to come in just about every size and shape imaginable, from ¼-inch-diameter spheres to foot-long stick shapes and most geometric configurations in between. Certain shapes are more or less standard, and are known by various names.

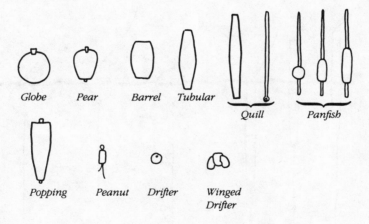

Float Shapes and Names

A float's size and shape affect its buoyancy, its castability, its posture in the water, and its resistance to being pulled under. Slender, tapered shapes cast better because of their lower wind resistance, and they are more sensitive than globular shapes. Weighted floats are particularly popular among those who cast floats and fish them actively.

Float sensitivity is important. A sensitive float signals bites better, it gives a nibbling fish less chance to work the bait off the hook, and it doesn't offer so much resistance to being pulled under that a timorous fish can feel the hook or otherwise sense that something is amiss. In special circumstances, sensitivity may not be of primary importance. If you are float-fishing live suckers for muskies or Florida largemouth bass, for example, a high-buoyancy float is often more desirable than a more sensitive one because the big float inhibits the bait's swimming and causes it to writhe and wriggle, sending out those low-frequency vibrations that attract predators.

A float's ultimate buoyancy is dependent upon the density and volume of its material, but its sensitivity is very dependent upon shape as well. At the surface, part of a float is above the water and part below. When a fish tugs on the hook, the float sinks by degrees and the fatter the float is, the greater the volume of buoyant material that must be pulled under per unit length of effort.

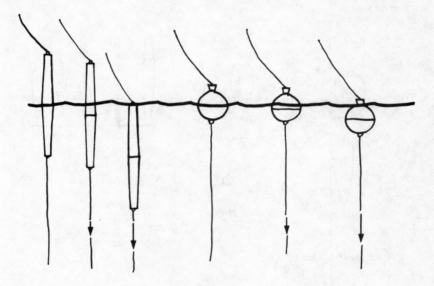

Float Shape and Sensitivity

A 2-inch-diameter globe bobber and a stick float that is 9 inches long by ¾ of an inch in diameter are virtually identical in volume, and if they were made of the same material they would be equally buoyant. But the stick float would be much more sensitive. If a fish pulled hard enough to drag an inch of bobber underwater, it would feel all of the spherical bobber's buoyant resistance, but only 60 percent of the stick float's—assuming both floats were half-submerged before the fish bit.

Ideally, a float should be of such a size that it can be pulled below the surface with very little effort on the part of the fish. Slender floats offer much less resistance and greater sensitivity than do the more rounded shapes. Long, slender floats can be rigged to float on their side—so that they stand up at first nibble, to float mostly below the water so that a light bite will take them under, or to float almost anywhere in between. Spherical floats simply can't be "tuned" for sensitivity (the only exceptions are those hollow, spherical, or ovoid spinning or casting bubbles—these have stoppered ports which allow the addition of water to increase casting weight and decrease buoyancy).

Stick, pencil, quill, and other slender floats are better at signal-ling light bites because they are taken farther underwater than a fatter float would be. Even the slightest touch can wiggle a long, slender float back and forth. Quill floats are generally the most sensitive of all floats, but they can't support much terminal weight. Many panfish floats incorporate a round, pear-shaped, or tubular body (for buoyancy) and a long, quill-type stem (for bite signaling); it's a good compromise. Other compromises between globes and quills include the various oval, tubular, cigar-, and barrel-shaped floats. In the right sizes, they are moderately sensi-tive.

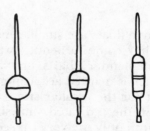

"Compromise" Float Designs

American anglers tend to use bobbers that are much too large. A big bobber isn't sensitive enough to signal really light nibbles, and it offers the resistance that can scare fish away or give them the leverage they need to steal your bait. And big bobbers are easily blown about in the wind, inevitably resulting in a bait's being carried away from your target area.

The Carbonyte Float System

This British float *system* is just about tops in versatility, sensitivity, effectiveness, and cleverness when it comes to light-tackle float-fishing for panfish, trout, and any other species that is hook-shy or sensitive to float resistance. I emphasize the word *system,* because that is what sets the Carbonyte float head and shoulders above the other well-balanced and sensitive floats.

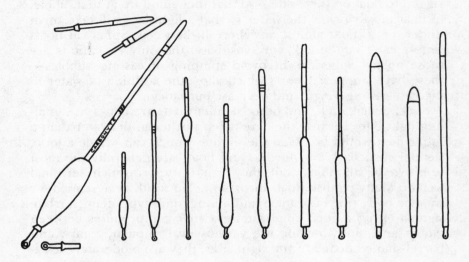

Carbonyte Floats

Carbonyte floats are small, sensitive floats made of a semi-rigid plastic. They come in about forty sizes, from a plain quill to all lengths of slender shafts on various sizes of oval or tubular bodies. Each is marked according to the size of the split shot it will support. (For the smaller sizes, check a fly-fishing shop or catalog.) When the indicated shot size is used, the float will be submerged until only the very tip section of its shaft shows above the surface. This gives the float incredible sensitivity and enables the angler to rig each float precisely. For visibility, the tip section is brightly colored while the rest of the float is jet black.

If that were all there was to it, I would refer to Carbonyte floats as a series rather than a system. But each float is made in three snap-apart sections, for interchangeability. The tip sections come in several colors, so you can select one that will stand out against the color of the water you are fishing. The other end of the float

—the eyelet by which it is attached to the line—also snaps out. This permits a change of float sizes to meet changing conditions and to accommodate different size baits without having to retie or rerig each time. Just snap on a new float, change split shot, and resume fishing. You can't beat it. Finding Carbonyte floats isn't easy. Few tackle shops stock them, and I know of just one mail-order source: Stump-Knocker Tackle Distributors, 300 North 34th Street, Decatur, Illinois 62521.

Float Attachments

Methods of attaching a float to a line or leader are as variable as the floats themselves, if not more so. Except for a few methods, the names aren't standardized and many are just variations of others. Most allow for adjustment of the float's position without having to retie, but a good many floats must be threaded onto the line before the rest of the terminal rig is tied. Obviously, the most versatile attachment devices are those that allow for attachment, detachment, or adjustment of position without any retying.

Some attachment systems are more secure than others—rubber bands, open eyes, and simple slots are the least secure of all. On those floats that employ wire springs, eyes, clamps, and so on, beware of any nicks, burrs, or rough edges that can damage line. I prefer those that use stainless steel, Monel, marine brass, or other corrosion-resistant metal wire, particularly when fishing salt water, brackish estuaries, alkaline lakes, or acid swamp-fed waters or reservoirs. Most floats are made for freshwater use, so be especially cautious when shopping for floats you intend to use in salt water.

Some Float Attachments

The spring-loaded metal hook that is used on the ubiquitous plastic spherical bobber tends to kink or crimp line, as do several other, similar attachment devices. Kinked lines and leaders cause trouble. After enough kinks have been set into the terminal end of your monofilament line or leader, you had better cut it off and retie your terminal rig.

Most center-hole floats have to be threaded onto the line before the rest of the terminal gear is attached, but slotted versions are more versatile. Center-hole floats that use a looped string are commonly employed as underwater floats, particularly in surf fishing, but many panfishermen like to use string floats on top. Fish-n-Good Tackle Company makes a float stringer for reinserting the threading strings, but you can also use a sewing needle, bait needle, or piece of thin wire leader pinched in a sharp Vee.

BOBBER BASICS

Float-fishing is effective only when it is done right. I can't cover all the different ways you can use a float or bobber, nor can I provide all the details for the methods I do cover. Each float rig lends itself to numerous variations and refinements. So let me outline some of the basics that can be applied to virtually all forms of float-fishing.

Depth Control

Depth control is crucial to successful angling. Depending upon water temperatures, seasonal life-cycle patterns, available cover, and the nature of the bottom, a given species of fish might be suspended at almost any depth. During the spring and fall turnovers in freshwater lakes and ponds, fish might be scattered throughout the water column, but usually you will find a given species within a rather restricted depth band. Some have diurnal or daily cycles, feeding shallow at dusk and dawn, say, and holding deep during the day. It pays to learn as much as you can about the habits and requirements of the fish you are after. Each species has a temperature-tolerance range, a comfort range, and a peak-activity range. If you are catching perch at a given depth, you might be fishing a few feet above a school of walleyes. If you are catching rainbows in a lake that also has brook trout, go deeper if you want to find the specks.

Electronic fishfinders or sonar depth finders are great for locating fish, but not all of us own one. I don't. A thermometer is the next best way to locate good fishing depths. Those expensive recording thermometers are great (I don't have one of those either) but a plain glass thermometer is good enough. Tie a thermometer on the end of your line, rig a float some distance up the line, lower away and wait a few minutes. If you are fishing from shore in a deep lake, cast the thermometer out as far as you can and take a reading as deep as is practical. Then subtract about ⅝ of a degree Fahrenheit for each foot of additional depth.

If you have neither sonar device nor thermometer, you can use an adjustable bobber to fish at various depths until you start catching fish. A single fish may not give you the answer you are looking for, but if you catch two fish in short order at the same depth, you are in business.

Fixed Floats

Fixed floats are those that are attached more or less securely to a line, whether they are adjustable or not. If you are casting, 5 or 6 feet is about as much fishing depth as you can use with fixed floats, because few anglers can handle more line than that dangling from the rod tip at the beginning of the cast. Even then, the float and the sinker tend to fly through the air swapping ends and absorbing the energy that was put into the cast. If you are casting, you would be better off using a sliding float.

For lowering a line into the water from a boat, bridge, or pier, fixed floats are fine. You can fix your bait as deep as you like, as long as you attach the float when the line is on its way down and remove it when you are reeling in.

Sliding Floats

When you can use a slip-rigged float you will find it to be a handier, more versatile, and less troublesome piece of tackle than its fixed-position sibling. Because you can reel your terminal rig right up to your rod tip when fishing a sliding float, you can fish deep without any hassle and cast almost as well as you can with a floatless bottom rig.

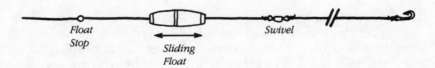

Float Stop   Sliding Float   Swivel

Sliding Float

And yet, for certain kinds of float-fishing, a fixed float works better than a sliding one. I think a fixed popping cork has it all over sliding variations. Fixed floats are also better when cast-and-retrieve fishing, "drift-fishing," or working a fly with a spinning bubble. And you will find that sometimes a sliding float isn't as easy to handle with spinning or spincast tackle as it is with revolving-spool or casting tackle. Most other times, though, I'll choose a sliding float over a fixed one.

To fish a sliding float, the line must be threaded through a center hole, eyelet, or some other attachment device so that the float slides freely on the line. Then a float stopper of some sort, preferably adjustable, must be added to arrest the float's travel at some predetermined depth. There are numerous patented float stops on the market; the best known is the Fin Bobber Stop, which is nothing but a tiny, flexible spring and bead. Float stops are easy to make. Some anglers like to tie a piece of rubber band onto the line, while others prefer to use a short piece of fishing line. The double overhand knot is perhaps the easiest and fastest stopper knot to tie. At first it will take some experimentation before you can predictably cinch the knot down just tight enough to keep the stopper from being pushed out of place by the float, but loose enough so that you can slide it along the line by hand. A small bead on the line between float and stopper minimizes the chances of the knot's becoming jammed in the float's eye, center hole, slot, or whatever.

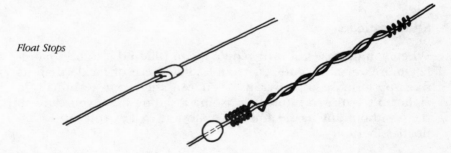

Float Stops

Because the line is pulled off a fixed-spool reel across looped strands, any sort of knot, spring, or other stopper will tend to interfere with the line's springing off the spool during the cast. This is enough of a problem that I don't much care to use sliding floats on spinning tackle, unless I am fishing shallow enough that the stopper won't be wound onto the reel spool before casting. That limits your fishing depth to about the length of your rod. On conventional or revolving-spool tackle (in which the line is

stripped off in line with the strands) you can fish as deep as you
want with a sliding float. I haven't tried it much deeper than 20
feet, by which point the long-distance telegraphy of vibrations
gets to be a little fuzzy. The deeper you fish, the less valuable the
float becomes as a visual indicator of what is going on below. But
it still retains its primary importance as a controller of fishing
depth.

If you fish with a metered or color-coded line, you can use a
freely sliding (unstopped) float to fish various depths on the same
cast until you find the fish. Just count the colors as they disappear
into the water and remember what color you were on when the
fish started biting. After you land that first fish, tie a float stopper
into the line right where it entered the water when the fish hit.
This method works better close to the boat or shore; on long casts
you will have trouble seeing the line colors way out at the float.

When fishing shallow, you can use stoppers above and below
the float—about 2 feet apart, say—to make it easier to change
the float's surface position without taking your bait too far out of
the feeding zone. Put a couple or three *noisy* glass or hard-plastic
beads between the float and the bottom stopper and you can get a
nice clicking sound each time you snap your rod tip. This clicking
imitates the sounds made by pistol shrimp and other crustaceans
that are favored fish foods in southern waters. If you are too lazy
to make your own, Boone's Shad Rig Float may be the ready-
made answer you've been looking for.

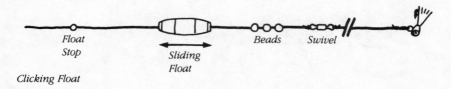

Float
Stop

Sliding
Float

Beads

Swivel

Clicking Float

Float-Fishing the Bottom

Bottom-fishing usually entails the use of a weighted terminal rig,
and few fishermen would think of the float as part of a bottom-
fishing rig. But on really bad bottoms that are choked with weeds,
broken rocks, brush, drowned timber, stumps, and other debris,
you will lose a lot of terminal tackle to snags if you fish the bottom

with conventional rigs. A float can be used to keep a bait just above the trouble, which may still be within the primary feeding range of most bottom species.

If the current isn't too strong you can use a *surface* float to fish fairly deep bottoms—up to 25 feet or so. You will need to use a sliding float with a float stop of some sort. Then you can reel your rig right up to your rod tip and cast quite some distance as well. If casting distance is important, you will have to experiment with sinker weights and float sizes to come up with the optimal total casting weight and buoyancy/stability tradeoff. It sounds trickier than it is, but it doesn't take long to find the right combination, and often your first hunch will be right.

FIREBALLS AND DRIFT BOBBERS

Sometimes water depths, strong winds, or currents make it impractical to use a float at the surface. But if you need to keep your bait off the bottom—to protect it from snags or bait-stealers— you can use a submerged float. The simplest are the little barrel- and cigar-shaped string floats and the spherical corks (called fireballs when they are large) that are often painted fluorescent red or yellow. Fireball rigs are favored among bait-fishing surfcasters from southern New Jersey down to Georgia because the glowing corks attract fish as well as elevate the bait. There has even evolved a surface-fishing version that has gained a lot of adherents among those who stalk the coast for bluefish. It is called a bluefish topwater rig by the Dragon Fly Company, and it is nothing but a fluorescent barrel- or popper-shaped cork skewered

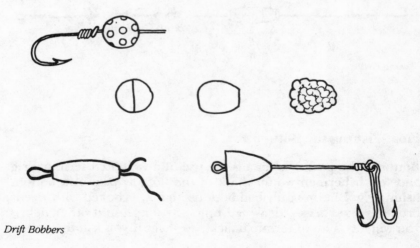

Drift Bobbers

onto a bait-needle wire that has an open-shank double hook at the other end. When fished like a popping plug with a whole dead baitfish, it is deadly. Smaller versions work almost as well in fresh water for bass and pickerel, and I imagine they would be effective on pike, too.

The idea of combining fish-attraction with buoyancy in a bobber has been elevated to a high plane by western steelhead and salmon fishermen. Out there, these dual-purpose submerged floats are called drift bobbers or drifters. Some variants have other names. Whether drift bobbers should be considered floats or lures is a question worth debating, but I decided to cover them here because they are so frequently used in conjunction with other baits and lures.

The so-called corky drifter is the steelheader's version of the East Coast fireball, a painted cork ball that is fished on the leader ahead of yarn lures, salmon eggs, live baits, or lures of various sorts. Cherry bobbers are similar, but may be pear-shaped and are often made of wood, hard plastic, or closed-cell foam. Luhr Jensen's Okie-Bobs and Gooey-Bobs are made of soft plastic and resemble gobs of salmon eggs; the latter are impregnated with a scented liquid that oozes out. As the drifter becomes more bait than bobber, the shapes become more wedgelike, so that Yakima's Wobble-Glo is about midway between cherry bobber and wobbling plug, and Grizzly's Li'l Guy is closer in form and function to Flatfish, Lazy Ikes, and similar plugs. But they can be fished differently.

Drift bobbers, unadorned or accompanied by bait, can be trolled, cast, or just still-fished or drifted in a fast current. If the steelheader uses enough weight so that the bobber stays in place and wobbles in the current, the technique is called plunking. If the whole rig bounces along the bottom with the current, it's called drifting. In trolling, drifters usually are fished behind a

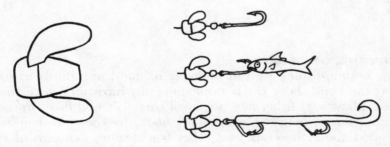

Winged Drifter

herring dodger, rotating flasher, cowbells, or other activating attractor.

Winged drifters are midway between drift bobbers and spinners. The best known is Yakima's Spin-n-Glo, a thimble-shaped plastic drift bobber with flexible rubber wings that cause it to spin in moving water. Winged drifters may be fished ahead of live or dead natural baits, hair and feather lures, yarn, skirts, tube lures, plastic lures of all sorts, or hooks that are plain or dressed. They're sold principally as steelhead, salmon, and trout lures out West, but I have used various sizes of winged drifters to good effect on the East Coast against crappies, bass, bluefish, brook trout, and shad, and in Alaska on pike.

FLOATING JIGS

A floating jig looks like a ball-type leadhead jig except that the head is a cork ball. Floating jigs have become very popular in the walleye country of the Middle West, usually in conjunction with a slip-rigged walking sinker. Floating jigs come plain, dressed with feathers or bucktail, or adorned with plastic worms, grubs, leeches, and other look-alikes. All work very nicely. Handy as the floating jig is, you can use a tiny cork ball, a small string float, or one of the drift bobbers to accomplish the same thing—often at a lower cost.

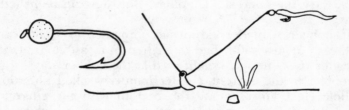

Floating Jig

BOTTOM-RIG SUPPORTS

Any bottom-fishing rig can be made to stand upright or to support the hook above the bottom simply by incorporating a small float. Many surf fishermen use small barrel-shaped floats in their terminal rigs, between sinker and hook, to keep the bait suspended above the crabs and other bait-stealing denizens of the bottom. The buoyancy may be added to the main stem of a bot-

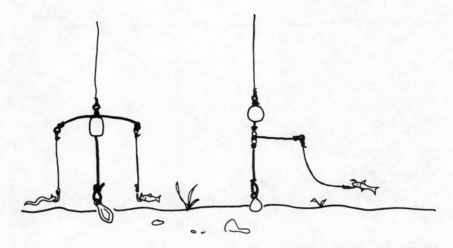

Bottom-Rig Supports

tom rig, in which case it often is called an Angling Jenny (actually a trademark owned by the Oberlin Canteen Company). Such rigs are very easy to design and make, either at home or on the spot.

ACTIVE FLOAT-FISHING

According to mossbound tradition, bobbers are used only on still waters by catnapping worm-drowners. Those who prefer to fish more actively will discover that floats are perfectly suited to their more restless styles. Natural and artificial baits of many different sorts can be fished almost as actively beneath a float as on a free line. A large sliding float allows a shorebound angler to jig lures vertically in waters that otherwise would be accessible only to jig fishermen using boats. Or you can cast and retrieve a bait (instead of still-fishing it) while using a float; that way you can cover a lot of water at a prescribed fishing depth.

On fast-flowing streams and in tidal inlets, floats can be used to suspend baits that are fairly ripping along at some distance above the bottom. Cast up and across the stream and let the current carry your bait downstream naturally. When the float begins to swing in toward shore, reel in and cast again. When fishing inlets for fluke or southern flounder—or a good many other species, for that matter—you can use a fairly large float to drag your baits right along or just above the bottom. This approximates the drift-

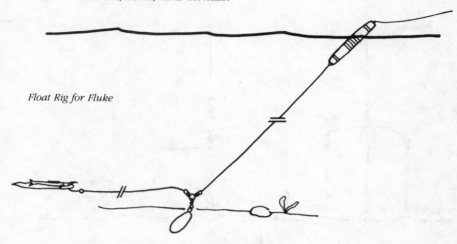

Float Rig for Fluke

fishing technique that boat anglers prefer when fishing for *Para-lichthys* species.

Steelhead fishermen on Western rivers use sinkers that will bounce along the rocky bottoms in fast current, and they often employ small floats on the leader between the sinker and the bait to keep the hook from fouling the bottom and to present baits in the steelhead's feeding zone. The geometry is the same as that described above for bobbered bottom rigs; only the method of employment is more active. The technique works on species other than steelhead trout and can be used effectively on eastern streams and in salt water, too.

Spinning and Casting Bubbles

When spinning tackle became popular in the U.S. in the 1950s, many anglers with casting outfits wanted to try the new spinning lures, which were much too light for their rods and reels. And the new breed of spinfishermen wanted to go even lighter, to use flies and other super-light lures that even their buggywhips couldn't cast. So the spinning bubble was invented.

Now available in all sorts of shapes and colors, the classic spinning bubble is round, oval, or teardrop-shaped, molded of clear plastic for camouflage. The simplest casting or spinning bubbles are nothing but buoyant clear-plastic forms with wire eyes on each end, but the best have stoppered ports so that water can be added. The addition of water increases the casting weight and decreases the buoyancy. When completely filled with water, most bubbles are neutrally buoyant, which means they neither sink nor float but go wherever the currents buffet them.

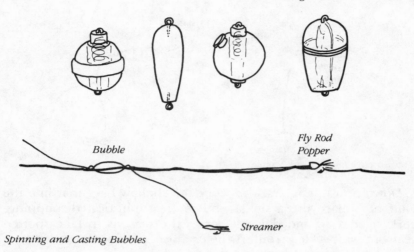

Spinning and Casting Bubbles

Various attachments more sophisticated than screw eyes are used on modern spinning bubbles. The Hank Roberts A-Just-A-Bubble has a center hole with a piece of surgical rubber that is twisted about the line to hold the bubble in place. The Newell Sink-R-Float has an interesting opposed-hook arrangement on each end that allows for easy attachment and detachment of looped lines, leader, and hook snells for fixed-depth fishing.

If you happen not to be carrying any spinning bubbles and want a heavy, neutral-buoyancy "float," try using a plastic sandwich bag and water. It won't be terribly pretty or durable, but it will work. California surf fishermen sometimes use this clever rig when they want to fish live bait at or near the surface and need to get the bait out beyond the breakers.

Popping Corks

In the Northeast where I live, surf fishermen like to meet the earliest arriving striped bass each spring with what they call broomstick rigs. A broomstick rig is nothing but a piece of wooden dowel (or broomstick) to which screw eyes have been fitted fore and aft. To match the dainty diets of the spring schoolies, a streamer fly, small bucktail jig, tiny lube lure, or similar bogus bait is attached via a dropper line to the rear eye and the "broomstick" is tied onto the fishing line at the front end and worked like a popping plug. After those first few days of the new season, most Yankee surfmen put their broomstick rigs away until the following year. The rigs will work all year long, however.

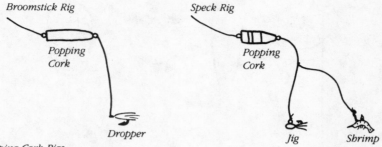

Popping-Cork Rigs

Down South, anglers who work the shallow bays that line the Gulf of Mexico use a similar, but more sophisticated, popping-cork rig day in and day out across the seasons to take spotted seatrout or speckled trout. As befits a fishery of some refinement, mere broomsticks are not used. Instead, a whole array of special floats have been developed. Popping corks come weighted and unweighted, in various sizes and colors, made of wood, cork, balsa, foam plastic, and hollow hard plastic. Some have eyes on each end to which line and leader must be tied; others use pegged center holes for attachment, and still others employ various mechanically sophisticated methods of attachment.

Because of the great variety of popping corks on the market, I risk oversimplification by singling out a few types for mention. Certainly the Plastilite Corporation and its affiliated Mobile Balsa Co. offer the greatest variety of popping corks (and other floats as well, for that matter) on the market. Besides the floats listed as

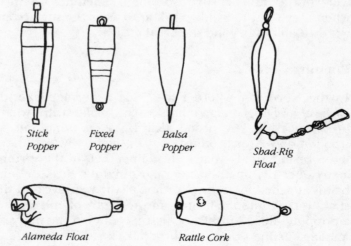

Popping Cork Types

popping floats in the Plastilite catalog, you will find a lot of Gulf anglers using various of the pencil, barrel, and tubular floats for the same purpose.

Boone's Shad Rig Float is a special-purpose "popping" float (actually a splashing, clicking float) that has gained a lot of adherents. Cotton Cordell, whose Big O crankbaits set the bass-fishing world on its ear a few years ago, makes an interesting molded-plastic popping cork with a built-in rattle chamber. The Cordell catalog lists it as the Rattle Cork, but the specimens I have are marked Plunker.

The most versatile popping corks I have seen are the Alameda floats out of Texas. Made of tough Styron plastic, the Alameda float has a patented attachment design that allows for easy attachment or removal and for rigging the float fixed or sliding. Very clever. Alameda floats come in five sizes, weighted and unweighted, and are well streamlined for good casting. The head design is unusual and creates a nice popping and splashing. The small, unweighted Alamedas are gaining popularity among freshwater anglers in the Southwest because of their visibility and tip-up sensitivity for still-fishing. This float is better designed than some of the popping plugs I have used.

Float-Fishing Lures

Most float fishermen use live or at least natural baits, which is right and proper, but it would be a mistake to overlook the often deadly combination of bobber and artificial lure. Among the lures that can be fished to good effect beneath a float are leadhead and diamond jigs, shad darts, streamers, wet flies, ice jigs (sometimes called panfish jigs), small spoons, spinners, and all sorts of plastic worms and baits. Certain ice-fishing lures that aren't quite jigs—

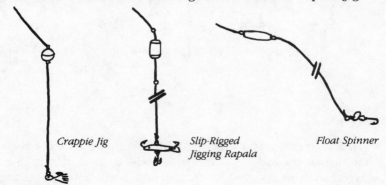

Crappie Jig   *Slip-Rigged*   *Float Spinner*
                    Jigging Rapala

Some Float-Rigged Lures

like the Rapala Jigging Lure—are very good in warm weather under a slip-rigged float. So are the so-called jump baits like Mann's Little George, Mister Twister's Zinger Shad, and Heddon's Sonar.

Crappies are easily taken, once you locate a school, by fishing small bucktail or marabou jigs beneath a float. All-black and all-white jigs have worked well for me, but now and then a black-and-white version has paid off handsomely; some crappie experts swear by yellow jigs. Such float-and-jig rigs may be fished by twitching them along slowly, twitching only occasionally, or merely allowing them to bob up and down with the waves. Crappies are aggressive little devils, but give that jig too much action and you will turn them off. Tie the jig directly to your line without using any hardware or leader. Tipping the jig with some natural bait usually improves the action.

Many float fishermen like to use tandem rigs, with a baited hook on one leader and a jig on the other. If one rig consistently takes more fish, then switch both leaders to that which is working better. Tandem rigs can use combinations of artificial lures, without any bait; a jig and a spoon or a jig and a spinner, say.

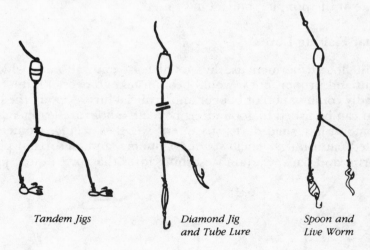

Tandem Jigs

Diamond Jig
and Tube Lure

Spoon and
Live Worm

Tandem Float Rigs

In a current, any number of lures may be fished below floats that are anchored in place or slowly drifted down. Spinners, winged drifters, skirted lures, and small wobbling plugs are your best bet here. Grizzly's Li'l Guy is a really splendid lure for this kind of fishing, which steelheaders call *plunking*. Any spinner may be used, too, including winged drift bobbers such as Yakima's Spin-n-Glo. So far steelheaders and salmon fishermen out West have been the biggest devotees of this kind of fishing, but the technique will work anywhere. Experimenting in various streams, I have caught bass, perch, pickerel, crappies, sunfish, bullheads, and golden shiners. In fairly fast currents, better leave off the float and stick to a straight plunking rig. Float plunking works best from a boat, bridge, pier, or other platform athwart the current. Inlet jetties and long points of land sometimes provide the right angling position vis-à-vis the current flow.

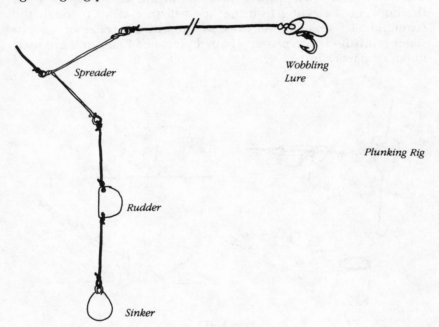

Spreader

Wobbling
Lure

Plunking Rig

Rudder

Sinker

There are dozens of other ways to fish floats actively, and the resourceful angler can figure out most of them without my help. One outrageous example: float-fishing dry flies. Most spinfishermen who use spinning bubbles to cast flies fish streamers, nymphs, or wet flies. With a little casting practice you can handle dry flies as well. You won't get the delicate presentation of the true flycaster, so be sure to cast well upstream of your target and let the current carry the float and fly down to the feeding trout. Purists will shudder, but it works.

MAKESHIFT FLOATS

The time-honored cork bottle stopper has lost none of its effectiveness as a fishing float over the years, nor has the piece of buoyant wood picked up on the spot. Neither one is particularly versatile, but both work well. Scraps and beads of foam plastic are very good. Saltwater anglers who drift big baits in chum lines for bluefish and sharks often suspend their baits from big chunks of scrap closed-cell foam. But a float big enough to support a whole menhaden or jack will give a fighting fish too much resistance, so the foam is rigged to break away. To make a cheap breakaway float, just make a couple of slits in the foam with a knife, and wrap your line twice around the foam in the slits. When you set the hook on a striking fish, the line will slice clean through the foam. Smaller versions will work as well in fresh water or on saltwater panfish. Those peanut-shaped pieces of foam that are used in packing work fine.

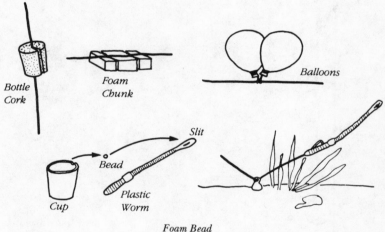

Bottle Cork

Foam Chunk

Balloons

Cup

Bead

Slit

Plastic Worm

Foam Bead

Makeshift Floats

Even smaller pieces of foam plastic can be put to good angling use. If you happen to have a stock of plastic worms that were made before the high-flotation types became popular, you can turn them into floaters that are very handy for fishing submerged weed beds. Just make a small slit in the worm's tail and stuff it with a small bead of plastic foam pinched from a coffee cup.

Toy balloons enjoy some popularity among saltwater anglers, particularly shark and king-mackerel fishermen. Balloons are extremely buoyant for supporting big baits, are extremely visible in oceanic chop, and are cheap enough for one-way use. Most balloon fishermen depend upon water pressure to break the balloons when the fish sound. But broken balloons can jam in roller guides and tiptops. Instead, tie balloons into your line with cheap cotton string, which will usually break first. Balloons are sometimes used as floats in fresh water; in his tackle company's catalog, Dan Gapen suggests using balloons to drift baits well out into the tailwaters below the big hydroelectric dams on reservoirs. These cold, well-aerated, and turbulent waters often harbor large populations of outsize fish.

Anglers who dote upon other types of floats and float-fishing techniques will probably be miffed that I haven't covered their favorites, but editorial space is finite. The important thing for every angler to know is this: The float is a versatile, effective, fun piece of fishing tackle that can be adapted to virtually every style of fishing, in fresh or salt water, on small streams, large lakes, or the ocean itself. Get yourself a collection of floats of different types and sizes, learn to use them, and figure out your own approaches to float-fishing. Don't be misled by tackle-shop stocks into thinking that the ubiquitous red-and-white plastic globe is the most useful type, nor by angling snobs into believing that float-fishing is for the inept, the lazy, or the infirm. The float isn't an angling panacea—nothing is—but it can be deadly effective when nothing else works. If you haven't been float-fishing since you were a kid, treat yourself to a reacquaintance with one of the finest and most dramatic forms of fishing there is.

6

Between the
Lines

Not many angling authorities include line in their definitions of terminal tackle, usually restricting themselves to those things that are tied onto the end of the line. If I were writing a dictionary entry on terminal tackle I probably would omit line, too, but I don't see how one can discuss the rigging and use of terminal tackle without also discussing the line that holds everything together. Like the hook, line is simply synonymous with angling. Anyway, the fishing line you use has so much effect on your terminal tackle and rigs I don't see how we can ignore it. Let's just say that line is a transitional item of tackle, belonging partly to the terminal tackle it supports and controls and partly to the rod and reel with which it works in the presentation of bait and the fighting of fish.

To hear Du Pont, Berkley, Gudebrod, Cortland, Sunset, and the other line-makers tell it, line is the single most important piece of fishing tackle, the one that usually spells the difference between success and failure. I'm not ready to go quite that far, and the line makers' self-interest is altogether obvious, but I wouldn't want to quarrel with the basic merit of their argument, either. Line *is* terribly important in fishing.

When I was a kid growing up in Illinois and fishing the Kankakee River, I used nothing but cheap line because I couldn't afford any better, but I'm not sure the "good" stuff was all that much better back then. These days even the cheap, budget-grade lines available to contemporary pennypinchers are probably better than the premium lines I couldn't afford on my schoolboy fishing budget. But stay away from the mill-end spools with the unknown names and the cheapo lines of uncertain quality and indeterminate physical properties. There is an incredible quality gap between the best premium lines and the worst budget lines, but the price differential is relatively moderate. You get more value for your money from the premium lines, which are cheaper in the long run because they last longer and deliver more hassle-free fishing.

"Premium" isn't an easy word to define, as beer drinkers well know. That it always means "better" and "more expensive" is taken for granted, but knowing where to draw the line is something else. You can be sure that the well-known, heavily advertised, and expensive brands are premium lines, and you can rest assured that the very cheap bargain-basement specials—the lines that sell for several hundred yards to the dollar—are not. In between these extremes, things aren't altogether clear.

According to the folks at Berkley & Company, a line is a premium one only if it is manufactured with exacting quality control and if it exhibits uniform and superior diameter, tensile strength, stretch, knot strength, and other physical properties.

At Du Pont the attitude about "premium" is more tolerant and catholic, even though Du Pont makes and sells nothing but top-of-the-line premium Stren monofilament and Prime cofilament lines. Someone in Du Pont's public-affairs office told me that any line that is made from high-quality raw materials, that is manufactured with good quality controls, that adheres to the acceptable quality levels in basic line properties, and that is backed up by at least some research on the part of the manufacturer deserves to be called a premium line.

No matter where the distinction is drawn, you had better stay away from the real cheapo lines, because their quality is so uneven. Some of the bargain-basement specials began life as premium lines but have been reincarnated under new brand names by companies who buy and relabel old, chemically deteriorating lines. If you stick to the top-dollar, top-of-the-line brands you won't go wrong. In the medium-price ranges you will have to rely upon word of mouth and your own experience.

In the Northeast, the favorite monofilament line among surfcasters, trollers, and others who ply the waters of the Atlantic Ocean, Cape Cod Bay, and Long Island Sound for striped bass, bluefish, tiderunner weakfish, bonito, bluefin tuna, and other briny brawlers is undoubtedly pink Ande. Ande sells a tournament-grade line, but it is expensive so you seldom see it away from the multimegabuck offshore cruisers. Recently, Ande introduced a new super-soft line that is thinner and limper and has strength, but regular Ande still holds sway in the market.

Regular Ande is a bit stiff and large in diameter—which gives it the toughness saltwater anglers admire—and some line manufacturers don't think it is a truly premium line. Whether that attitude stems from high standards, snobbishness, or sour grapes I can't say. At any rate, to most Ande users, that pink line is just about the finest stuff that ever came out of a test tube. (On the West Coast, saltwater anglers feel the same way about Maxima Chameleon.)

Party-boat fishermen and others in the Northeast who toe the budgetary line are fond of Handy Line, a pink monofilament that is sold at very modest prices by Jeros Tackle. I know fishermen who use pink Ande on their surf and trolling rods and pink Handy on their cod rods and other rigs intended only for sinker-bouncing clam baits. They would have apoplexy if they had to use Handy line on the surf or trolling sticks. The fact of the matter is, both Jeros and Ande buy their pink monofilament from the same manufacturer in West Germany and, so far as I have been able to determine, there is no difference between regular-grade Ande and Jeros's Handy Line, angler attitudes notwithstanding. (As an anonymous wit at Jeros Tackle penned in the margin of a letter I sent them, asking this very question, "Ande is handy, but Handy is Ande.") There really is no accounting for personal taste. For my taste, Ande, Handy, and Maxima are a bit too stiff, but I use Maxima a lot in fly-fishing leaders.

LINE PROPERTIES

Before you can select the proper line for your kind of fishing (and if you are an average angler I suppose I should have pluralized both *lines* and *kinds* to accommodate the variety of your fishing), you have to know what to look for. Whether it is intended for blue-water trolling or dry-fly fishing, whether it is made of metal wire or soft filament, whether it is of single- or multiple-strand construction, a line will exhibit a set of physical properties that, measured against the demands at hand, translates into the line's angling characteristics. It is essential that you understand these physical properties because, unless you can analyze a line's exhibition of them, you can't begin to assess its suitability to the fishing you want to do. It doesn't take much analysis to know that a lead-core line isn't going to work very well when ultralight spinning for small-stream trout; but if you need to go way down deep in the Pacific Ocean for chinook salmon, how does that lead core stack up against wire, monofilament, and Dacron trolling lines?

Materials engineers might quarrel over my omission of certain physical properties and the names I have decided to give some of those I have chosen, but here are the basic physical properties of fishing lines that concern anglers most:

- Breaking Strength
- Diameter
- Density
- Visibility
- Flexibility
- Elasticity
- Shock Resistance
- Abrasion Resistance
- Knot Strength
- Durability

The properties aren't listed above in any particular order of importance, because that is something only you can determine according to the particular demands of the angling conditions at hand and your own idiosyncrasies. As you'll see, these physical properties are intimately interrelated, some going together like heat and light, others working at cross purposes.

Breaking Strength

The actual physical property that best measures a line's bearing strength or tenacity is probably tensile strength. But tensile strength is measured in units of force per cross-sectional area (usually pounds per square inch). That doesn't tell the average angler on the dock much that is very helpful, and it only works on solid, single-strand lines. Besides, tensile strength is rarely listed on line spools anyway. Most of the materials used to make fishing lines have tensile strengths on the order of 100,000 pounds per square inch, give or take a few thousand (but copolymer or nylon "alloy" monofilaments such as Berkley's Trilene and TriMax lines may have tensile strengths that exceed 120,000 psi). Tensile strength is a bit difficult to translate into fishing strategy, so line manufacturers label their supply spools with breaking strength, the weight the unknotted line can support. Usually that strength is listed in pounds, but the U.S. is gradually switching over to the metric system, so you had better memorize that 1 kilogram weighs about 2.2 pounds.

TEST STRENGTH

Breaking strength is usually listed as test strength, or simply test. It is a sort of guaranteed breaking strength and in most cases the actual breaking strength of the line will be anywhere from 10 to 30 percent higher. Most manufacturers test their lines dry, but some test them wet, and it makes a difference you won't be able to determine except by experience because the labels rarely distinguish between the two testing methods.

LINE CLASS

World-record hunters don't use "test" lines; instead, they use what are called "class" lines. The International Game Fish Association keeps world records by line-strength classes—1, 2, 4, 6, 8, 10, 15, 24, 36, and 60 kilograms, corresponding to 2, 4, 8, 12, 16, 20, 30, 50, 80, and 130 pounds—and for a fish to qualify as a line-class record the line must break at or under the weight of its class, otherwise the fish is pushed up into the next heavier line class. More than a few records have been lost this way. Class lines are labeled according to line class—"15kg class," for example, or "IGFA 30 lb"—and the makers guarantee that the lines *will* break, when wet, below but within 5 or 10 percent of the listed class weight.

Diameter

This, too, is a function of tensile strength. But, in a braided or multi-stranded line, diameter also is affected by how tightly the strands are laid or woven in the manufacture. Alas, few manufacturers list diameters on their labels. That is a shame, because line diameter affects many things: a reel's spool capacity; wind resistance (and therefore distance and accuracy) in casting; water drag (which affects the depth that can be attained at a given trolling speed or the weight necessary to anchor a still-fished line in a current); the bulkiness of knots (and therefore the amount of friction and trauma they're likely to encounter when sailing through the rod guides); and, of course, its visibility to spooky fish. If line manufacturers listed diameters on their supply spools (as they do in Europe), anglers could make better and more intelligent line choices. This information might enhance sales of such exceptionally fine-diameter lines as Royal Bonnyl II, Trilene XL, Ande Super Soft, Siglon, and Sigma monofilaments; Micron, Invincible, and Gamestar braided lines; Tel-A-Depth, Nicro, and Almet 304 wire lines.

In general, the smaller the diameter, the better. Fine-diameter lines increase spool capacities, cast better, troll deeper, and enable you to hold bottom in a current with less sinker weight. They may also be less visible, about which more later.

Diameter can be measured accurately only for solid, single-strand lines that are round in cross section, like monofilament and single-strand wire. Braided and multistranded lines cannot be measured precisely, and any diameters listed for them must be approximations. The first time I tried to measure braided Dacron trolling line diameters, I thought something was wrong with the micrometer because I got six different readings in as many different spots along a 1-foot piece of line.

Density

Density, too, applies only to solid, single-strand lines because it is measured as mass per unit volume. Density affects a line's weight, sink rate, and responsiveness to moving air or water. Generally, multistranded lines have a much lower *effective density* than single-strand lines made of the same material, because of their larger diameter and the tiny volume of air trapped in the spaces between the strands.

Specific gravity is a convenient way of expressing density because it is a factor by which a given solid material exceeds the density of water. (Remember, though, that seawater is slightly more dense than fresh water, having a specific gravity of about 1.025 compared to fresh water's 1.0.) The specific gravity of mono-filament nylon (or the essentially identical Perlon from Europe) ranges from 1.07 to 1.15, whereas the metals used to make solid-wire trolling lines come in at 7.9–8.0 for stainless steel,

8.53–8.86 for brass, 8.84–8.88 for Monel, and about 8.91 for copper. The lead used to make lead-core trolling lines has a specific gravity of approximately 11, but the effective density of the line is less than that because of the braided nylon or Dacron jacket.

Visibility

When it comes to visibility, angling attitudes seem to be stronger than the scientific evidence at hand. Most fishermen feel that a line ought to be invisible underwater, but no scientist has been able to demonstrate conclusively that very many fish are frightened or otherwise affected by a line's visibility. As for shadows cast by a line, the evidence is fairly strong that at least some species— brown trout and bonefish, for example—can be spooked by the shadows cast by line. Still plagued by the folk conviction that visible lines scare fish, I tend to use uncolored, transparent leaders with the highly visible, often fluorescent, lines that I prefer. More superstition than science here.

Why the high-visibility line? Because I have to see a line to be able to control it properly. Against dark waters and foliage, white or very light lines are quite visible. In bright light, against tropical skies and white sandy bottoms, very dark lines will stand out. But for sheer visibility, nothing quite beats the fluorescent lines that glow like the devil's own fire. My special favorite was fluorescent-orange Stren. Now Stren comes in just two fluorescent hues: golden yellow and clear/blue. Du Pont's new Prime comes in fluorescent aqua and the company recently added a clear, nonfluorescent Stren to its repertoire. Several other monofilament lines are now available in various fluorescent hues. Berkley even used to make its Medallion braided-Dacron trolling line in fluorescent green. The ultraviolet light that activates fluorescence will penetrate perfectly gin-clear water at high noon in the tropics to a depth of about 45 feet. The water-penetration curve of sunlight is one the geometers and statisticians call asymptotic, and that means light penetration falls off very, very quickly as the sun moves away from its dead-overhead position at noon. In murky water or in midmorning or midafternoon, fluorescent line won't glow deeper than 4 or 5 feet.

Most fish possess some degree of color vision, but a line's color isn't all that important to its underwater visibility. Its opacity is much more important, particularly in the casting of shadows. Monofilament lines that are fairly transparent probably are the least visible to a fish, whether seen against the sky, against the bottom, or as a shadow. Wire and braided lines are opaque, but they are available in various camouflages. Brown wire, for example, won't glint in the sun and frighten wary fish or attract misdirected strikes from bluefish, muskies, pike, mackerel, sharks, or other species that are attracted to flashiness.

Marked or metered lines should be considered briefly. Many lead-core trolling lines, a few monofilaments, and some Dacron lines come marked so that you can tell how much line is out. This can be a real help in determining trolling depth of a bait or lure or in presenting a bait at a level where the fish are known to be holding or feeding. Some, like Sunset's Marked Flexon monofilament, have a color mark every so often, every 10 feet in the case of Flexon. Others change colors entirely every 10 feet or 10 yards. Among the lines in this last category are Sunset's Rainbow Dacron trolling line, Gladding's Cor-Les coated Dacron, and quite a few lead-core trolling lines. Among these last, some of the best are Sunset Tel-A-Depth, Gladding Mark Five Invincible series, Cortland Kerplunk, and Gudebrod Metered Lead Core. Most of the deep trollers who use wire lines mark their lines with paint, colored plastic tape, permanent-ink felt markers, or some other means, so they will know how much line they have out and therefore how deep their baits are running.

Flexibility

In monofilament lines this quality usually is called limpness; in wire trolling lines, softness; and in structural metals, beam stiffness. By whatever name, it isn't difficult to understand, but in materials as soft, limp, or flexible as most fishing lines, it can be difficult to measure and compare. Naturally, wire lines are the stiffest and braided multifilament lines the limpest, but making distinctions among lines of the same or similar type can be pretty subjective. If you can *feel* a difference in flexibility, that difference is probably very large.

The more flexible a line is—up to a point—the easier it is to manage on a reel. However, on spinning reels a certain amount of stiffness is desirable so that the line will spring off the fixed spool easily, in properly sized coils and at the right speed. If it's too wiry it will leap off in great, self-knotting spaghetti messes. The stiffer a line is, the more prone it is to take sets and kinks, both of which can drastically affect its angling performance.

A softer, more flexible line will generally allow a lure or live bait more freedom of action, but when it comes to giving a lead-head jig, a popper, or similar lure the proper action by manipu-lating the rod, some anglers feel that a little stiffness in the line helps.

When flexed back and forth at the same spot continuously, wire lines become work-hardened and brittle. Better use a rod that has a soft tip section and let out a few inches of line every so often. Monel lines generally are much softer and more flexible than stainless steel, but Weller's Soft Flex stainless trolling wire is a re-markable exception. Multistranded wire lines are more flexible and less prone to kinking than solid wire strands.

Most monofilaments are advertised as being super limp, be-cause consumers seem to think that limpness is the mark of qual-ity (which might have been true a decade or more ago), but there are remarkable differences between brands. Garcia's Royal Bon-nyl II, Berkley's Trilene XL, Cortland Nylorfi, and the new Ande Super Soft are the limpest premium monos I know. The stiffest are such monofilaments as Sunset's Amnesia (a fly-fishing shoot-ing line), Buck Perry's No-Bo trolling line, Ande, Maxima, and some of the super-tough lines like Triple Fish, a Perlon trolling line lately favored by some big-game fishermen.

Elasticity or Stretch

All fishing lines will stretch to some degree. Stretch is both good and bad in a line. Insofar as it keeps a line from breaking under pressure, it is good; if it keeps you from feeling a bite, from set-ting the hook, or from controlling a running fish, it is bad.

Of the materials used to make fishing lines, the stretchiest is nylon. Most wire trolling lines won't stretch much more than 5 percent (although a really soft wire can stretch as much as 20 percent), but the wires won't return to their original length and diameter. This is called plastic deformation. It weakens trolling wire, and you ought to use monofilament shock leaders and soft-tipped trolling rods to help prevent it.

Nylon is much stretchier than Dacron, Micron, or most of the other polyesters and so-called poly-synthetics. All but the worst brands of nylon are heat-treated and prestretched, and the best premium lines have been able to keep the ultimate stretch under 20 percent. Cheap mono lines may stretch as much as 35 percent. Dacron, Micron, and similar lines will stretch 10 to 15 percent.

There is another major difference in the way nylon and Dacron stretch. Nylon stretches almost uniformly from zero to breaking stress, whereas Dacron does most of its stretching during that last 25 percent of stress. Under normal fishing pressure, then, Dacron, Micron, and similar lines are virtually stretch-free.

Shock Resistance

This property is also known as impact resistance. Shock or impact is the sudden, violent loading of stresses. In fishing, shock usually occurs as a sharp jerk, when a big fish hits a trolled lure, when a fisherman strikes to set the hook, when a battling fish jumps. A 130-pound-class trolling line will support 130 pounds (actually, 120 to 125 pounds) without breaking, if the weight is hanging still at the end of the line, and the skillful big-game fisherman can land a fish weighing more than 1,000 pounds on 130-pound line. But a 15-pound weight will break that line, if the weight is dropped any great distance. Try it yourself, using 10-pound-test line and 1-pound weight. That pound might have to fall several feet before it will break the line, but it will break it.

The stretchier the line is, the more impact resistance it will have. But a line with poor knot strength will break at the knot even if the unknotted portion of the line survives. This serves to illustrate the interrelatedness of these physical properties, something we'll discuss a little later.

Abrasion Resistance

Fishing lines are subject to pretty rough treatment at the hands of sharp teeth and scales, coral reefs and barnacle-encrusted rocks, rusting wrecks and pier pilings, rough-stemmed weeds and brush piles, gnarled stumps and gritty bottoms. Abrasion resistance is a line's ability to withstand all that rubbing, chafing, wear, and tear. Some materials are more resistant than others, of course: Hardness is usually the key, but line construction is a major factor. Solid, single-strand lines are much more resistant to abrasion than multistranded lines made from the same material. Stranded lines are less smooth than single-strand lines, so they won't slip over hazards as easily, and those fine strands are much more easily severed.

Wire lines are obviously more abrasion-resistant than soft lines, but the multistranded wires are surprisingly prone to abrasion failure. Braided-wire lines seem to hold up better than twisted wire, with cable-laid wire somewhere in between. Nylon coatings help. Among the soft lines, nylon monofilament (Perlon, too, for that matter) is tops for abrasion resistance. All other things being equal, the thicker a mono line is, the more abrasion-resistant it will be, which gives some of the thick, stiff bargain lines some advantage in fishing wrecks and reefs. But smart anglers who stick with the all-around quality of premium lines will find as much abrasion resistance as in lines like Ande, Maxima, TriMax, Trilene XT, and Les Davis Super Velux. Nylon is nylon, the chemists used to say, and the only way you can improve its abrasion resistance is by making it thicker. Then the wizards at Du Pont came out with *new* Stren in 1979, a monofilament that was identical to Stren Mod. II in every respect except abrasion resistance. The new Stren is not only more abrasion-resistant than old Stren, it's more abrasion-resistant than any other soft line on the market at this writing. Naturally, Du Pont won't let the cat out of the bag, but Dr. John Hansen, director of research for Du Pont's Stren Division, has said the difference is in the polymer itself and isn't some sort of super-slippery or armor-plated coat.

As for the braided lines, Gudebrod pioneered by coating its G-T Dacron line with Teflon, Du Pont's incredibly slippery tetrapolyfluorethylene. It doesn't make the line tougher, but the Teflon does let it glide over some abrasive hazards without frayage. (Les Davis has done something similar with siliconized Super Velux monofilament.) Several other makers of Dacron trolling lines have since followed Gudebrod's lead. Gladding has come up with its unusual Cor-Les Dacron, which sports the same bonded vinyl plastic coating found on many fly lines. Lead-core trolling lines, which have a braided nylon or Dacron jacket around the lead core, are available uncoated, coated with vinyl or urethane plastic, or with a fly-line-type bonded coating.

Knot Strength

As a rule, knotting a line weakens it. Some knots weaken lines more than others, and some lines take knots better than others, but a knot generally will be the weakest link in your line. Knots weaken line because the loops, coils and turns of a knot cause the line to cut into itself under pressure. The knots we use in fishing have been developed over the years to perform well under various sets of conditions. Many of the modern fishing knots were developed to get around monofilament nylon's very poor knot strength when it first appeared after World War II. Over the past two decades, though, mono's knot strength has been improved considerably. Today, its slipperiness, which can allow a knot to pull loose under pressure, may be a more important consideration than its differences in chemical and molecular structure. Virtually all of the knots that have been developed for monofilament work well in braided lines, and have forced most of the old angling knots out of the picture. A few knots are difficult to pull up properly in braided line, which isn't as slippery as monofilament.

All lines *claim* superior knot strength, but there is quite a range. Again, premium lines are generally better than the budget-grade lines. Some of the cheap lines have good knot strength, but others don't. Virtually all premium lines have superior knot strength. Garcia's Royal Bonnyl II has relatively poor knot strength among the premium monofilaments, but it's still better than most of the cheap lines. I use Royal Bonnyl II when I want a very fine, very limp line, and by sticking with high-strength knots I haven't experienced any difficulties in fishing the Garcia line. But when the going gets rough, give me Stren or another line that has exceptional knot strength.

Braided lines which have a hollow core (virtually all Dacron trolling lines, Micron, and nylon squidding line) can be spliced as well as knotted. It will take a little practice to get the hang of splicing, but it is easy enough. Splices are smoother, smaller, and less prone to jam in rod guides and underwater hazards than knots. I haven't had the opportunity to test spliced lines on an Instron tensile-strength tester, but I am told by people in the line-making business that splicing a line reduces its breaking strength by a few percentage points. I'll wager that most anglers who have learned to splice a line can make line splices with more consistency in strength than their knots.

Durability

Premium lines that are well made from first-line materials are more durable than cheap, sloppily made lines, of course, but some materials and types are more durable than others. No line will last forever. Line manufacturers don't want to say in writing how long their lines should last, because so much depends on how the lines are used and stored. The average angler probably can get by with changing lines every season (or two, if you are lucky), so long as you keep cutting back the battered end. Tournament anglers typically change lines every day, and some big-game fishermen respool after every fish landed or fought.

Wire lines are the most durable, but they are subject to corrosion, kinking, work-hardening, plastic deformation, and metal fatigue. Stranded wire lines also are subject to abrasion and unlaying.

Old organic-fiber lines like cotton, silk, and linen were subject to rot and had to be removed from the reel periodically, rinsed, and wound onto a ferris-wheel-like drying frame to dry. The synthetics—nylon, Perlon, Dacron, Micron, and so on—won't rot, but they are subject to chemical deterioration. Constant wetting and drying is tough on line, and so are all the stretching, rubbing and other things that go on during fishing.

Most anglers know that sunlight is bad for nylon monofilament, which ought to be exposed to direct sunlight only when necessary. Sunlight affects all synthetic lines, so store your loaded reels and supply spools out of the sunlight. And, salty as it may look, traveling for hours to and from the fishing grounds with the fully rigged rods on a roof rack or stuck in the topside rod holders only exposes your line to unnecessary photochemical deterioration. High heat is death on synthetics, too, so a shady spot that is reasonably well insulated or ventilated is your best bet for storing line.

Lead corrodes rather rapidly in salt water. So don't use lead-core line in the briny deep, unless you are willing to remove it from the reel spool at the end of each trip, rinse it well in fresh water, and hang it out to dry. Otherwise the lead will corrode very rapidly in the saltwater-soaked "sponge" of the braided jacket, leaving you with a line that is lumpy from a broken core and a lot less dense than it used to be. A less dense line won't sink very fast or very deep, which is why you are using lead core in the first place.

Monofilament is quite durable, but it is subject to setting because of nylon's "memory." If you fish with a spinning, spincast, or sidecast reel, or if you troll a lot or cast spoons and spinners, you will probably retire a lot of mono line because of twists that become set on the reel. The best preventive medicine I know is the use of a small Sampo ball-bearing swivel. The best cure is to trail the twisted line—*without* any terminal tackle attached—through the water or the grass.

Modern fishing line is extremely durable and needs only a bare minimum of maintenance and care. Changing line once a year won't break anyone's bank. If you want to change it more frequently than that, buy your line in bulk spools and you will save a lot of money.

Interrelatedness of Line Properties

These physical properties of fishing line are not independent of one another. Indeed, they are quite intimately interrelated. Diameter and breaking strength, for example, increase and decrease together within different lines made of the same material. When it comes to multistranded lines, of course, some manufacturers manage to lay or braid their strands more tightly than others, producing a slightly thinner line in the same strength. Knot strength, on the other hand, suffers a bit as diameter and breaking strength increase. It doesn't make much difference up to 20 pounds, but above that test strength knots won't hold as well because the turns taken in the thicker material can't be pulled up properly.

Within a given type of line, the following properties should increase as you go up in breaking strength: diameter, weight, visibility, abrasion resistance, and overall durability. At the same time you can expect decreases in flexibility and knot strength. Elasticity and shock resistance, which are measured in percentages, should remain essentially unchanged, as they are a function of the line material's physical chemistry. In monofilament lines, limpness, stretch, and shock resistance go hand in hand within a given diameter. The limper a line is made, the stretchier and more impact- or shock-resistant it will be. And some of the chemicals that are added to the polymer to increase limpness also decrease knot strength; I can't think of a single, super-limp mono line that is noted for its superior knot strength, though some are more affected than others. Knot strength isn't a chemical or physical property of the nylon itself. It is added after the line is extruded by manufacturing processes that are dark, deep, and closely guarded secrets.

Wet vs. Dry

Wire lines aren't affected by wetting, because they don't absorb water. But soft lines do, and line properties change when wet. Nylon absorbs more water than Dacron or the other polyesters, and so is more affected by it. According to Du Pont, nylon monofilament that has been soaked for two hours will exhibit these changes in performance:

Breaking Strength	10–15%	Loss
Stretch	20–50%	Increase
Shock Resistance	Some	Increase
Limpness	60%	Increase
Abrasion Resistance	50%	Loss
Knot Strength	10–15%	Loss

Dacron line absorbs only about half as much water as nylon lines, so isn't changed as much. But nylon and Dacron lines have inherently different characteristics to begin with (as do monofilament and braided lines), so you have to consider things carefully. For example, Dacron line can get awfully hot under the thumb when "thumb-stalling" a long cast or a running fish, simply because it doesn't carry back with it as much cool, heat-absorbing, slippery water.

Alloys, Copolymers, and Cofilaments

Before we compare monofilament and braided lines, note that the polymer chemists have thrown us a few curves. Several monofilaments are actually copolymers or "alloys" of different nylon polymers. Berkley's popular Trilene lines use "a patented nylon alloy formulation." Aeon copolymer, which has been adopted as the leader material of choice by a lot of fly-fishermen, is a blend of nylon 6 and nylon 66 polymers. Berkley's new TriMax line is a tripolymer, but again the company isn't handing out the recipe. By blending polymers, manufacturers hope to give their line a more desirable balance of properties than can be obtained with a single polymer. Du Pont has taken a different tack; their new Prime is a cofilament, a nylon monofilament sheath coextruded around a polyester core.

Du Pont and Berkley chemists and copywriters each claim complete superiority for their products. According to Berkley, Trilene has 20 percent more tensile strength than single-polymer monofilament lines, and TriMax 40 percent more. And there are two different Trilene formulations: XL, which is blended to be extra limp, and XT, which is blended to be "extra tough." Du Pont claims that Prime has the abrasion resistance, shock resistance, surface slipperiness, and casting manageability of nylon monofilament, with the low stretch and high sensitivity of a braided

Dacron line. And each company is certain that its approach is the right one.

Du Pont says it is too difficult to extrude copolymer or alloy monofilaments with uniform characteristics. In turn, Berkley claims that its TriMax tripolymer is "a fully cohesive composition that will not separate or pull apart like cofilaments."

Not being a chemist, I can't judge the relative merits of the claims. The proof, I say, is in the fishing. Between Stren and Trilene, I like Trilene XL's manageability but prefer Stren's dependability from spool to spool. But I haven't fished enough with TriMax and Prime to have an opinion about either one. So, let's get back to general principles.

MONOFILAMENT VS. BRAIDED LINES

If you pay any attention at all to sportfishing's version of "current events," you know there is a perennial controversy over the alleged superiorities of monofilament or braided lines. Well, there are differences, but assigning the pluses and minuses has to be a personal thing, because the differences between the lines must be judged against the needs and preferences of the individual angler and the physical demands made by the fishing conditions. I have tried numerous ways to quantify or at least to make objective some sort of comparison, and I have decided it is pretty much a waste of time. Once I even tried making a scorecard and it came out in a dead tie. Tell me where and how I will be fishing, and what I will be fishing for, and I'll tell you which line I think would be better *for me*, but I'm not sure you would be happy with my choice. I use and carry both types.

On fixed-spool (spinning, spincast, sidecast) reels, it is tough to beat a good, premium monofilament that has just the right balance between limpness and springiness. If it gets too limp you will lose some casting distance to line slap against the rod; too springy and you will lose a lot of fishing time to removing "wind knots" from your line. You *can* use soft, braided lines on these reels, however. The so-called "braided monofilaments" or "polyfilaments" would be a good compromise except that they are so thick, decreasing reel capacity, casting distance (and accuracy, in a crosswind), and sink rate, while increasing visibility and the sinker weight necessary to hold bottom in a current or to attain the desired trolling depth. Some are better than others, however; the braided poly-synthetics (such as Gudebrod's Supernatural Bass

Line) are generally finer and more translucent than the braided monofilaments.

On revolving-spool or conventional reels—and it makes little difference whether you are talking about casting, squidding, trolling, or boat reels—you can use either braided or monofilament lines, because the extra limpness of braided line won't interfere with casting efficiency and the extra springiness of monofilament isn't likely to cause any trouble. So you can afford to choose the line according to its characteristics, not according to the requirements of the reel.

Some of the supposed differences between mono and braided lines actually are differences between nylon and Dacron. Those differences have been covered pretty well in the preceding pages of this chapter, but maybe we ought to summarize them. Nylon is stretchier (and therefore more shock-resistant), absorbs twice as much water, is somewhat more prone to photochemical breakdown in sunlight, and has slightly less knot strength. Dacron tends to be hotter on the thumb than nylon, and is less affected by wetting, because of the difference in water absorption, but Micron and some of the other polyesters are not as hot as Dacron. As for the patented poly-synthetics, they can't be categorized because of their diversity and, frankly, I haven't yet had enough experience with them to say very much about them. Most of those I have seen were more nearly like Dacron than nylon. But Perlon, the European polymer, is so nearly identical to nylon you can ignore any differences.

A few companies still make braided linen Cuttyhunk line. Linen is an organic fiber, so it will rot. Therefore it should be removed frequently from the reel, rinsed thoroughly in tap water to remove the rot-producing organisms, and wound onto a line drier. The same goes for braided silk, a line still used by some tournament distance casters. Ditto for braided cotton, which is a generally poor fishing line (if you have any, I suggest you divert it to tying parcels for the mail).

Linen Cuttyhunk hasn't disappeared entirely because it has some remarkable characteristics. It stretches hardly at all (which makes it a powerful and sensitive line, albeit one with no cushion against sudden shock), has superior knot strength, and its tensile strength actually increases when it's wet. If you are willing to put up with the necessity of wetting the line before you can cast it and with removing, rinsing, and drying the line at the end of every day, using Cuttyhunk is the quickest route to being recognized as an old salt.

Now let me get on with the differences between monofilament and braided lines, regardless of the materials used. If you are under thirty-five or forty, you probably don't have much experience with braided lines. Monofilament commands more than 90 percent of the fishing-line market in this country! Only in fishing for giant tuna (where Dacron is favored) and in deep trolling (where wire and lead core dominate) does monofilament trail the field. Except for fly fishing, of course.

Stretch

Braiding fibers or filaments usually results in a less stretchy line, partly because of differences in molecular structure of fine fibers and extruded monofilaments, partly because of the friction binding of the individual strands in braided lines. So braided nylon casting or squidding line is slightly less stretchy than nylon microfilament (but still stretchier than braided Dacron or Micron). Du Pont's Prime cofilament is a special case. Because of its polyester core and nylon sheath, it stretches like a braided polyester line in the beginning but has the ultimate stretch of monofilament Stren.

Twisted lines are less stretchy than single-strand lines of the same material, but stretchier than braided ones. As there are very few, if any, twisted soft lines today, the observation applies more to wire lines, which will be discussed shortly in a separate section.

Diameter

Diameter of a line is a function of the material's tensile strength, of course, but also of its construction. A braided nylon line is usually larger in diameter than a monofilament of the same test strength. This is especially true in the case of nylon squidding line, which often has a hollow core to allow for splicing. The larger diameter, as well as the trapped air bubbles and lower effective density, makes braided nylon a slower, shallower sinker than monofilament, and more subject to wind resistance in casting and water resistance in trolling.

Braided Dacron is usually larger in diameter than a monofilament of the same strength, but it may not decrease a reel spool's capacity. In fact, if monofilament and hollow-core Dacron lines are wound onto identical reels under the same winding tension, the Dacron-loaded reel ought to hold about 8 to 12 percent *more* line, because of the compressibility of the braided line. Monofilament won't compress unless it is wound onto the spool under great pressure, in which case you will have two very serious problems. First, the coils of the nylon laid on under heavy pressure are going to dig down into the coils below. This would insure knots, tangles, snarls, and backlashes, were it not for problem two. Because nylon exhibits what is commonly called "memory"—that is, an ability to return to its original configuration—monofilament that is laid on under heavy pressure, and which will be stretched to some degree, is going to try to contract to its original, unstressed length. This will exert such incredible forces on the reel spool and sideplates that it will destroy the reel, crushing the spool or "exploding" the sideplates.

Cortland's Micron line—like Dacron, a polyester braid—is even finer in diameter, so you can wind more Micron onto a given reel than any other soft line of the same strength. Among the Dacron lines, Gladding's Invincible Bluedot comes closest to Micron in fineness of diameter. The fine diameter is a real plus in trolling, casting, and bottom-fishing in strong currents.

Ah, but nothing in life comes free, and the relatively small diameter of most top-quality Dacron lines exacts its price. A few years back, when Du Pont switched from its standard, high-bulk Dacron fibers to finer, high-tenacity fibers, many braided-line-makers started having trouble delivering lines that wouldn't snap considerably under their rated strengths. The fineness of each fiber makes it more vulnerable to fraying, chafing, abrasion, and friction heat failure. Recent improvements in the high-tenacity Dacron fibers have helped to cure the problem, as has the practice of some linemakers to lubricate the individual fibers or strands before braiding.

Abrasion Resistance

Monofilament and other single-strand lines win hands down. For a given material, abrasion resistance is almost entirely a function of the thickness of that material, and the fine, individual strands of multifilament lines abrade easily and rapidly. Monofilament, besides being thicker, has a hard, smooth surface that will slide over things, whereas braided lines offer a softer, more textured surface, just the sort of thing that lets abrasive objects do their stuff.

Among the braided lines, it doesn't seem to make much difference whether the line is braided of nylon fibers, fine monofila-ments, Dacron, Micron, any of the new synthetics, or old-fashioned linen or silk; all will abrade at about the same rate —fast. Gudebrod's G-T trolling Dacron has a Teflon finish, and that helps it to slide over fairly smooth surfaces, but it doesn't armor-plate it by any means. In other words, Teflon might help to prolong a braided line's life under good conditions, but it isn't going to stop a coral branch from sawing its way through. Lately other companies have followed Gudebrod's lead with Teflon-fin-ished lines.

Among the monofilaments there is quite a range of abrasion resistance, with Du Pont's third-generation Stren topping the field, followed closely by Maxima, Ande, Handy, Trilene XT, Tri-Max, Velux, Hawaiian Perlon, and so on. The softest monos are usually the least abrasion-resistant, but the premium brands— Royal Bonnyl II, Trilene XL, Flexon, Nylorfi, Mason Super Soft, and Perflex, to name a few—will still be considerably more abra-sion-resistant than the best braided lines.

Shock Resistance

Almost completely a function of line stretch, shock resistance among the braided lines varies considerably (from stretchy nylon squidding line through low-stretch Dacron to no-stretch linen and silk), but monofilament nylon is tops. Its stretch and its lack of all those individual strands strangling one another guarantees its first-place ranking in this department.

All nylon lines have a certain amount of inherent shock resis-tance because of their stretchiness, but some seem to get theirs more from sheer toughness. It is this very toughness which makes such relatively thick, stiff lines as Ande and Maxima so popular. Recently, on my first *successful* outing for Atlantic salmon, on northern Quebec's Whale River, I learned what a difference this toughness could make. After losing two hooked salmon to (*a*) a sudden run that came just as I had finished reeling up the slack line and (*b*) a jump that came right down on the tippet, I aban-doned my favorite trout-fishing tippet material—supple Nylorfi —and tied on some relatively wiry Maxima in a heavier test strength. I hooked, and landed, a 12-pound salmon on my next cast. I used the same tippet material the rest of the trip and never broke another tippet. Maxima has now become my salmon-fish-ing tippet material, for sure.

Knot Strength

As long as you don't select one of those double-dozen-coil knots that can only be pulled up properly in slippery monofilament, I'd have to give a very slight edge to braided lines. The edge isn't as great as it used to be, but it's still there. If the braids and mono were absolutely even in knot strength, I'd tip the scales a bit in favor of the hollow-core braids because of their spliceability. Splices aren't stronger than the best knots properly tied, but they are neater and more streamlined, and therefore marginally more resistant to failure because of the hard knocks that can damage or deform knots.

Visibility

All other things being equal (namely, color and opacity), monofilament has a slight edge because of its smaller diameter and the smoothness of its surface, which isn't going to be mottled by all those miniature shadows and highlights. Actually, monofilament's edge is larger because of the wider variety of colors available, from clear nylon to jet black, not to mention fluorescence, camouflage, color metering, and every shade imaginable. So if visibility (either high or low) is an important factor, mono gives you more to shop for.

Braided lines won't glint in the sunlight or act like mirrors, so they can be pretty subtle in the water. For bottom-fishing, consider the color of the water and the bottom, including vegetation, if you are selecting a line for low visibility. But for trolling, or any form of fishing above the bottom, remember that a fish will see the line from below against the bright background of the sky.

Flexibility

The limpest monofilaments are like wires compared to the braided lines. Berkley and Company's technicians have measured beam stiffness or modulus of elasticity in fishing lines and Paul Johnson tells me that most of the braided lines are testing within a few percentage points of 50,000 pounds per square inch, whereas Berkley's monofilaments, including very limp Trilene XL, fall into the range of 150,000 to 225,000 psi. (Stren tests at about 200,000 psi, Maxima Chameleon at about 230,000, Ande at something over 280,000, and Sunset's Amnesia shooting line at more than 600,000 psi beam stiffness.) Fly lines are the limpest of all, Johnson says, coming in at 15,000 to 20,000 psi.

The limpness of braided lines makes them somewhat less than ideal for spinning, but they can be used. The limpest monofilaments are ideal on baitcasting and other revolving-spool reels. Use the springier monos and you can expect trouble, no matter how educated your casting thumb is.

Within each material and configuration category (wire lines excepted), the thinner a line is, the more flexible it will be. However, there is considerably more difference in flexibility between, say, 15- and 45-pound mono lines than between the same tests in braided lines.

Some lures and baits work better on soft lines, others on lines that have a little stiffness to them. If you have determined that a given lure or bait-fishing technique isn't working particularly well on ultraflexible braided line, try using a fairly stiff, fairly long monofilament leader. If that doesn't work, switch to mono line.

Durability

Given the same treatment in fishing and storage, a monofilament ought to outlast a braided line, principally because of fraying and abrasion in the latter. However, line twist can be a problem with mono line. When I am being super-sneaky in small, clear trout streams and fishing ultralight spinning tackle without any sort of terminal hardware other than a hook, I get a lot of line twist. If I can use a Sampo ball-bearing swivel, my mono lines last longer.

However, if you seldom fish and your tackle, including line, spends most of its time being stored in a shaded room that isn't subject to extreme variations in heat and humidity (either of which tends to shorten a line's life), you will have better durability with braided line. Mono's actual shelf life seems to be shorter, perhaps because of the monomerization of the nylon. Whatever the reason, monofilament ages less gracefully. In its prime, though, it will slug it out longer than any braid.

Sink Rate

Monofilament, hands down. Its smaller diameter, smoother surface, round cross section, and solid construction (without entrapped air bubbles) allow it to sink deeper and faster. The same principles apply to wire lines; a single strand of solid wire will go deeper faster than any twisted, braided, coated, or lead-core wire.

Buoyancy and water drag seem to be more important than density or weight in determining sink rates. Some few braided lines are touted as being designed to sink fast, but I'm not sure I understand how they work. I haven't used them enough to say much about them. Naturally, a line that is braided around a hollow core will be more buoyant than one that is braided around a twisted core. Of all the braided lines I have tried, hollow Cortland Micron is the one that sinks deepest and stays down better with the least weight. Its diameter is very fine and its tight braid minimizes the roughness of the surface. Some water-friction test figures I have seen would seem to show that Micron is about as efficient as the same-strength but larger-diameter monofilaments.

For top-water fishing with small poppers and delicately balanced surface lures, I believe that the more buoyant, less water-absorbent braided Dacron line is at least marginally superior to monofilament and braided nylon lines. It is sort of the baitcaster's and spinfisherman's answer to the floating lines so favored by dry-fly fishermen. Incidentally, when you want a line to be truly buoyant, try rubbing it with dry-fly line dressing.

Manageability

This is a real can of worms. Conventional wisdom says the softer braids ought to be more manageable, but have you ever tried to pick a bad bird's nest or backlash out of fine-diameter braided line? Not only are the knots tighter, but your fingernails and calloused fingertips are going to abrade that line. I believe that any distinctions in overall manageability are going to have to be made by you, according to your tastes, talents, and idiosyncracies.

When you get into something as stiff as wire, though, there isn't any question that the multistranded lines are easier to manage, and that lead core is the best behaved of all.

If you experience behavioral problems with monofilament, try going to a different brand, perhaps one that is limper or that has less "memory." (Until chemistry catches up with promotion, the last-named is a can of worms.) On the other hand, maybe you need a stiffer, more springy line if you are spinning. And by all means, if you are using and having trouble with cheap, bargain-basement mono line, get rid of it and spool up with some fresh premium line! On baitcasting and other revolving-spool reels, you might want to try one of the oval monofilaments. These cannot be used on spinning and other fixed-spool reels. The few oval monofilaments on the market (Cortland Mono-Worm and Sunset Uni-filament, for example) are premium lines, and they are designed to lie flat on the revolving spool. Once twisted, however, they are awful, so be sure to use a good, dependable, small ball-bearing swivel when fishing with spoons, spinners, and other lures and baits that tend to revolve.

Ice-fishermen and those who go out on the North Atlantic in midwinter for cod and "frostfish" (a name often applied to whiting, which is itself a misnomer for silver hake) may experience quite serious line-manageability problems. These problems are magnified by frost-numbed fingers. Monofilaments stiffen with the cold and become awfully wiry. For years, ice-fishermen worried whether the cold-stiffened monos were more brittle. They aren't, according to tests made by Berkley. Trilene actually became tougher as it stiffened. Winter fishermen who like mono would do well to use a very limp, premium line like Trilene XL, or one of the monofilaments specifically intended for ice-fishing. The best of these probably is Sunset's new Hot Line, a limp mono that is coated with a waxlike substance to keep ice from adhering. It also is color-metered for judging depth accurately, with alternating 5-foot sections of black and red.

Braided lines are limper still, so some winter anglers prefer to use them. Besides being more manageable, braided Dacron is much more sensitive to those feeble winter nibbles than limp, stretchy monofilament. The problem here is icing. Even though Dacron isn't very water-absorbent, it ices up rather easily because of all those little droplets of water trapped between the fibers. Because the braided surface isn't as smooth and slippery as that of mono, Dacron line is susceptible to freezing up on the reel spool. To offset these problems, Gudebrod and a few other companies wind fairly short lengths of their Teflon-coated Dacron trolling lines onto small spools that are ideally suited for ice-fishing.

Cost

In any given quality range, monofilament is nearly always cheaper. It isn't any cheaper or easier to make than braided line (in fact, just the opposite is true), but its popularity gives it the advantage of mass volume and the cost savings that usually accompany mass marketings. Besides, with so many brands on the mono market, discounting is rampant. You seldom see braided lines being sold at a promotional discount.

The Envelope, Please...

If you just tot up the advantages and disadvantages outlined above, mono comes out ahead, which probably explains its popularity. However, braided lines do have significant advantages under certain conditions, so don't hesitate to use them. If you miss a lot of strikes because you can't seem to set hooks properly, try switching to braided Dacron and your score should improve immediately. And low-stretch Dacron may be just the ticket if you are jigging or bottom-fishing with a soft rod that won't telegraph the bumps and light nibbles: Before selecting a line, analyze carefully the demands that are being imposed by the angling conditions and by your own tastes, techniques, and limitations.

WIRE AND WEIGHTED LINES

Trolling deep is a problem, because it is difficult to make a line sink deep and stay down. And, frankly, it isn't nearly as much fun as fishing on top. But when the fish are sulking down deep you have to go down after them. If you own your own trolling boat, downriggers may be your best bet for getting down to those lurking chinook salmon, lake trout, and striped bass. But if you fish alone you will need one of those expensive, electric-powered models so you can retrieve the trolling weight and tether cable while both hands are full of battling fish.

If, like me, you are boatless, then downriggers are out. Strike-release sinkers and diving planers have their advocates, and I use them both on occasion, but they put an awful lot of strain on the tackle and on your arms and back. Wire lines, including lead core, get down deep without the strain and the extra weight.

All of the wire lines are more difficult to use than soft lines and require special care and a bit of practice. They aren't alike, however, and their efficiency seems to be inversely related to their manageability.

Wire lines will stretch some, but metal isn't very elastic and so won't return to its original length. A wire that has been stretched is a wire that has been weakened, so it is a good idea when trolling wire lines to use soft, flexible rods and monofilament shock leaders. As all of the wire lines are considerably more expensive than soft lines, don't fill a monster-sized reel with wire line. Use only as much as you need—100 yards usually is sufficient, although Great Lakes salmon fishermen may use as much as 200 yards—which will be attached to a backing line of monofilament or braid.

Wire Types

We can break the whole field down into three major types: (1) solid or single-strand wire, (2) stranded wire, of which there are three subtypes—twisted or cable-laid, braided, and coated wires —and (3) lead core. They aren't interchangeable.

SOLID WIRE

Nothing gets down deeper, faster, or more efficiently than solid, single-strand wire, and it stays down better than almost anything else. Its efficiency is a combination of its density and diameter, and you can stir up quite an argument among anglers or engineers as to which is the more important factor.

Solid wire is tough to handle, there is no denying it. It lies coiled on the spool like a spring, ready to leap off the instant you throw the reel into free-spool without keeping adequate thumb pressure. Smart trollers leave their clicks on when spooling out wire, and some even stick the rod in a holder, set the reel drag very light, and pull the wire off hand over hand. No precaution is too great, unless your tastes run to picking apart metal bird's nests. When wire line twists, it kinks, and each kink is a weak spot in the line, so use swivels—more than one, and better make them ball-bearing Sampos—in your wire trolling rigs.

Solid wire line is the most resistant of all lines to abrasion, but it isn't abrasion-proof. A nicked wire line can develop little burrs that scratch and slash, so wear gloves when handling wire.

Don't confuse soft, relatively thick trolling wire with thin, hard, spring-tempered leader wire. Leaders made of trolling wire will cause baits and lures to run awry, and as for spooling wire leader onto a trolling reel—well, that is the sort of mistake no one makes twice in one lifetime. Lazy anglers may get away with barrel-turned loops and eyes in heavy leader wire, but *always* use haywire twists to make connections in trolling wire.

Many angling authorities say that at normal slow-trolling speeds—3 to 4 knots—a 30-pound-test wire line will troll 1 foot down for every 8 feet of line out. I have asked several wire-liners about this and most think the ratio is at least ten to one. Troll a little bit faster and you might run it up to twenty to one or worse. Experiment; don't rely on hearsay, no matter how eminent the authority.

STRANDED WIRE

Because of its larger diameter, its lower effective density, its trapped air bubbles, and its rougher surface (which gives water friction a better fingerhold), multistranded wire won't troll as deep as solid wire. And it is considerably more expensive. Nonetheless, some anglers like it because it is easier to manage—more flexible, less subject to kinking, less prone to fatigue failure. But twisted lines are much more subject to abrasion, and the finest uncoated wires will develop a wire fuzz that can cut hands and jam in rod guides and tiptops, particularly those of the roller type.

Twisted lines are those in which the wire strands are simply twisted tightly together. Seven-strand wire, also called 1×7, is the most common type, although the lightest tests usually are 1×3. There is quite a difference between brands of stranded wire regarding the relationship of test strength to diameter. Assuming the strands are twisted together equally tightly, the thinner a stranded wire line is, the stiffer it is likely to be.

Cable-laid wire, usually just called cable, is twisted wire of a more complicated sort. Individual strands are twisted into bundles and then several bundles are twisted together. The best-known type is called 49-strand, 7×7, or aircraft cable. Other types include 3×5, 3×7, 5×5, 6×19, and 6×37. Cable-laid wire is less apt to become untwisted under stress and torque, but under extreme duress it can become unlaid. Because its individual strands are finer, it is somewhat more prone to abrasion and fuzz. Most cable-laid trolling lines are big-game cables, intended for use on marlin, tuna, sharks, and swordfish. But some trolling cables see use on smaller fish, in fresh water as well as salt. Cable-laid wire is usually thicker and more supple than a plain twisted wire of the same test strength.

Braided wire isn't very common, because of its large diameter and a somewhat greater stiffness than that of twisted-wire lines. But some trollers like it because it just won't come unlaid and because it is very difficult to kink. Usually braided of individual strands that are thicker than those used in twisted or cable-laid wires, braided wire is more abrasion-resistant. Its construction can't be described because it varies so from one manufacturer to another.

Coated wire is stranded wire, usually 1×7, that has been coated by a nylon, urethane, or vinyl plastic. It is the thickest and least dense of all the true wire lines, and therefore the least efficient for getting deep. But its ease of handling has won some advocates. As long as that coating remains intact, the wire won't abrade, so the line can be safely handled without gloves. And you can use coated wire line with any kind of rod guides. (Bare wire requires the use of case-hardened roller guides or ring guides of tungsten carbide, silicon carbide, or aluminum oxide.) But once that plastic coating gets abraded, watch out. Frayed coatings can jam in guides and tiptops, too.

Some anglers won't use coated wire because they think the coating bears some major portion of the stress and that, once the coating becomes frayed, the line will be severely weakened. Actually, the coating is there only to "insulate" the wire core; the rated test strength is based completely on the wire strength.

LEAD CORE

Lead core is the easiest of all the "wire" lines to use and is my favorite in fresh water. It will corrode in salt water, however, and so needs to be removed from the reel, rinsed, and dried after each outing. Lead-core line is nothing but a nylon or Dacron line braided around a core of lead wire. The wire does the sinking and the jacket provides the strength. It is quite large in diameter, and increased water drag offsets the advantage of lead's great density. Only at extremely leisurely trolling speeds—just barely under way—will lead core sink as deep as solid wire.

But lead core won't kink, it doesn't spring off the reel spool, you don't need to use special guides or gloves, and it is just plain well behaved. Once the lead core gets broken, however, the line does get lumpy and more difficult to manage.

Some lead cores, like Sunset's Tel-A-Depth, are uncoated, so you can pinch the lead core out of the last couple of inches and splice the braided jacket as you would any other hollow-core braided line. Many lead-core lines are coated, with vinyl or urethane plastic, to protect the jacket from abrasion. Gladding's Mark Five Special has a bonded-plastic coating like that used on fly lines. Even with the coatings, lead core is the most likely of the weighted lines to fail under abrasion, so don't drag it over the rocks and coral reefs. A long leader of tough monofilament is a good idea.

Most, but not all, lead-core lines are metered. That is, the color of the braided jacket changes every 10 feet or 10 yards so you can keep tabs on how much line is out. This is very handy.

Metals and Materials

The materials used to make wire trolling lines greatly affect their performance. Among the true wire lines, several metals are used, including stainless steel, Monel, and copper. The wires used to make lead core are essentially alike, but the braided jackets of nylon or Dacron perform very differently.

STAINLESS STEEL

Stainless steel is the strongest of the wires used to make trolling lines, and its fine diameter helps keep it down. But it is stiffer and more difficult to handle than the other wire materials. The softest stainless-steel wire I've seen is Weller's Soft-Flex, which isn't all that much stiffer than some Monel lines I've handled.

Solid wire, seven-strand, cable, coated wire—all types are available in stainless steel. Most are bright finish, but a few are available in brown or darkened finishes. I've heard that a blue wire is available on the West Coast, but I haven't been able to track it down.

The grades of stainless steel used to make trolling wire—Types 302 and 304—are quite corrosion-resistant in salt water and virtually immune to rust in fresh water. Specific gravity is 7.9 and tensile strength of the soft-drawn wire is about 85,000–100,000 psi. Stretch can vary a good deal, depending how the wire was drawn and how much it is annealed—as much as 35 to 50 percent.

MONEL

Monel metal is a nickel-copper alloy, trademarked by International Nickel Company. It is softer and more manageable than stainless steel, even more corrosion-resistant in salt water, and heavier (specific gravity of 8.46 to 8.88, depending on the exact alloy used). But it isn't as strong (tensile strength 63,000–85,000 psi), so its diameter will be larger than a stainless steel wire of the same strength. It is also about as stretchy, the factor ranging from 35 to 48 percent.

Monel would have to be counted superior to stainless steel as a trolling wire, but for two drawbacks. In salt water, Monel will cause most other metals it comes in contact with to corrode galvanically (see Chapter 11), whereas stainless steel polarizes with most other metals and therefore doesn't affect them very much. So, when trolling in the sea, be sure any hardware you attach to Monel wire is made of stainless steel or Monel, or is heavily nickel-plated. Monel wire is roughly twice as expensive as stainless steel. The best source I know for budget-priced, top-quality Monel trolling wire (and stainless steel, too, for that matter) is the Jelliff Corporation of Southport, Connecticut, whose advertisements appear regularly in fishing magazines.

Most of the Monel trolling wire you see in tackle shops is solid, single-strand wire, but several companies make stranded or braided Monel. U.S. Line Company in Westfield, Massachusetts, also makes dark Monel, which is good in stained or murky waters. Benco Wire Product's Fab-U-Line brand of trolling wire is one you don't run into everywhere, but it is just about the most diversified line I've seen, covering stainless steel, Monel, and copper. All three metals are available in solid, stranded, and braided forms.

COPPER

Copper line isn't used in salt water, because it will corrode, but it is popular in certain freshwater locales for its superior suppleness and weight (specific gravity 8.91). Since it isn't very strong (tensile strength on the order of 35,000 psi), it has to be quite thick. In 30-pound-test, copper line will have a diameter of approximately 0.032 inches. In the same strength, a solid stainless wire line would run about 0.020, Monel 0.020 to 0.022, and lead core 0.034 to 0.036. Given those diameters, I think lead core would be the better choice for a supple line because it is softer and more flexible than copper and will sink deeper.

LEAD-CORE JACKETS

Most lead-core lines have a nylon jacket braided over the lead core, but a few are Dacron-jacketed: Sunset's Tel-A-Depth and Gladding's Mark Five, for example. The Gladding lines come in two types, regular and special, the former having a vinyl outer coating and the latter a bonded, flyline-type coating. Sunset's line is uncoated so the lead can be pinched out and the coreless jacket spliced.

Dacron-jacketed lead core is, in my estimation, so superior to the nylon-jacketed type that it should be the first choice of any lead-core troller. Remember, Dacron stretches only half as far as nylon, and most of Dacron's stretch comes in the last part of the stress curve. The lead wire core is stretchier than either fiber, but the lead isn't elastic, and it won't snap back to its original length. Therefore, a lead-core line that has been stretched will have a deformed and broken core, and it will be lumpy and more difficult to manage. The broken lead wire actually promotes abrasion of the braided jacket.

Otherwise, there isn't much difference between nylon and Dacron for strength, abrasion resistance, and other characteristics (although a Dacron-jacketed line might be marginally smaller in diameter). As for the choice between coated and uncoated lines, suit yourself. The coating adds to the line's thickness, but makes it a little more slippery in the water. Those factors tend to balance each other. The plastic-coated lines are more resistant to normal abrasion, but the thin plastic coating won't keep the line from being sawed in two against a sharp granite reef or the rusting hulk of a barge or derrick.

TOPWATER TACKLE FOR WIRE-LINE TROLLING

I've already touched on this a bit, but a few points are worth summing up.

Rods

Rods for wire-line or lead-core trolling ought to be fairly soft and flexible, to help keep the inelastic lines from stretching. In the case of lead-core line and coated wire, regular guides and tiptops will do, but when using bare wire line be sure your rod is outfitted with good carbide or aluminum-oxide ring guides or case-hardened roller guides.

Reels

Capacity must be adequate to handle at least a hundred yards of wire line and at least that much backing line (the latter may be monofilament or braided soft line testing about 20 or 30 percent more than the wire, mainly because you don't want to lose the whole length of that expensive wire if things get out of hand). The spool should be wider or deeper than normal. The deep, narrow spool is traditional in wire-line trolling, the theory being that the looser the wire is wound, the more manageable it will be. Recently, though, wire-liners have gone to wide-spool reels because it is easier to pick the inevitable wire jams out of them.

The reel spool should be strong enough to handle the loads generated, and that pretty much rules out plastic spools. As for aluminum spools, avoid them when wire-lining in salt water because any of the metals—copper, stainless steel, and especially Monel—will corrode the aluminum very badly. Stainless-steel spools are best, but brass spools that are heavily plated with hard chrome are also good.

FLY LINES

Fly lines are different from all other fishing lines. In fly-fishing, it is the weight of the line that is cast, not the weight of the lure. Flies are essentially weightless. Balanced tackle is important in all types of fishing, but it is most important in fly-fishing. The balance between fly rod and fly line is especially important. Which is chosen first, the rod or the line? As in the case of the chicken and the egg, it all depends. If size and wind-resistance of the fly, fishing depth, or maximum casting distance is the prime variable, then the line is chosen first, the rod being selected according to its ability to cast the chosen line well. On the other hand, if the size or strength of the fish is the key issue, or the presence of rocks, reefs, or other underwater hazards, a rod that can handle the fish is selected first, then a line that will flex the rod properly in casting. (Actually, it's a little more subtle and complicated than that, but this is close enough for our purposes.)

If you've ever looked at fly lines before, you know they aren't rated by breaking strength or diameter. Strength of the line isn't an issue, because fly tippets (the bitter end of the leader that is tied to the fly) are intentionally the weakest links in fly-fishing gear. The fly-line diameter will vary according to size and manufacturing decisions. Look at a packaged fly line, and you will see a code that contains a combination of letters and numbers. A DT6F code means you have a double-taper, 6-weight, floating line. Fly rods are labeled according to the weight (and sometimes the taper) of the lines they can handle.

Weight

We'll look at weight first, because it's the variable that most affects rod selection and fly size. All fly lines are rated according to the weight in grams of the forward 30 feet. All fly-line manufacturers conform to the size and weight standards established by AFTMA (the American Fishing Tackle Manufacturers Association). AFTMA has established such standards for fly lines rated from 1 to 15. One- and 2-weight lines would be considered "stunt" lines by most anglers. Three- to 8-weight lines are used by trout fishermen, while bassmen generally use sizes 6 through 9. Salmon fishermen prefer rods and flies that require 7- to 10-weight lines, while saltwater flyrodders can usually be found casting 9- to 12-weight or heavier lines. The ranges and variations take into account a lot of variables, including angler skills and idiosyncracies. Until you've packed a good bit of flycasting experience under your wader belt, rely on the advice of a good fly-fishing shop in selecting and balancing rods and lines.

Tapers

Fly lines are sorted by taper into five categories, but there is actually a good bit of creative variation here, from manufacturer to manufacturer. The experts know why they might choose, say, a Cortland 444 line over a Scientific Anglers Air Cell Ultra, but I rely upon the sage advice of the fellow who sells them to me or upon my whim of the moment.

A fly line's parts are named according to their position within the profile of the taper.

Parts of a Fly Line

LEVEL (L)
Level lines, because they are cheap, are often advertised as beginners' lines, but I can't imagine a worse fly line for a beginning flycaster. They are difficult to cast and present a fly with maximum clumsiness and commotion. Avoid them.

DOUBLE TAPER (DT)
Because they cast well, make delicate presentations, and can be reversed when the front end of the line begins to show wear and tear, double-taper lines are the most popular. As the name implies, these all-around fly lines are symmetrically tapered fore and aft.

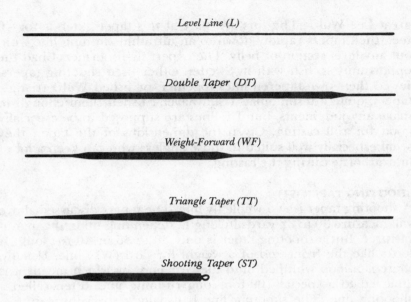

Level Line (L)

Double Taper (DT)

Weight-Forward (WF)

Triangle Taper (TT)

Shooting Taper (ST)

Fly Line Tapers

WEIGHT-FORWARD (WF)

A weight-forward fly line's taper is, as the name suggests, biased heavily toward one end (even though the first 30 feet will weigh the same as the same portion of a double-taper line). Because they can be cast faster and farther and take up less space on the reel spool (all these advantages accounted for by the thinner cross-section of the running-line portion following the taper), they are favored by experts. They cannot, alas, be reversed when they begin to wear out, and they are more difficult for duffers like me to cast delicately. Each manufacturer seems to have a different idea of the ideal taper, and some give their variants such names as long-belly or rocket or torpedo taper; but they are all rated WF.

Saltwater and bass-bug tapers are also called blunt weight-forward tapers, and they have shorter, steeper tapers that do a better job of casting big, bulky, wind-resistant flies. These, too, are officially rated WF by AFTMA.

TRIANGLE TAPER (TT)

This is a special sort of weight-forward (but not officially WF) asymetrically tapered line invented and manufactured by the great Lee Wulff. The forward part of this taper extends for 40 feet, then tapers rapidly down to an ultrathin running line without any level section or belly. The expert fly-fishermen I had the opportunity to fish with in Sweden either used shooting tapers, sewed their own tapered lines together, or fished Wulff triangle tapers, quite a testimonial. I still haven't fished them enough to make any judgments, but TT lines are supposed to be especially good for roll casting. Given the dimensions of the taper, they seem especially well suited to those anglers who can keep a lot of line airborne during the casting.

SHOOTING TAPER (ST)

A shooting taper isn't a whole fly line. The tapers discussed above will measure 30 to 35 yards in length, depending upon the manufacturer. But a shooting taper is only 30 to 35 or 40 *feet* long. It looks like the front end of a weight-forward (WF) line. Usually, there is a loop whipped onto the rear end, by which means it is attached to a special 100-foot-long running line, often called a shooting line. The shooting line is usually a specially manufactured level fly line that is very thin, but it may also be a monofilament or braided line. Mono shooting lines (often ultra-stiff, sometimes flattened-profile lines made especially for this purpose) can be cast the farthest, but only in the hands of experts. The rest of us are better off using a level-taper-type shooting line. Don't get into a casting contest with a fly-fisherman who uses shooting tapers; he will almost certainly be a seasoned expert. More of us tyros should try shooting tapers; they're great. Especially for sinking lines.

Density

The last part of a fly line's classification nomenclature refers to its density. (Not its weight; in the case of fly lines, "weight" refers only to the first 30 feet, no matter how heavy the whole line feels in your hands.)

FLOATING (F)

Floating lines are made with buoyant, closed-cell foam cores that cause them to float on the water. They are by far the most popular and useful of the fly lines. (Their popularity exceeds their utility, because sinking densities are much more difficult to cast.) Even wet flies, streamers, nymphs, and other sinking flies can be fished effectively on floating lines.

INTERMEDIATE (I)

These neutral-density or very-slow-sinking lines are not very popular, but they are extremely useful. More fly-fishermen ought to use them. Designed to present a fly just below the surface, intermediate lines cast thinner shadows than floating lines underwater on sunny days. Their maximum effective fishing depth is two to three feet, depending upon the current and the hydrodynamics of the fly.

SINK-TIP (F/S)

Also called floating/sinking lines, these are floating lines that have tip sections that sink. The length of the sinking tips will vary from 10 to 20 feet. A lot of fly fishermen find them easier to cast and to handle than full sinking lines. I can't cast either and have gone to high-density shooting tapers, which I can sort-of cast when the wind and the stars are in the right quadrants.

SINKING (S)

Sinking lines are full fly lines that sink along their whole length. When the fish are feeding deep, they are the most efficient lines to use... *if* you can cast them. I can't. But too much of my fishing is done mentally, while bound to the desk. Those who get out on the water and practice with them swear by sinking lines.

Sinking lines are made in at least four densities, I through IV, their sink rates varying from just less than two to more than five inches per second, their ultimate fishing depths depending upon your patience, the speed of the current, and what sort of fly you are using. Slow-sinking (Type I) lines are good to about five feet; fast-sinking (Type II) lines to about ten feet; extra-fast-sinking (Type III) lines to twenty feet; and super-fast-sinking (Type IV) lines to maybe thirty feet in still waters.

SHOOTING HEADS

These are ultra-fast-sinking shooting tapers, typically very short (just a few feet long, and usually tied between the end of the fly line and the butt of the leader), and built around a lead core. Shooting heads are rated by weight (450 to 800 grams) and sink rate (7 to more than 10 feet per second). Some fly-fishermen use short sections of lead-core trolling lines, but the best shooting heads are tapered, usually with the thickest, heaviest section in the rear. Either type is difficult, and even dangerous, to cast. I won't use them—too inept and cowardly.

Coating

The inside of a fly line, the core, is what makes it float or sink, but the outside coating is what causes it to sail through the rod guides. Most fly lines have a fairly hard, slick plastic coating that is bonded onto the core. I can tell you from experience that this coating will suffer fatally if you leave your fly lines in the trunk of a car on a hot, sunny day. To keep your line shooting through the guides, keep it clean. Numerous gunks, pads, and the like are available for cleaning lines. All work.

Color

The precise hue of a fly line isn't important, but it is often what causes fly-fishermen *A* and *B* to disagree violently over the relative desirability of fly lines *C* and *D*. Choose a line you can see well under the fishing conditions you expect to encounter. Some of the most vividly colored fly lines were made first for the purposes of photography and were put on the market only after fishermen seeing those photos in the fishing magazines started asking for them. My fly lines cover the whole color spectrum, from dark brown to fluorescent cerise and yellow. The best reason to carry different colors is to help you to remember your different densities.

END OF THE LINE

No matter what anyone tells you about this or that line's being *the* best line, forget it. A line might be the best choice for a given situation or a given set of conditions, but no line rates at the top for everything. Premium monofilament might be as close as we'll ever come to a do-everything line, and even before I started collecting lines to test for this chapter I routinely stocked my shelves with half a dozen different brands of monofilament alone, not to mention the Micron, Dacron, nylon squidding line, stainless and Monel wire, and lead core. Now that I've taken up fly-fishing, I find myself using a lot of different brands, densities, and tapers of those lines, too. And I love all the color choices available in fly lines.

7

Take Me to Your Leaders

To HEAR some fly-fishermen tell it, leaders are a subject of never-ending mystery, a search for the ultimate taper and perfect tippet that is not unworthy of consideration alongside the Arthurian quest of the Grail. Nonsense? Of course; the practical angler need not wallow in mystique, whether the subject is leaders or anything else. On the other hand, flycasters have good reason to be concerned about their leaders, and other anglers might profitably spend a little more time than they usually do, deciding whether they need to use a leader at all and how to select and tie the right leader for the job.

Simply put, a leader is nothing but a certain length of material —usually a synthetic polymer or a metal wire, sometimes both— between the fishing line and the terminal hook or lure. There are no hard-and-fast rules regarding all the variables of material, length, strength, color, and so on, nor is there anything like a true consensus among angling experts on these details. There are, however, standards and common-sense guidelines that are worth knowing and within which the individual angler will still have plenty of room for exercising personal option.

The basic and ultimate reason for using a leader is to change in some significant way the nature or physical properties of the terminal end of the line that is connected to the baited hook or lure.

Leaders may be stronger or weaker than the lines to which they are attached, stiffer or more supple, of the same, similar, or entirely different material. Leaders may be long or short, simple or complicated, constructed of one or several pieces of leader material. Before attempting to thread one's way through this thicket of options, it pays to be a bit analytical about leaders.

"SELF LEADERS"

Except in fly-fishing and trolling, leaders are not absolutely and universally required in sportfishing. If the line you are using has the necessary properties of strength, durability, size, visibility, flexibility, and so on, you might just as well use the line itself as a leader. Some anglers and angling authorities refer to such lines as "self leaders." If you are fishing live bait on reasonably light tackle for such species as trout, panfish, striped bass, bonefish, yellowtail jacks, seatrout, carp, small tuna, permit, cobia, or even redfish or channel bass, it often makes sense not to use a separate leader, because all of the species named (and others, besides) can at times be quite leader-shy. If, however, you are using braided or other opaque lines, it usually pays to use a more translucent monofilament leader, even if it has the same diameter or test strength as the main line. There is very little scientific evidence to suggest that leader *color*—even fluorescent color—much affects fish, but I have plenty of practical evidence that shadows cast by opaque lines often scare fish, particularly some of the wary or timorous species listed above.

If you are going to use your fishing line as a self leader, that line had better be a dependable, high-quality monofilament. Ordinarily, the terminal end of the line is the only part that a fish gets a chance to look over, so you want a line that behaves well, trailing through the water without any of the undue looping or curling that can draw a fish's attention to it. Keep an eye on the end of a fishing line that is being used as a self leader and cut it back at the first sign of fraying or abrasion. If you are going to fish without a leader, better stick to particularly abrasion-resistant premium lines. (See Chapter 6.)

If you have decided you need a leader—and we'll get to the various reasons for needing leaders a bit farther on—you will have to choose among the leader materials currently available. Silkworm gut, tarred line, and other traditional options have pretty much fallen by the bankside, so what follows is restricted to monofilament and wire.

MONOFILAMENT LEADERS

Nylon monofilament is far and away the most common leader material in use today, and for good reason. As a general rule, monofilament should be your leader material of first choice; opt for wire leaders only when mono ones won't do. Various synthetic polymers—nylon, Perlon, and others—are extruded as mono-filaments and used in fishing, but they are so chemically and physically similar we needn't distinguish among them.

Some monofilaments are sold specifically for use as leaders. They may or may not differ from the monofilaments that are packaged and sold as fishing lines. Sometimes only the labels and packages are different. If a mono can provide the physical prop-erties you need in a leader, then fret not whether the manufac-turer labeled it as leader material or fishing line. There are a lot of merchandising tricks in the tackle trade, and the confusion they cause among consumers is awful. Fly leaders excepted, the things that usually distinguish a monofilament line from a mono-filament leader material involve the balances stuck between such properties as limpness and stiffness, diameter, color, and so on, rather than any inherent differences in the properties themselves. Tynex, the nylon monofilament that is often used to tie saltwater terminal rigs, is one of the few monofilaments that is used exclu-sively for leaders (if terminal rigs can be considered specialized leaders); Du Pont actually extrudes Tynex for use as a bristle in paint and toothbrushes.

Monofilament has many properties and qualities that make it the best all-around leader material. Chapter 6 covers those prop-erties in some detail. But those that chiefly interest us here are its high tensile strength, its good resistance to abrasion, the stretch that provides the necessary cushion against shock or impact fail-ure, its blend of flexibility and stiffness, its ease of handling, and its transparency or translucence. Mono is relatively cheap and can be purchased almost everywhere. And it is available in a stagger-ing range of types and colors, enabling the angler to purchase a leader material that can provide just about whatever he is looking for. Monofilaments are extruded in test strengths that range from less than 1 pound to well over 1,000 pounds, but 400-pound-test is about the heaviest mono leader generally in use even among big-game trophy hunters who troll the blue waters far offshore.

You used to see some braided monofilament leaders and hook snells, but they have virtually disappeared from the marketplace, having been replaced by single-strand mono or so-called T-cord, which is nothing but nylon tennis-racket-stringing material. Braided mono leaders were used principally in saltwater bottom-fishing, to wean old-timers away from the traditional tarred lines.

Excellent as monofilament is, it has some drawbacks as a leader material. It isn't as rugged as wire and won't survive as well when confronted by sharp teeth, rusty wrecks, barnacled rocks, coral reefs, and other hazards. And polymers like nylon are subject to photochemical deterioration and to some chemical attacks to which wires are immune. While monofilament can be knotted without much loss of its listed test strength (*if* the right knots are used and tied well), the stiff, heavy monofilaments often used for shock and big-game leaders can be awfully difficult to tie well. Monofilament that is difficult to knot can be crimped with the sleeves that are actually meant to be used on stranded wire and cable leaders, but crimp sleeves that are cinched down too tight can nick and weaken monofilament, and those that are crimped too cautiously will allow the slippery, stretchy nylon to slither out of their grasp. When crimping heavy monofilament, you must proceed with extreme caution and use two or even three sleeves per crimped connection.

WIRE LEADERS

It isn't so easy to be general about leader wire because of the variety of metals used the way they are drawn and treated, and the differences between solid and stranded wires. In general, though, wire is tougher and more durable than monofilament when it comes to coping with sharp teeth and other abrasive hazards. It also sinks more rapidly and will troll deeper. And it isn't subject to photochemical deterioration or to damage by diesel fuel, certain insect repellents and sun lotions, or the other things that can wreck monofilament.

However, wire has so many offsetting disadvantages it must be regarded as a special-purpose leader material, rather severely limited in its acceptability. It is generally more expensive than monofilament, and not so widely and readily available. Its diameter may be larger or smaller in the same test strength, but it always is opaque and casts detectable shadows, no matter how well it is camouflaged in the water. Since wire is stiffer and more dense than mono, it can seriously inhibit or dampen the action of a live bait or lure. Line twist is even more seriously damaging to wire than to monofilament, and wire leaders are also subject to kinking, setting, work-hardening, and fatigue failure. All wire stretches to some degree, and, being inelastic, it can't rebound to its original length and diameter. Wire so stretched usually is weakened because of necked-down spots (thin places where, because of the thinner diameter, the wire's actual breaking strength has been reduced). Most wires cannot be knotted successfully, so you have to use special twists and crimped connections. Wire is relatively difficult and sometimes dangerous to handle, and the wise user of wire leaders wears gloves. Finally, wire is subject to corrosion, particularly in salt water, where it is much more often used.

Wire Metals

Carbon-steel piano wire is the strongest, stiffest, thinnest leader material available, virtually always in solid (single-strand) construction. It isn't so popular anymore because of its high susceptibility to rust and corrosion. When the wire is tinned it is fairly corrosion-resistant, but bright and reflective.

Stainless steel has pretty much replaced piano wire because, in the grades used to make leaders, it is very resistant to saltwater corrosion and is almost immune to rust or corrosion in fresh water. Its tensile strength is about 3 to 10 percent less than that of piano wire, depending upon how it is drawn and treated. Stainless steel is not very reactive in salt water, so it can be joined to most other metals without corroding or being corroded by them because of galvanic reaction. Stainless-steel leaders are available in solid and multistranded forms, the latter in twisted, braided, or cablelaid configurations. Virtually all of the nylon-coated wire leaders presently available are made of stainless steel.

Brass is seldom used for trolling lines or leaders, but the Weller Company makes a blackened, extremely supple brass leader in 3 × 5 cable-laid form called Ultraflex. Brass corrodes too rapidly for serious consideration by saltwater anglers, but fresh water doesn't much harm it. Brass wire is softer, weaker, and heavier than carbon- or stainless-steel leader wire.

Obviously, stainless steel is the leader wire you are most likely to use, although some bluewater traditionalists prefer piano wire.

CORROSION RESISTANCE OF LEADER MATERIALS

In the following ranking, the most corrosion-resistant of the "raw" materials used to make leaders is ranked first; the most corrosion-prone is ranked last.

1. Monofilament
2. Stainless Steel
3. Tinned Piano Wire
4. Brass
5. Piano Wire

Note, however, that in the case of metals, their precise rankings depend upon the exact alloys used and whether the leader is fished in fresh or salt water. In salt water, for example, a high-zinc yellow brass would be subject to dezincification, a form of corrosion so destructive that this alloy would rank dead last for ocean fishing. See Chapter 11 for a discussion of galvanic corrosion, to see how joining dissimilar metals in salt water affects their corrosion potentials.

Solid Wire

Solid or single-strand wire is manufactured and sold as trolling line or leader material. Don't confuse the two, even if the labels of some manufacturers do. Trolling lines are soft-drawn and annealed to make them supple and easier to handle on a reel. In this form they have about the same tensile strength as monofilament, which makes them very nearly identical in diameter, although the wire is more visible because of its opacity. A soft-drawn wire leader will set itself into curves, bends, spirals, and all sorts of shapes that destroy lure action.

Hard-drawn, tempered leader wire is extremely strong and stiff. It is the finest-diameter leader material you can buy in any breaking strength or test. It is available in nineteen sizes, the smallest being no. 2 (0.011 inches in diameter, and testing 27 or 28 pounds) and the largest, no. 20 (0.045 inches and 315 to 397 pounds, depending on the brand). The ultimate test strength of each size depends on what alloy the manufacturer selected, how the wire was drawn, and how much it was hardened or tempered. In solid and stranded wires, beware of statements that this brand or that is thinner than the competition, because it depends upon which size or test you are talking about.

All wires are opaque and will cause shadows, but solid wires cast skinnier shadows than stranded wires. Solid wire is available in a range of finishes or colors; the bright finishes are highly reflective, but some stainless-steel leader wire has a dull gray, nonreflective finish. Brown finishes are available in a number of shades, from coppery bronze to dark coffee brown, and you can find blued and blackened wires, the former being generally twice the cost of the latter.

Solid wire is not easy to handle. Its stiffness makes it tough to twist into connections without the aid of pliers (or special wire-twisting tools), and it kinks rather easily. If you use pliers or wire snips to cut wire, the ends will be very sharp and hazardous. Learn to break the wire by bending it back and forth, and you won't cut yourself on it nearly so often. Solid, hard-drawn wire is extremely resistant to abrasion, but when it does get nicked the burrs can slash ungloved hands. There is a myth afloat that you can't join wire directly to monofilament, because the former will cut the latter, so many anglers always use a swivel to separate the two. The place where line joins leader is often a good place to use a swivel, if you need one, but it is a far better idea to learn how to make a safe, strong wire-mono connection: Use a haywire twist to put a loop in the end of the wire, then tie on the monofilament using an Albright knot. (See Chapter 10.) Done properly, it is a 100 percent effective connection.

Stranded Wire

Many fishermen who like to use wire leaders prefer stranded wires to solid-wire leaders because they are more flexible and easier to handle, less subject to kinking, work-hardening, or fatigue failure. But stranded wire is thicker and therefore more visible, slower sinking, shallower running, and much less resistant to abrasion. The fine-diameter wires that are used to make stranded wire or cable are individually more susceptible to abrasion and breakage, partly because they are thinner and partly because they usually are softer-drawn wires. When stranded-wire lines and leaders become frayed, they are weakened appreciably, and the metal fuzz can cut hands and jam in rod guides and tiptops (particularly the roller types).

Nylon-coated leaders are very popular because the nylon jacket makes them easier and safer to handle, effectively more supple, and somewhat easier to crimp. But the plastic jacket also makes the wire thicker, less dense, and more subject to water drag, so it won't sink as fast or stay down as well in a current. A frayed nylon jacket is not particularly hazardous, but it can scratch or burn hands and jam in guides and tiptops. Once the jacket is frayed or removed, the stranded wire core is exposed to the same abrasion as unclad wire.

A few anglers—including some really good ones, who ought to

know better—won't use nylon-clad wire because they think that, once the nylon jacket has been cut, the wire loses half of its breaking strength. This simply isn't so. The nylon jacket is not a stress-bearing part of the package, and the listed test strengths are based solely on the wires inside the jackets.

Stranded wires are available in many of the same finishes as solid wires, and the nylon-jacketed ones *could* be colored in any hue of the spectrum, but color conservatism is the rule in leaders. On the West Coast, saltwater live-bait fishermen are very fond of short, blue-nylon-clad, stranded-wire leaders. On the East Coast, black-clad and black-finished wire leaders are just beginning to gain favor among those who fish the murky depths and stained or dirty waters, replacing the bright wires that still dominate the market there.

As far as I can tell or have been able to find out, there is very little difference among the fine wires that are used to make the individual strands, whether the stranded wire will be used to make trolling line or leader material. The acceptability of the final product is not so much a matter of the individual strands used, but of the way they are put together.

TWISTED WIRE

The most common of the stranded wires, twisted wire is simply a wire made by tightly twisting a certain number of strands into a neat bundle. Twisted wire is sometimes miscalled cable, but, as we shall see later, cable-laid wire is different. Of the twisted wires, seven-strand wire is by far the most common and the most readily available. (Note here that seven-strand wire is a generic type, whereas Sevenstrand is a trademarked brand, one of the very best.) Seven-strand stainless steel is available in all the metal finishes described above, either unclad or nylon-coated. Test strengths vary from 18 to 250 pounds, and the diameters of each test vary considerably from brand to brand and even within the brands. The Sevenstrand Tackle Corporation actually makes its 8- and 12-pound-test twisted wires in three-strand construction.

Seven-strand wire is reasonably flexible. The precise degree of flexibility depends upon the hardness and diameter of the fine strands used. When twisted wire gets twisted again during fishing, it can become kinked or the strands can become separated; either situation results in leaders that are weak and unwieldy. Most seven-strand wires are of stainless steel, but Monel and copper trolling wires are made in this form and are sometimes used to make leaders.

CABLE-LAID WIRE

For the ultimate in wire flexibility, ultrafine wire strands are twisted in bundles and then several of the bundles are twisted together to make cable-laid wire or just plain cable. The finer the individual strands and the greater number of them used to make a cable of given strength, the more flexible the cable will be. The most common cable configuration is called 7×7 (because it is made by twisting together seven bundles of seven-strand wire) and 49-strand aircraft cable (because the same stuff is used as control cable in light airplanes). Other popular cable configurations include 3×7, 6×19, and 6×37; in each case the first number indicates the number of bundles used and the second,

LEADER MATERIALS RANKED BY PHYSICAL AND OTHER PROPERTIES

(all comparisons by equal or similar test strengths)

	MONO FILAMENT	SOLID WIRE	TWISTED WIRE	COATED WIRE	CABLE-LAID WIRE	BRAIDED WIRE
Fineness of Diameter	4	1	2	6	3	5
Limpness or Flexibility	1	6	5	4	2	3
Weight	6	5	3	2	4	1
Sink Rate	6	1	2	5	3	4
Shock Resistance	1	6	5	4	3	2
Abrasion Resistance	6	1	4	2	5	3
Kink Resistance	1	6	5	4	2	3
Twist Tolerance	1	5	4	2	6	3
Ease of Handling	1	6	5	2	3	4
Color Range	1	3	4	2	5	6
Economy	1	2	3	4	5	6

NOTE: *Rankings are not precise because of variables within types and materials, between brands, and a general reordering of rankings from very light to very high strength leaders. Therefore, it is more important whether a leader material is very high or very low in rank, not how it compares to the leader materials immediately above and below it in rank. These rankings are weighted to reflect typical or average values across the spectrum of test strength.*

the number of strands in each bundle. The last named, 6×37, is the most flexible of all wire cable leaders. Most cable-laid leaders are used in big-game trolling, in tests ranging from 60 to 800 pounds. Weller's Ultraflex brass cable comes in 3×5 configuration and in three test strengths (27, 45, and 60 pounds), and is used in fishing for muskies, big pike, gar, and giant catfish.

Cable-laid wire is the most susceptible of all the wire leaders to fraying and abrasion. For this reason, among others, cable leaders are most popular among bluewater fishermen who troll surface lines many fathoms above the bottom in open water. The flexibility and resistance to kinking of cable are what these anglers seek, as well as the fine diameters and super strengths.

Severe twisting can unlay cable construction, making the leader subject to kinking, abrasion, cutting, shock failure, and fouling in the sections thus unlaid. Unlaid cable also can be hazardous to handle. On bluewater fishing cruisers, the mate who handles the leaders is called the wire man, and he always wears gloves.

Virtually all cable-laid leaders are made of stainless steel.

TYPES OF LEADERS

You can pigeonhole leaders into all sorts of different categories, but to keep the number down to a manageable lot I am going to do it by function. By thus cutting down on the number of leaders that require description, I shall be omitting a few of the really special-purpose leaders, but it still leaves plenty of leaders to look at.

Fly Leaders

Though I don't in general have much to say about terminal tackle for fly-fishing, I can't ignore fly leaders entirely. After all, aside from the flies themselves, fly lines and leaders are about all the terminal tackle there is in fly-fishing. Besides, leaders are of first-rank importance in the art of casting and presenting an artificial fly with the long wand.

Flycasting is different from all other forms of casting. When you use a levelwind or spinning reel, you are casting the weight of the lure, bait, or sinker, which pulls the line from the reel. In flycasting, though, it is the line that is being cast, so the line must be thick and heavy. For really long-distance casting, some fly-fishermen use fly lines that have the bulk of their weight in the forward part of the line. Obviously, since delicacy of presentation is the very heart and soul of fly-fishing, it just wouldn't do to tie a dainty fly onto the end of a thick, heavy fly line. Some sort of leader must always be used in fly-fishing.

The typical fly leader is a tapered one, very thin and delicate in the forward section or tippet, thicker and stronger in the aft section or butt. It would be difficult to tie a cobwebby tippet onto a plastic-coated fly line; hence the need for the tapered leader. Some tackle companies make and sell knotless tapered leaders, and they are handy, but the resourceful fly-fisherman had better know how to tie his own. It isn't difficult. The average fly leader ranges from 7½ to 9 feet, but expert fly-fishermen may adjust to special conditions and go as short as 3 feet or as long as 15 feet. In a typical tapered leader, the butt section (which may actually be two sections of monofilament, one heavier than the other) should occupy about 50 to 60 percent of the leader's total length. The tippet should represent about 20 percent of the total length, and the remaining 20 to 30 percent is devoted to progressive graduation in diameter from butt to tippet.

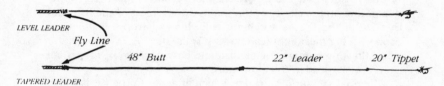

LEVEL LEADER

Fly Line

48" Butt   22" Leader   20" Tippet

TAPERED LEADER

Typical Fly Leaders

All sorts of tricky knots—nail knots, needle knots, rolling splices, and what have you—have been devised for assembling leaders and joining them onto fly lines, but you really needn't learn them. (See Chapter 10 for knot-tying tips.) The Uni-knot will suffice, both for tying the leader onto the fly line and for joining together the various sections of a tapered leader. Or you can make quick-change leaders by making loops in the ends of the various sections of leader and using girth hitches (also called lark's-head and interlocking loops) to join them together as needed. The surgeon's loop knot will do just fine in the leader material; as for the end of the fly line, you can either learn how to whip an end loop or join a short, looped butt section of leader onto the fly line with a Uni or other knot. Plenty of fly-fishermen will tell you that all those interlocking loops and loop knots will foul up your casting, pick up weeds, get caught on twigs, and scare fish; but so eminent a fly-fishing authority as Lefty Kreh uses and recommends using loop-connected fly leaders, so you will be on safe piscatorial ground.

So much for the mechanics of assembling fly leaders. Now, how about their physics and geometry?

Whole books have been written about fly leaders, and I am sure more will be. I am going to be so reckless as to try to boil the whole subject down into just a few paragraphs. If you are really new to fly-fishing, three courses of action are open to you: (1) Stick to the pretied tapered leaders that are carried by most tackle shops. Many of them come with some sort of advice on how and when to fish them, and if the shop specializes in fly-fishing, the clerk or proprietor ought to be able to furnish expert guidance. (2) If you want to tie your own, better latch onto one of the good fly-fishing books available or, better still, onto a knowledgeable fishing companion. (3) Be content with the words of general wisdom that follow, which were furnished by and are reprinted with the permission of Scientific Anglers/3M Company, a very knowledgeable outfit when it comes to fly-fishing:

> Most fly-fishermen use tapered leaders from 7½ to 9 feet long, depending on the clarity of the water, the wariness of the fish, and the size of the fly. As a general rule, heavy (strong) leaders are used with big flies; light leaders with small flies. A 7½-foot leader is usually long enough for panfish and bass. Most trout fisherman prefer a long leader, 9 feet or more.
>
> The final section of a leader, which attaches to the fly, is called the tippet, and should be at least 20 inches long. The tippet will become shorter every time you change flies and should be replaced when it's less than 14 inches.
>
> Tapered leaders can be purchased at most tackle stores, or you can make your own. The commercial variety comes in two forms, knotless or hand-tied. One drawback with the knotted leader is that weeds and debris have a tendency to hang up on the knots and make casting and playing the fish more difficult.
>
> If you wish to tie your own leaders, there are kits available with spools of different diameter monofilament and complete instructions. You generally start with a 36- to 40-inch section of heavy mono, approximately half the size of the line tip, and then knot in shorter sections of decreasingly smaller diameter until you have tapered down to the desired length.
>
> Finding the right leader construction to best fit your casting style and fishing needs will take some experimenting. But it's worth the effort.

A typical trout leader might go something like this: A butt section of 36 inches of 30-pound-test mono, followed by a 24-inch section of 20-pound, 12 to 18 inches of 15-pound, 12 inches of 12-

pound, and 6 to 12 inches of 6-pound, finished off with a 20-inch tippet of 4-pound-test.

Panfish and bass fishermen often use a 6- to 7-foot level leader in 6, 8, or 10 pounds, but purists tend to stick to tapers: 36 inches of 30-pound test, 24 inches at 20 pounds, 12 inches at 15 pounds, 12 inches at 12 pounds, and 6 to 12 inches at 10 pounds, with an 18-inch, 8-pound tippet.

For big largemouth bass, and for general saltwater fly-fishing, a heavier tapered leader is called for: 36 or more inches at 30 pounds, 30 inches at 20 pounds, 12 inches at 15 pounds, and a 24-inch tippet at 12 pounds.

Heavy saltwater fishing for tarpon, big snook, sailfish, and larger game requires the use of longer, heavier leaders, usually with a heavy shock leader rather than a light tippet at the fly end. It is almost impossible to prescribe a general-purpose heavy-duty saltwater leader, but this one should see you through a lot of heavy fishing: 72 inches of 30-pound for a butt section, followed by 24 to 36 inches at 12 to 15 pounds, and finally a heavy shock leader of 12 inches or more, depending upon the hazards.

Fly-fishermen experiment endlessly with these formulas, hoping to find a leader that will turn the fly over properly at the end of the cast to present it delicately and accurately. The new braided-butt leaders are by far the best things I've ever used. Despite their greater expense, I hardly use anything else now.

Tapered Leaders

Tapered leaders aren't solely the domain of the flycaster. Many of the leaders commonly used by anglers of all sorts are nothing but tapered leaders. For example, if you use a monofilament leader that has a short section of much heavier mono on the terminal end to guard against sharp teeth, gill covers, or scales, you are using a tapered leader. Some angles might call such a dual-purpose, two-part leader a *composite leader,* but I am restricting that term to leaders that are made from two or more different materials: monofilament and wire, for example. If a leader is made from two or more sections of leader material, with different strength or diameter but essentially similar chemical composition, then it is a tapered leader.

Anglers of all stripes could profit from using tapered leaders in many situations. If, for example, you are deep-trolling with large-diameter lead-core line followed by a long, fine-diameter mono leader (as you might when trolling deep for small kokanee salmon), you could get a better, more secure connection by tying a heavier butt section of leader to the lead-core and then tapering down in diameter to the fine leader.

Those who use long, heavy shock leaders for surfcasting know how difficult it can be to make neat, secure knots using two monofilaments that are wildly different in diameter or stiffness. Doubling the line from the reel helps (it also represents one approach to making a tapered leader), but you still might want to use—instead or in addition —a short butt section that is intermediate between the line and leader in diameter or limpness.

As described in the section on Fly Leaders above, a multipart tapered leader can be connected via interlocking looped sections, but I'd rather use slim, streamlined knots when fishing down near the bottom or around weed beds, brush, and other snags.

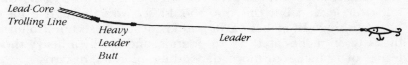

Lead-Core
Trolling Line

Heavy
Leader
Butt

Leader

Tapered Trolling Leader

Light Leaders

A leader that is finer in diameter and lighter in test strength than the main fishing line is a light leader. Fly-fishermen call it a tippet. Light leaders are invariably made of monofilament which is usually clear or translucent. You might use a light leader for several reasons: To give a small, light, delicately balanced lure or bait more freedom of action than would be afforded with a stiffer, heavier line or leader; or to provide an invisible, gossamer-thread leader when fishing for leader-shy species like brown trout or bonefish (particularly if you are using braided line or dark, opaque monofilament line). Whenever you find yourself forced to use line that is awfully heavy for the species at hand, tie on a light leader and you will get more strikes and catch more fish. Light leaders needn't be very long—2 to 4 feet is standard.

When fishing with a light leader, don't forget to adjust your reel drag to the test strength of the leader, rather than of the line. I've lost more than a couple of nice fish because of this oversight. If you are casting, and the test of the leader is lighter than the line test recommended for the rod action and casting weight you are using, be sure to use lob casts instead of snap casts or you will break the leader at the power peak of the casting stroke. I've lost lures and terminal rigs to this oversight as well.

Whether a clear or translucent monofilament leader of the same test strength or diameter as a braided line should be called a light leader is an interesting semantic question, but it is of no particular importance to the practical angler. What is of consequence is failure to use such a leader—no matter what you call it—on bright days in clear or shallow water when opaque lines cast fish-scaring shadows. Leader color may make no difference to fish, but if you suspect that they are avoiding your offerings because they can see the leader, don't hesitate to tie on a clear, translucent, or otherwise color-camouflaged leader. Always go with what gives confidence. I am convinced that the angler's confidence can be more important to angling success than scientific relevance.

Bite Leaders

I am calling any leader that is designed to prevent line failure in the face of sharp teeth a bite leader. Some angling authorities might classify these among the shock leaders, but I am restricting that term to those leaders that are intended to absorb the shock or impact of sudden, violent stress loads.

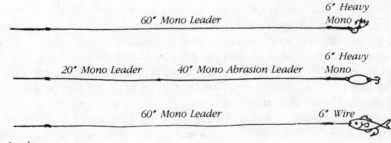

Bite Leaders

Bite leaders are common in saltwater fishing, particularly when baited hooks rather than artificial lures are used. Many species that inhabit the ocean and its arms have sharp teeth. If the teeth are numerous, set close together, or bladelike in shape, wire leaders are preferred. But if the teeth are spikelike and spaced rather far apart, then either wire or heavy monofilament may be used. In fresh water, only muskies, pike, and large walleyes merit the use of wire bite leaders, although some anglers prefer light wire to heavy mono when fishing for pickerel with light tackle.

Most of the time, bite leaders should be fairly short, from 6 inches to 2 feet long. If you need a longer leader to protect your

line against abrasion, don't use wire just because you have selected a wire bite leader. Instead, make a two-section, dual-purpose composite leader. Wire can do all sorts of untoward things to
the terminal end of a line, and you should try to minimize your
use of it.

Saltwater fly-fishermen and those who ply the long wand for
pike will really like the Climax Wire-Tip leaders designed by Fred
Arbona and Jon Olch. A short section of nylon-coated, multistrand wire is attached via an Albright special to the tippet end of
a tapered monofilament leader. Crimp sleeves are supplied, so
you can attach your fly. A neat solution to an old and thorny
problem.

Bluefish sometimes go beserk once they are hooked, destroying
lures and somehow managing to attack several feet of line with
their teeth. Still, I'd rather risk losing these occasional savages in
favor of getting many more strikes by limiting wire bluefish
leaders to 2 feet or less. You will be safe from biteoffs by most
blues and you won't be sacrificing your fishing action for the sake
of guarding your line against that almost mythically malevolent
chopper blue, should it happen onto your bait. Anyway, no wire
leader is long enough to fend off a barbaric bluefish that is on a
real rampage.

A lot of fishermen use wire leaders when they would be much
better off using stout, stiff, hard-finish monofilament. Virtually
all good pickerel anglers use mono bite leaders and many of the
best pike and walleye anglers use mono most of the time, opting
for wire bite leaders only when they are after real trophy fish.
The heaviest, stiffest monofilament is lighter, more supple, and
probably less visible than wire. Du Pont's new Stren is extremely
abrasion-resistant, without being very stiff or large in diameter.
Unless I need the stiffness of special leader-material monofilament, I often use clear Stren to make up leaders.

Multistranded bite leaders have gained some favor among
freshwater anglers, particularly those who fish for pickerel, pike,
and walleyes. Instead of using wire or a single strand of heavy
mono, they make bite leaders by tying together several strands of
lighter-test leader, or even strands of the fishing line itself. The
theory is that a spike-toothed fish is likely to part such leaders a
strand at a time, and even if all the strands but one are severed,
the skillful angler with a deft touch ought to be able to land a fish.
Those who use these leaders say they affect lure action less than
single strands of heavy mono.

Keep an eye on your bite leaders, for even solid wire won't last forever. I have watched sharks cut heavy cable leaders and gang-ings as if they were made of spaghetti. Less well-endowed toothy critters can do almost as nasty a job on your leaders. Discard a bite leader as soon as it shows real evidence of wear and tear, but don't let the frayed nylon on a coated-wire leader upset you too much.

Shock Leaders

Many angling authorities lump together as shock leaders all the leaders that are intended to absorb physical punishment, such as mechanical abrasion, cutting by sharp teeth, excessive tensile stress, and true shock or impact loading. Rather than fly com-pletely in the face of tradition and risk misunderstanding for the sake of mere accuracy, I am going to gather most of these leaders under this single heading, but I will distinguish among the chief types.

Dacron
Trolling   Wire Leader   Mono Shock Leader
Line

Shock Leader

TRUE SHOCK LEADERS

Shock or impact is a *sudden,* violent increase in stress. In fishing, such shocks occur at the moment of the strike, just before the reel drag starts slipping, when the hook is set on a strike, when a trolled bait or lure is suddenly panic-stopped by the strike of a heavy fish, when a trolled hook encounters a snag, when a hooked fish makes a sudden and desperate rush for freedom after a momentary lull, when it shakes its head violently or jumps (particularly if it lands upon the line), when a fish slips from the gaff as it is being lifted from the water, and when a thrashing fish is being lifted without the aid of a gaff or net. To withstand these shocks, a leader must either have a large surplus of unstressed strength in reserve or it must have built-in forgiveness or shock resistance.

The most dependable shock resistance in a line or leader is elasticity or stretch. Monofilament is, therefore, the best material to use in a true shock leader, because it is the stretchiest and most elastic of the leader materials. A 130-pound-test length of any material ought to be able to lift a 130-pound weight off the floor. But a limited-stretch material in that test strength, like Dacron or hard-tempered leader wire, will snap if a 15-pound weight is dropped 16 feet before the line comes taut. Even monofilament would be shock-stressed awfully close to its breaking point under those conditions.

A shock leader need not be particularly long, nor need it constitute the entire length of the leader. If you need, say, a wire leader to guard against sharp teeth or severe abrasion, a 2-foot length of heavy-test monofilament spliced somewhere into the leader might suffice to protect line and bite leader against shock or impact stresses. The higher and more violent the expected shock loads, the longer and stronger the shock leader ought to be. The limper and stretchier the monofilament, the better it will be as a shock leader. If you are trolling with monofilament line, perhaps it alone will be able to handle the shock load of the strike. Even so, it might not be able to withstand the shock load once you get a big fish close to the boat. The rubber trolling snubber is a type of shock leader. Whenever you are using Dacron or polyester line and a wire leader, you had better have some sort of snubber or monofilament shock leader between them, unless your tackle is quite a bit overstrength for the fish you expect to catch.

CASTING SHOCK LEADERS

Surf fishermen and other distance casters often use long monofilament shock leaders to absorb the very high loads that are generated when they are casting heavy weights great distances with long rods. These are typically twice as strong as the main line and long enough so that a few turns of shock leader will be on the reel spool when the lure or sinker is dangling in proper position for casting.

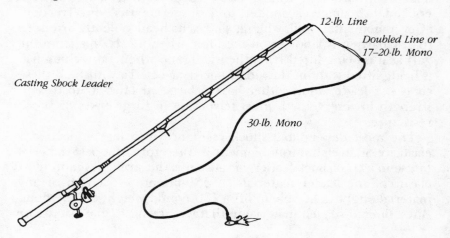

Casting Shock Leader

12-lb. Line

Doubled Line or 17–20-lb. Mono

30-lb. Mono

A shock leader enables the use of a fairly light-test line, which will increase casting range because of its reduced line drag and air resistance. Casting shock leaders are very popular on the salty coasts, but relatively few freshwater anglers seem to know about or use them. True, they aren't as necessary on the inland streams and ponds, but they are very useful when you want to use lines that are a wee bit lighter than recommended for the rod. Under such conditions, you must either use shock leaders for casting or resort to lob casts and settle for reduced distance. I sometimes even use long shock leaders on ultralight spinning tackle, as long as I need the distance and the fish I am after aren't leader-shy.

OVERLOAD LEADERS
When fishing from bridges, piers, and other places high above the water, and where gaffs and nets aren't practical, it can be a good idea to use long, strong leaders that will enable you to reel fairly heavy fish right up out of the water. Such leaders should be made of monofilament of a test strength sufficient to bear the weight of the largest fish you are likely to catch, and they must be long enough to reach from the reel to the water. It is actually better to use a bridge gaff or net, of course, because the heavy leader may adversely affect the allure of your bait or scare off wily old lunkers. But in a pinch it can save the day. Don't overdo it on leader strength, however. If you manage to catch a fish of truly heroic proportions you had better resort to alternative measures—leading it around obstacles to shore or figuring out how to get down to the water with a gaff or net. If you try lifting a real heavyweight out of the water, the hooks may tear out of its mouth or your rod tip may break. Remember, *all* your tackle must be taken into account when you are putting together a winning combination. Go too heavy here and too light there, and you will have a problem.

Sometimes the only way to catch big fish in really heavy cover, without going home for heavier tackle, is to approach the cover quite closely and stealthily, use a long overload leader to yank the fish out of the cover, and then let it steam off into open water for the fight. This is high-risk fishing, however, and it takes a lot of skill and at least a little luck to make it succeed. You will seldom be able to overpower really big fish on test strength alone because of the relative frailty of their mouth tissues. You whip a big fish by tiring it with the reel drag and the flexure of the rod, and you overcome mismatches in the fish's favor by following it in a boat or on foot. I have watched surf fishermen cover a half-mile of beach as they walked or ran up and down during the battle.

Until the International Game Fish Association (IGFA) changed its rules—which now prohibit "catching a fish in a manner that the double line never leaves the rod tip"—some unethical, but record-hungry trophy hunters would use maximum-length doubled lines and super-heavy overload leaders to take big fish from shallow water on very light line. They would use, say, 60-pound-test leader material to catch fish of maybe 15 to 35 pounds. That the leaders were tied to 6- to 12-pound-test lines made no real difference, because the fish were yanked aboard on the overload leader alone, the light line never coming into play. Until IGFA rewrote its rule book, such catches could and did qualify as world records in those line classes. I don't know how such "sportsmen" could sleep at night. Without regard to rules and records, the use of an overload leader as some kind of meat-fishing hand line is unconscionable.

Abrasion "Shock" Leaders

I use the word "shock" in this category only because most other anglers and angling writers do. Fully half of the time, when you hear someone advocating the use of a "shock leader," it turns out he really means an abrasion leader. Abrasion is bad news, but it isn't shock.

Fishing around wrecks, rocks, coral reefs, barnacle-encrusted pilings, bridge abutments, shellfish beds, heavy brush piles, stump fields, flooded timber, and other such hazards, your line is subject to an awful lot of abrasion. Even sand bottoms can abrade line fairly fast. Most of the abrasive beating will be absorbed by the last few feet of your line, which ought to be protected. To guard against fraying and abrasion failures, you need to use abrasion leaders. And anytime you are fishing a braided line, you really ought to use a monofilament leader because multifilament lines are much more susceptible to abrasion.

When it comes to abrasion leaders, you can waltz into all sorts of controversy over the relative merits of monofilament and the various kinds of wire. Certainly solid wire is the most abrasion-resistant of all leader materials and soft nylon polymer the easiest to abrade. As a rule of thumb, though, I'd stick to fairly heavy, stiff, hard-finish mono unless the abrasive hazards are purely awful. Stranded-wire leaders offer quite a varied range of resistance to abrasion; the most easily abraded are those made with the slenderest individual strands. Nylon-clad wire is less likely to fray than bare, stranded wire, but once the cladding wears through, it's back to square one.

An abrasion leader should be no longer than it has to be. If sharp scales or sandpapery hides are the problem—as they would be if fishing for tarpon or sharks—then your abrasion leader needs to be about as long as the largest fish you are likely to catch. On the other hand, when fishing for snook and other species that have razor-edged gill covers, the abrasion leader need be only as long as the fish's head. More often, though, abrasion hazards will be environmental rather than biological. You can't protect your line against every conceivable abrasion hazard, so forget super-length leaders. Restrict your abrasion-leader length to cover the worst of the hazards—the ones that mostly attack the last few feet of line. If a lot of your line will be exposed to abrasion, be sure your reel is loaded with a monofilament line that is particularly resistant to the hazard: For example, Du Pont Stren (especially the new clear, nonfluorescent version), Les Davis' siliconized Super Velux, Berkley Trilene XT, Maxima, Ande, or any good, tough line that has a reputation for being abrasion-resistant. These lines make good abrasion leaders, too.

Sometimes it is a good idea to tie long, tapered leaders to cope with abrasion. To your line, attach a reasonably long butt section of mono leader that is heavier or more abrasion-resistant than your line; its exact length depends upon the extent of the hazard. To this butt section, join a shorter, even more durable monofilament leader—very heavy-test line or special leader material. Finally, if things are really going to be tough, tie on a short length of wire leader. Don't try to play it safe by using wire for the entire length, because that would inhibit lure action or bait freedom enough to sorely limit the number of strikes or bites you will get.

Caution and common sense, each balanced against the other, are your best guidelines when making abrasion leaders. Some fishermen forgo them altogether, preferring to lose a few fish, a few lures, a few terminal rigs, in favor of the faster fishing they can get on a leaderless (self-leadered) line. I use abrasion leaders, mostly of monofilament, but they are seldom longer than 6 feet even in rugged saltwater fishing, because most of my reels are spooled with abrasion-resistant line in the first place.

For some fishing, though, wire leaders have a definite place. Large sharks, for example, are very difficult to land on anything else, and some of the big ones can bite through wire. Many big-game fishermen like to use cable leaders, which offer a balanced compromise between the ruggedness of wire and the suppleness of monofilament. The use of stranded-wire leaders is, I think, overdone by inshore fishermen. Most snook fishermen prefer wire over monofilament for their leaders, partly because old *ro-*

balo's gill covers have such razor-sharp edges, and partly because so many snook anglers feel that single-strand wire gives them more power and control than stretchy monofilament for yanking snook out of the mangrove jungles. But snookers keep their leaders short and light; 6 to 24 inches of no. 3 to no. 6 wire is standard. Freshwater anglers who do battle with toothy, rough-scaled gar often use composite leaders with a short wire bite leader and a longer abrasion leader of tough monofilament (less often, of stranded or nylon-clad wire). Tarpon fishermen seldom use wire—the good ones never do—but they use long, tapered leaders that are designed to cope with both abrasion and shock. The typical tarpon leader employs a long butt section that tests at least 30 pounds and might go as high as 60 pounds when heavy tackle is being used to subdue really big tarpon. A 3-foot terminal section of much heavier mono—from 50 to 100 pounds, depending upon the weight of the tackle and of the fish—is added because the terminal section will take most of the beating.

Trolling Leaders

Like fly-fishermen, trollers have to use leaders virtually all of the time, and they have evolved almost as many different kinds of leaders—and nearly as much mystique about them. Most trolling leaders are pretty long. The best trolling lines have limited stretch, which means they also have limited shock resistance. A stretchier leader will better withstand the sudden shock when a big fish puts the brakes on a moving bait. Unless a long leader is used to restore the necessary horizontal stability, weighted trolling lines will keep a bait or lure from producing its best action and from traveling straight and level through the water. And big-game trollers need long, strong leaders that will enable them to subdue huge fish when they are close to the boat.

DEEP TROLLING LEADERS

Those who troll with heavy sinkers, diving planers, wire lines, or lead core to get their baits down deep must use long monofilament leaders, sometimes as much as 50 to 100 feet long. These leaders will keep their baits running level and true, give them freedom of action, and absorb the shock of the strike. They are also less visible than wire and lead-core lines. Salmon trollers in the Pacific Northwest (and, to a lesser extent, in the Great Lakes) have established fairly uniform standards for leader lengths and weights, but elsewhere in the country and on other species one

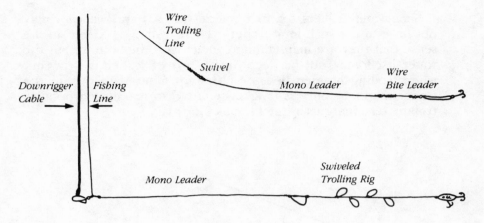

Typical Deep-Trolling Leaders

has to go pretty much on logic, common sense, and the advice of local experts.

The typical trolling leader is a tapered leader. The long leader that is attached to the trolling line usually is followed by a leader that makes up the trolling rig itself, and it may involve all sorts of keels, attractors, and other bits of hardware. Sometimes composite leaders are used in trolling, with wire bite leaders, rubber trolling snubbers, wire spreaders and umbrella rigs, monofilament droppers and trailers.

A snubber, in case you haven't seen one, is nothing but a length of latex rubber tubing (not unlike the surgical tubing that is used to make tube eels and similar lures), through which is run a longer length of strong, heavy-duty line (often linen Cuttyhunk line or braided Dacron). The line is tied to two swivels, both of which are attached to the ends of the rubber tubing. When a fish strikes, the tubing stretches, absorbing the shock, but the heavy line inside will hold the fish in case the tubing breaks. Very clever. Trollers who don't use snubbers have to use a short section—maybe 3 to 6 feet—of very heavy monofilament as a shock leader.

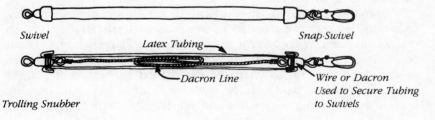

Trolling Snubber

Shoalwater trollers for such species as bass and walleyes may not have to use such long leaders. Their trolling is "deep" in the sense that they are maintaining contact with the bottom, but the water itself may not be deep. Some sort of leader is necessary when trolling braided lines or ultralimp monofilament, but the leader might be only as long as required to make such popular trolling terminal rigs as the famous Lindy rig.

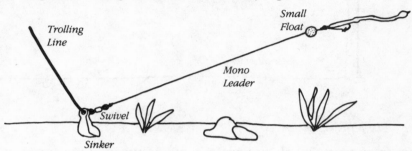

Bottom-Trolling Leader

BIG-GAME TROLLING LEADERS

Most bluewater trolling is done on the surface, using monofilament or braided lines and skipping baits or lures. Here, long, very strong leaders are necessary to absorb the direct punishment of big, strong-jawed, acrobatic fish, and to give the boat crew a terminal connection that is strong enough and tough enough to bring oceanic behemoths to the gaff. Once a pelagic gamefish is brought close to the boat, the final maneuvering is done by hand-lining the leader. Thus, the flexure of the rod, the clutch of the reel's drag, and the stretchiness of the line are no longer available to cushion the shock of sudden, desperate lunges. Actually, big-game leaders are nearly always composite in construction, because virtually all big-game anglers use a fairly long section of doubled line in front of the leader itself. However, in traditional offshore terminology, a distinction is always made between the "double" and the leader.

Under the rules established by the International Game Fish Association, leaders must conform to certain specifications if a fish caught on them is to be considered as a world record. In recent years, IGFA has expanded into freshwater and fly-fishing as well as saltwater angling, so virtually any record fish must be caught on a leader that passes IGFA muster. Like other rule-making bodies, IGFA changes its rules and regulations from time to time,

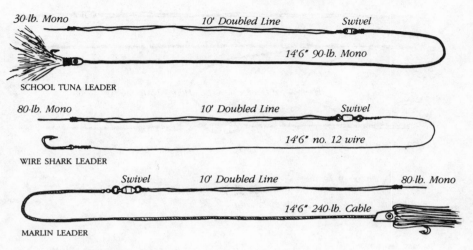

30-lb. Mono   10' Doubled Line   Swivel

14'6" 90-lb. Mono

SCHOOL TUNA LEADER

80-lb. Mono   10' Doubled Line   Swivel

14'6" no. 12 wire

WIRE SHARK LEADER

Swivel   10' Doubled Line   80-lb. Mono

14'6" 240-lb. Cable

MARLIN LEADER

Typical Big-Game Trolling Leaders

so it is best for the would-be record angler to check on the current leader specifications. Most recently, IGFA changed its leader specifications to unify the requirements for fresh- and saltwater fishing, and to bring fly-fishing tippet classes into conformity with other light-tackle leader rules.

The big-game leader itself may be made of any of a variety of materials, in various strengths. Monofilament, solid wire, stranded wire, coated wire, and cable all have their adherents. If there has been a discernible trend in recent years, it has been toward the use of nylon-clad stranded wire. Once the *leader,* not the doubled line, reaches the rod tip, IGFA rules permit one or more people to handle the leader to help bring the fish to gaff. On most charter boats, the mate in charge of this job is called the wire man, which tells you which materials are traditional. Depending upon the tackle used and the size and species of fish, these leaders may test anywhere from 40 to 400 or more pounds.

In catch-and-release tournaments, composite release leaders are used. The baited hook is attached to a short wire leader that is in turn attached, often via a heavy-duty snap, to the rest of the leader. After the fish has been brought alongside, identified and verified, its length and weight estimated, and a tag placed to aid in scientific investigations of oceanic gamefish, the fish is unsnapped and released. Sometimes the leader is simply cut close to the mouth with side-cutting pliers. (Whenever and wherever you are fishing just for fun, you might consider rigging similar release leaders. A fish that is released with a hook and a stub of leader in

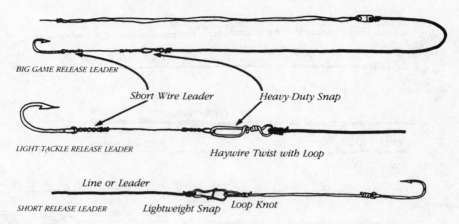

BIG GAME RELEASE LEADER

Short Wire Leader Heavy-Duty Snap

LIGHT-TACKLE RELEASE LEADER Haywire Twist with Loop

Line or Leader

SHORT RELEASE LEADER Lightweight Snap Loop Knot

Release Leaders

its mouth has a *much* better chance of survival than does a fish that has been hauled aboard for handling and unhooking prior to release. In such cases, don't use stainless-steel hooks or treble hooks of any metal, because corrosion helps the fish to shake the hook, and a three-pronged hook can become so securely lodged in a fish's mouth that it will drown or die of starvation before it can rid itself of the hook.)

Snells

A hook snell is a leader of a special type. Seldom very long, snells are nearly always made of monofilament, although it is possible to use other materials, including wire and so-called T-cord. The typical snell is looped at the top end, for easy connection to the line, leader, or snap. The other end is, of course, snelled to the hook shank (the British call it snoozing, and the snell is called a snood). The principal reason for using a snelled hook is to insure that the setting force is applied along the shank, resulting in a line of penetration that is close to that designed into the hook. If a hook is dangling from a knot at an angle, or free-swinging from a loop, there is no telling what the line of penetration will be when you set the hook. Snelled hooks offer another advantage, too: quick changes. When you are fishing for species that tend to take the bait deeply—bullheads and catfish, for example—it is a lot quicker to unsnap a snell and snap on a new snelled hook than it is to struggle with pliers or a disgorging tool to get the hook dislodged.

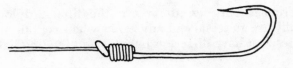

Snelled Hook

Few fishermen know more than one way to snell a hook but there are at least ten methods. Some, including the traditional method, are whippings, but others more closely resemble knots. No one need learn ten methods of hook snelling, but it's nice to have a couple or three in one's repertory. (See Chapter 10.)

Hooks best suited to snelling have knobbed or spaded shanks, or ringed eyes that are turned up or down. If hooks with regular or straight ringed eyes are used, the snell should *not* pass through the eye of the hook; in such cases, pretend that the eye is just a shank spade or knob.

TERMINAL RIGS

A terminal rig—which could be considered a special kind of leader—is nothing more or less than the whole arrangement of terminal tackle pieces used in any given angling situation. It can be as simple as a single hook tied onto the end of a leaderless line, or it can be as complicated as a full-bore trolling rig with long, compound leader, special sinker, trolling rudder or keel, snaps and swivels, a cowbell or herring dodger, primary lure, dropper fly, and whatever else might come to mind. There is virtually no limit to the number of ways all the bits and pieces of terminal tackle can be combined in a terminal rig, although I suppose a competent mathematician could peer into your tackle box and compute some staggeringly astronomical figure for the whole range of possibilities. After a point, though, you get into very subtle and sometimes arcane variations on, and refinements of, a more manageable number of basic rigs. The common themes are easier and better to learn than their myriad variations, anyway.

Sometimes the variants are important enough, from the angler's point of view, to merit separate mention, and sometimes not. Geometrically speaking, there isn't a lot of difference between, say, a mackerel tree, a pompano pier rig, a Seth Green lake trout trolling rig, a Chincoteague shad rig, and a tandem jigger rig. Piscatorially speaking, though, they are sometimes worlds apart. On the other hand, while old salts along the Northeast coast can, and do, make fine distinctions between porgy and tautog rigs, they are both just tandem bottom rigs for sure; the only differences between them are the fine and logical ones that usually are necessary in any event when rigging up for different species that have different habitats and feeding habits.

Commercially Pretied Rigs

Most of the saltwater anglers I know, and some of the freshwater ones, too, use—at least part of the time—those commercially pretied terminal rigs you see in virtually all tackle shops, tackle catalogs, and tackle departments of discount department stores. There really isn't anything wrong with that, as long as the rigs are selected with intelligent care, which often isn't the case. I've seen a lot of anglers who never seem to use anything but the commercial rigs, and their selections often reveal anything but discrimination on their part.

Not all of the pretied rigs on the market are well made. Some are made of cheap, shabby materials. Others are assembled without much care. Still others are not well thought out in terms of design. And most have too much hardware and too many extra bits of "jewelry."

Sevenstrand, Sampo, and a few other specialty tackle companies make and sell snelled hooks, pretied leaders, and simple terminal rigs that are quite good. Sevenstrand's are pretty much designed specifically for West Coast angling tastes and tend to be fairly short. They are made of quite thin, blue nylon-covered wire, and they also incorporate small, very short-shanked hooks and action rings. They can be used with equal effect almost anywhere wire leaders are necessary or desirable (and they seldom are). Sampo's, quite naturally, are well swiveled. They also aren't quite so uniregional in orientation. But Sampo does have a few rigs and leaders aimed at specific regional markets.

Speaking of regional markets and preferences, which the tackle companies must try to satisfy if they want to stay in business, this is as good a time as any to reiterate that the customer isn't always right. Anglers can be very stubborn consumers, tough to budge from mistaken habits. Having noticed one day that Sampo's muskie leaders are made with a Sampo ball-bearing snap-swivel on one end and a Rosco barrel swivel on the other, I wrote to ask why the barrel swivel was used, as the ball-bearing swivel's much greater efficiency would prevent the barrel swivel's ever turning. Jack Spriggs, then Sampo's president, gave me this answer: "As for our muskie leaders, we make them that way at the request of our customers in the Wisconsin and Minnesota territory. I agree

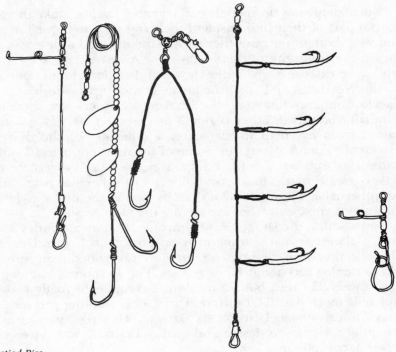

Pretied Rigs

with you that there is no good reason for the Rosco swivel." Give
the customer what he wants, the law of commercial survival says,
even when he's wrong. Unfortunately, that thinking dominates
the fishing-tackle trade, which isn't much of a boat-rocking business, so outmoded ideas and strange idiosyncrasies in angling
tend to persist.

Berkley also makes a fairly extensive line of leaders and simple
rigs, as do Weller, Pequea, and a host of other tackle companies
and suppliers. For many of these companies, rigs constitute a
small but apparently profitable sideline, something they sell
mostly to discount-store chains whose buyers wouldn't know a
walleye from a Warsaw snapper, let alone a trolley line from a
tandem rig. To accommodate the discount stores, which place
very large orders, some tackle companies rather indiscriminately
stencil their rig packages with various market-region names
("bluefish rig," "snapper rig," "catfish rig"), no matter what sort
of planning went into the design and manufacture of the rig.
Caveat emptor is definitely the watchword in shopping for commercially pretied rigs.

Some companies do specialize in terminal rigs, or make them a central part of their business, and their rigs tend to be well made and well thought out. But they supply the demand as it exists, so they make some pretty dumb rigs, too. At least their selections tend to be extensive, giving the thoughtful angler a lot of options. In the Northeast, J.T. or Scotchman brand rigs made by Jeros Tackle Company dominate the market, and there are similarly dominant brands in other regional markets. Jeros's rigs run the gamut from excellent to mediocre, a reflection of the diverse market the company services. Some of the most popular J.T. salt-water rigs employ T-cord, crimped sleeves, big swivels, lears, sinker-release snaps, beads, and all sorts of other hardware and paraphernalia. These are by no means among the best rigs Jeros makes, but apparently they are among the most popular.

Down South, the Dragon Fly Company of Sumter, South Carolina, is almost as market-dominant as Jeros is up North. Dragon Fly's selection of pretied rigs is even more diversified than Jeros's, whose catalog lists about 80 or so rigs. The Dragon Fly catalog I have shows 234 rigs, but I am told the company actually makes and sells more than 500 different rigs, not counting the special ones for private-label customers. Dragon Fly's rigs, like Jeros's, are quite varied as to design and quality, but most are extremely clever in conception.

Aqua-Clear Products of Atco, New Jersey, makes a really ingenious line of rigs. Aqua-Clear's product line is limited to just six basic types, tied in variations for various fresh- and saltwater species; striped bass, bluefish, weakfish, fluke, winter flounder, sea bass, porgy, cod, pollack, trout, panfish, bass, crappie, perch, catfish. As the species names imply, these rigs are aimed principally at the Northeast and Middle Atlantic markets. But don't let the monickers fool you; the rigs are much more versatile than their names suggest. In overall geometry, these are fairly basic rigs that may be used to take a wide variety of species. For example, according to Aqua-Clear president Bob Shaw, the fluke/weakish rig has been proved effective on several other East Coast species, including croaker, red hake (ling, in New Jersey), silver hake (the Garden State's whiting), channel bass, sheepshead, tautog (blackfish), seabass, and haddock. Field tests have produced similar results for the other rigs, too. Aqua-Clear rigs are distinguished by particularly long leaders or hook droppers and by a clever and patented T-shaped standoff that makes each rig's geometry adjustable.

Many other companies make terminal rigs, and some of them are very good. I can't possibly name them all—for one thing, I

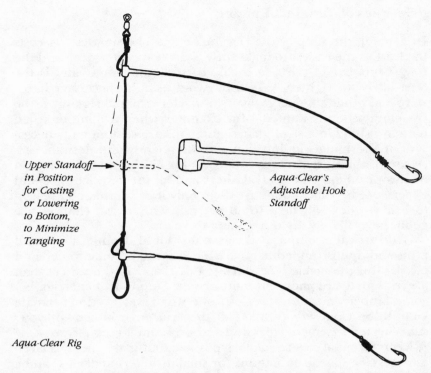

Upper Standoff in Position for Casting or Lowering to Bottom, to Minimize Tangling

Aqua-Clear's Adjustable Hook Standoff

Aqua-Clear Rig

don't know very many of them, as so many of these fine manufacturers are small, regionally restricted companies—but their omission shouldn't be considered as a discouragement against buying their wares.

Although it is possible, acceptable, and sometimes even desirable to use commercially pretied rigs, most of the time you will fare better if you tie your own. It's easy enough, and a lot cheaper. And you can design and tie terminal rigs to meet your own angling idiosyncrasies or the peculiar demands of your fishing hole. Besides, the terminal rigs you make yourself can be better, stronger, and less visible than the ones you can buy. If you are accustomed to using pretied rigs now, tying your own might seem a bit of a bother at first, but it won't take long for you to get the hang of it. Once you do, chances are you will never go back to using the commercial variety.

Perhaps the chief advantage in tying your own terminal rigs is that doing so pretty much forces you to think about what you are doing. And thinking is just about the best and most effective fishing technique I know.

Principles of Terminal Rigging

In general, the simpler the rig, the better. The simplest rig costs the least, is the easiest to make, offers the least water drag and the fewest number of parts to break, corrode, or tangle, and is the least likely to frighten wary fish. Avoid using unnecessary hardware and other angling gewgaws. Swivel a terminal rig only if the swiveling action is wanted—for example, when trolling or when bottom-fishing in a strong current. Snaps are seldom truly necessary in a terminal rig, but they can be a handy and desirable accessory if their use isn't overdone. As for beads and spinners and macaroni tubing and pearl flashers and all the rest, let logic and experience be your guide; use them only if you have good reason to believe they will help to attract fish. Otherwise, chances are good they will only discourage and dissuade.

Geometrically complicated rigs with a lot of dropper loops and arms and multistranded parts are more apt to become fouled and tangled (in the tackle box, during a cast, and in the water) than are rigs that are more straightforward. Monofilament rigs become limper and more tangle-prone when wet, so don't dangle your Rube Goldberg creation in the arid environment of your superheated basement workship and proclaim it tangle-free.

Keep terminal rigs as small as possible, but make them as large as necessary. On clean bottoms for small fish, terminal rigs can be very short and made of really wispy, lightweight materials. Go longer and stronger as bottom and other hazards increase. In a simple bottom rig, the hook dropper can be fairly long, though, as it sometimes helps to get the baited hook away from the sinker and main fishing line.

Abrasion resistance can be a real plus in a terminal rig, so select your rigging material with care when still-fishing or drifting over broken bottoms, or when trolling or casting for species that have sharp teeth or scales. That does not necessarily mean that wire or coated-cable rigs are called for. Most of the time, a heavy-duty monofilament rig will do very nicely. Metal should be used very sparingly in terminal rigs. Sales figures show that far too many anglers, in fresh water as well as salt, use those commercially pre-tied rigs that are fabricated of nylon-coated, multistranded wire.

While we're on the subject of metal in terminal rigs, let me get a couple of things off my chest. Those heavy-wire gadgets called umbrella rigs (also known as spider rigs, gorillas, and coat hangers) ought to be banned from sportfishing. Sure, an umbrella rig that is towing a dozen or more hooked surgical tubes

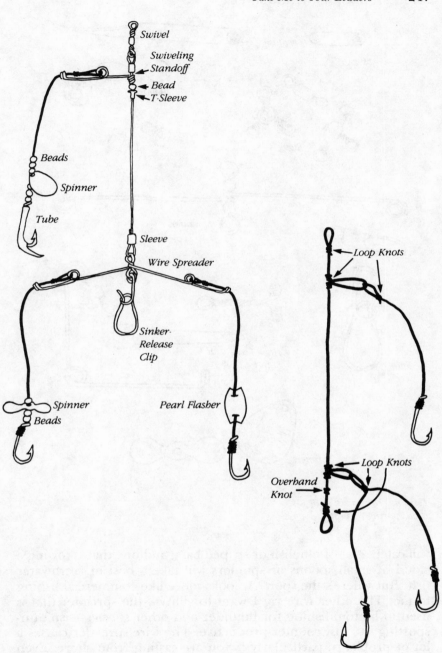

Swivel

Swiveling
Standoff

Bead
T-Sleeve

Beads

Spinner

Tube

Sleeve

Wire Spreader

Sinker-
Release
Clip

Spinner
Beads

Pearl Flasher

Loop Knots

Loop Knots

Overhand
Knot

Simplifying the Complicated Rig

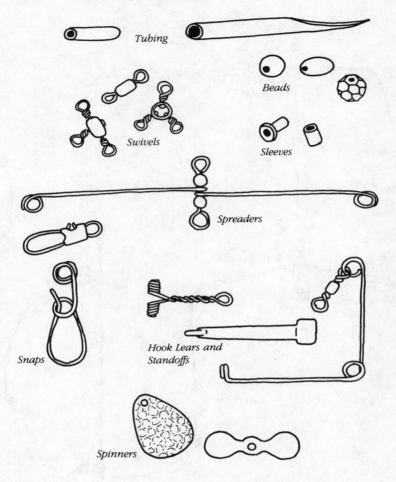

Terminal Hardware to Be
Used Sparingly in Rigs

will catch a lot of bluefish or striped bass, and one that is towing a cloud of small spoons or spinners will take a host of freshwater fish. But where's the sport? It looks more like commercial fishing to me. The other wire rig I want to villify—the spreader that is used in bottom-fishing for flounder and other species—isn't unsporting; it's just counter-productive. The wire spreader causes a lot of problems, particularly if you are casting from shore. Even when lowered straight down from a boat, bridge, or pier, it will cause tangling and fouling. If you must use more than one hook,

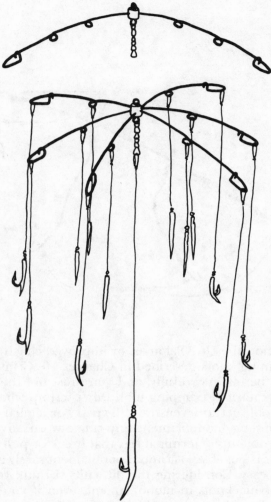

*Umbrella and
Coat-Hanger Rigs*

try a simple tandem rig or, even more effective, use the really clever three-hook flounder rig that was popularized (if not invented) by New Jersey angling writer Milt Rosko. The "extra" rubber-core sinker needn't be very heavy—a fraction of an ounce will do—because it isn't there to help sink the whole rig, merely to get those hooks right down on the bottom.

Use a small number of good knots you can tie well when fabricating your own terminal rigs. You won't need many: A good loop knot (the surgeon's loop is my favorite), a strong and dependable

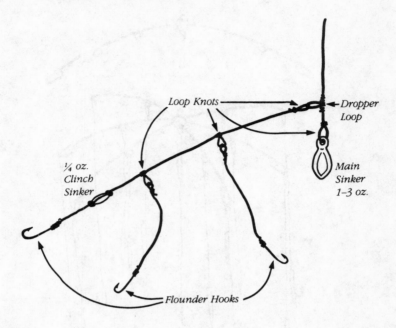

Loop Knots — Dropper Loop

¼ oz. Clinch Sinker

Main Sinker 1–3 oz.

Flounder Hooks

Rosko Rig

terminal knot (the Uni, Palomar, or improved clinch), and any of the line-joining knots described in Chapter 10. Crimped connections must be made carefully, and you must use the proper size sleeve and the right crimping tool. Don't scrimp when you buy a crimping tool; get a Sevenstrand Type C or similar instrument. As for crimping monofilament, my single-word advice is Don't, unless you dote upon terminal rigs that break or pull apart under pressure. It is possible to crimp monofilament safely and securely, but it isn't easy. Considering the difficulty, I think you would be better off tying knots in monofilament, even if you have to use pliers to pull the knots up in thick, stiff leader material.

In salt or brackish water (and even in some "fresh" waters that are very acid or alkaline), be sure to use corrosion-resistant metal parts. Several brass alloys and high-quality nickel-plated parts will do, but it's a good idea to stick to stainless steel in saltwater. Monel metal is at least as corrosion-resistant as stainless, but the nickel-based alloy will cause other metal parts to corrode. (See the section on galvanic corrosion in Chapter 11.)

8

Fooling
Fish

FISH-ATTRACTING SMACKS strongly of both art and science without being precisely either one. Like the true arts, attracting fish allows for plenty of personal freedom of expression (while at the same time requiring a lot of discipline), and some people seem to be born with more knack for it than others. In the dog-day doldrums of a summer afternoon, fish-attracting can be so downright mystifying as to seem almost like one of the black arts. However, while it isn't precise or empirical enough to be a pure science, the attracting of fish is based upon the common-sense practical application of certain well-known scientific principles. The angler who would outfox fish consistently had better learn a bit about them. The principles are simple enough, even if the sciences themselves aren't.

Take piscine ethology, the most important of the sciences involved in angling. Sounds arcane, but it's nothing but the study of fish behavior. In other words, you need to know a little something about the habits and behavioral patterns of the fish you are after. You can't plan an effective fishing strategy until you know where the fish are likely to be and how they will probably react. The more you know about fish behavior, the better, but don't think you have to know everything. No one does—not even the single-species specialists. You can study your ethology in books or at the feet of some grizzled old gaffer, but most of it you will learn on your own, through trial and error, by watching and wondering every time you go out fishing.

Once you get to know your fish a little, and begin to understand how and why they do some of the things they do, you will need to know something about lures and other terminal attractors to turn that ichthyological knowledge into angling know-how. Knowing all about statistics and trivia can turn anyone into a self-made baseball *expert,* but it takes practical knowledge about the proper application of bat and glove to become a baseball *player.* Some good ichthyologists are pretty sorry fishermen because, no matter how much they might know about fish, they don't know enough about fishing tackle to put their scientific lore to good piscatorial use. But every good fisherman is at least a middling-fair ichthyologist.

PREDATION AND SENSORY PERCEPTION

Behavior in fish is nothing but a pattern of responses to sensory stimuli. No matter how wily they seem, fish are fairly short on brains, and they don't really think in the same sense that we do. Fish are creatures of habit and instinct; they don't cogitate, they react. The smartest fish can't possibly outthink the dumbest fisherman, but even the smartest angler can outthink himself. Fishing is not a battle of wits. Relax in the confidence that you are many times smarter than the wisest old fish you will ever encounter.

A fish's repertoire of instinctual response patterns is fairly limited, but its battery of sensory equipment can be quite impressive. What some fish can detect in their watery world is almost uncanny. Some sharks, for example, have special sensory organs that allow them to detect the very weak bioelectric fields that are created in water by virtually all living organisms. It has been calculated that in some sharks those organs are so sensitive they could conceivably detect the electrical current flowing between two flashlight cells that were separated by several miles of water. Live bait is the only thing a fisherman can use to appeal to this special sense—which some other fish might also possess—but don't be too surprised if someday a bioelectric lure shows up in the tackle shops. Lure designers and tinkering fishermen are always looking for new ways to fool a fish.

Fish possess other sensory mechanisms that are considerably less esoteric than electroperception, but their sensory abilities are in some cases almost as remarkable. Fishing live bait is effective—

because a writhing minnow or squirming worm can appeal to virtually all of a fish's senses—but it isn't always practical. Anyway, some of us get our biggest angling kicks out of fooling fish with bogus baits. A hunk of wood or metal or plastic might not smell, taste, or feel like anything a fish is used to eating, but it can be made to look, sound, and *seem* right. Through the intelligent selection and rigging of lures and other terminal tackle, you can appeal to or confuse a fish's senses so that it will strike at your ersatz offering.

A well-designed, carefully selected, and properly fished artificial lure can call fish in on most if not all of a fish's senses at once, though. While all fish have all of the senses described below, there are remarkable differences among species in the relative dominance of the senses. Some fish, called sight-feeders, rely principally upon their sense of vision to locate food. Most sight-feeders have large, prominent eyes, and most are predators (that is, they single out and attack living, free-swimming prey). Scent-feeders follow scent trails to find their food. They tend to be bottom-feeders rather than active predators (sharks are a notable example to the contrary), and many of them live in dark or deep waters. As you might suspect, scent-feeders have fairly large nostrils, which are often situated rather far apart, to provide the olfactory equivalent of depth perception.

However dominant a single sense may be in a fish's feeding patterns, though, the other senses can't be ignored. Most fish home in on food from afar by following current-borne scents or vibrations. As feeding fish get closer to their targets, other senses come into play. Once a sight-feeder gets in really close, it may not be able to focus its eyes properly, so other senses will take over—smell or touch, for example. If a lure looks good but smells wrong, even a sight-feeder may reject it at the last moment. Few lures actually smell good, so the angling goal is to appeal so strongly to a fish's other senses that its instinctive response patterns will overpower its last-minute suspicion that something is amiss.

Predation and feeding aren't the only behavorial response patterns that are triggered by a fish's sensory perceptions. Fish also use their sensory input to find mates and fellow travelers, to navigate, to avoid predators, and in other behavioral syndromes that make up their life cycles. The smart fisherman will take these into account, too. In some circumstances, a lure must be very flashy and noisy to communicate its seductive message through boiling and roiled waters. At other times, a lure's noise and flash is just so much sensory static; it might even signal "predator" rather than "prey." Lures intended to pass as bait or forage species ought not to flash and thrash too boldly in situations where prey species would be more circumspect; they must not approach larger fish without hesitation, beat their way rapidly upstream, or swim too strongly across current. A small lure that is fished improperly can frighten off even quite a large fish. But don't be too timid, either.

I am convinced that fish strike at baits and lures for many reasons other than to feed upon them. I think it is likely that other than predatory factors are involved in strikes against artificial lures a majority of the time. Curiosity, fear, anger, self-defense, territorial defense, petulance—all these things can cause a fish to attack a lure. Female largemouth bass will hit lures when they are on their nests and aren't feeding, but only if the lures are placed and worked so that the sow bass are irritated enough to attack but not enough to flee. Getting just the right amount of feistiness into a lure to provoke a bedded bass into striking is a real art, one I haven't yet come close to mastering. Shad, kokanee salmon, and other plankton feeders are regularly taken on spoons, spinners, flies, and other bait-imitating lures. Why they will bite such bogus baits is uncertain, but it is obviously some sort of instinctive response pattern to the sensory stimuli. When shad are in fresh water—which is when most anglers catch them—they don't feed at all, not even on plankton. Yet they aren't particularly difficult to catch on lures of various types.

As far as the sportfisherman is concerned, it is an academically moot point whether a fish strikes at a bait out of hunger or other predatory instinct, or whether it is just testing, challenging, eliminating, or warning an unwanted source of irritation or anxiety. Whatever the nature of the response, once triggered by a sensory stimulus, a fish tends to react in a set behavioral pattern. Once the train of events is set in motion, it often doesn't need further stimulus to be taken to its predetermined outcome. If, however, contradictory sensations subsequently get through to the fish's brain, the response pattern may be aborted if the contradictory stimuli are strong enough. Fooling fish isn't a great mystery, but it isn't duck soup, either.

Hearing

Hearing tends to be much more acute in fish than it is in human beings. Many fish have true ears and can detect actual sounds, but some cannot. Still, all fish can "hear" by detecting subaural vibrations and pressure waves in water. This characteristic is almost as

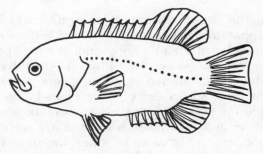

Lateral Line Sensory System in Fish

much touch as hearing, because it requires the use of special sensory organs that are scattered along the lateral line, which is externally visible in many fish. Some fish can detect such vibrations miles away from their source. Most lures are designed to create vibrations and pressure waves, which may or may not be audible to the angler. Irregular, low-frequency vibrations apparently are most attractive to fish, ostensibly because they resemble the vibrational patterns given off by fish that are thrashing in distress. As most fishermen have discovered for themselves, erratic, stop-and-go retrieves are often much more effective than steady reeling when fishing lures. Fish that aren't feeding and that are ignoring natural baits can be enticed to attack a vibrating lure, so the response pattern can't be motivated entirely by hunger.

Vision

Some fish see quite well, others poorly. Although the sharpest-eyed fish probably don't see as well in water as we do in air when it comes to visual acuity, the perception of detail and image sharpness, many can outperform human beings in their ability to spot things in darkness, and to detect masses, shapes, and motions in the murk. Scientists have concluded that certain night-feeding sharks, and perhaps some other fish, have such good dim-light vision they can probably see things at or near the surface by *star*light!

Whether fish have good color vision is a controversy that has raged within the scientific community for years, and no definite answer is in sight. It is apparent that many species can distinguish certain colors, but there is quite a range of color-vision ability among those species that have been tested. Some are more color-perceptive than others, and certain colors seem more detectable or at least more interesting than others. Black bass are notoriously fond of red, and the catch records kept by Jim Maxwell, formerly president of Grizzly Tackle, strongly suggest that salmonids have definite color preferences in lures, Pacific salmon apparently being more color-fickle than western trout. Based on samples of about a thousand of each species, Maxwell's records reveal that 94 percent of his lake trout have been caught on lures that were finished in silver, pearl, chartreuse, or combinations thereof; 86 percent of his steelhead (anadromous rainbow trout) fell for pink, red, orange, and combinations of these colors with silver and pearl; brown trout much preferred (77 percent) brass, copper, and brass-and-copper metallic lures, and among the true colors, chartreuse-and-red combinations. Coho and chinook salmon didn't show such strong color preferences, but 41 percent of Maxwell's salmon were taken on lures that combined either blue or green with silver or pearl.

Obviously, catch records like Jim Maxwell's are less than scientific and are skewed by the colors of the lures customarily fished. Southern bass fishermen are overwhelmingly partial to purple, black, dark blue, and smoky gray plastic worms for largemouth bass (and my more limited experience confirms the effectiveness of their choices), but you hardly ever see anyone casting purple plugs to bass. Don't draw too many firm conclusions about color preferences in fish until you have tried all the possible combinations and permutations of colors, lures, species, and fishing conditions. Even my rusty math suggests you won't live long enough to try them all, so your color choices in lures will have to be intelligent hunches rather than statistical certainties.

Smell

All fish have nostrils, but the other physiological mechanisms of smell vary considerably from family to family. Smell is seldom inconsequential, and it can be extremely important in predation and food-locating. Few lures come with built-in odor, but some plastic worms and other soft-plastic lures have various smelly substances molded into them. Whether the fruit flavors that are incorporated in some plastic worms actually attract fish is uncertain at best. More likely, they serve to mask the human smells that might otherwise scare fish. Many fish seem to be repelled by human odors (with the possible exception of saliva), and anglers who smoke are thought to emanate the most fish-repelling smells. Excessive bare-handling of baits, lures, and other terminal tackle isn't likely to increase one's chances of angling success. Carry one of the patented goos or lotions to clean and deodorize your hands, or use ordinary toothpaste.

And beware of sunscreens and bug dopes that repel fish as well as ultraviolet rays and biting insects. Berkley's new Blockaid sunscreen is a good solution, as are the citronella-based repellents. DEET is a great insect repellent, but it smells terrible and ruins monofilament and fly lines.

Taste

Common sense tells us that most if not all fish have a sense of taste, but scientists are uncertain whether fish taste in precisely the same sense we do. Probably they have a more limited sense of taste and don't savor their food the way we do ours. At any rate, when a fish mouths a bait or lure, it can tell fairly quickly whether the thing is edible. So you can't afford to dawdle in setting the hook on a strike against an artificial. Many fish—particularly those with mouth barbels, like members of the cod, catfish, and nurse shark families—have taste organs located outside their mouths, so they can taste an angler's offering without actually mouthing it. Some of those "bumps" you feel and miss are just that, fish bumping their external taste organs up against a bait or lure to test its palatability.

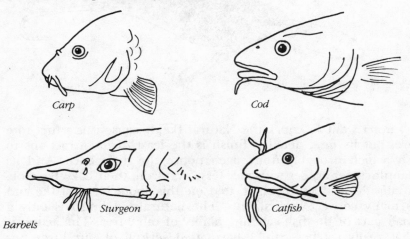

Carp

Cod

Sturgeon

Catfish

Barbels

Touch and the Common Chemical Sense

Fish have a sense of touch, for sure, and they also have what physiologists call the common chemical sense. The chemical sense is somewhat related to senses of both taste and touch, but it's a little difficult to describe precisely what it is and how it works. If some acid were dropped on your skin, your sense of touch would feel it hit and tell you it's wet; your common chemical sense is what would let you know that it burns. These two senses in fish are not very important in fishing, for it is difficult to figure out how to turn either of them to angling advantage.

LURE VARIABLES AND THEIR IMPORTANCE

Not so very long ago there burst upon the fishing scene a new lure called the Natural Ike. Its shape was a little unusual, but the thing that struck you immediately was its finish—as lifelike as the paint job on a really good fish mount. The thing was so darned pretty, you just had to buy one. But angling skeptics wondered whether the thing would catch fish. Natural Ike turned out to be a real fish-catcher, and its market success set the whole industry on its ear. Other lure manufacturers rushed their own "naturalized" plugs onto the market. Soon, even spoons, spinners, and jigs were being given the photo-print treatment.

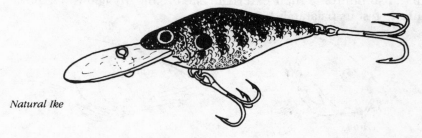

Natural Ike

I don't want to knock the Natural Ike, because it is a first-rate lure, but its fine, detailed finish is the least of its attractions to fish, which probably don't even notice the difference. And its manufacturer agrees with me. Jesse Waldron, then Lazy Ike Corporation's product manager, told me this about Natural Ike and its many copycat look-alikes: "The naturalized finish is only a small part of the fish-catching ability of our lures. The action is what really catches fish. I have used several of our lures unpainted, just colored with magic markers, and in various colors from phosphorescent to purple, all with equal effectiveness." As they say, it's the sizzle that sells the steak.

Few of the skin-deep things that are done to lures add very much to their fish-catching ability. This isn't to say that color and finish are worthless or that action is everything in a lure. But there is a pecking order in the variables that help bogus baits to fool, attract, tantalize, irritate, seduce, or otherwise goad a fish into striking. In my reckoning of eight lure variables, color and pattern rank seventh and eighth, respectively. Action ranks just third on my list, but it is a very high third because the first three variables stand way above the other five in importance. This is how I define and rank the variables that make lures work:

1. Running Depth
2. Speed
3. Action
4. Size
5. Visual Contrast
6. Shape
7. Color
8. Pattern and Finish Detail

Running Depth

I rank most important the depth at which a lure runs. No matter how natural a lure looks, how enticingly it wriggles, how interesting it smells or sounds, it simply won't catch fish if you fish it where they aren't. Being cold-blooded creatures, fish depend upon water temperatures to control their own body temperature, and the temperature of water is pretty much a function of its depth. Fish will often travel a considerable horizontal distance to grab a bait (generally much farther after a natural bait than a lure), but few will move up or down more than a tiny fraction of the distance they might be coaxed into moving laterally. Most fish have a rather limited range of preferred temperatures, and you can expect to find them holding or feeding in waters of those temperatures *most* of the time. A thermometer or temperature probe of some sort can be invaluable in finding fish. (See the chart on page 451 to determine the preferred temperature ranges for various species of food and game fish.)

Most anglers carry lure selections that run the gamut of sizes, shapes, and colors, but some forget to take running depth into account when selecting lures. Many plugs and other lures are designed to run at a specific depth, and you will want at least one lure in each depth range, but most spoons, spinners, and jigs are more versatile because they can be fished on top, on the bottom, or anywhere in between. Among plugs, the most versatile are the neutral-buoyancy, "countdown" types such as the Countdown Rapala, Rebel Suspend-R, and Arbogast Hustler.

Speed

Some will argue that a lure's speed isn't as important as its action, or that speed is just a single facet of a lure's action, but I disagree on both counts. In the case of those lures that have no built-in action—the jigs, jerk baits, and others the angler must manipulate with the rod tip—lure speed obviously is independent of lure action, each being produced by the angler rather than by the manufacturer. As for lures with built-in action, they may or may not lend themselves to variations in fishing speed. The Helin Flatfish is a terrific lure at slow speeds and will catch fish by just hanging virtually motionless in the water; at high speeds, however, the Flatfish is too frenetic and the similar-looking Lazy Ike is a better choice. Many of the newer big-game trolling lures—the jet lures, konaheads, and so on—are designed to skip or "smoke" properly only at certain trolling speeds.

To see how important a lure's fishing speed can be, try fishing Texas-rigged plastic worms in a pond that contains both bass and pickerel. Work the worms ever so slowly, in the languorous southern style, and you will catch bass and pickerel; speed up the retrieve so that the worms bounce and slide briskly along the bottom, and you will catch almost nothing but pickerel.

As a rule, the warmer the water, the faster you fish a lure. This is true up to a point and as long as the water temperature is within the range preferred by the fish you seek. But if the water is really warm, slow down; too much heat causes most fish to become torpid and lethargic and to go off the feed. Under such conditions, only the patiently fished and barely moving lure stands a chance. In hot water, fish will sometimes strike lures out of petulance, even if they won't blink at a natural bait that is fished right in front of their snouts.

In stream-fishing, the best lure speed is that of the current. Stream predators expect to find their food tumbling or coasting along with the current. They never look for it to be sprinting upstream.

Action

As I define it, action does not include speed or running depth *per se*. Otherwise, action is the whole pattern of lure behavior: the way it moves, the noise it makes, the bubbles or vibrations it creates. Many lures, including the so-called crankbait plugs, come with a lot of action built in by the manufacturer, but others need to be manipulated by the angler. Most lures are at least amenable to a little angler enhancement, and will work better when twitched and tweaked, rather than just reeled in steadily. Plugs like the Rapala and certain other well-known and successful crankbaits will catch fish almost equally well whether they are trolled or retrieved at constant speed or fished with an active, "educated" rod tip.

Study any literature or tips that come with a lure, because many luremakers offer excellent advice on how to fish their lures, the result of field testing. Still, don't take a manufacturer's word as gospel; it's only good, sound, seasoned advice. Follow it, of course, but do some experimenting of your own.

Size

There is an old angling adage that says big fish like big baits. Like most adages, this one is only partly true, only some of the time. Juvenile fish tend to be more aggressive and less cautious than larger, older fish of the same species; the behavioral differences between the ages are more pronounced in some species than in others. Baby sunfish are notoriously reckless and will chase lures that are as big as they are. But to catch huge sunnies, you sometimes have to resort to really tiny jigs, spinners, and flies. If it took big bait to catch big fish, fly-fishermen would never catch trophy specimens. Some of the very best lures for jumbo salmon —lures like Grizzly's Li'l Guy—aren't much bigger than the lures I use on crappies in small ponds.

Li'l Guy Salmon Lure (Actual Size)

Most fish—the plankton-strainers not included—do tend to prefer the largest meals they can handle *easily*. I stress easily because in the fish-eat-fish world there exists a very fine line between starvation and sufficiency. A fish burns up a certain amount of energy just living and breathing, and a certain amount more stalking, chasing, capturing, subduing, and digesting its prey. If a fish has to work too hard finding and getting food, it may burn up more energy than the food provides, which would lead to certain starvation. Given their tight energy budget, fish will seek out the largest food for the least effort.

Like every rule, this one has its exceptions. Each species has its own food preferences, modified by the givens of its habitat.

Smallmouth bass prefer smaller prey than largemouths (as befits fish with smaller mouths), and stream smallmouths want smaller prey than do their lake-dwelling counterparts. Fish in a certain habitat may get used to feeding upon the abundant prey of a certain size and become loath to tackle anything larger. In a small stream, where the dominant forage species are tiny insects, nymphs, and darters, a brown trout may not show much interest in running down big plugs or fat bass bugs. But brown trout in a big, deep lake will eat almost anything and grow impressively large in the process. Those who stalk Flaming Gorge Reservoir's tackle- and record-busting browns (upward of 30 pounds) routinely troll muskie and saltwater plugs that are almost as big as the stocked hatchery trout most of us are used to catching.

Study the fish you are after, learn about their food preferences and how they go about predation, and select lures accordingly.

Visual Contrast

By visual contrast I mean a lure's position on the brightness–dullness scale—its flash and pizzazz. Whether brightness or high visual contrast will help or hinder your fishing in a given situation isn't one of those things about which one can safely be dogmatic. The flashy, high-contrast lure that gets a lot of action one day can scare fish away the next.

Usually, high visual contrast makes a difference. When the fish aren't hitting, try switching from a bright, flashy lure to a more subtle version, or vice versa. Expert anglers tend to fish bright, flashy, and chrome-plated lures in clear water on sunny days, and dull, dark, and brass or copper lures in dingy waters or on cloudy, overcast days. For some species, though, the opposite trends are followed; top shad fishermen use chromed spoons and spinners on overcast days and hammered brass or copper lures when the sun is shining. Shad seem to be more frightened than attracted by flashiness.

The red-and-white Daredevle spoon probably has caught more fish in more waters for more anglers than any other single lure in

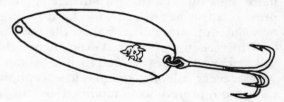

Dardevle

a given color pattern. How much the bass-attracting red color helps is debatable, but the Daredevle's overall appeal isn't. Its action set the standard for spoons, and its visual appeal is optically exciting and apparently appetizing as well. The alternating flash of the chromed underside of the spoon and the chiaroscuro pattern of the top side's barber-pole striping create an optical effect that probably resembles, to a predatory fish, the shimmer of a frantic baitfish's iridescent scales. Resemblance to the natural iridescence of most small fish is what makes the prismatic, fluorescent, and pearl finishes so particularly effective at times.

LIGHT

Phosphorescent and light-emitting lures have been around a long time, but they hadn't turned all that many anglers on until the last decade or so. When South Florida fishermen discovered you could catch swordfish at night by fishing deep with Cyalume Lightsticks rigged above, below, or inside dead or plastic squid baits, people sat up and paid attention. Now, chemiluminescent lures are rather widely available but perhaps most popular in the Pacific Northwest. LumaLure Manufacturing probably has the biggest and best-known line of light-emitting lures: diving and trolling plugs, spoons and spinners, hootchies, salmon trolling flies, jigs, squid jigs, artificial spawn sacs, and even plastic worms. The LumaLites that make them work come in two sizes and four colors. If you haven't tried fishing deep or at night with light-emitting lures, you're in for a real treat.

Shape

Fly-fishermen have made a virtual fetish out of "matching the hatch" of stream-side insects in their selection of flies. When it comes to matching the *shape* of principal forage species, other anglers probably ought to follow suit. Target-feeding and other behavioral experiments by ichthyologists and ethologists have pretty well confirmed that many, and perhaps even most, species of fish can discriminate very well between shapes. Fish that have been trained to strike a rectangular target to be fed become confused when triangular or diamond-shaped targets are substituted. (Experiments have shown that black bass and certain other species react with alarm when suddenly confronted with strange, unaccustomed shapes like stars, so be a bit careful about the obviously discernible geometry of your terminal rigs.) A lure's shape needn't be precisely equivalent to that of the dominant forage species present, but I doubt you would be well advised to fish long, thin tube lures when the fish you are after are gorging themselves on gizzard shad or butterfish, both of which are short, flat, and more or less hatchet-shaped.

Some anglers are convinced that potbellied or "pregnant" lures are more attractive to predatory fish than are flatter-tummied versions. I can't find much scientific evidence to support this claim, but one can't ignore the almost phenomenal success of the fat, "alphabet-type" crankbaits like the Fred Young/Cotton Cordell Big O and its myriad imitators and variants. The Big O's potbellied shape affects its buoyancy and wriggle at least as much as its appearance, and I suspect its different action is what really attracts fish.

Color

The importance of color in fish predation is debatable. You can marshal evidence and experts on both sides of the question. Most will agree that a great many fish can see certain colors—at least in clear, shallow water by bright daylight—but beyond that things get pretty murky, literally as well as figuratively.

One thing is certain: Fishermen vastly overrate lure color, probably because they don't understand how colors show up in water. Take the case of red. It has been demonstrated scientifically that black bass are excited by and attracted to the color red. Hence, the popularity of red-headed and red-striped lures in fresh water. But how come all-red lures aren't popular? And why do so many bass fishermen troll red lures very deep? Red shows up as black or gray once a lure goes just a few feet beneath the surface. In 40 feet of perfectly clear water at high noon on a bright day, black and red plugs would be virtually indistinguishable. However, a color's *density* may be quite important, more important than its hue, because the density affects how light or dark its gray will appear long after its actual color has disappeared.

Years ago, Michigan biologist Stan Lievense developed a system he called spectrum fishing, which enables a fisherman to use lure color to maximum advantage. Spectrum fishing is nothing but a lure-selection strategy based upon the optical properties of sunlight in water. Pure "white" sunlight contains all the colors in the visible spectrum, plus invisible wavelengths like infrared and ultraviolet. Each color behaves differently as the light passes through air or water, depending upon its wavelength. Short-wavelength colors like red do not travel well. There is actually very little red color in sunlight early in the morning or late in the afternoon; the rosy glow you see in the sky is the red that has been absorbed by the atmosphere as the sunlight traveled through it. Similarly, red is the first visible color to be absorbed by water as the light penetrates the depths (infrared disappears first, but that's of little concern to lure-color selection, although it does explain why the uppermost foot or so of water is so much warmer than that which is below).

With these optical principles in mind, and after testing his theories in the field, Lievense came up with the following suggestions as to lure-color selection:

Before 8 A.M. and after 6 P.M., use blue, green, white, or silver lures. Use black lures at night, though, particularly if you will be fishing on or near the surface.

After 8 A.M., follow this progression of colors to high noon: yellow, orange, fluorescent red, red. Reverse the order in the afternoon.

In dirty water, use blue and green lures. But in brown-stained waters such as are commonly found in swamp-drained areas, go for yellow and brass.

Given the bright, full-spectrum light of high noon, use red lures if the fish are in shoal water, yellow or brass lures if the fish are suspended in mid-depths, and blue, white, or silver lures if they are holding deep.

Don't expect spectrum fishing to work wonders for you; after all, color isn't one of the primary variables in lure selection. But you can count on its helping you to get what little help there is out of those wonderfully attractive colors you pondered over so long in the tackle shop.

Lately, the tackle shops and catalogs have been invaded by color-coded lures and tackle boxes in support of an electronic gadget called the Color-C-Lector. This measures light penetration in water and relays the information to a dial that has color bands rather than numbers. Resist the temptation, for this fad too shall pass. It's a lot better and cheaper to learn the principles behind spectrum fishing.

Pattern and Finish Detail

The last variable worth worrying over in lure selection is pattern or finish detail. And it's seldom worth worrying over. Like me, you probably can't resist those new, photo-finish, "naturalized" lures, even if they do cost more. But, pretty as the things are, natural-finish plugs won't improve your catch or mine unless everything else about them—running depth and action, size, visual contrast, and shape, sometimes even color—is in the right ball park and the lure is being fished at the proper speed. Then, and only then, *might* the natural finish make a dime's worth of difference.

Older, more stylized lure finishes raise interesting and perhaps unanswerable questions. For instance, will a polka-dotted lure arouse a fish's predatory curiosity, or will it frighten the fish away? I doubt anyone knows for sure. The polka dots might add a little verisimilitude and gustatory interest if the fish you are after are used to dining on spotted, speckled, or mottled forage species. Perhaps the same considerations apply to stripes, bands, bars, and other patterns. Just don't get too hung up on the notion. I once had an Abu Reflex spinner in a black-spotted yellow finish that was incredibly effective on the bass, pickerel, and crappies in my backyard pond, even though I couldn't find any forage species in the pond that even remotely resembled it. After losing the spinner to an underwater snag, I replaced it with another, and another, and another. None of the replacement Abu Reflexes in the same pattern worked half as well. There must have been something else that made my lost lure so special, some little quirk in its action, perhaps, or the way its partly shiny, partly tarnished blade reflected light.

There are a few angling experts who are strongly convinced that bold details on lures are a very bad idea, that such touches make wary old trophy fish very suspicious. Perhaps they are right, but two finish details are, I feel, helpful in lures. The first, but lesser, of the two is the thin splash of red that represents a minnow's gills. Again, this isn't something that is going to salvage an otherwise misbegotten bait, but, if everything else is working right those red crescents can sometimes make the difference between a follow and a strike. Much more important, however, are eyes. I like eyes on virtually all my lures—plugs, spoons, jigs, spinnerbaits, spinners. Not so much for the realism, as for the target appeal. Bass—both black and striped—and some other predatory fish tend to aim their strikes at the eyes of their prey. When I played football, coaches were forever telling me to aim

Eyes and Gill Slits

my tackles at a ball-carrier's gut, not his swiveling hips, feinting shoulders, or juking legs. A wriggling, writhing baitfish can put as many moves on a pursuing predator, but its eyes will always give away its position, direction, and speed. A great many small fish, and particularly tropical reef fish, have black dots and other fake eyes located near their tails, to confuse predators.

When I am repainting and refurbishing lures anyway, I will often add eyes if the lures came eyeless from the factory (usually just a circle of yellow paint with a big, black dot in the middle). But I seldom bother to paint eyes on a new lure. Eyes are, after all, merely the most effective option within the least important category of lure variables.

ATTRACTIVE ODDS AND ENDS

Fish-attracting is accomplished primarily through the skillful use of the appropriate natural baits (which are outside the scope of this book) or artificial lures (the various types of which are surveyed briefly in Chapter 9). But many baits and lures can be enhanced, under the right conditions, by the addition of a little attractive something extra. Having learned this, some anglers fall into the trap of always adding some gimcrack or gewgaw to a lure or bottom rig. They have missed the point almost entirely. The properly selected bait, properly fished, ought to be attractive enough, most of the time. But there are times and conditions that lend themselves to experimentation with attractive little extras. If the fish aren't having any of what you are offering, and you have run out of substitutes, then maybe you had better resort to baubles, bangles, or beads. It's good to have a few tricks up your sleeve, as long as you use them sparingly and intelligently.

Baubles, Bangles, and Beads

All sorts of colorful little things can be added to a terminal rig to increase its visibility and—one hopes—its attractiveness to fish. I hesitate to go very deeply into this, because too many anglers already overdo it, particularly saltwater bottom-fishermen. Moderation is the key to success here.

BEADS
Whether they are made of glass, plastic, metal, or painted wood, beads work principally because of their flash and color. When fished for trout, salmon, and a few scavenging species, they might

Round   Faceted   Oval   Tri-Bead   Tee

Beads

be mistaken for fish eggs. Unless I want the buoyancy of wood, I prefer beads of the other materials because they sink well and because they make noise when rattled against one another. When shopping for beads in a tackle shop, I will roll them around in the palm of my hand to see how they sound. Many crustaceans that are favored as food by sportfish make snapping and clicking sounds. Even in waters that are devoid of these knuckle-cracking arthropods, clicking beads seem to work better than silent ones, perhaps because they sound like snapping jaws.

Spherical beads are standard, of course, but faceted beads are favored by some, and I know some kokanee-salmon trollers who swear that nothing works as well as pearl-colored oval beads. In recent years—an innovation of the offshore trollers in Hawaii—tri-beads have come into great favor and general usage among the high-speed trollers of the bluewater fleets. Many of Seven-strand's most popular big-game lures feature strings of these beads inside hootchy skirts. A string of tri-beads makes a unique sound—a gritty, clattering swish, something like the sound the surf makes on a pebble or shell beach—and big-game fish apparently like it.

Kokanee, shad, perch, and many other species can be taken on an unbaited terminal rig that is simply three or four colorful beads strung on the leader ahead of an unadorned, but flashy, gold-plated hook.

TUBING

Tubing can be used to make primary lures—as in the case of surgical-tubing eels and mackerel tubes—but smaller pieces can also be used to dress up other lures and terminal rigs. Many salt-water bottom-fishermen like to use short pieces of bright plastic or latex tubing on the shanks of their baited hooks or on the leaders or droppers just above the hooks. The tubing seems to work for some anglers, but not for others.

The jig-and-teaser combination is a venerable and effective one in the Northeast among cod and pollock anglers, and has seen both sport and commercial service on halibut and other species as well. It is nothing but a short tube lure, fashioned around a bent-shank hook that is rigged just forward of a diamond jig.

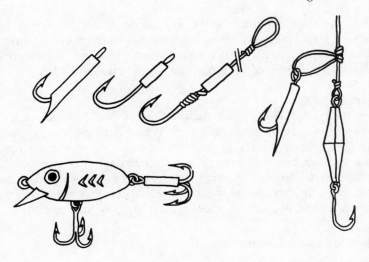

Tubing Rigs

Even on plugs and other lures, in fresh or salt water, a bright red piece of tubing on the shaft of the aftermost treble hook can sometimes make the difference between catching fish and just fishing. But only sometimes.

FLAPPERS

Flappers are those little teardrop- or heart-shaped pieces of colorful plastic or brightly plated metal that flicker from the hooks of various lures. Swedish Pimple jigs come packaged with these little flappers, and so do many Hildebrand spinners. If the flappers aren't too large, they won't unbalance the lure or encourage short strikes. In fact, I think that sometimes they help direct strikes at the hook itself.

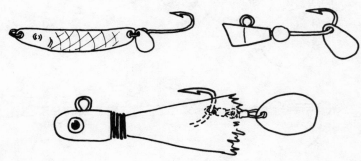

Flappers

The tiny flappers don't work as well on heavy, saltwater lead-head jigs. In such cases, when I want a tail flapper of this sort, I'll rig onto the jig hook a tiny snap-swivel to which is attached a small spinner blade, often a hammer-finished Colorado.

SPINNERS

Sometimes a whirling blade will call attention to a moving bait that might otherwise be overlooked. When drifting or casting into inlets for fluke (summer flounder), I like to rig natural baits behind a spinner blade of some sort. I particularly like the wobbling action imparted by rotor-type blades, but a lot of fluke fishermen prefer regular clevised blades. (See Chapter 9 for a more complete discussion of spinner blades, their rigging and use.)

Pork Rinds and Plastics

Many single-hook lures—jigs, spoons, spinners, spinnerbaits, poppers, even flies—can be made to produce on slow days by tipping them with a piece of pork rind, a small plastic worm, or a soft plastic bait tail. Some anglers use them on treble-hooked lures as well, but I find that a single pork rind or plastic trailer on a treble hook often causes the lure to run crooked, destroying its fish-catching action. A tiny pork-rind strip on each of a treble's

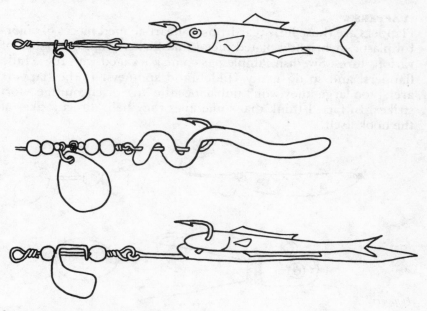

Spinners in Terminal Rigs

barbs—now that's another story. Sometimes it works well, sometimes it doesn't. You will have to experiment to see whether triple-tipping upsets a lure's hydrodynamic balance.

As for plastic worms and bait tails, I will have a lot more to say about them in the next chapter. Here, let me just note the major distinctions between plastics and pork rinds. Generally, plastic worms and bait tails are more flexible and less durable than pork-rind baits of similar design. The flexibility gives them more action, most of the time; sometimes, the stiffer action of a pork rind

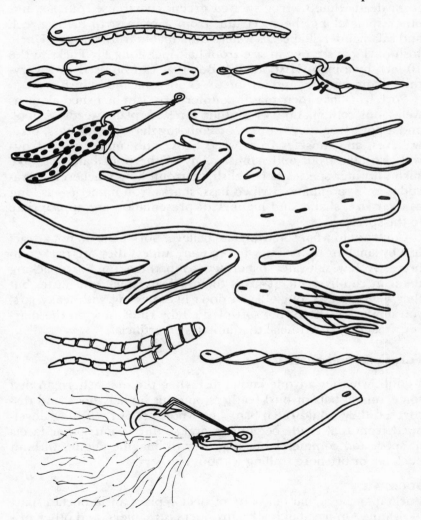

Pork Rind Baits and Pork Rind Kicker

is what's wanted. Try pork rinds and plastics on Johnson Silver Minnow spoons and you will see what I mean. Plastics come in a wider variety of sizes, shapes, and colors, but the pork rinds aren't really wanting in any of those departments. As a rule of thumb, pork rinds and plastics can be substituted freely for one another.

The General Motors of pork-rind manufacturers is the Uncle Josh Bait Company of Fort Atkinson, Wisconsin. I doubt whether Uncle Josh invented pork-rind baits, but the company sure wrote the book on them. Available now is all sort of shapes and colors— from dead white to frog-spotted green, chartreuse, purple, and other spots along the spectrum; from a plain strip to frog, eel, and salamander shapes, as well as unnamable frilly things—Uncle Josh pork baits range in size from half-inch-long Fly Flicks to the 10-inch-by-2-inch Offshore Big Boy that can be used for everything from muskies and tarpon to school tuna and billfish.

Pork baits, like their plastic counterparts, can be fished alone as well as in combination with other lures. A plain weedless hook and a pork frog, pork chunk, or Pollywoggler will take bass, pike, walleyes, and muskies from weed beds. The smaller pork frogs will also take trout and panfish. Any of the pork baits will take such saltwater species as bonefish, seatrout, king mackerel, barracuda, jacks, pompano, striped bass, sharks, you name it—as long as their size, shape, and manner of presentation are appropriate to the species.

Contrary to what some anglers believe, pork baits do not attract fish by smell or taste. They haven't any, unless they are packed in brine. A few saltwater fishermen soup them up by repacking them in cod-liver oil. It gives them a fishy smell and taste, but they won't last as long. If you don't like messing with leaky jars, you might try one of the soft-plastic fake rinds now on the market. Imagine, an artificial that imitates an artificial.

Fur, Fuzz, and Feathers

I doubt whether anyone knows just when the first fisherman tied some animal hair or bird feathers onto his homely hook and discovered they would catch fish. The whole art of fly-fishing developed from that crude beginning, and so did various other facets of sport and commercial fishing. Try to imagine jigging without bucktail, or offshore trolling without feathers.

BUCKTAIL
Bucktail—the actual tail hairs of deer—plays an important part in fishing. On jigs, tail hooks, droppers, streamers, and other primary lures, bucktail and other animal hairs are very important as

primary fish-attractors. Even in bait-fishing, bucktail-dressed hooks can play an important part. The Chincoteague flounder rig is nothing but a standard high/low bottom-fishing rig that uses a leadhead (usually bucktail) jig or heavy spoon instead of a plain sinker, and two bucktail-dressed hooks on which are impaled the standard flounder baits (usually strips of fish or squid, live or dead baitfish, or combinations thereof). Up North, where the local *Paralichthys* species is known as summer flounder or fluke, similarly dressed hooks work as well on locally popular fluke rigs.

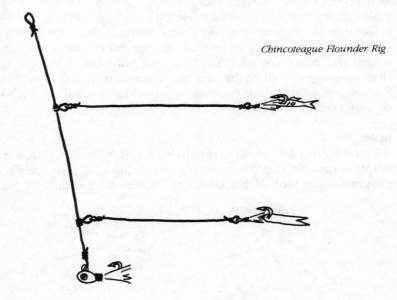

Chincoteague Flounder Rig

Besides true bucktail, other animal hairs have been and are used. Polar-bear hair was once favored by fishermen because of its real or imagined superiority, but its use is happily a thing of the past. Squirrel hair is very good, as are various other mammal pelts—muskrat, seal, ermine, otter, lynx, and rabbit among them —but my conservationist conscience prevents my using some of them.

SYNTHETIC FIBERS

In recent years, various synthetic "hair" fibers have been used to replace natural animal hairs. In some cases, the switch was made because of cost. But since most of the synthetic fibers are made from petroleum-based chemicals, escalating oil prices have caused some manufacturers to switch back to natural hairs. Most of the fake furs are more durable than most natural-hair dressings, a virtue that hasn't been lost on those who jig for bluefish, barracuda, and other toothy warriors. And some of the newer synthetic fibers—FisHair and Dynel, for example—"breathe" (undulate) almost as nicely in the water as polar bear and other now-*verboten* dressings.

Synthetic fibers come in various grades and types. The crimped, fuzzy grades "breathe" best, but there are times when the long, sleek look of the straight, uncrimped fibers is what you want. Sometimes straight, monofilament nylon fibers are used to make short, brushlike hook dressings and jig tails of surprising effectiveness. Permit jigs and Chincoteague flounder rigs work better if bristly nylon rather than longer, more sinuous synthetic or natural hairs are used to dress the hooks. For fishing fairly shallow waters by daylight, the incorporation of a few strands of fluorescent fishing line can make a bucktail-type dressing or fly especially effective.

ROPE

Various kinds of rope—polypropylene and braided nylon, for example—can be used as ersatz-bucktail hook dressings. To approximate the look of bucktail, rope has to be partially or wholly

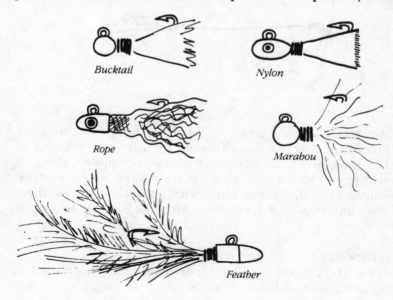

Bucktail

Nylon

Rope

Marabou

Feather

Jigs with Various Dressings

unbraided or unraveled and fluffed up. Down on the Gulf of Mexico, king mackerel and cobia specialists have developed a whole fishery around their rope jigs. This is a field that lends itself to a lot of experimentation and handcrafting.

FEATHERS
Feathers of all sorts—from homely chicken features to exotic fowl plumes—are used to make commercial tuna jigs, offshore trolling lures, muskie spinners, streamers, and artificial flies of all types. Conservation and protection of endangered bird species in recent years has limited or outlawed the use of certain previously popular feathers, but true sportsmen are stoically resigned to it if not actually delighted; only the worst fish hogs are dismayed.

Some bluewater fishermen troll hookless feather teasers to lure billfish and tuna up to the boat, then drop rigged natural baits back to the attracted fish. Others prefer to do both the luring and catching with feathered jigs and trolling lures (which often are referred to as Japanese feathers). When sand eels (sand lance or launce) abound in coastal waters, mackerel-tube lures are especially effective as trailers on leadhead jigs and tin squids when the tubes are adorned by single long, thin feathers and maybe a wisp of nylon FisHair. That's a trick I picked up from Dr. John B. Lapetina of Norfolk, Virginia, whose Doctor J lures have done so incredibly well on so many species over the years.

Feathers aren't as often used as natural hair or synthetic fiber dressings on baited hooks, but they aren't unknown. A little hackle tied high up on the shank near the eye of a bait hook can be very helpful in making that little angleworm or cricket even more interesting to behold. Almost anywhere bucktail or synthetic "hair" is used, a touch of feathers will do almost as well.

MARABOU
The downy plume feathers of the marabou, an Old World stork that also is known as the adjutant bird, are among the most active and effective hook dressings you can imagine. Whether all of the "marabou" plumes sold today still come from such storks I don't know for sure, nor do I much care. No matter what the source, marabou plumes really work. For marabou to develop its characteristic and winning performance, it must first be wetted, then squeezed dry between the fingers. A good marabou plume will pulsate slowly and voluptuously with every little movement of the current or of the dressed hook. It's great stuff.

YARN

It isn't really hair, fur, or feathers, but yarn is used in much the same way. Salmon, steelhead, and trout fishermen out West, and a few other anglers elsewhere, use bits of yarn in front of spawn sacs, individual salmon eggs, cherry bobbers, and other baits (natural or bogus) to add an extra attractive dimension. Red, orange, and yellow are the colors most often used (often in fluorescent dyes), but other colors will work too, particularly lime and chartreuse greens. Special yarns are made (or at least packaged) for fishing, but I suppose cheaper knitting yarns could be used. Angling yarns are made so they won't mat in the water. Most come in handy, center-feed dispenser tubes.

One of the best ways to rig a hank of yarn on a hook is to use a cinched loop. Thread a bead onto line or leader, then tie the loop knot of your choice. If line and bead are chosen with care, the bead will slip along the looped line with enough resistance that it can be used to cinch a piece of yarn up against the hook eye. Otherwise, just knot the yarn around the hook shank or leader.

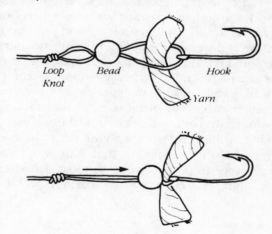

Loop   Bead   Hook
Knot

Yarn

Cinching a Yarn Rig

Skirts

When I was a kid, Arbogast's rubber-skirted lures (Hula Popper, Hawaiian Wiggler, Hula Dancer, and so on) seemed utterly unique to me, but I suppose there were other skirted lures around. Now, of course, skirted lures are everywhere, particularly skirted spinnerbaits. There is a reason for this proliferation of skirted lures: They catch fish. And the skirts are durable, generally more so than natural or synthetic hairs and fibers.

What I didn't know when I was a kid is that the skirts alone can be used, *sans* any lure, on various terminal rigs in combination with natural baits. Offshore trollers have known this for years. They call their giant skirts hootchy skirts or hootchies, the reference being, I suppose, to hootchy-kootchy rather than hula dancing. And bluewater anglers have been rigging hootchy skirts over or ahead of balao and mullet baits for a long time.

The argument can be made that a saltwater hootchy skirt closely resembles a squid, whereas a Hula Skirt resembles nothing found in fresh water. Logical as it is, the argument doesn't hold water. Skirted baits and lures will catch fish in fresh water as well as they will in salt. Regionally, fresh-water anglers rig skirts immediately ahead of sucker and big shiner baits for muskies and lunker largemouths. Maybe the skirt resembles a frog; who knows?

Some of the skirts on today's market are made of rubber, others of vinyl. In warm water, either type will work as well, although a really good vinyl skirt might have a slight edge in action. But in cold water, plastic skirts stiffen slightly, dampening their fish-enticing action, whereas rubber or latex skirts will remain flexible and lively. But don't write the plastics off entirely for coldwater fishing. The North Atlantic Ocean off New England is nothing if not cold, and the PVC (polyvinyl chloride) Tee-Zer Tail skirts from Fishfinders are well known and effective in those waters.

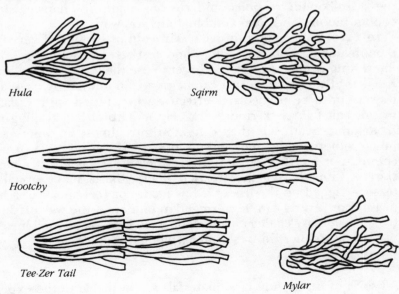

Hula

Sqirm

Hootchy

Tee-Zer Tail

Mylar

Skirts

"Worm plastic"—that soft, fleshy stuff used to make plastic worms—has been used with mixed results in skirts. Mister Twister's Sassy Skirt, a multiarmed version of their famous twist-tail worm, failed in the marketplace, although it was successful enough in the water to insure some less well-known copies or look-alikes that can still be found in various parts of the country. Lately, Burke's Sqirm Skirt has been causing a stir. It's a little difficult to describe, but if you can imagine a combination spider-web-hydroid-fireworks burst made of soft, fleshy plastic, you have some idea of what a Sqirm Skirt looks like when it's spread flat. In action, it has to be seen to be believed. It isn't as durable as the latex or vinyl skirts, but it keeps its flexibility in cold water better than either, and it will catch fish with the best of the skirts.

A fellow out in San Jose, California, named Frank Hauck has invented or at least markets something he calls Living Rubber Skirt Material, and it is so darned clever I am willing to forgive its rather dingy colors. In ready-to-tie form, Living Rubber comes in inch-wide bands of various lengths. Look closely, and you will see that the wide bands are scored longitudinally. Tie three or more wide bands of appropriate length to a jig, spinnerbait, hook, or whatever, using line, twine, or wire; split each wide band in half, stretch the bands until taut, then snip them at the fingertips with scissors. Voilà! Instant hula-type skirts. Easy as pie, cheaper than the store-bought versions, and custom made in whatever sizes, configurations, and color combinations you want.

In a real pinch, you can make skirts out of strands of very fine monofilament. Combine colors and test strengths for the most interesting results. And don't forget to use the fluorescent colors.

Skirts of various materials can be rigged in numerous ways, and they seem to be particularly effective when fished with a plastic worm, bait tail, pork rind, pork eel, or natural bait trailing out from underneath. Or they can substitute almost anywhere you might otherwise be tempted to use a pork rind. A worn or chewed-out bucktail can be given a new lease on life if a small skirt is slipped over the frazzled fibers. Skirts make excellent teasers (rigged up the leader a few inches or feet ahead of a bait or lure) or several can be so rigged in tandem—the way offshore trollers rig daisy chains of squids or hootchies—and used instead of cowbell spinners in freshwater trolling.

Tantalizing Tapes

All sorts of interesting tape materials are available to the experimentally minded modern angler. The fishable tapes are essentially waterproof and will stay on pretty well through the wear and tear of normal fishing. Some of them are fluorescent, others are phosphorescent, and still others are prismatic. I use them all, and I especially like the prism tapes for fishing by day and the glowing phosphorescent tapes for fishing by night or at any time of day in really deep water. The prism tapes are fairly expensive, so you might not want to stock your tackle box in all the available colors. My favorite is silver, because its iridescence sparkles with all the colors of the rainbow, including gold. Prism tapes come in geometric and fish-scale patterns, but I doubt fish notice the difference. It is their flashiness that counts.

You can use all these tapes to dress up lures (don't forget spinner blades), turn sinkers into auxiliary attractors, make floats or bobbers more visible, and even fashion some quick, crude "flies" in a pinch. For night fishing, the phosphorescent tapes can also be used to make gaffs, landing nets, tackle boxes, and other gear more easily locatable. And a piece wrapped around the barrel of a rod's tiptop guide can make light bites and nibbles easier to detect when bottom-fishing after dark.

Scents and Oils

Most fish follow their noses in feeding, at least part of the time. But until recently, few artificial lures appealed to a fish's olfactory sense. In fact, lures that have been fondled by human hands are more often repellent to fish. When I was a kid, we always kept dropper-bottles of anise oil in our tackle boxes, to make our baits

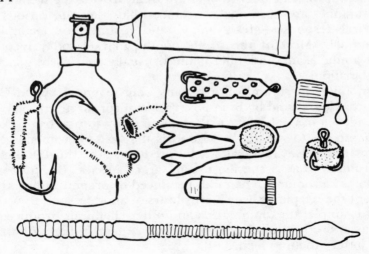

Scents and Scented Lures

and lures more attractive. I suspect that it was effective mostly because it masked human odors. Anise oil is still used, but it has been replaced by a whole spectrum of scents and oils.

Mann's Jelly Worms were perhaps the first widely popular scented lures. I am not sure that bass really dote upon dewberry, watermelon, marmalade, and some of the other fruit flavors molded into the plastic worms, but they certainly help to mask human odors, and they do work.

Other tackle manufacturers turned to fish and bait oils. All sorts of bottles of messy, stinky oils started turning up on the market about ten years ago. Even a few lure manufacturers got into the act. Numerous plugs and trolling lures were made with cavities that could carry little sponges or cotton balls that had been soaked in these scent oils. A company called Applied Oceanographic Corporation used to make a line of Chumin lures that used pellets of freeze-dried chum in their cavities. Mold Craft's old Reel Eel had natural eel oil molded into the plastic.

Recent studies in olfaction in fishes turned up all sorts of information that has been pounced upon by the tackle manufacturers. It was, for example, discovered that the component of human smell most repellent to fish was the amino acid L-serine. Other amino acids, being the building blocks of protein, are highly attractive to fish. Scientists investigating the ability of salmon to return to their natal streams decided that it was the memory and recognition of the stream's smell. And it has been theorized that population-specific pheromones are what provide the scent trails. Pheromones are hormonal substances that stimulate various behavioral responses—fear, anger, and mating, for example—in animals. Most of the scents on the market today incorporate amino acids and pheromones, usually in closely guarded combinations.

Dr. Juice, the brand of attractant scent invented by Dr. Greg Bambanek and sold by Blue Fox Tackle, incorporates three types of pheromones. The first is the one used by forage fish to keep their schools together; the second is the fear pheromone given off by small fish under attack by predators; the third is the sex pheromone that is specific to the target species. Dr. Juice also contains kairomones, chemicals produced by organisms but which benefit the recipients, which are always of another species. A relevant example: the amino acids and other chemicals produced by plants and other lower organisms reduce fear in higher animals and induce them to feed.

Today, you can buy jigs, spoons, spinners, plugs, plastic worms and baits, even unattached hooks, which have absorbent areas for the purpose of carrying some of these new scent juices. For the past couple of years, scents have been *the* hot new thing in terminal tackle. Some anglers love the stuff, others hate it. Still others, myself included, don't pay the subject much attention.

Teasers, Trolls, Dodgers, and Flashers

Those who fish for large gamefish know that really big fish often dote upon rather small bait—bait that might be too subtle in its appeal to attract their attention from afar. But a big, provocative bait often will attract more follows than strikes. The solution is to combine a smallish bait with a bigger, noisier, flashier, more active attractor. Bluewater anglers who troll the surface of the open sea for billfish and tuna usually drag big, splashy, hookless teasers behind their transoms to lure the pelagic gamesters up into the hooked baits or lures.

The hottest teasers in use today are called birds. Made of wood, foam plastic, or soft plastic, birds differ from other teasers in their possession of angled wings that really send the water flying. One day while fishing Cape Cod Bay for giant tuna with Mold Craft's Frank Johnson (designer and manufacturer of the Soft Bird) and M & M Tackle's Steve Moreton (popularizer and manufacturer of the spreader-bar rig), we had three Soft Bird spreader-bar rigs out. Each rig had 13 Soft Birds, only one of which was Pro-Rigged with hooks. It looked as if we were towing a bunch of those gang lawnmowers that golf courses and ballparks use. What a grand commotion! If only there had been some feeding tuna about....

Deep trollers seeking salmon and big trout usually resort to tying into their terminal rigs a lake troll (cowbell), herring dodger, or rotating flasher. Cowbells or trolls are nothing but large spinner blades rigged in tandem, often with a rudder or keel added up front. Herring dodgers and flashers look very much alike—something like long, slender trolling spoons—but the former dart from side to side while the latter travel along spinning and doing barrel rolls. Both impart some of their action to the bait (which may be a whole or cut fish, dead natural bait, a small plug, spinner, spoon, streamer, fly, or vinyl squid), as well as sending out all sorts of sonic signals and brilliant flashes. Cowbells, dodgers, and flashers must be well swiveled to prevent line twist, and they must be tied into the rig some distance above the bait—anywhere from one to several feet.

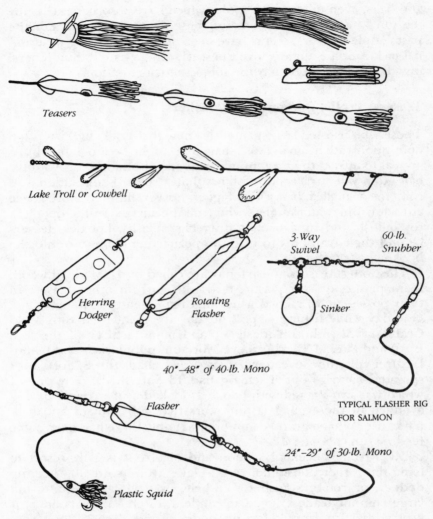

Teasers, Trolls, Dodgers, and Flashers

Attractors Far Afield

Keep the principles of fish predation and sensory perception fixed in your mind, and your eyes peeled, and you will be surprised how many innovative ideas in fish-attraction will come to you. Craft and hobby shops, the sewing and notions departments in discount stores, even supermarkets and hardware stores are veritable cornucopias of fish-attracting ideas.

*Aluminum Foil
Crumpled
Around
Hook Shank Inside
Clear Latex Tube*

*Electrical Wire
Insulation on
Hook*

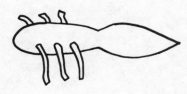

*Rubber-Band Legs
Added to Plastic
Grub*

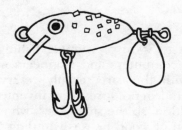

*Craft-Shop Glitter
Glued
onto Plug
Body*

Miscellaneous Added Attractions

9

A Survey of Lure Types

ACCORDING TO MADISON AVENUE, fishing lures are designed by sophisticated computers and engineers with PhDs, and are manufactured with the care usually reserved for fine instruments. According to legend, lures were invented quite by accident. It was James Heddon, so the story goes, who invented the fishing plug when a chip of wood he was whittling fell into Michigan's Dowagiac River and was immediately attacked by a big bass. Similarly, the spoon lure supposedly was invented by some nameless and hapless fellow who was lunching in his boat on some lake somewhere when he dropped one of his bride's silver spoons overboard, only to watch it disappear into the toothy maw of some gigantic pike or ravenous muskie as it fluttered toward the bottom. Would that fish-attracting were that simple! But, however romantic or oversimplified these stories are, I suppose the first lures were probably discovered or invented under such rustic conditions, probably a long time before James Heddon was born. And, while I doubt that the computerized industrial wizards of Route 128 and Silicon Valley have much competition to fear, lures these days are designed and developed as much by engineering calculation as by angling hunch.

Of all the different kinds of terminal tackle, lures are surely the most varied, the most widely advertised and heavily promoted, the most subject of myth. A lot of what passes for "information" about lures was dreamed up by some pin-striped copywriter who may or may not be a fisherman. So, while the lures themselves have become more "scientific," the lore about lures has become more like science fiction.

Whole books have been devoted to lures without even beginning to exhaust the subject, and one probably could write a book-length manuscript just describing the important differences and similarities among the myriad types of lures, without even getting down to the nitty-gritty of how best to use them all. In this chapter, there is room only for the briefest survey of the most common lure types.

PLUGS

Originally, plugs were made of wood, but these days they may be made of numerous other materials—hard or soft or foam plastics, solid or hollow metals, glass, rubber, even some space-age materials that are difficult to categorize. Whatever material is used, the plug is usually shaped to resemble something that is presumably attractive to fish, although sometimes a plug's resemblance to prey isn't apparent until it is set in motion. One-piece or jointed, fabricated of strange combinations of homely and exotic materials, often with interchangeable parts or riggings, plugs have become so varied in recent years that traditional distinctions among the various types are becoming blurred. However, differences in plug performance are still as important as ever.

Swimming Plugs

Often called crankbaits, wobblers, or swimmers, the swimming plugs usually have some sort of writhing, wriggling, wobbling, or swimming action built into them. Fishing them is mostly a case of casting them out and cranking them in, or dragging them behind a moving boat. But skillful anglers know that, for all the know-how of the top lure designers, crankbaits will often work better and under a wider range of angling conditions when the fisherman varies retrieval speeds and gives his rod tip the right dance or waggle. In the beginning, this means trial-and-error experimentation, but it doesn't take long to discover the winning combinations of lures, conditions, and tip-waggling techniques.

It probably isn't fair to ignore all the other dozens of effective shapes now available, but three types are about as good as they come: long, slender "Finnish minnows" exemplified by Rapalas and Rebels; the potbellied "alphabet plugs" originated or at least popularized by the Fred Young/Cotton Cordell Big O; and the flat, curved swimmers like the Flatfish and Lazy Ike. Each produces its own kind of swimming action, appealing to a wide variety of species and effective under a wide range of conditions. Within each body shape and style, there are available a great many variations on the swimming action typically associated with the shape. Jointed or "broken-back" variants of the torpedolike Finnish minnows have an extra-frantic action that sometimes will take fish that ignore the more sedate swimming of the single-piece lures.

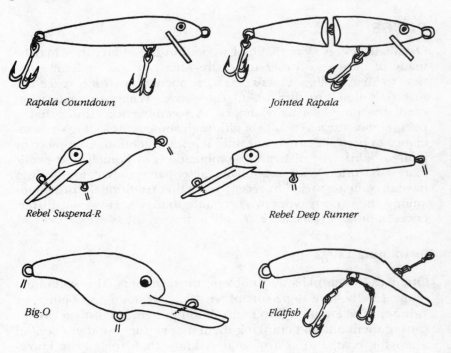

Rapala Countdown   *Jointed Rapala*

Rebel Suspend-R   *Rebel Deep Runner*

Big-O   *Flatfish*

Swimming Plugs

Swimming plugs may be designed to float or to sink at rest, and some manufacturers and fishermen make their primary distinction between floating and sinking swimmers, but running depth is the key variable to a swimming plug's angling performance. Most expert anglers mentally pigeonhole or physically separate their swimming plugs as surface, shallow, medium, or deep swimmers. It makes good sense.

Especially versatile are the countdown plugs (those that sink at a specified rate and that will maintain that running depth when trolled or retrieved at appropriate speed) and the neutral-buoyancy swimmers (those that will dive to a certain depth once the retrieve is begun, and that will maintain that depth when the retrieve is stopped). These two types of swimmers give the careful angler the ability to fine-tune his fishing depth to match almost any angling condition he encounters.

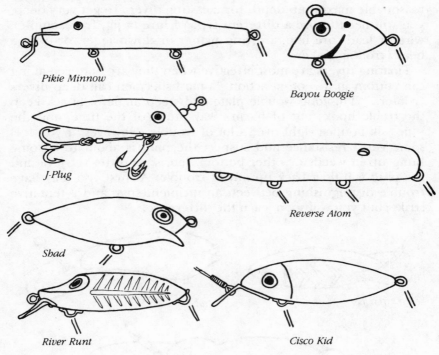

Other Swimming Plug Shapes

Floating Divers

Some deep-diving plugs sink at rest (and may be classified as deep-running swimmers), but others will dive deep only when in motion and will float back to the surface if the retrieve is stopped. Floating divers are easier and, I think, mostly better to use. Ordinarily, it is best to begin the retrieve with a sharp lift of the rod tip and then to follow by medium-slow cranking of the reel, rather than the supersonic cranking that is widely believed to be necessary. Most of the deep divers come with some sort of paperwork or instructional labeling to let you know how deep they are designed to run. If you buy one that isn't so labeled, better ask a knowledgeable salesperson or angler before trusting that it will dive to the bottom of your favorite lake.

Hydrodynamics being what they are, it is practically impossible to design a diving plug that will get down as deep as 35 feet on its own. For most practical purposes, 12 feet might be considered a reasonable maximum depth for a casting diver. To get very deep, you will need to use a different type of lure (a jig, for example), wire or lead-core line, a diving planer or downrigger, or even a heavy trolling sinker.

Floating divers are most effective when they are bounced along the bottom in a rooting action. Some fishermen call deep divers "rooters." The long wobble plate and steep angle of attack keep the treble hooks out of harm's way much of the time, and the plug will bounce right over a lot of trouble. However, if you feel some extra resistance and suspect the plug is about to become hung up in weeds or other bottom debris, stop the retrieve and the plug will float back up out of trouble. At first you may have trouble distinguishing between an incipient snag and a tentative strike, but you will soon learn the difference.

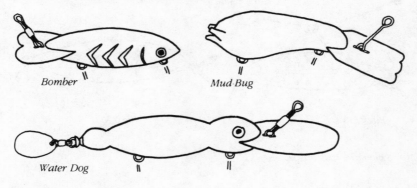

Bomber

Mud Bug

Water Dog

Floating Divers

Few of the surf fishermen I know carry floating divers in their shoulder bags, probably because so few surf-size divers are available. And it is difficult to fish rooters in the surf because of the extra resistance of the big diving plugs. However, considering how many littoral predators stalk the surf zone feeding on mole crabs (sand bugs) and other bottom-burrowing creatures, the rooter is a good bet on sandy ocean shores. Just don't try to fish one in really heavy surf or the extreme resistance of the plug will make it tougher to "land" than a fairly decent-sized fish. Be sure, when surf-fishing rooters, to use a rod that has some backbone to it and line that is perhaps one class heavier than you might otherwise use.

Darters

The name "Darter" is actually a trademark owned by the Creek Chub Bait Company. Their Darter is one fine lure for sure, but the name has come to be applied by most anglers to other plugs of similar action, no matter who was the manufacturer. Darters float when at rest and will swim at or near the surface with a rolling, wobbling action when retrieved slowly and steadily, but it is their more typical side-to-side dashing and darting that gives them their special appeal. To get that action, the angler retrieves the lure at moderate or faster speeds, whipping the rod tip smartly as he reels.

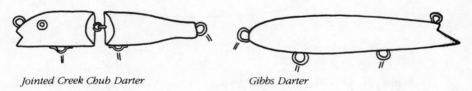

Jointed Creek Chub Darter   *Gibbs Darter*

Darting Plugs

Unlike swimming plugs, darters do not have long wobble plates. Instead, their action is carved or molded into the basic body shape. A notched lip, often combined with a long, sloping forehead, is what makes the darter tick.

On broad-finned, fairly flat-bodied fish that rely more upon maneuverability than speed to run down their prey—fish like the striped and black basses—darters are terrific lures. They aren't as effective on the straight-ahead speedsters like barracuda and pickerel or other members of the pike family.

Popping Plugs

Poppers are great fun to use and extremely effective, too, but it takes a bit of practice to get that fish-calling sound and action just right. Sometimes you want a subtle little "bloop," and other times you want an explosive "POP!" A well-designed popper can deliver either sound. Most popping plugs have a flat or concave face, and an experienced popper fisherman can look at a popping plug's face and know just how it will sound and what kind of bubbles, splashes, or spray it will produce.

For bass fishing on dark summer nights, hardly anything will beat a black popper, but you had better practice the action during the daytime, when you can see what is going on.

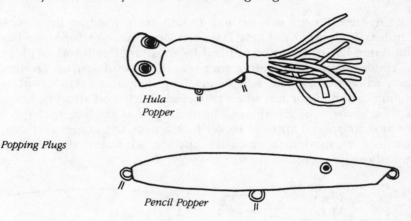

Hula
Popper

Popping Plugs

Pencil Popper

Most poppers float at rest, and are most effective when allowed to rest between pops until the radiating ripples of water die away. Many of the anglers I have watched are too impatient to fish their poppers that deliberately; they miss a lot of strikes by popping their plugs too frequently. It takes nerves of steel to develop the Joblike patience it takes to properly fish a popper around lily pads, weed beds, and brush. But it's worth it.

In the ocean's turbulent surf, where speedy, noisy retrieves are necessary to attract a fish's attention, and where casting distance is an important consideration, popping plugs may be weighted so heavily that they sink when at rest. If you are new to surf-fishing, this will take some getting used to, but the trick is to begin cranking the reel just *before* the popper hits the water, and to crank that reel handle and whip that rod tip as if your life depended upon it. Surf-fishing with poppers is as sweaty and athletic as freshwater popping is contemplative and nerve-wracking. The pencil popper—a long, slender popper that is more heavily weighted in the rear—is a particular favorite of surf and saltwater boat casters.

Surface Disturbers

This category is a real catchall; it includes almost any surface-running plug that attracts fish by disturbing the surface with splashes, waves, ripples, gurgles, or whatever. Poppers and surface swimmers and darters are, technically speaking, surface disturbers, but they are important and different enough to merit the separate mention above.

In general, surface-disturbing plugs work better on calm waters, but some are noisy and splashy enough to work well in a chop or even in heavy surf. My favorite weather conditions for fishing surface disturbers are those that give the surface of the water just a bit of texture: no chop, and certainly not waves; just a kind of wrinkly calm with maybe a ripple here and there. On mirror-smooth surfaces, it takes extreme subtlety in fishing surface disturbers of any type.

Most, but certainly not all, surface-disturbing plugs can be pigeonholed into one of these subcategories. Even Mold Craft's Soft Bird teaser can be rigged with a single hook and fished as a surface-disturbing lure. All sizes are great for trolling offshore, and the smallest Soft Birds can be cast or trolled in fresh water for bass, pike, and other fish.

CHUGGERS

While most surface disturbers have little or no built-in action and must be manipulated enticingly by the angler, chuggers can be reeled in steadily, without any twitching of the rod tip. Arbogast's Jitterbug and Heddon's Crazy Crawler are among the most venerable and best known of the chuggers, testimony enough to their effectiveness. Either one's attractiveness to fish can be enhanced

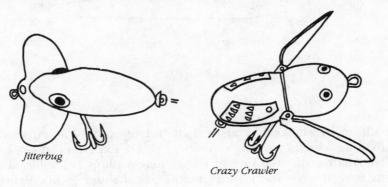

Jitterbug

Crazy Crawler

Chuggers

by artistic rod-twitching, but they will also catch fish in the hands of tyros who simply cast them out and crank them in. The Jitterbug, particularly in black, is my all-time favorite lure for night fishing in fresh water; its plop-plop-plopping sound enables you to locate it on the darkest nights.

STICK BAITS

At the opposite extreme from the chuggers are the stick baits, surface-disturbing plugs that have absolutely no action other than that imparted by the angler's manipulation of the rod tip. For this reason, stick baits are better fished by day than by night, at least until you get so good at it you can manipulate a stick bait by feel and sound rather than sight.

Some of the so-called stick baits aren't stick-shaped at all, but more nearly resemble bombs and other fairly bulky objects. But all of them work virtually alike, floating at rest (either flat on the surface or vertically), and sliding straight along the surface under steady reeling, with none of the commotion or action it takes to attract fish. But, when twitched and jerked along in an erratic, stop-and-go fashion, they will take an incredible range of species, in both fresh and salt water, under a wide variety of conditions.

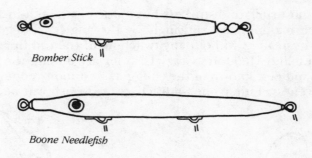

Bomber Stick

Boone Needlefish

Stick Baits

Often overlooked by anglers, stick baits can be as effective as anything else in an angler's armory. An experienced stick-bait fisherman can make one of these lifeless plugs resemble almost any sort of prey species imaginable, from squid to needlefish to gizzard shad.

PROPELLER PLUGS

Some stick baits are equipped with propellers fore, aft, or both (some popping plugs also have incidental propeller-blade spinners on the aft hook eye shank), but some propeller plugs are stubby little things. No matter what their shape, propeller plugs get much of their fish-attracting effectiveness from their whirling, gurgling propellers. The Arbogast Dasher is a good example of the propeller-equipped stick bait. The Dasher's fore-and-aft propeller blades are counter-rotating; that is, they spin in opposite directions, one clockwise, the other counterclockwise. This helps prevent torque and line twist and gives the plug a desirable trueness in movement.

Among surface freshwater lures, the little-known Helin Fishcake has become one of my special favorites. It is a stubby, barrel-shaped lure that has the tiny, outriggered treble hooks that are so familiar on Helin's more popular Flatfish. The strange propeller blade on the Fishcake (which looks something like a two-bladed version of those plastic pinwheels children love) is capable of making all sorts of noises and disturbances of the water's surface, and the plug can be fished as a popper or chugger as well. It is one of the most versatile and effective lures I have used. Why it is no longer made is a real mystery.

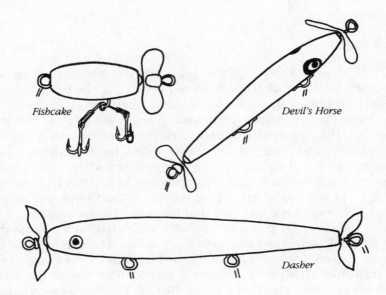

Fishcake

Devil's Horse

Dasher

Propeller Plugs

CRIPPLED MINNOWS

Like "Darter," this might also be a registered trademark, but plugs from a number of manufacturers are called crippled or injured minnows by most anglers. Usually shaped like a small baitfish, these plugs float on their sides at rest, their treble hooks dangling from the tail end and the middle of one side. When they are moved forward, crippled minnows may dive slightly beneath the surface, dart slowly from side to side, or wobble erratically. Some have propeller-blade spinners, usually mounted on the tail end. Naturally, the lures are made to resemble small baitfish in distress, in both shape and action. They are best fished in a slow, erratic, stop-and-go fashion, with plenty of pauses in between movements. You will know when you get the action down right, because predators will jump all over them.

Prowler   Dorado

Crippled Minnows

Jerk Baits

Stick baits, propeller plugs, and some other surface disturbers are sometimes called jerk baits, but I am restricting the term to those underwater plugs that have no action of their own and that must be worked by the angler. Perhaps the best known of all the jerk baits are the lipless MirrOlures. Retrieved steadily, they will vibrate tightly and send out some sonic waves, but when jerked and twitched along, they are among the most effective lures in the angling arsenal. It will take some practice to become truly adept, but the practice is worth every minute. The Chopper Stopper from Fishfinders is a jerk bait that looks like a cross between a jig and a tube lure. It has a slab-sided lead body molded around a big jig hook. Stretched over this body is a short piece of large-diameter plastic tubing. The resulting lure looks something like a butterfish or menhaden, casts well, and comes through the water with all sorts of loops and swoops and gyrations in response to a little action of the rod tip.

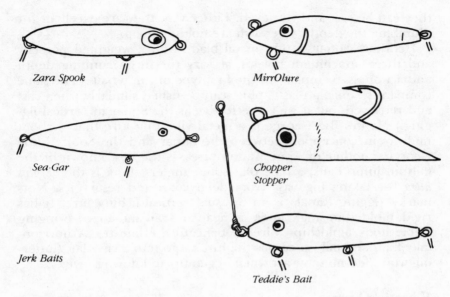

Zara Spook

MirrOlure

Sea-Gar

Chopper
Stopper

Jerk Baits

Teddie's Bait

Jump Baits

These lures are a little difficult to categorize, and might as logi-
cally be called jigs as plugs. However you choose to classify them,
get to know jump baits because they are versatile and effective
fish-catchers. Most of them can be fished vertically, like jigs, or

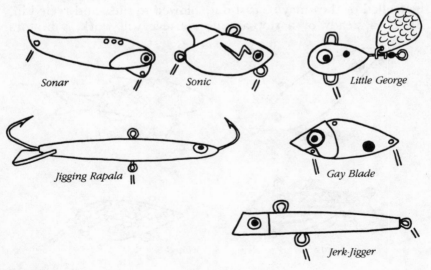

Sonar

Sonic

Little George

Jigging Rapala

Gay Blade

Jerk-Jigger

Jump Baits

they can be cast and retrieved. Either way, they are excellent for plumbing the depths when fish are holding deep.

Heddon's Sonar, a thin metal blade with a weighted potbelly and three attachment holes that vary the lure's running depth and action, is exemplary of the first type of jump bait. (The same company's Sonic, a plastic plug, can be fished similarly when cast and retrieved, but it isn't as effective as the Sonar in vertical jigging.) Mann's Big George is a metal vibrating lure that is about midway in conception between the Sonar and the Sonic. Little George, another of Tom Mann's lures, is the best known of the tailspin jump baits, a type that some anglers think is the *ne plus ultra* for taking big bass from deep lakes and reservoirs. Normark's Jigging Rapala is an unusual vertical-fishing lure. It has rigid, molded-in single hooks at head and tail and a free-swinging treble hook amidships, directly beneath the line tie. A horizontally flattened tail fin causes the lure to go into a circular, fluttering wounded-minnow act when jigged up and down slowly.

Vibrating Lures

The line separating jump baits from vibrating lures is a fine one, but vibrators are usually molded of hard plastic and are similarly related, either in action or function, to some swimmers and divers and even to certain jerk baits. Most vibrators are slab-shaped, and look something like sunfish. Like true crankbaits, vibrators may be trolled or they may be cast out, allowed to sink, and reeled in. Either a steady or a stop-and-go retrieve will work. Vibrators

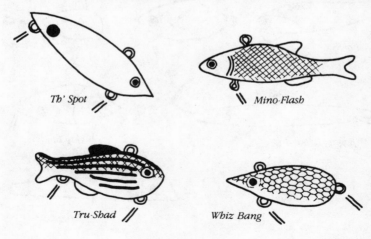

Th' Spot

Mino-Flash

Tru-Shad

Whiz Bang

Vibrating Lures

don't have much swimming action, just a tight, frenetic writhing that emits high-frequency sonic waves and audiovisually resembles the semiparalytic tremors of a stunned baitfish. There are a lot of good vibrating lures on the market, some of which have built-in rattle chambers.

Miscellaneous Metal

Certain metal lures are virtually impossible to categorize, and they are lumped together here only for convenience. The Fred Arbogast Company seems to specialize in them. Their Hawaiian

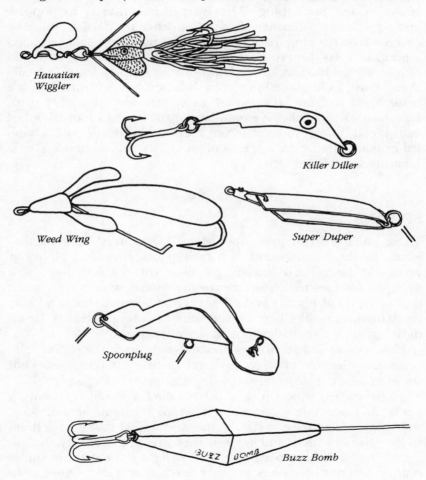

Hawaiian Wiggler

Killer Diller

Weed Wing

Super Duper

Spoonplug

Buzz Bomb

Miscellaneous Metal Lures

Wigglers have been around so long, fishermen have forgotten just how strange they are. Spinners? Jigs? Buzzbaits? No matter what you decide to call them, they are fine fish-catchers. The old South Bend Super Duper (now manufactured by Luhr Jensen) is another unclassifiable chestnut. It's sort of a spoon, but it has the swimming action of a plug. Buck Perry's aptly named Spoonplug —which has been described as looking like "a tromped-on shoe horn"—virtually revolutionized bass fishing by introducing the concept of "structure fishing." Most of Buck's fishing rudiments have been applied with good success to spoons, plugs, jigs, plastic worms, and other baits, but there are plenty of bassmen who swear by the Spoonplug. The Buzz Bomb that is so popular among salmon fishermen from California to Alaska could be called a free-running, flattened diamond jig, or it could be called a jump bait. Its fluttering action on the fall imitates the struggles of a wounded baitfish, and salmon can't resist it. Johnny O'Neill's Weed Wing looks something like a Johnson Silver Minnow with a rotor blade in front. It's a good, noisy lure for fishing lily pads. Les Davis's Killer Diller is exemplary of the lures fashioned out of bent metal tubing, most of which are used by West Coast salmon fishermen, although a larger look-alike is popular among Texas king-mackerel fishermen.

SPOONS

To no one's great surprise, spoons are metal lures shaped somewhat like the business end of a tablespoon. However, plenty of variations have been introduced since our hapless folk hero dropped his first mate's silverware overboard, and today spoons may be made of plastics and other nonmetallic materials and may be shaped more like bent butter-knife blades, elm leaves, or almost anything else that's thin and slightly cupped.

Most spoons will revolve as they move through the water—necessitating the use of a good swivel to prevent line twist—but some dart from side to side or wriggle along in a single plane.

The standard spoon lure is often called a wobbling spoon, a name that accurately describes the typical spoon action. Most wobbling spoons are of a size, shape, and weight that enable them to be cast accurately and far but they are as effectively trolled. Super-thin trolling spoons that are too light to be cast are sometimes called flutter spoons, another descriptive name. Other trolling spoons are given a variety of names, some which describe their actions, and others, like the bunker spoon, in celebration of the bait species they imitate. Super-heavyweight spoons might be called almost anything: jigging spoons, muskie spoons, dunkers, slabs. These may be cast, trolled, or jigged. Sometimes spoons are used to trail streamer flies, in which case the spoon serves not as the primary lure but as an attractor in the manner of the herring dodger or rotating flasher.

There are many good spoons on the market today, but the most effective spoon of all must be the Eppinger Daredevle. I am confident that no other single lure has caught as many fish in fresh and salt water as the red-and-white candy-striped Daredevle. It will catch fish almost anywhere. In weed-choked shallows, though, the traditional favorite is the Johnson Silver Minnow, particularly when it is used to trail a strip of pork rind from its weedless single hook. And recently I have discovered another candidate for the Angling Hardware Hall of Fame: the Williams Wabler, a spoon that requires a little more work to fish properly but which seems to entice, infuriate, or captivate almost everything that swims. In the Northeast where I live, tradition almost demands that on opening day the spin-fisherman after trout use Acme's fish-shaped Phoebe spoon. Being a born iconoclast and experimenter, I would invariably start the season fishing something else; almost as invariably, I would switch to a gold Phoebe because I would soon tire of practice casting while watching everyone else catch fish. From day two, I can catch trout on other spoons and spinners and lures, but on opening day it always seemed to take a Phoebe. Now I prefer to avoid opening-day crowds and to use a fly rod for trout. It's just more fun.

On a fishing trip to Alaska with Morry Israel of the Alaska Sportfishing Lodge Association, I discovered two spoons that are truly indispensable for salmonids. Everyone seemed to be using Blue Fox Pixee spoons for coho salmon, and I soon found out why. They were far more effective than anything else I had in my tackle box. Give me a ¼- or ⅓-ounce Pixee with a pink or orange soft-plastic insert, and I'll show you an eight- to twelve-pound coho. The writer J. L. Jenkins, who was along on the trip, introduced me to the Lobo spoon, a vaguely fish-shaped fluorescent-orange spoon that was lightyears ahead of everything else for taking pink (humpback) salmon. Since then, John has told me that on a trip to northern Canada he discovered Lobo spoons were equally irresistible to big, brawling, sea-run Arctic char. Pixees and Lobos now dominate my salmon spinning box and probably ever shall.

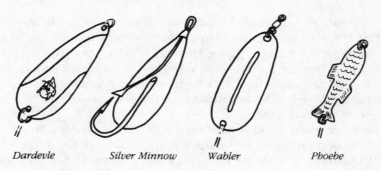

Dardevle   Silver Minnow   Wabler   Phoebe

Great Wobbling Spoons

JIGS

A jig is a weighted lure, nearly always metal, that can be fished vertically, but some are as effective when cast and retrieved through the water with an up-and-down action or when bounced along the bottom. And in recent years new types have been added to the jig-fisherman's armory that have wobbling or swimming actions built into them. Most experienced anglers rate the jig as the single most indispensable lure there is, the one lure they would take along if they could take only one. The angler who knows how to fish a jig can take almost any fish out of any water at any time. It takes more than a day's practice to develop this degree of competence, but it's well worth the time it takes to learn how to make a jig do its various dances.

Vertical jigging can be hard work if the water is deep and the jig heavy, but a good jigger will outfish a live-bait angler. Before going out to fish the deep cod grounds in the North Atlantic, where the jigs run to 16 and 20 ounces and the fish to 50 pounds and up, many jig-fishermen will do calisthentics as if they were working out in preparation for a heavyweight bout. If you aren't used to vertical jigging, working even a quarter-ounce jig can strain seldom-used muscles. Deep-jigging for amberjack is so strenuous, it ought to be an Olympic event. And vertical jigging can be frustrating; you can't see the lure and, until you get the hang of it, it doesn't feel like much, either. There is nothing like a graphite rod with its stiff action and sensitive touch for deep vertical jigging. If your budget restricts you to fiberglass, be sure to use a rod that is fairly stiff and has a "fast" action. Otherwise, you won't be able to give that distant jig enough action without tiring yourself out.

A jig's weight determines how well it will sink in a fast current or how far it may be cast, but its shape can be important, too. Its shape will also influence its action. Many jigs have absolutely no action in the water, except that which the angler gives it by skillful manipulation of the rod tip; other jigs, particularly those that are

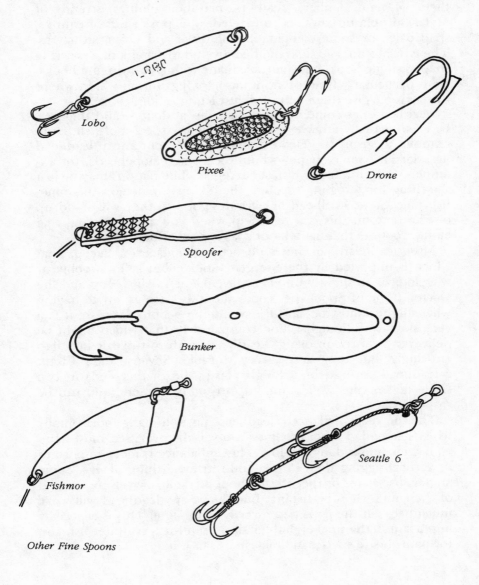

Other Fine Spoons

thin or flattopped or bent or curved, have some waggling or wobbling action.

Leadhead Jigs

Sometimes called bucktails, in deference to the traditional tail dressing, leadhead jigs usually consist of two parts—a molded head and an attractive tail section that might be fashioned of synthetic or natural fibers, feathers, marabou plumes, strands of Mylar, soft plastic bait tails, unraveled rope, pork rinds or chunks, strip baits, or some combination of these and other attractors. The typical leadhead jig is molded around the shank of a specially shaped single hook, but some are made with free-swinging hooks. I am particularly fond of swinging-hook jigs in salt water, where the currents give them extra fish-attracting action.

Leadhead jigs come in various shapes and sizes, and they can be used virtually anywhere on virtually any species of fish, from crappies to groupers. Head shape can be important in leadhead jig selection. Some shapes—butterbeans and slopeheads, for example—will sink faster in fast currents, while flattops may be just the thing for waggling through the "skinny" water on the bonefish flats. Some leadhead jigs are designed so they will stand up on the bottom; this is a real help when you are bouncing a jig along a bottom that has a lot of snags or other debris.

Most leadhead jigs have no action whatsoever, except that which is imparted by the energetic angler, but a few wobble or waggle ever so slightly upon retrieve. Gapen's Ugly Bug and the Doctor J line of Spoon-Jigs come about as close as any to having what might almost be called a swimming action. Even so, it is a very slow, very limited action compared to that which might be delivered by a spoon or jig. Leadheads with soft-plastic tails flap enticingly, but they aren't very durable. Sevenstrand's Clout, a leadhead covered by a tough plastic sheath that ends in two sickle tails, swims well, stands up to toothy critters, and can be cast or trolled.

The perfectly balanced leadhead jig will hang horizontally when suspended from the line. You will discover that most hang with their hooks dangling low. This imbalance is more important in vertical jigging than in cast-and-retrieve fishing of jigs. Some anglers use snaps or (perish the thought!) snap-swivels on the end of their line when jig-fishing, but almost any leadhead will work much better if the jig is tied directly to the line. This is especially important in the smaller, lighter sizes used for freshwater fish and for panfish-size species in brackish or salt water.

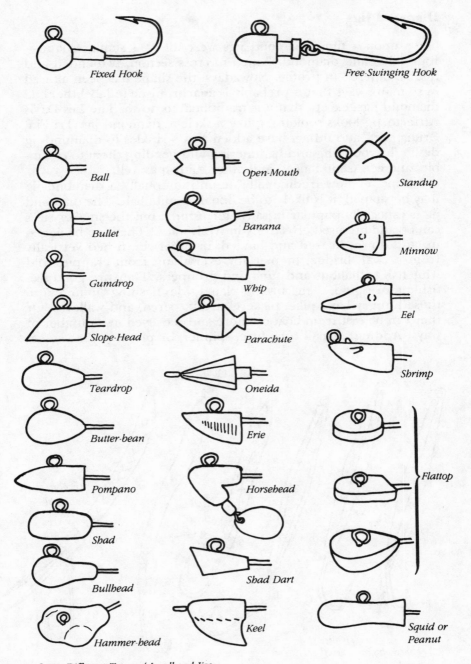

Fixed Hook

Free-Swinging Hook

Ball

Bullet

Gumdrop

Slope-Head

Teardrop

Butter-bean

Pompano

Shad

Bullhead

Hammer-head

Open-Mouth

Banana

Whip

Parachute

Oneida

Erie

Horsehead

Shad Dart

Keel

Standup

Minnow

Eel

Shrimp

Flattop

Squid or Peanut

Some Different Types of Leadhead Jigs

Diamond Jigs

Once upon a time, diamond jigs were all of a similar shape—four-sided and diamond-shaped in cross section, two-ended and double-tapered in profile. Nowadays, the shape has been altered in so many ways that it probably is anachronistic to label them all diamond jigs, except that it is traditional to do so. The Les Davis Attracto Jig looks something like a skeletal diamond jig. Tri-Fin, Bridgeport, and others have added new wrinkles to diamond-jig design by rounding and hammering and bending them to resemble sand eels (sand lances) and other baitfish as well.

No matter how traditionally or untraditionally a diamond jig may be shaped, it is likely to be one dynamite bait. The diamond jig is especially popular in saltwater fishing, but the smaller sizes can be and are used effectively in fresh water. They can be jigged up and down, heaved and hauled, or otherwise fished vertically from a boat, bridge, or pier for everything from crappies and whitefish to halibut and tuna and groupers. They are good ice-fishing lures, too, their chrome-plated sides flashing "minnow" to those hungry bass, pike, pickerel, trout, perch, and walleyes. Or they can be cast from boat or shore and retrieved in a number of ways. Adding a small tube lure, spinner, or piece of yarn some-

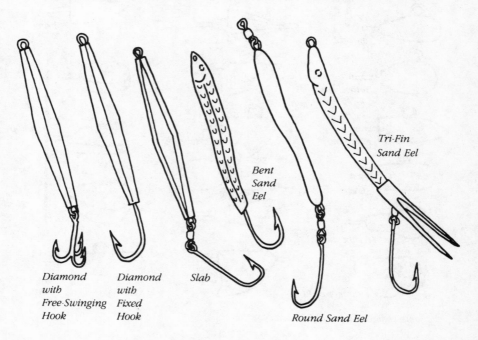

Diamond
with
Free-Swinging
Hook

Diamond
with
Fixed
Hook

Slab

Bent
Sand
Eel

Round Sand Eel

Tri-Fin
Sand Eel

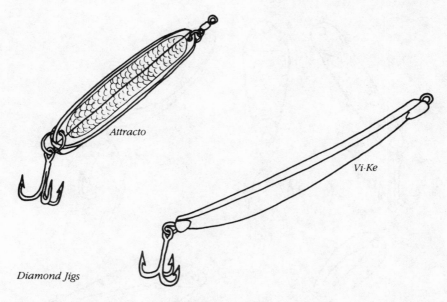

Attracto

Vi-Ke

Diamond Jigs

times enhances a diamond jig's appeal, as can a small piece of natural or stink bait.

The bent jigs known as Norwegian, Scandinavian, Viking, or banana jigs are just variants of diamond jigs. They come in fairly large sizes and are popular along some coasts among those who fish really deep wrecks and reefs for cod and pollock.

Knife-Handle Jigs

As their name implies, these jigs are shaped somewhat like tableknife handles, being thinner and flatter than diamond jigs. Designed to be cast far and to come through the water with a bit of a wobble, most knife-handle jigs are made of solid lead or stainless steel or brass, and they are usually chrome plated, painted, or otherwise finished. The Hopkins lures (both No = Eql and Shorty types) are the best-known examples, and the Kastmaster and similar lures are flatter, wedgier variations on the same theme.

Along the nation's littoral, knife-handle jigs have all but replaced the old block-tin squids that once dominated the surfman's arsenal. Some surfmen with a fondness for tradition call knife-handle jigs "tins" or "squids." When casting distance is more important than swimming action, the knife-handle jig is a good bet. Even when distance isn't necessary, the knife-handle jig can be fished vertically like any other jig.

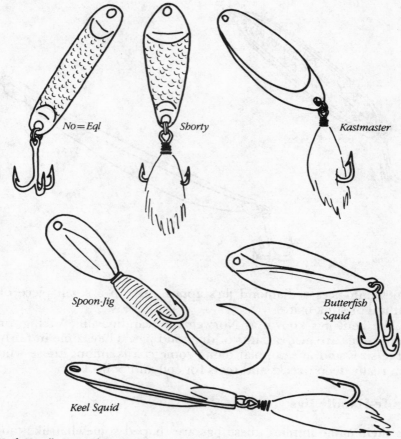

No=Eql
Shorty
Kastmaster
Spoon-Jig
Butterfish Squid
Keel Squid

Knife-Handle Jigs and Tin Squids

Sling Jigs

This is a category few fishermen will recognize, and I confess to having coined the name out of thin air. If these jigs have a generic name, I have yet to hear of it. Included here are the long, slender, thin lead jigs that will out-cast even the knife-handle jigs: Bagley's Salty Dog Spoon, the Mann-O-Lure, Luhr Jensen's Nordic, Lindy/Little Joe's Yo-Bo, and Arbogast's Triton are excellent examples of the type. Some of these are made of malleable lead, so they can be bent by hand to make them spin or wriggle or dart through the water. It takes some trial-and-error experimentation to get a winning configuration, but the flexibility is a worthwhile plus. Most have painted or plastic finishes, but the Nordic is available in prismatic and phosphorescent finishes as well, both of which can be especially effective under the right conditions. If you haven't tried these sling jigs before, you might want to start with a Salty Dog Spoon because Jim Bagley puts a lot of good angling tips on the back of his package.

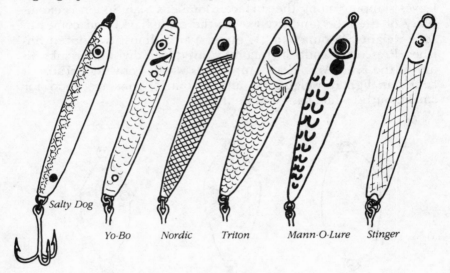

Salty Dog   Yo-Bo   Nordic   Triton   Mann-O-Lure   Stinger

Sling Jigs

Tin Squids

Knife-handle, sling, and even diamond jigs have virtually driven the old block-tin squid into extinction, but as long as there breathes a surf fisherman who ever used a tin squid there will be holdouts. Generally speaking, all that has been said about fishing the previous three jigs applies to tin squids. But there are differences. For one thing, tin is lighter than lead, brass, or stainless, and so won't cast as well. But a tin squid doesn't have to be reeled in as rapidly to keep it from fouling the bottom. Like the malleable-lead sling jigs, tin squids can be bent a bit to change their swimming actions and other hydrodynamic characteristics. But the chief advantage of tin is its satiny luster, not at all like the bright glare of chrome plate. Some fishermen swear that tin's subtler sheen is more attractive to fish, less apt to scare them off.

Maybe so, maybe not, but it sure is prettier. Tin tarnishes rather easily, but it polishes up easily; just rub it in the sand.

Slab Spoons

Despite the name, these are jigs—short, fat, flat lead jigs that can be fished vertically or cast and retrieved. If you have a reel with a high-speed retrieve ratio, you can even get one of these leaden leaves skipping along the surface. Bomber's Slab Spoon is exemplary of the type (and even owns the trademark) and comes in four weights (⅝ ounce to 2½ ounces) and almost two dozen finishes. Prescott's Leadbelly (manufactured by a division or subsidiary of the Fred Arbogast Company) is worth knowing because it comes in lighter weights (⅛ and ⅜ ounce) that are good for smallmouths, white bass, and panfish.

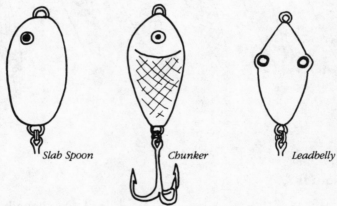

Slab Spoon   Chunker   Leadbelly

Slab Spoons

Ice and Panfish Jigs

These are nothing but tiny trout and panfish hooks to which are attached minuscule bodies (usually flattened in shape so the mini-jigs will flutter as they fall). Sometimes they are embellished by a little tuft of hair or shred of feather, and some have a Lilliputian spinner blade attached. Originally intended for vertical fishing through the ice—and still extremely popular for that purpose—these little jigs are now known to be deadly fish-takers twelve months a year. You needn't fish them vertically, either. With casting weight added as necessary 18 inches or so up the terminal rig, they can be cast and retrieved in stop-and-go fashion, letting them fall and flutter periodically. If you aren't a purist, you can even cast them with a fly rod. Or they can be fished beneath a float (which ought to be twitched fairly frequently), or used as droppers in front of another, larger lure.

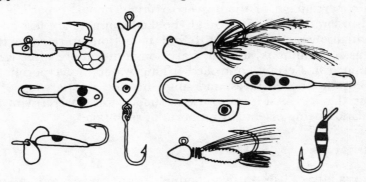

Ice and Panfish Jigs

SPINNERS

The word "spinner" means two things: An accessory spinner blade that is intended to be fished in conjunction with, and as an attractive accessory to, a natural or artificial bait (which use was discussed briefly in Chapter 8); and a lure whose attraction to fish is chiefly a function of the flash and vibrations caused by a rotating spinner blade. The latter definition is the one that concerns us here, although the basic principles of spinner design and rigging can be put to good use when fishing accessory spinners. As for the spinnerbait lures that have become so popular in recent years, they are sufficiently different and important to merit separate consideration in the section immediately following this one.

I am convinced that it is virtually *de rigueur* to use a swivel when fishing spinners. Change that "virtually" to "absolutely" if you are fishing with spinning or spincast equipment. Spinners generate a lot of torque, torque twists lines, and twisted lines foul up fishing. The swivel should be small and efficient. Nothing beats a tiny Sampo ball-bearing swivel for spin-fishing spinners. The swivel can be located almost anywhere in your terminal rig, but it will have less adverse impact on the balance and minnow-imitating look of the spinner if it is tied into the rig about a foot or so above the lure. However, if you are fishing for bass or pike with fairly

heavily weighted spinners—in the range of, say, ⅜ to ¾ ounce—
you can locate the swivel right down at the spinner without untoward consequences. I hate to admit it, but in such cases you
could even get away with attaching the spinner directly to the
tiniest of snap-swivels.

Most spinners come with treble hooks, but I like to switch a
certain percentage of them over to single hooks, especially for
small-stream trout fishing. Single-hooked spinners are less apt to
foul themselves on the cast or to foul the bottom on retrieve; they
are easier to unhook, and they are sometimes more effective in
hooking fish. Certain controlled fishing waters don't permit the
use of gang-hooked lures, and single-hooked spinners are often
among the very best lures to use in such places, the resident fish
population being essentially ignorant of such fakes.

Blade Basics

Spinners attract fish on two channels: sight and sound. A spinner's flash may suggest the glinting scales of an escaping baitfish,
or it may be attractive in the abstract sense of appealing to a fish's
curiosity or triggering a self-defense mechanism. Rotating spinner blades make a churning sound that even the human ear can
hear, but their sonic appeal includes those subaural, but definitely
detectable, vibrations and pressure waves fish can sense with their
lateral-line organs. Spinner blades come in all sorts of sizes,
shapes, styles, finishes, and colors, each of which has its own set of
angling pluses and minuses. It isn't necessary to analyze each,
because certain principles apply across the design spectrum.

BLADE SIZE AND SHAPE

A spinner blade's size and shape affect its rotational speed and
angle, its audiovisual appeal, and its effective fishing speed. Up to
a point, the wider and shorter the blade, the slower it will revolve,
and its rotational angle will be very high. Long, narrow blades
spin faster and tighter than short, wide ones, and are less apt to
be fouled by thin, stringy weeds.

The larger a spinner blade's surface area, the more resistance it
will encounter in moving water. That means it won't sink as fast
or stay down as well in a current, and upon being trolled or retrieved it will ride much higher in the water than will a similarly
weighted blade that is long and narrow. The greater resistance of
the larger blade also means that it will turn more easily and at
slower speeds than will one whose shape is more svelte. However,

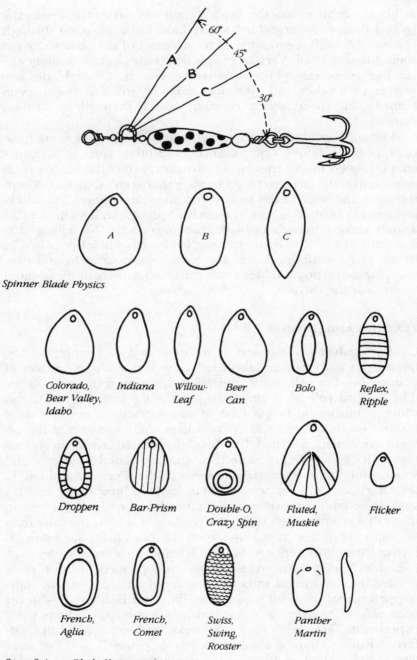

Spinner Blade Physics

Colorado, Bear Valley, Idaho   Indiana   Willow-Leaf   Beer Can   Bolo   Reflex, Ripple

Droppen   Bar-Prism   Double-O, Crazy Spin   Fluted, Muskie   Flicker

French, Aglia   French, Comet   Swiss, Swing, Rooster   Panther Martin

Some Spinner Blade Shapes and Names

as blade size increases the extra weight will offset the geometric factor; thus, very large blades may have to be whipped through the water at high speed, at least at the outset of the retrieve, to get them turning at all. Very large spinner blades have a tendency to act like actionless spoons or planing boards. Some blades are thicker than others, and the thicker blades will sink faster, swim deeper, and need more running speed than their skinnier cousins.

Most spinner blades are symmetrical in design, but some have cups, bubbles, hooks, crimps, kinks, and other sorts of asymmetries designed in. All these little variations affect the blade's rotational and sonic characteristics in ways that aren't easy to assess in the store and which can't be covered adequately here. The wackiest-looking blade I've seen is Grizzly's Susie-Q, which employs an acutely kinked, hyperbolic blade that spins crazily. No telling what it sounds like to fish. Some spinner blades have holes punched in them. These doubtless affect the blade's sonic patterns and produce fish-attracting bubbles when retrieved rapidly in the aerated water near the surface.

PLATINGS AND FINISHES

Gold and silver platings are most often used on spinner blades, but copper and brass are also used, as well as a whole rainbow of painted finishes. All will work well at different times and places. The general rule of thumb is to use the lightest, brightest, and shiniest finishes on bright days or in clear waters, and the dark finishes on dull days or in dingy waters. Alas, sometimes the reverse treatment is called for. Shad fishermen are quite accustomed to using highly reflective, chrome-plated spinners and spoons only on overcast days or early in the morning and late in the afternoon, and copper- and brass-colored lures in the midday sun. Some trout fishermen have noticed that early in the season in small streams, when trout are feeding more on nymphs than on minnows or insects, dark-painted spinner blades are more effective than chrome-plated or even bright-finish brass blades.

Besides the smooth-surface plated and painted finishes, spinner blades come in all sorts of hammered, fluted, waffled, stair-stepped, prismatic, and stippled designs and finishes. I've never been able to analyze the optical physics involved, so do as I do: experiment. Try them all. Each works variously well under different fishing conditions. After a while, you will develop your own hunch system about using the various types.

Selecting Spinners

Whether spinners work better with or without hair, feathers, plastics, pork rinds, or other tail-end tantalizers is a subject fit for gathering around a potbellied stove on a cold winter's night. Spit and chew, chew and spit—it's six on this side of the argument and a half dozen on that. It's the same with beads versus brass bodies on the spinner shaft. Suit yourself; the fish won't mind all that much. Just be sure the size is appropriate to your quarry and the angling conditions, and that you don't upset the spinner's balance by skewering a heavy plastic worm or pork rind on one barb of a treble hook (single-hooked spinners work better with such dressings). If what you have selected doesn't work, try another type. One thing is certain: If there are fish about, and if you are trying hard and intelligently enough, you will catch them on spinners.

Spinners come in a myriad of types and brand names from the tackle companies, but most can be lumped into the categories that follow. Now and then the odd spinner almost defies categorization, but deserves mention—Eppinger's Notangle, for instance. It's just a clevised spinner with a conventional blade painted in red-and-white Daredevle fashion, but its wire shank is bent at a 45-degree angle in front of the blade, and that makes the difference. The bent shank gives the lure a keel-like stability in running, preventing line twist and making the Notangle and Worth's similar Musky Fin better suited than most spinners to trolling. Virtually any spinner type can be so stabilized, as long as its wire shank is long enough. And that usually means making your own.

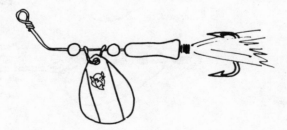

Offset Spinner

Making spinners is easy, and you can save yourself quite a bundle while customizing lures to your own fishing. But don't expect your first ones to look as nice or work as well as the top-brand ones you buy. It takes a little practice. All you need is some wire, split rings, hooks, swivels, clevises, beads or brass bodies, and spinner blades—all of which are available in tackle shops and catalogs. You will need a pair of long-nose pliers, too, preferably round-nose ones; an inexpensive wire-bending jig or one of those hand-cranked wire-forming machines is handy, but not essential. Handcrafting spinners is as easy as twisting eyes in wire and stringing beads.

SWIVELED SPINNERS

The simplest swivels don't even use wire shafts and special parts like clevises, just swivels and split rings. The spinners will work better if they are tiny ball-bearing Sampos, but good-quality barrel swivels will suffice. Hildebrandt's Flicker-Spinner is of this simple type—just two swivels connected in tandem with a split ring, to which is attached the spinner blade. (And a tiny snap-swivel or swivel and split ring can be used effectively to mount spinner blades in terminal positions on the arms of spinnerbaits or trailing behind hooks or lures as flap-tail spinners.) Know that a swiveled blade won't look or sound the same as it would rotating on a clevis. It will be different, but not necessarily better or worse.

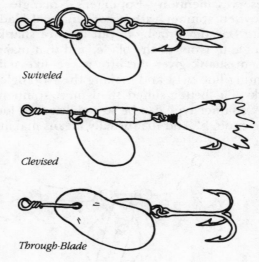

Swiveled

Clevised

Through-Blade

Spinner Types

CLEVISED SPINNERS

Most spinners are made so that their blades swing about a wire shaft on a clevis, which is nothing but a U-shaped piece of metal that gives the blade rotational freedom. Ordinarily, clevises are flanked by brass, glass, or hard-plastic beads, which serve as bearings and keep the rotating clevis from binding against the more angular surfaces of the stationary parts of the lure. At least one brand comes with a third bearing bead in the middle of the clevis's straddled legs. In salt water, stick to glass and plastic bearing beads if you can, because most of the brass ones will corrode and cause binding. Cheap stamped-and-folded clevises are also subject to binding, and their breadth offers some resistance in rotation. Round wire clevises with stamped and drilled ends are generally the best ones to use.

THROUGH-BLADE SPINNERS
Italy's Panther Martin is the best known of the through-blade spinners. In these lures, the blade doesn't swing about the axis of the wire shaft on a clevis or swivel; instead, the shaft passes directly through a hole drilled in the blade near one end. The Panther Martin's blade is also made with a compound curve—part concave and part convex—so that it sets up a unique pattern of sound waves and vibrations. Some Panther Martin copies are on the market now, but I haven't tested them, so you might want to stick to the P.M. brand.

For trout, panfish, and bass, Panther Martins are very good. I haven't tried them much on larger species, but I know that the larger sizes—20 and 28—are not the easiest-turning spinners around; I find I sometimes have to begin the retrieve in a sprint to get the big blades rotating. Panther Martins use thinner wires and generally more corrosion-prone metals than most other top-brand spinners, so don't expect them to last forever, or even for a whole season in salt water.

ROTOR-BLADE SPINNERS
The rotor is a special type of through-blade spinner, and there are two basic rotors: single- and double-wing. The oldest of the lot are propeller blades, which are the simplest of the *double-wing or symmetrical rotors*. They also produce the least interesting sonic-wave patterns, so you will seldom see a spinner that uses a single propeller blade as its sole attractor. Its body shape or hook dressing is likely to be equally or more important in attracting fish, and twin propellers are more sonically attractive than a single blade. After propellers, the most common double-wing rotors are those bell-shaped blades that are usually called bass buzzers by freshwater fishermen, and stingray or manta spinners by saltwater anglers. Like propellers, these blades revolve evenly about their

midline wire axes, setting up regularly pulsed vibrations, which are only moderately attractive to predatory fish that are tuned in on the irregular vibrations of critters in distress. However, the bell-shaped buzzers produce a lot of commotion and even bubbles, and work well at or near the surface where racket is more important than irregular wave pulses in attracting the attention of fish. Recently, some saltwater trolling lures with buzzer blades in front of vinyl skirts have hit the market.

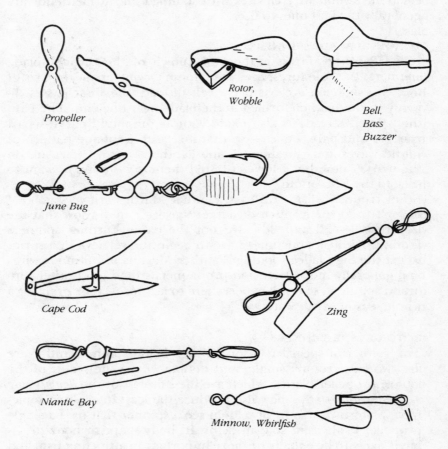

Propeller

Rotor, Wobble

Bell, Bass Buzzer

June Bug

Cape Cod

Zing

Niantic Bay

Minnow, Whirlfish

Rotor-Blade Spinners

The winged drifter or spin bobber is a special type of rotor-blade lure. Because the drifter's body is buoyant, it is best fished on a long dropper line attached a certain distance above a sinker that is trolled or drifted along the bottom. This gives precise depth control. Or the winged drifter can be used in plunking, a form of river fishing made popular by western steelheaders. In plunking, a drifter-and-sinker rig is cast out into a swift current and still-fished. It works best near the edges of eddies. The spin bobber's wings are made of soft rubber, so its sonic allure is very subtle. Its fish appeal is as much visual as aural, and the winged drifter comes in many colors and color combinations. Spin bobbers may be rigged directly on monofilament leaders and droppers as well as on wire shafts and may be used ahead of bucktails, plastic worms, pork rinds, or other artificial or natural baits.

Single-wing or asymmetrical rotors are even more interesting than their double-wing relatives because they set up an irregular wave pulse that apparently resembles the thrashing of forage fish in distress. They also produce an agitated wobble of the shaft and lure. Oldest and probably best known of the single-wing rotors are the June Bug spinner, that perennial favorite of Great Lakes area walleye fishermen, and its saltwater cousin, the Cape Cod or Niantic Bay spinner so beloved of old salts who troll New England's coastal waters for striped bass and pollock. Good as these chestnuts are, I prefer the newer rotors whose blades have a curved pitch to them. Only a few single-wing rotors of this new type are used in the manufacture of ready-made lures—Worth's Nova and Hole-in-One spinners come to mind immediately—but they are easy to make. My favorite fluke rig for casting into inlets employs a single-wing rotor blade in front of two gold or red beads and a bucktail-dressed single hook that carries a so-called "fluke sandwich" of sand eel and a strip of either squid or pork rind (or a plastic worm in a baitless pinch). Aggressive summer flounders love this combination of aural, visual, and olfactory treats, and (knock on wood!) I've not yet been skunked or even outfished at an inlet while using this rotor-activated terminal rig.

TANDEM SPINNERS AND COWBELLS
Some spinners come equipped with more than one blade, and the extra thrashing can help in some cases and be a hindrance in others. Twin spinners mounted in tandem so that they rotate in opposite directions can help prevent torque and line twist; a good thing in trolling especially. Probably the widest use of multiple

blades, though, is in attracting the attention of fish to a primary lure that is trolled behind a string of spinner blades. In the Great Lakes and Pacific Northwest especially, these lake trolls or cowbells are very popular for trolling salmon and lake trout. Some of the multibladed lake trolls use "regular" spinner blades like the Indiana and Colorado, but numerous special blades have been developed for these cowbells, among them the Ford fender and Doc Shelton. The trailing lure can be a streamer, vinyl squid, whole minnow, cut bait, or almost anything else, but it is essential that swivels be used—at least one aft of the cowbell and one forward. And it is a good idea to use a trolling rudder, keeled sinker, or some other stabilizing weight.

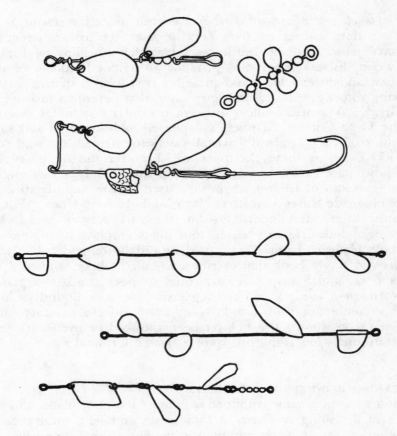

MultiBlade Spinners: Tandems and Cowbells

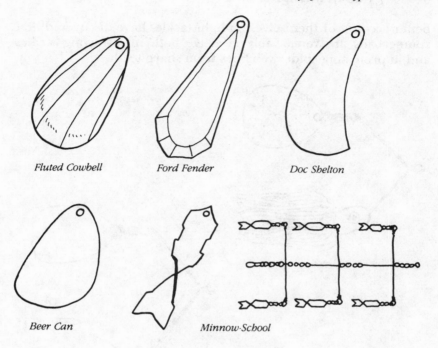

Fluted Cowbell   Ford Fender   Doc Shelton

Beer Can   Minnow-School

Special Cowbell or Lake Troll Blade
Designs

SPINNERBAITS

Were it not for the phenomenal success of plastic worms in recent
years, I suspect that spinnerbaits would be the hottest "new" lures
around. They aren't really new, though. The jig-and-spinner has
been around for years, and the spinnerbait is nothing but an adaptation. In both cases, a Y- or V-shaped wire form is used to
separate a spinner blade and a jig body. If the wire form has a
spinner blade at the end of one long arm and a snap closure at
the other, it's a jig-and-spinner; if the jig body is molded right
onto the wire form, it's a spinnerbait. For brevity, I'm going to call
them all spinnerbaits. However you decide to call them, they are
deadly. It is difficult to imagine a more universally effective lure.
Few saltwater anglers use spinnerbaits, and I don't know of many
that are made big enough, strong enough, and durable enough to
withstand the rigors of saltwater fishing, but it is easy to make
your own. And pike and pickerel fishermen who like to use light
lines and leaders (the smaller members of the *Esox* tribe give a

better account of themselves on light tackle) have discovered that spinnerbaits are remarkably effective both in attracting strikes and in protecting spiderweb lines from sharp teeth.

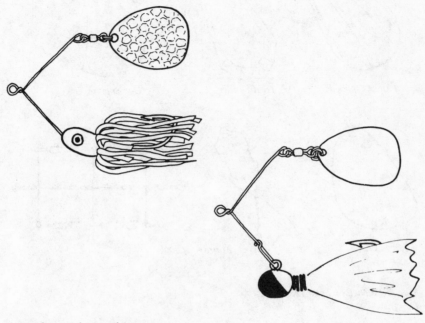

Spinnerbait and Jig and Spinner

Spinnerbaits can be trolled or retrieved steadily at various speeds, but they are at their best when fished in stop-and-go fashion so that they yo-yo through the water. The spinner blades flutter nicely on the drop, when many fish like to attack lures anyway, and wary gamefish that might not strike a falling jig will often go for a fluttering spinnerbait. When retrieved very rapidly, a spinnerbait can be made to whir and slosh noisily along the surface, a technique called bass buzzing that is very effective in and around shoalwater weed beds. I can't say enough good things about spinnerbaits; when things get really slow, I can almost always count on a spinnerbait to produce *something*.

Because of their wire forms, spinnerbaits are fairly weedless and they are stable enough to be fished without a swivel. However, although a spinnerbait won't cause line twist, it won't allow reel-induced twist to remove itself, so always use a swivel when fishing with spinning, spincast, or other fixed-spool reels.

Single-Blade Spinnerbaits

This is the standard spinnerbait, which can be used most of the time. The blade may be attached to the upper arm of the wire form on a clevis, or it may trail from the end of that arm on a swivel. The blade mountings affect the lure's performance. The clevis-mounted blade will swing in a wider arc and generate a busier audiovisual profile, making it the choice for trolling and steady retrieves. But the more flexible swiveled blade will flutter more limply on the drop, making it my choice for yo-yo fishing in deeper water.

In most cases, the wire form is V- or Y-shaped, but in some cases it's shaped more like the number 7, with the upper arm horizontal. The shape makes little difference. More important is the distance between spinner blade and hook. All spinnerbaits are pretty weedless, but the weedlessness is enhanced the closer the turning blade comes to the hook spear. Some anglers like to bend the upper arms of their spinnerbaits so that the turning blade gives the hook a little whack on every rotation; they figure the ticking sound adds to the lure's appeal.

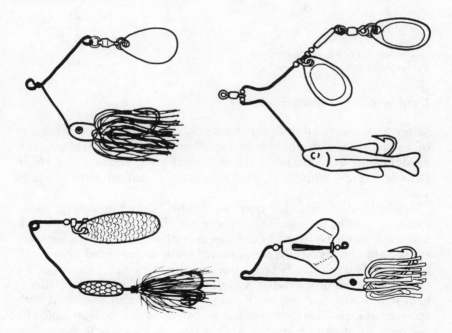

Spinnerbait Forms

Speaking of weedlessness in spinnerbaits, there is a very simple way to affix a quick-change weed guard onto the fixed-jig type of spinnerbait. All you need is a small rubber band. Attach the elastic to the attachment eye loop in the center of the wire form using a girth hitch, then stretch the band and loop it behind the hook barb. You'll rarely snag a spinnerbait so modified.

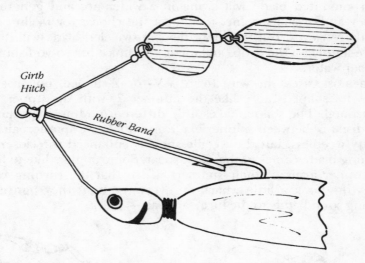

Spinnerbait Made Weedless by Stretching Rubber Band Behind Hook Barb

Double-Blade Spinnerbaits

When maximum commotion seems in order to get the attention of a jaded fish, a double-bladed spinnerbait can be just the ticket. Hildebrandt even makes a three-bladed spinnerbait—the Hilde Double Eagle—which employs a forward-mounted rotor blade as well.

Actually, there are two types of double-bladed spinnerbaits on the market. On the one hand, there are those spinnerbaits which use a normal wire form, to the top arm of which are attached two spinner blades; typically, the forward blade is mounted on a clevis and the aft blade trails from the arm on a swivel. On the other hand, some double-bladed spinnerbaits use a tripodlike, three-arm wire form, the two upper arms of which are festooned with spinner blades. The latter type is somewhat less weedless than the former, but it can be rigged so that the blades bang into one another as they turn.

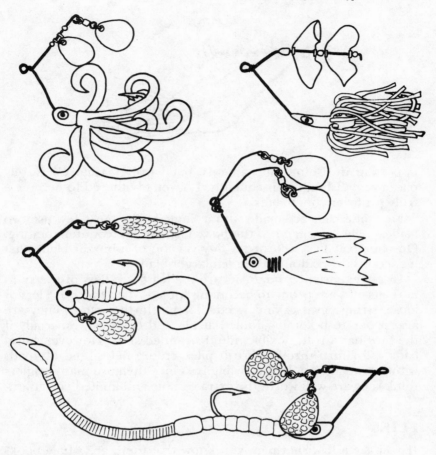

MultiBlade Spinnerbaits

Buzzbaits

Some bass fishermen call all spinnerbaits buzzbaits, because they can be buzzed along the surface with the aid of a high-speed reel and some elbow grease. The term is more properly restricted to those spinnerbaits which use bell-shaped, rotor-type blades. The buzzbait is designed to be fished with a rapid, steady retrieve. It isn't nearly as effective as a yo-yo lure. What the buzzbait lacks in versatility it makes up for in its effectiveness in rapid prospecting around weed beds, brush piles, and stump fields. Covering the maximum amount of water in the minimum amount of time is

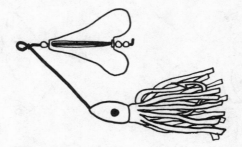

Buzzbait

important in fishing tournaments, but I prefer a more leisurely pace in my fishing. Consequently, I haven't bothered to become a truly proficient buzzbaiter.

Most buzzbaits are made with a single blade, but a few use two blades—always rigged so the buzzer blades are counter-rotating. One buzzbait I've seen had a tiny version of a buzzer blade that turned inside a cutout in a much larger blade.

In my experience, buzzbaits are the least weedless of the spinnerbaits and are prone to becoming fouled when there are lots of loose, stringy grasses and weeds floating in the water. They are also prone to becoming fouled at the end of a cast, especially if the lure has a soft, flexible, multi-stranded skirt. However, buzzbaits will churn through brush piles, stump fields, and lily pads without much trouble. Really big bass love them, so many anglers think they are well worth the extra trouble and limited versatility.

FLIES

If you are a fly-fisherman, you know that there are whole books on selecting and tying flies to match the streamside hatch of insects. And you know that those books haven't exhausted the subject. Besides, I am certainly no expert or authority on fly-fishing. However, every fisherman ought to know a little something about flies, which are terrific fish-catchers when used as droppers auxiliary to another lure or natural bait. Flies can be fished as primary lures on spinning, spincast, or casting tackle as long as they are trailed behind a spinning bubble, float, or surface lure on a length of ultralight leader material.

Dry Flies

Simply stated, these are flies that float. Tied to resemble insects just emerging from the nymph stage and about to take flight (or, alternatively, ephemeral insects that have just dropped onto the water at the end of their brief lives), dry flies are what matching the hatch is all about. They are usually tied with hackles to make them float high on the surface film of the water, but they also need to be treated with a special water-repelling dope to keep them from getting waterlogged. In flycasting, it is also necessary to use a foam-core or floating fly line. With other tackle, the floating bubble, bobber, or lure accomplishes the same thing.

Accuracy of placement and delicacy of presentation are the keys to fishing dry flies. Cast upstream of your quarry and let the current carry the fly down, twitching it ever so slightly now and then.

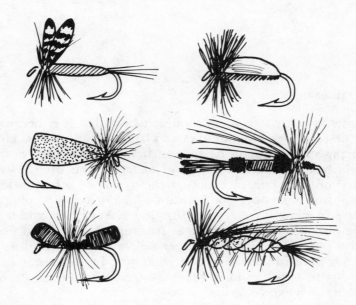

Dry Flies

Wet Flies

Wet flies are flies that sink. They aren't nearly as popular as dries, streamers, and nymphs in North America, but they are really big in Britain. On a trout-fishing trip to Scotland's Orkney Islands a few years ago, I discovered that Scots use almost nothing but wet flies, usually fished in threesomes on very long leaders. Effective but not a lot of fun, I think.

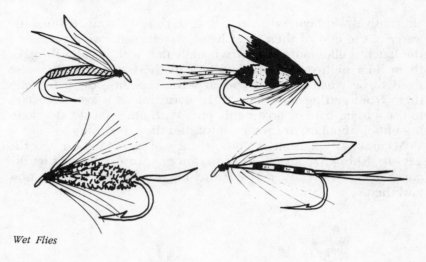

Wet Flies

Streamers

Purists say that streamers shouldn't be called flies because they are tied to resemble minnows and baitfish, not insects. However you pigeonhole them, be sure to have some streamers in your tackle box, no matter what kind of tackle you use. A streamer fished on a fly line, or trailing behind a jig or other underwater lure, or on a dropper line beneath a float or popping plug, is one of the deadliest lures around. Anglers after salmon and big trout have discovered that a streamer trailing behind a good wobbling spoon is a terrific bait. Eppinger sells a combination lure called the Sagamore Flasher Fly that is nothing but an ultrathin Daredevle-type spoon and a trailing streamer. It's great, but it's cheaper to make your own.

In salt water, dropper flies (usually streamers, to imitate sand eels and other small forage fish) are particularly effective. The largest striped bass ever taken in the surf—a 73-pounder—was taken on a dropper fly trailing from an eel rig. In the spring, droppered streamers will take almost any species that can be lured to a bogus bait, and throughout the year they will catch many kinds of fish. Among the commercially available saltwater droppers, I particularly like the Droppas sold by a Connecticut company called Angling Aids.

When fishing streamers in fresh water on spinning tackle, I find they are most effective, especially in rocky streams, when

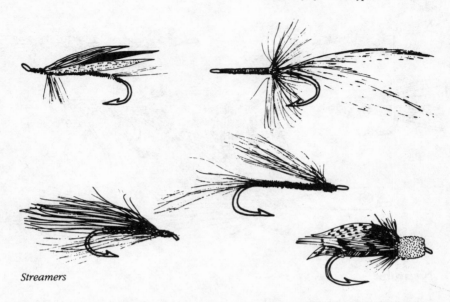

Streamers

rigged so they will drift or bounce along the bottom. The Muddler Minnow—a Don Gapen invention that looks like a cross between a bucktail (or marabou) streamer and a hair bug—is a real killer when fished this way, on everything from trout to bass and Atlantic salmon.

Bugs

There are two kinds of bugs: popping bugs and just plain bugs. Popping bugs—also called fly-rod poppers, bass bugs, and bass poppers—probably are the best known of the fly-rod bugs, even if some of them are made to resemble tiny frogs. Most are made with cork or sponge bodies, but a few are tied from other materials. Whenever fish are busting bait on the surface, but won't pay attention to your surface-disturbing or popping plugs, try trailing a fly-rod popping bug behind your plug on a five-foot leader. Dynamite.

The nonpopping bugs, which are known by a variety of names —hair bugs, for example—come in a variety of styles, shapes, and sizes. Some imitate insects, others frogs, others mice, and still others things I've never seen in real life. Fish love them. Perhaps the most famous line of hair bugs and popping bugs are those sold by the Gaines Company, but there are plenty of fine competitors.

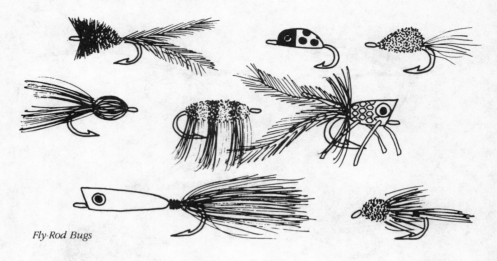

Fly-Rod Bugs

Nymphs

Like wet flies, nymphs sink and are sometimes fished on sinking fly lines, only this time the flies are made to resemble the larval or pupal stages rather than the adult insects. True nymphs are tied, like flies, but so many molded-plastic "nymphs" are on the market that confusion reigns in terminology.

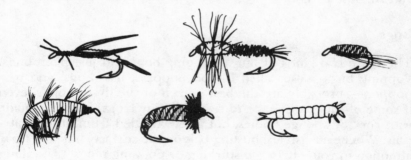

Nymphs

Nymphing, a special technique of fly-fishing on stream bottoms with nymphs, has swept parts of the country and has become a real specialty in Rocky Mountain streams. A good nymph fisherman can take trout in weather that would be considered a bit too cold by the average deer hunter; as long as the stream isn't iced over, it's fishable. In late winter and early spring, nymphs dominate trout diets in most streams, so smart opening-day anglers will forgo the dry flies and fish nymphs instead, either on a fly-rod or on bottom-bouncing terminal rigs with other tackle.

Weighted Flies

In flycasting, the weight of the fly is incidental; it's the fly line that is being cast. But some nymphs are slightly weighted so they will sink faster or deeper. Really heavily weighted flies are not intended for flycasting but for trolling and for casting on spinning, spincasting, and conventional tackle. Sometimes it is difficult to establish a fine line between weighted flies and jigs. But most jigs are made on special hooks, with the hook barb extending, scorpion-like, upward. Weighted flies are made on more conventional hooks, usually with the barbs hanging below the body of the fly.

Most weighted flies resemble heavy streamer flies. Optic-type flies, with large, round, plastic eyes, are intermediate between wet flies and weighted flies. The new epoxy flies that have become so popular on the bonefish and permit flats look something like the Phillips Wiggle Jig (a dynamite spinning lure on those same skinny waters), but they might be considered slightly weighted flies of a special type. Anglers other than flycasters will find weighted flies to be very useful, either as primary lures or as droppers.

Keel Flies

Keel flies are usually tied as streamers. They deserve separate mention because of their special hooks and their weedlessness. I don't know whether Wright & McGill invented the type, but their Eagle Claw keel hook certainly popularized the concept. The keel-fly hook has its shank bent or stepped so that the short, upper portion of the shank just below the eye is directly in line with the point. The weight distribution of a properly tied keel fly causes it to ride in the water with the point up, which makes it nearly weedless and snag-free.

The keel-fly hook's shape also, in the opinion of many, makes it less than an efficient hooker, so a lot of keel-fly fishermen sacri-

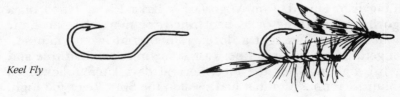

Keel Fly

fice a little of the weedlessness and some of the strength of the hook by bending the spear so the point is raked slightly upward.

Keel flies are fun to fish in treacherous waters because you can spend more time hunting for and battling fish and less time coping with snags. The keel fly makes an excellent dropper fly when casting to heavy cover or bouncing along rocky or weedy bottoms.

Plastic "Flies"

Whether a cleverly molded piece of plastic should be called a fly is an interesting linguistic question. More interesting to most fishermen, however, is how well they catch fish. Many of the best ones imitate nymphs and are so classified, but others ape ants, crickets, grasshoppers, spiders, grubs, caterpillars, horn worms, shrimp, crayfish, frogs, and minnows. At some point, the size and weight of the things disqualify them as flies, at which point they must be considered ultralight lures. In any event, they are very good and can be used to good effect by all anglers, not merely the wavers of the long wand.

Several years back, a fellow named Walt Rogers invented the Frisky Fly, a hard plastic "fly" that somewhat resembles a paper airplane in shape. On the retrieve, it comes through the water with a tight, almost violent wiggle, one that apparently sends out enticing sonic vibrations. After tiring of the tackle business, Rogers sold the Frisky Fly to Luhr Jensen and Sons. Then Walt got mad because he thought Jensen was inadequately promoting the Frisky Fly. So Walt invented the Bingo Bug. It looks like a Frisky Fly with a more rounded nose and with some chicken feathers molded into the wings. And darned if it isn't an improvement.

Both plastic flies can be trolled behind a sinker, cast on a spinning rod about 18 to 24 inches down from a split shot or two, or fished "as is" with a fly rod. Sinking or sink-tip lines work best, because the Frisky Fly and the Bingo Bug both have a tendency to plane and spin when fished in a fast current on a floating line. Either way they are pure hell to cast, being more than a little aerodynamic. Casting, you will look like a fool. Until you start catching fish. One day on Yugoslavia's Krka River, I tied on a Bingo Bug after three of us had fished for more than an hour without a strike. I caught a dozen rainbows in twenty minutes, often getting several strikes per cast, sometimes having three and four fish fighting over the lure. Several days later, following a ten-hour torrential rain that had swollen the Sora River too high, fast, and muddy for fishing, I took two of three brown trout we spotted under some willows, and no one else had so much as a strike or follow. Frisky Flies *should,* but probably won't, be available in your tackle shop; you have to order Bingo Bugs from Walt Rogers: 2803 Homedale Road, Klamath Falls, Oregon 97603.

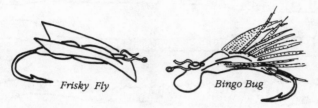

Frisky Fly   Bingo Bug

Plastic Flies

PLASTIC WORMS

The plastic worm has been the cause of the biggest tackle revolution since the introduction of spinning and spincast reels. Actually, though, plastic worms are a little older than fixed-spool reels, and ancestral rubber worms were listed in the Sears, Roebuck catalog at the turn of the century. But spinning tackle caught on first. Ironically, the popularity of the plastic worm among largemouth bass fishermen has probably done more than anything else to revive the popularity of the old levelwind multiplying (or "conventional") reel. The plastic worm has been a real sales boon to the tackle industry. As bassmen developed new and specialized techniques for fishing plastic worms, tackle companies have developed and marketed special rods, reels, hooks, sinkers, lines, you name it. I doubt that even the modern bass boat would be quite so popular were it not for plastic worms.

Before there were soft plastics, artificial fishing worms were made from rubber. But they were used primarily in saltwater fishing, and they weren't very good. For one thing, they smelled terrible. Texan Nick Creme pretty much singlehandedly invented the soft-plastic worm back in the early 1940s, and he got the idea one day while fishing, not for bass, but for steelhead. It was while he was watching those anadromous rainbow trout turn and follow the "milk" trails that are let into the water by spawn sacs of salmon eggs that Creme decided the rancorous scent trails of rubber worms just wouldn't do. So he set out to invent a better worm. Du Pont and others gave him advice and some chemicals, but it was Nick Creme who mixed and stirred and field-tested

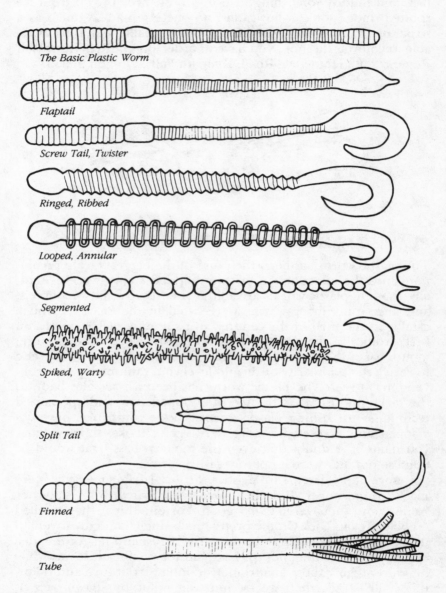

The Basic Plastic Worm

Flaptail

Screw Tail, Twister

Ringed, Ribbed

Looped, Annular

Segmented

Spiked, Warty

Split Tail

Finned

Tube

Plastic Worm Types

until he got it right. His first plastic worms weren't as good as the ones his company makes today, and they didn't revolutionize sportfishing overnight. But Creme kept developing and improving and proselytizing, and it paid off.

In recent years, all sorts of technological advances have resulted in numerous changes to the plain old plastic worm. In general, today's worms are softer, more flexible, and more appealing than the earlier worms. Some, following the path Tom Mann blazed with his Jelly Worm, have fish-attracting or human-masking scents and oils molded into them. Lately, all sorts of flaptails, screwtails, ridges, loops, annular rings, spikes, gimcracks, and gewgaws have been appended to the basic worm. For day-in, day-out bass fishing, though, it is hard to beat Creme's Scoundrel or Mann's Jelly Worm. Flaptailed and sickle-tailed worms are very good, but in waters that support pickerel and pike as well as bass you will lose a lot of worm tails. Even panfish will drive you nuts, nibbling at those fluttering sickle tails, particularly if they are fluorescent-colored. Fish them slowly enough, however, and you won't have much trouble. On balance, I like the active tails.

As for the newest, most outrageously modified plastic worms, I am of two minds about them. Some are very, very good, and some are horrid. The others fall somewhere in between. Knight's Tube Worm is especially good, but fairly expensive. Burke's Hookworm and Rebel's Ringworm are excellent examples of the "warty" worm types, but some of the other looped, ridged, lumped, and warted worms are a lot less active than their names and advertising claims suggest.

There are several ways to rig plastic worms, but Texas-rigging wins hands-down in my estimation. The virtual weedlessness of the Texas rig enables you to fish plastic worms in waters you simply can't fish with most other lures. You can fish a Texas-rigged plastic worm right in the middle of the weed beds and brush piles that used to be the stuff of anglers' nightmares. As for more open waters, where Carolina-rigged or gang-rigged plastic worms might enjoy a slight edge in action and fish appeal, I think it's more fun to fish plugs, spoons, spinners, or jigs.

In case you have been asleep in recent years, here is how to **Texas-rig** a plastic worm. First, slide a bullet-shaped slip sinker or tiny egg sinker onto your line. Next, tie on your favorite worm hook—I like the bent-shank models. Now, skewer the worm onto the hook in the method prescribed for the type of hook you are using. To save a thousand words, here is a picture on the next page.

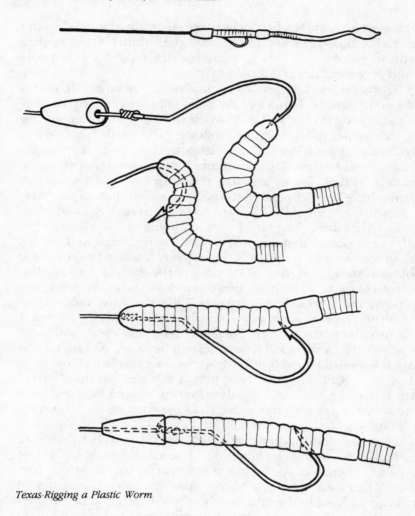

Texas-Rigging a Plastic Worm

The plastic worm must lie straight for the best action, and that usually means being very careful when it comes to inserting the hook point the second time. Note, too, that the hook point doesn't quite come through the worm the last time—unless you are fishing Ringworms, Hookworms, or other warty worms, in which cases the point can protrude a little.

To fish a Texas-rigged plastic worm, cast to cover, let the worm sink to the bottom (watching the line for the slightest sign of abnormal behavior, which often means a bass has sucked the worm in on its fall), then retrieve very, very slowly. You can crawl the worm along the bottom at a snail's pace, or you can hop it along very slowly. High-flotation worms seem to work best, because they look the most active. Plastic-worming will take some getting used to, and you can expect to miss a few strikes in the beginning. You will be unaware of even more strikes that happen very gently. It is a bit frustrating, but it is worth being patient because you will get a lot of strikes in the end.

If, while retrieving a plastic worm through weeds or other cover, you feel a little resistance, there are two schools of thought as to what comes next. Anglers who subscribe to the big-bang theory say to set the hook hard, right now! Some of those "strikes" will turn out to be weeds or snags, and you will lose some terminal tackle, but enough of them will turn out to be trophy fish to make the risk worthwhile. More cautious anglers say you should crank the line taut, but not too tight, and watch to see whether the line just sits there or moves a little. If it moves, set the hook *hard* and hold on for a real scrap; if it doesn't move, assume it's a snag and ease it free. The choice is yours.

When you set the hook, remember that you must drive the point through the plastic worm and into the fish's jaw. So set it hard, harder than you would when fishing another kind of lure. And keep your worm hooks filed especially sharp. The softer the worm, the easier it will be to set the hook properly, but the more likely it is that the rig will get hung up on a snag. Remember, Mother Nature serves no free lunches. Bagley's Hardhead worm is an interesting compromise; it is a blend of two plastics: the tail end is super soft, for maximum action, but the head end is a bit harder, for maximum weedlessness.

The typical worm rod, whether spinning or casting, has a stiff tip section, to make hook-setting easier and surer and to give the angler maximum bite-detecting sensitivity. Because of the need for sensitivity and power when fishing plastic worms, stay away from ultralimp, stretchy monofilament lines. Braided Dacron or Micron has plenty of sensitivity and power, but some of the best worm-fishing waters have too many abrasive hazards for braided line. Use new Stren or another abrasion-resistant mono with controlled stretch. Down South, where plastic-worming is a way of life, virtually everyone uses multiplying-reel casting gear. However, plastic worms can be fished on spinning tackle if the rod is stiff, and even some of the bass pros spinfish their plastic worms on occasion. If you choose to go the spinning route, you will wind up with a lot of twisted line (you can't use a swivel in a Texas rig), so plan on changing line fairly often.

Three worm-rigging variants are worth brief mention. If you toothpick the slip sinker in place some distance up the line, or use a fixed sinker, the Texas rig becomes a **Carolina rig.** This is a good way to fish a high-flotation plastic worm at some specific distance above the bottom or just along the upper fringes of a submerged weed bed. Remove the sinker entirely, and your **floating worm rig** becomes a super way of slithering worms across the surface of thick stands of lily pads and other aquatic weeds. Use a standard weedless hook—or even two or three such hooks rigged in tandem—pierced all the way through the worm, and you have a **worm-and-swivel rig,** so called because you tie a swivel into the line a foot or so above the worm. This rig is fished a little faster than Texas or Carolina rigs. I like the Texas rig so much, I haven't had much experience with worm-and-swivel fishing, but I have heard that this worm rig catches more but smaller fish than Texas and Carolina rigs. I wonder why?

Inevitably, the wear and tear of angling will take its toll of torn and tattered worms. The only good plastic worm is a new, fresh, untorn plastic worm. Period. So, once you get the hang of or get hung up on plastic-worm fishing, you will probably want to buy your worms in bulk bags rather than those three- and six-worm cards, to save money.

Plastic worms come in various thicknesses, a factor that affects action, hook setting, and the optimum hook size. The Jelly Worm, for example, is a bit thicker than average, a difference that is especially noticeable in the larger sizes. If you normally select a 1/0 Sproat hook for a worm of average thickness, you might want to go to a 2/0 for a Jelly Worm. And set the hook harder. The Wiggler Worm from Hanger Lure Co., a Southern California outfit that deserves nationwide renown, is super skinny; that gives it super action and allows the use of slightly smaller hooks than normal. If you want a super-active worm, but want to use a large hook, consider Jack Davis's Whip Worm, which has a round forward section but a long, thin, flattened tail section. It's a nice compromise.

Length makes a difference, too. Down South, a 6-inch worm is a small one. Up in New England, 4 inches is small, 6 inches normal. In the monster-bass lakes around San Diego, some guys think an 8-inch worm is a runt. Generally, the larger the bass, the longer the worm and the bigger the hook. However, stream fish generally prefer smaller, shorter worms than lake and reservoir fish. Some segmented worms—Burke's Buckshot, for example—are designed to be shortened by pinching off one or more seg-

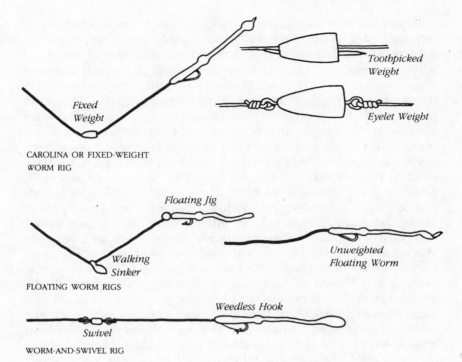

Toothpicked
Weight

Fixed
Weight

Eyelet Weight

CAROLINA OR FIXED-WEIGHT
WORM RIG

Floating Jig

Walking
Sinker

Unweighted
Floating Worm

FLOATING WORM RIGS

Weedless Hook

Swivel

WORM-AND-SWIVEL RIG

Other Plastic-Worm Rigs

ments from the forward end. (Never shorten a worm by cutting off its active tail end.) Virtually all plastic worms can be shortened by trimming the head end; the segmented worms are just designed for trimming in a hurry.

Color seems to be a more important variable in plastic worms than in most other lures, something I have experienced but can't rationally explain. Maybe it's because they are fished so slowly. At any rate, black, dark purple, blue, and red worms are the most popular colors, but smoke gray and the color known either as marmalade or motor oil are real comers. As for scents and flavors, I wouldn't worry too much about which ones to offer. Even Tom Mann, whose Jelly Worms started the whole flavored-worm business, admits that the scents do more to mask offensive human odors than they do to attract fish *per se*. In any event, scented worms are popular. There are even a lot of bottled scents, oils, and smelly potions on the market for doctoring unscented plastic worms. Anise oil is an old favorite, and budget-minded anglers would do well to try plain old cod-liver oil from the drugstore.

If you are new to plastic-worming, let me warn you that these new soft plastics are chemically incompatible with some, maybe even most, hard plastics. The soft worms will dissolve the hard stuff, so keep your plastic worms away from the plastic plugs in your tackle box. Watch those painted jig heads, too, because some use pigmented plastics rather than old-fashioned paint. As for the plastic tackle box itself, don't worry unless you have a dime-store cheapie or an old one (five or more years old, say), in which case it might not be made of one of the new worm-proof plastics.

Of the dozens of other things I could say about plastic worms —all of them good—I'll restrict myself to just one: experiment. Good as the Texas-rigged plastic worm is for bass, bogus worms can be fished in numerous ways to take many other kinds of fish. Most freshwater fish will take an intelligently fished plastic worm, and so will a lot of saltwater species. Gator Tails and big Jelly Worms are especially good in the salt. As long as there is some movement of or through the water to give it a flutter, a plastic worm can be used to take almost anything that swims. Plastic worms can be fished on all sorts of terminal rigs, on leadhead jigs, with popping corks, on single-hooked spoons and spinners. (Some anglers even impale worms on treble-hooked lures, but mine always rotate or behave strangely when so adorned.) Wherever you might be accustomed to using a pork rind, try a plastic worm. The action won't be the same as the rind's, but it usually will be as attractive. One interesting exception: I haven't yet tried a plastic worm that works as well as a strip of pork rind on the weedless Johnson Silver Minnow spoon.

OTHER SOFT-PLASTIC BAITS

A lot of other soft, wriggly creatures are made in soft plastics that are the same as or similar to those used in making artificial worms. Among the closest of the plastic worm's kin are the various eels, salamanders, snakes, leeches, and so on. Many of them can be rigged and fished as if they were plastic worms, with similar results. DeLong's Sneel and Bill Norman's Snatrix are good examples; both are especially good when rigged without a sinker and snaked across the top of a bed of lily pads. But others are made to be fished differently. Those made expressly for saltwater fishing are often made of plastic that is stiffer, harder, and more durable than that used for bass worms, and must be rigged differently. Creme's Sandworm, for example, is almost as soft and flexible as a freshwater worm, but its size and shape require that it be rigged with two or three tandem hooks, each with its point exposed. It's hard enough setting the hook on a bluefish or striped bass without having to drive the point through a mass of plastic first.

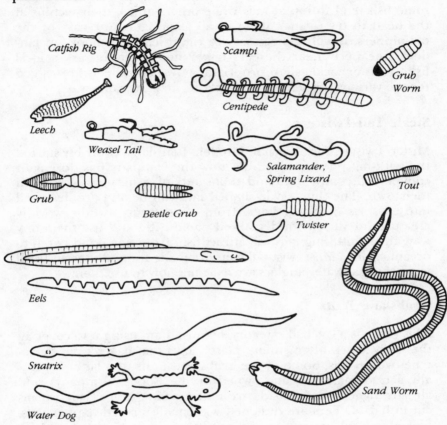

Catfish Rig

Scampi

Grub Worm

Leech

Centipede

Weasel Tail

Salamander, Spring Lizard

Tout

Grub

Beetle Grub

Twister

Eels

Snatrix

Water Dog

Sand Worm

Other Plastic Creepy-Crawlies

Eels

All sorts of plastic eels are available, but the best of the lot might still be one of the oldest—the Alou Eel. The action plate or wobble head gives the Alou Eel enough weight for surfcasting and enough action to fool almost anything that swims. Rebel and other tackle manufacturers turn out essentially similar eels. Some eels are made to be used on leadhead jigs, and therefore have only as much action as an angler gives them. Others, more flexible, can be fished Texas-style or, without any weight, as a skipping balao-type bait for offshore trolling.

The thing to remember when fishing big plastic eels is that some fish tend to nip at tails while others attack their victims at the head to try to suck them in all at once. In the case of the tail-nippers, it will be necessary to rig at least two hooks in tandem, one fairly near the eel's tail. When in doubt, ask a local fisherman or tackle-shop proprietor how natural eels are rigged for the various species. Rig your plastic fake the same way.

Sickle-Tail Twisters

Mister Twister, Inc., down in Minden, Louisiana, probably started the twist-tail phenomenon, but now the company has dozens of commercial competitors and thousands of fishermen who mold their own. The thin, sickle-shaped tails can be and are designed into all sorts of plastic baits, from earthworms to otherworldly creatures of various trademarked names. Rig and use them any way; their fluttering tails will attract fish, from tiny pond perch to oceanic giants. Most twist-tail baits are made for and used in fresh water, but saltwater anglers are learning how to use them.

Grubs and Touts

This really is a catchall category, because I am using it to cover all the fairly short, often stubby, plastic baits that haven't got sickle-type twister tails. Some of the grubs and touts (the latter is actually a trademarked name owned by the Boone Company) sold already rigged on jig heads are nothing but plain plastic worms cut in half. Others are designed with spade-shaped flapper tails, forked tails, all sorts of special configurations to make them wiggle. Beware of bargain-basement imitations, though. Despite their look-alike shapes, some have about as much action as a cigar butt. The good ones flap enticingly. You can't go on looks alone. Hanger's Weasel Tail is one of the crudest looking, but most effective, of the fork-tailed grubs.

Among freshwater fishes, crappies are particularly susceptible to white grubs and touts on leadhead jigs and spinnerbaits of appropriate size. They are so fond of these that you can save money without sacrificing much effectiveness by making your own. Just buy a tube of white bathtub caulking compound, squeeze out varying lengths of the white latex onto sheets of wax paper, and let them dry.

Salamanders and Lizards

Down in the Deep South, a lot of top bassmen swear by "spring lizards," which is Dixieland for newts and salamanders. To accommodate them, tackle companies have developed all sorts of plastic fakes. I must confess that I haven't had much luck with them, not even in ponds where I have seen bass feeding on salamanders rising to the surface. Maybe I'm not fishing them properly.

While some anglers, and perhaps most, Texas-rig their plastic salamanders as if they were worms, others prefer to fish them on leadhead jigs. Some few companies make special jigheads for them; a good example is Hanger's Water Dog Head, a coin-type jig hook.

Crayfish and Shrimp

Plastic crustaceans can also be Texas-rigged, if they are soft enough, but they are more commonly used with leadhead jigs and special weighted hooks. The harder plastic types are molded around hooks; for reasons I cannot understand, many of these are made with their hook points turned down, which makes them snag-prone. There are dozens of shrimp-tailed leadhead jigs on the market, and they all work reasonably well. But down along

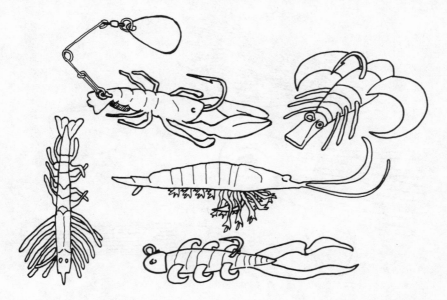

Plastic Crayfish and Shrimp

the Southeast coastline, anglers call them all Salty Dogs, which is fair testimony to Jim Bagley's plastic shrimp of the same name. In fresh water, I really like Burke's Crawspin—a spinnerbait-type lure that features a lifelike, soft-plastic crayfish.

Squids

Applied Oceanographic Corp. used to make a Chumin Squid which had a hollow, pellet-holding, soft-plastic body joined to a specially shaped jig hook. The leadhead was shaped like the forward end of a squid's mantle, fins and all, so it dove and swam when being trolled or retrieved. Too bad it disappeared. Among the ranks of saltwater fishermen, the plastic squid is almost as ubiquitously popular as the plastic worm is among freshwater anglers. And there are almost as many brands, types, styles, shapes, and sizes on the market. Some are leadhead jigs of one sort or another. Others are made to be used without a weighted head. Still others—the so-called vinyl squids—are about midway between molded squids and vinyl skirts in design. All will catch fish well. And for good reason: There is hardly a fish in the sea that doesn't routinely eat squid.

Mold Craft's Squirt Squid is representative of the many commercial examples of the molded-from-life baits that almost per-

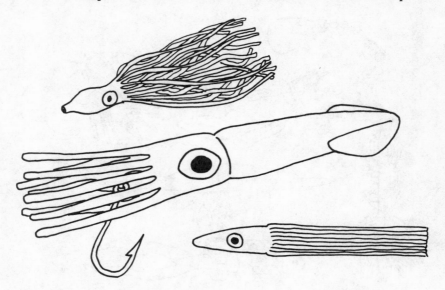

Plastic and Vinyl Squids

fectly resemble the real McCoy. It comes in four sizes, from 6 to 16 inches long, and in a whole array of colors, including a phosphorescent one I like a lot. The Squirt Squid has a hollow central chamber that can be baited with a cotton ball (or even a tampon) soaked in fish oil or one of the newer fish-attracting scents, or that can be used to house one or more egg sinkers for fishing fast or deep. Steve Moreton's M & M Tackle has made spreader-bar squid rigs pretty standard in the giant bluefin tuna fleets. Depending on their size, he rigs from 8 to as many as 21 Squirt Squids (only one of which carries a hook) in a rig.

On the West Coast, salmon fishermen swear by vinyl squids of various sorts. A Martin Twinkle Fly or Grizzly Li'l Octopus trolled behind a rotating flasher or herring dodger is extremely effective on chinooks and coho, and the latter is effective on steelheads when drifted or "plunked" in fresh water. Offshore trollers everywhere use giant-size vinyl skirts called hootchies, often rigging several of them in tandem as a daisy chain of squid baits. Most hootchies are designed for surface trolling, but a few tackle companies have made variants that are intended for fishing deep, either jigged or deep-trolled. The Killer Squid by Fishfinders is an excellent example of the type.

Baitfish

Fished alone, few of the molded plastic baitfish will catch much of anything; they just don't have the action that turns fish on. But plenty of molded minnows have been incorporated into lures of great effectiveness particularly in jigs. Burke's Wig-Wag Minno, the Blue Fox Vibrotail Minnow Jig, and Mister Twister's Sassy Shad are among the most dependable fish-catchers in my tackle box. As for the spinners that incorporate molded minnows, I have more luck if I remove the fakes and replace them with the real thing.

Molded baitfish can be trolled with telling effect on marlin and other big-game species, as long as they are rigged to skip along the surface with a lot of splash and commotion. Honestly, though, I think it is the surface commotion rather than the molded likeness that attracts the fish.

Blue Fox Tackle is importing the Red Gill lures from Cornwall, England. Over there, these lures, which are made to resemble sand eels and pilchards (which are closely related to herrings or sardines), are used mostly in deep jigging, but American fishermen are having all sorts of fun trolling and casting them. Red

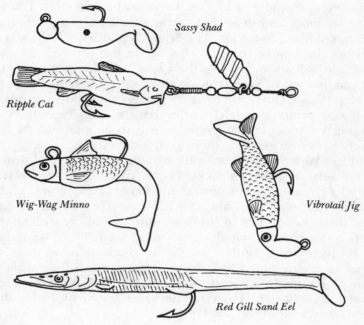

Sassy Shad

Ripple Cat

Wig-Wag Minno

Vibrotail Jig

Red Gill Sand Eel

Plastic Baitfish

Gills look real, but more importantly, their thin, floppy tails with the patented tip shape are effective. Because they resemble needlefish, halfbeaks, and sauries, big Red Gill Sand Eels can be trolled offshore for such game fish as dolphin, sailfish, and white marlin.

Burke's Flex Plugs, sort of midway between soft-plastic baitfish and plastic plugs, have a lot of the former's feel and the latter's action. (No matter how good a plastic lure *looks*, remember what Duke Ellington wrote: "It don't mean a thing if it ain't got that swing!") The topwater Flexes are available in weedless versions, a doubly nice idea from Bing McClellan.

Frogs and Mice

Most of the plastic and rubber frogs might better be classified as soft plugs, because the best of them are designed to kick and swim and otherwise carry on like a frog-imitating plug. But they are plastic, so they are pigeonholed here. I don't happen to be a frog-bait fisherman of any great experience, but from my eavesdropping on angling conversations around the country I think I can safely report that Bill Plummer's Super Frog is the odds-on favorite in the field. It really is a dandy lure, with its high-flotation body, its clever weedless hook, and its thin, fluttering legs.

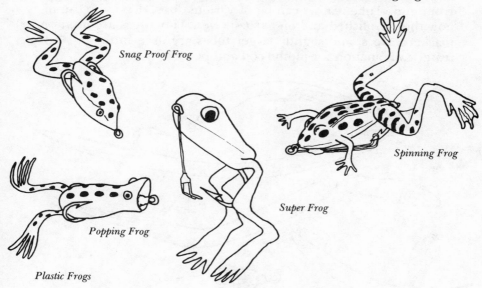

Snag Proof Frog

Spinning Frog

Popping Frog

Super Frog

Plastic Frogs

As for plastic mice, you will have to satisfy your own curiosity, because I have never been tempted to try one. Back when I was a kid I used to fish a flocked mouse plug that was made, I think, by Heddon, and that uneventful series of experiences rather dampened my interest in mouse-imitating lures.

TUBE LURES

Not quite plastic lures, because they are often made of latex-rubber surgical tubing, the tube lures have won a lot of adherents over the years. I don't know why, but tube-lure fishermen tend to be among the most dogmatic of anglers, giving nothing away to dry-fly fishermen when it comes to smugness. Those who drag half a dozen or more tube lures behind umbrella rigs tend to be the worst of the lot, but I must confess to a bit of intolerance myself when it comes to umbrella rigs. I can't fault the tube-lure legions on logic: Tube lures really are good, and sometimes they will catch fish when nothing else will. But I just can't see using umbrella rigs, which turn sport fishing into meat fishing.

The basic tube lure is the teaser. It is a relatively short lure, fashioned from a piece of tubing that isn't more than 4 or 5 inches long. It is usually slipped over a hook that has a long bent-aside shank. And it virtually always incorporates a swivel on the front end. Tube teasers can be of various sizes, depending upon how they are fished and on what species. Tiny tubes are used on mackerel trees, and slightly larger tubes are used in the jig-and-teaser combination for jumbo cod and pollock.

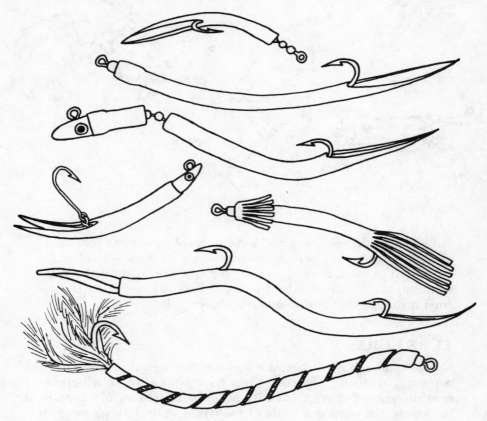

Tube Lures

Tube eels may be quite long, 16 inches or more. They usually incorporate two or more hooks, at least one of which is usually a bent-aside Limerick. Swivels are nearly always incorporated to prevent line twist (tube eels must spin to attract fish), and some are outfitted with egg sinkers or other weights at their front end, for casting weight and to take them down where the fish are.

Most saltwater anglers I know make their own tube lures. They do it not only to save money but also to customize the lures to their own specifications. Surgical tubing comes in a range of diameters, flexibilities, and colors. If there is a secret to making (or maintaining) tube lures, it is keeping them bent. Their bent shape makes them spin, and spinning is all the action they have—unless, of course, one is built around a wobble plate or action head. Long tube eels ought to be stored in loose coils, to make sure they keep their shape. The bent-aside shank hooks help give tube eels their action and are virtually necessary on the short teasers.

Of the commercially available tube lures, one is sufficiently different to deserve mention: Mr. V's Spir-eel. This is a spiral-cut lure that is made from tough, fairly inflexible tubing, and it is virtually indestructible, even when fishing for sharp-toothed species. Bill Burton of the *Baltimore Sun* wrote that he took twenty-seven big bluefish on a Spir-eel with only acceptable fraying of the lure. Most hard plugs won't take twenty-seven chopper blues without suffering major damage.

BIG-GAME TROLLING LURES

While many of the lures used by bluewater trollers can be pigeon-holed into some of the groups listed above, a few are sufficiently different to merit brief mention. In some cases, the differences are great. There is nothing quite like the teaser in other forms of fishing. A teaser is nothing but a hookless, vaguely baitlike object that is trolled behind a boat to attract fish. Once the marlin or sailfish are lured in close, the durable teaser is reeled in and rigged natural baits or more delicate artificial lures are dropped back to the fish. A teaser may be a skirted or feathered affair, or it may be a pluglike piece of wood or plastic—even a beer or soda can. The important thing is that it skip and dance along the surface in the fashion of, say, flying-fish.

Some of the differences that count are smaller. To the casual tackle-shop browser, most of the big-game lures may look like oversize skirts or vinyl squids. But to the veteran bluewater angler, important differences in detail count for more than do the resemblances to squid. When a lure is being splashed along the surface of the ocean at high speed, audiovisual performance is more meaningful than looks alone.

Size, weight, and especially the shape of a big-game trolling lure's head determine how the lure will look and sound to fish.

The head's design will cause it to skip or to dive, and to behave properly only within a certain range of trolling speeds. Most of the names given to the head shapes are registered trademarks (many of them owned by Sevenstrand Corporation, which makes some of the finest trolling lures), but most fishermen use them as if they were generic classifications. Perhaps Sevenstrand and the others will forgive me if I resort to angling tradition and do so, too. Blunt bullethead lures are generally designed for moderately slow trolling speeds, in the range of 5 to 8 or 10 knots. If the bullethead lure has feathers instead of a plastic body, it will probably be called a Japanese feather or Jap feather. These trolling feathers are only superficially related to the feathered jigs used to fish down below. If the bullethead's nose cone is long and slender, shaped more like a .30-06 projectile than like a .45 caliber slug, the lure will work properly at speeds well above 10 or 12 knots. These are the lures often used for trolling tuna and marlin. A big, thick head with a scooped-out face is called a Kona lure or Konahead, and it's a medium-speed lure that can handle 8 to 10 knots. The new jet lures are real speed demons; they can be trolled at speeds between 10 and 17 knots, sometimes even higher. Many of these big-game lures are innovations of the pioneering bluewater anglers in Hawaii.

When Frank Johnson started making Mold Craft lures, his Soft Head was a pointed-head plastic trolling lure that came with instructions and a template for cutting the head at various lengths and angles. That didn't work well, because fishermen couldn't cut straight and the lures trolled at a yaw. Now Johnson makes an extensive line of molded trolling baits, including daisy chains, spreader-bar rigs, and a new split-tail mackerel. Flagships of the Mold Craft fleet are the flat-headed Hooker, one of the most popular trolling lures in use today, and the Soft Bird teaser and lure. Give Mold Craft a pat on the back for innovative creativity but a rap on the knuckles for the company's lamentable backing of the crassest sort of big-buck fishing tournaments.

The old-fashioned cedar plug isn't as popular as it used to be, now that all those pretty Hawaiian lures have hit the market. But the cedar plug is a lot cheaper and almost as effective, and it is about as versatile a lure as can be found. It resembles a small torpedo or medium-large cigar with a heavy lead nose and a hollow cedar body. It can be fished plain or painted, with fixed or trailing hooks, unadorned or trailing skirts, feathers, bucktail, plastic worms and eels, strip baits, or whatever else strikes an angler's fancy. And when the winds are blowing fresh onshore and the bluefish are feeding out beyond the first breaker, you can turn a cedar plug into a real gale-force surf plug by rigging it on a wire leader with the lead-weighted end aft.

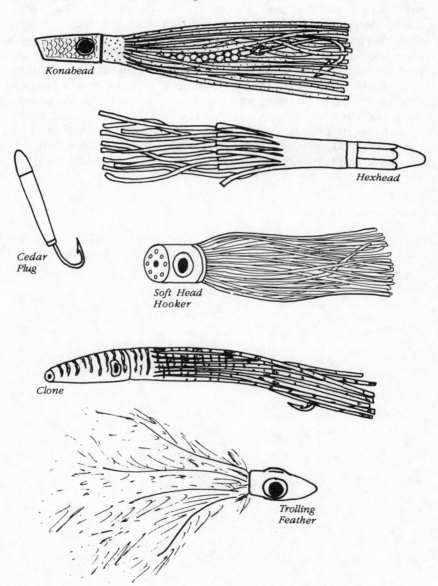

Konabead

Hexhead

Cedar Plug

Soft Head Hooker

Clone

Trolling Feather

Big-Game Trolling Lures

This survey by no means exhausts the subject of lure types, and it barely scratches the surface of their proper and effective use. When using an unfamiliar lure for the first time, it pays to read the instructions that are printed on the package or that come inside the box. If the lure you want to try doesn't come packaged with instructions, ask the tackle-shop proprietor for advice. If you are shopping in a discount department store, though, don't expect the clerk to be a fount of piscatorial information. Chances are he can barely distinguish between a popper and a bobber. Once you know what you want, and how to use it, go ahead and shop the discount department stores for the best price. Every fishing penny counts. But when you are "just looking," stick to the good tackle shops. The expertise costs a little more, but it is usually worth the premium.

10

Thou Shalt Knot

FOR MOST OF US, frail human beings that we are, tackle manufacturers are convenient scapegoats. We tend to look to our tackle to
explain away our fishing failures. When it comes to knots,
though, we are on our own. We can't fairly saddle tackle manufacturers with much blame or credit for our knots.

It is surprising how many otherwise expert anglers are just earnest bunglers when it comes to knots. Some don't even know how
bad their knots are. Because of their great skill in the manipulation of tackle and the fighting of fish, they can compensate for
their poor knots with a manual tour de force that keeps them
from losing too many fish. That's all right, I suppose, but it is a lot
easier to learn to tie knots well than to learn those compensatory
skills and techniques.

It has been estimated that there are some three thousand different knots, each with its own assets and liabilities. Some are just
new wrinkles or variations on others, of course, and some have
little or no application in angling. Eliminating the nonfishing
knots and the fishing knots that aren't very good, we still find
hundreds of knots in the potential repertoire, and that's too
many. The practical angler only needs to know how to tie a small
number of knots. But he must know how to tie them well.

Many of the good old knots that served fishermen well for gen-

351

erations were what are known as jam knots. They achieved their strength and security by jamming strands of line together or against a hook eye, wire loop, or other tackle connection. They were fine when lines were braided of linen, cotton, silk, and other organic fibers. But, in synthetic fibers and filaments like nylon and Dacron, such knots tend to cut themselves in two. So, a whole new generation of knots was invented to accommodate nylon monofilament and other synthetic fishing lines. These are the so-called direct-pull or wrapped-turn knots that are formed by wrapping or turning the line over itself rather than by folding or looping it. Don't worry if you can't tell the difference. Most of the knots we use today were developed specifically for use in synthetics.

At the same time these new knots were being developed, chemists were working on new formulations for the synthetics, so that lines made from them wouldn't have such a strong tendency to self-destruct when knotted. Today's monofilaments aren't anything like the snap-crackle-and-pop monos of years gone by. Still, some fishing lines have more knot strength than others (see Chapter 6), and the knots themselves have their own inherent strengths, so it is essential to use fishing lines of high knot strength, to select good, strong knots, and to tie those knots well.

In general, the same knots may and should be used in monofilament and braided lines, whether the lines are made of nylon, Perlon, Dacron, Micron, or other polymers, polyesters, or "poly-synthetics." Note, however, that some of the multiturn knots that will pull up neatly and easily in slippery monofilament can be a bit more difficult to tighten well in braided lines because of the greater compressibility and surface friction of the braids. As you experiment, you will learn which knots give you more trouble than they are worth in braided lines.

Most of the modern knots were developed for general fishing rather than for ship-anchoring or big-game trolling, so they are best tied in the lighter, thinner lines. Knot strengths typically fall off rapidly in lines that test higher than 20 or 30 pounds, unless the knots were designed to be tied in higher-test lines. Because the heavier lines are thicker and stiffer, it becomes increasingly difficult to pull the knots tight enough to seat the wraps, turns, or coils against one another properly. A good many knots are best tightened with pliers rather than fingers in the high-test lines.

Of course, knots aren't terminal tackle or even tackle at all. Why, then, devote so many pages to them in a book about terminal tackle? Because you can't use the tackle without them. If your knots don't work properly, then neither will anything else that is covered in this book. Knots are the weakest links in the average angler's entire armory, yet even an awkward klutz who was cursed with ten left thumbs and no mechanical aptitude can become a proficient tier of knots. I am living proof of that. Knot-tying is one of the few areas in which you can compete on an even footing with the high rollers who can afford the finest and most expensive tackle, and with just a little practice and experience you can go head-to-head with the famous, world-class anglers whose other repertoire of skills will take years to match.

KNOT-TYING PRINCIPLES

Before we get to the nitty-gritty of tying knots, let's cover a few basic principles that apply to all knots.

Practice makes perfect, and perfection isn't too good when it comes to knots. Before adding a knot to your angling repertoire, be sure you have practiced tying it at home until you are sure you can tie it well under the adverse conditions that often prevail while angling.

The first step in tying a good knot is to form it properly. The strands of line must cross each other on the proper side, the wraps and turns must be made in the proper order and direction, and the number of wraps or turns must be correct.

Form your knots carefully. Don't rush them, because haste definitely makes waste in knot-tying. Tying speed will come naturally with practice and experience.

After a knot has been properly and carefully formed, it must be tightened or drawn up properly, otherwise it can become deformed and weakened. First, lubricate the knot and the line with water or saliva, then tighten it. Each knot must be pulled up tight according to a prescribed procedure, holding this part and pulling that; get it backwards, and you will be pulling the knot out of shape, weakening it severely. Above all, pull your knots up with a slow, steady, continuous pull; don't jerk them tight or use hesitant, unsteady, stop-and-go pressure when tightening. If the knot must be drawn up tight in several stages, use a single, slow, steady pull in each stage.

Be careful that you don't damage the line while you are forming or tightening your knots. Pliers, teeth, and even fingernails can make fatal nicks in the line that are almost impossible to detect. Pliers should only be applied to tag ends of knots or to hooks, swivels, snaps, or other hardware, not to the standing part of the line, a loop, or any other integral part of the knot itself.

Having formed and tightened a knot properly, clip the tag ends as close to the coils as the knot will allow. An eighth of an inch is more than sufficient in most knots; if a knot requires closer or looser trimming, I'll say so. If tag ends are left unnecessarily long, they can become fouled in weeds, line guides, and other tight places.

Before fishing a knot, examine it carefully, looking for loose loops, gaps between coils, and other deformities. If it doesn't look right, cut it out and start over again. Be sure to check your knots periodically, several times each fishing day. Watch for signs of loosening, deformation, abrasion, fraying, and general wear and tear. Cut out suspicious-looking knots and retie.

KNOT ANATOMY AND TERMINOLOGY

So that we can zip through knot descriptions and tying instructions with a minimum of words, here are some fictional knots labeled with many of the terms I'll be using:

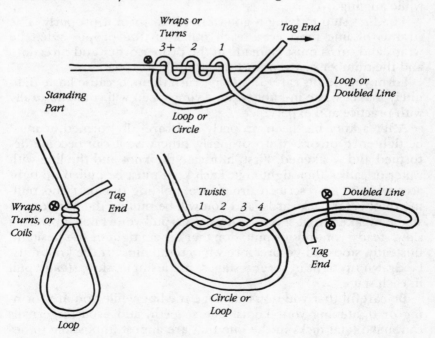

Knot Anatomy and Terminology

Note that I'll be numbering the wraps or turns in the order they are taken. Use the number of turns specified, otherwise you risk weakening a knot or making it unnecessarily bulky. However, if the last number is followed by a plus sign (+), it means the number of turns illustrated is the minimum recommended, but that more turns may be taken without trauma.

An X in a circle indicates where a knot must be held in the fingers, so that it won't come undone during the tying.

The arrows indicate which parts ought to be pulled (or pushed), and in which direction, during the tightening.

TIES THAT BIND

Not many years ago, each branch of angling had its own knot armory. Fly-fishermen had their Turles and nail knots, big-game trollers their Bimini twists and offshore swivel knots, surfcasters their key loops and Albright specials. All these are excellent, special-purpose knots, and I have included most of them, but in recent years the trend has been toward simplification, toward using the same knots across the board in fishing. It is tough learning to tie a great many dissimilar knots. I have decided to ignore some of the old standbys in favor of simplicity and standardization. Choose your knots carefully, and learn to tie them well.

I suggest you learn one complete knot *system* and as many or as few of the others as you feel like tackling. You really could get by using nothing but the Uni-knot system, but the others I have included come in handy from time to time.

UNI-KNOT SYSTEM

Vic Dunaway, editor of *Florida Sportsman* magazine, author of several authoritative books on angling, and fishing expert of the first order, is the father of the Uni-knot *system*. The basic Uni-knot itself has been around for years, known in this country as the Norm Duncan loop knot and in Australia and New Zealand as the hangman's noose. A variant, the whipped snell, might have been around even longer. Nevertheless, give Dunaway credit for recognizing the latent possibilities in the principle, and for turning a good little knot into a rational knot system that can be used in virtually any angling application. In most of its variant configurations, the Uni-knot will retain at least 90 percent of the unknotted strength of a line that has good knot strength. In cheaper lines of lower knot strength, the Uni might dip down to as low as 80 percent in some variations. In premium lines that have superior knot strength and that test below 20 pounds, you can tie a 100 percent Uni-knot the first time you try it.

The Uni-circle is the basis of the whole system, so study these configurations and commit them to memory. That will make learning all the variations a lot easier.

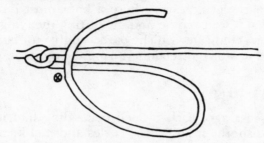

Uni-Circle

Basic Uni-Knot

The basic or terminal Uni-knot will deliver 90 to 100 percent of the unknotted line's breaking strength, depending upon the inherent knot strength of the line and its diameter or test strength. It can be used for attaching just about any type of terminal gear to a line or leader: hooks, lures, flies, snaps, swivels, sinkers.

1. Run the end of the line or leader through the eye of the tackle for at least 6 inches and form a Uni-circle. With the tag end of the line, make *six* turns around the doubled line at the top of the circle, working back up the line away from the hook, lure, or other tackle.

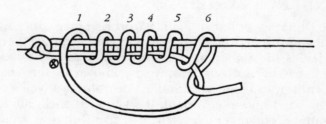

2. Holding the doubled line or loop at the point where it passes through the eye (marked X), pull the tag end in the opposite direction until the six turns are snugged, but not tightened, into a neat barrel around the line. Wetting the whole knot first will produce a smaller, neater, stronger knot. Don't pull too hard at this

point. Just snug the wraps down. The tightening of the knot comes in the next step. The heavier and thicker the line is, the less neat your snugged-coil barrel will look.

3. Grasp the standing part of the line above the knot, while holding the hook or lure in the other hand, and pull on the line to slide the lubricated knot up against the eye. Continue pulling on the standing line until the knot is tight. Trim the tag end very closely, because the Uni-knot will not permit any line slippage within the knot.

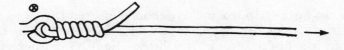

Uni-Knot Loop

This knot—the Duncan loop or hangman's noose—is just about as strong as the basic Uni-knot (although it may be considerably weaker in lines of less than good knot strength) and is tied the same way, but it is tightened differently. Steps 1 and 2 are the same as on page 356, so we'll begin with step 3.

3. Pull on the standing part of the line to slide the knot toward the eye until a small loop of the desired size is achieved.

4. Tighten the loop in place by pulling hard on the tag end with pliers; you won't be able to tighten it sufficiently by hand. Don't jerk the tag end or you will damage the line. Clip the tag end to about ⅛ inch above the coils.

The Uni-knot loop will give a lure more freedom of action than any of the jam or cinched-down terminal knots. Under the normal stresses of casting and retrieving, or trolling, the loop knot will remain in place. Once a fish is hooked the knot will slide down against the eye, closing the loop and providing slightly greater security against impact failure. Du Pont tests have shown that in 14-pound-test line it takes about 5 pounds of pull to close the loop. To reopen the loop, work the coils back up the line with your fingers, taking care not to nick the line with your nails.

Some flies and streamers, small spoons and jigs, and most swimming plugs work better when they are tied to the line with a loop knot, like the Uni.

Uni-Knot Splice

To join two lines of approximately equal diameter, the Uni-knot is easier to tie than the better-known and more common blood knot, but it is just as strong. It will test about 85–95 percent. If you double each of the lines to be joined, then tie the doubled strands as if they were single strands, it will test at 95–100 percent.

1. Overlap the two ends of the line 6 to 8 inches. Take one of the ends and form the Uni-circle, crossing the overlapped lines about midway along the overlapped distance.

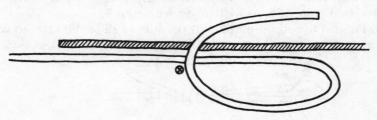

2. Tie a six-turn, basic Uni-knot around the two lines. Pull the tag end away from the overlapped portion to snug the wraps down. Remember, don't overdo it at this point.

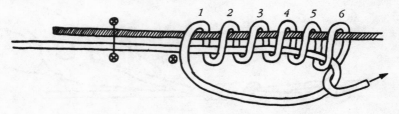

3. Now, take the other loose end and, as in steps 1 and 2, tie another Uni-knot and snug the coils down.

4. The two snugged-down knots and the strands of line between them must be lubricated prior to this next step. Pull the two standing lines in opposite directions to slide the knots together. Without overstressing the line, pull as tight as possible, then snip the tag ends close, within 1/16 inch. You can minimize the chances of the knot's jamming in a rod guide by clipping the tag ends at a 45-degree angle.

For most angling purposes, the Uni-knot splice may safely be tied without doubling the lines. But for tough service, tying it with doubled lines is better. If you do use the doubled-line approach, the tag ends to be clipped will include two single tags and two loops. Study the next variant for details.

Uni-Knot Leader Tie

To attach a leader that is considerably heavier than the line, but no more than four times greater in diameter or pound-test, this variant of the Uni-knot will preserve at least 95 percent of the line's unknotted strength, and perhaps all of it. This knot may be used instead of the Stu Apte—improved blood knot or the offset nail knot; it is as strong as the others and easier to tie.

1. Double the end of the line (not the leader) about 8 inches and overlap this doubled line and the single strand of leader by about 6 inches. Make a Uni-circle *with the doubled line* and tie a *four*-turn Uni-knot around the leader and doubled line.

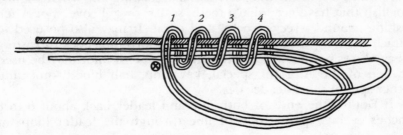

2. Snug the coils down by pulling on the loop of the doubled line.

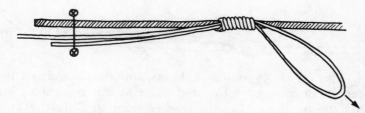

3. Now form a Uni-circle with the leader and tie a *three*-turn Uni-knot around the doubled line and leader. Snug the coils down.

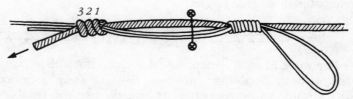

4. Pull both standing parts of the line and leader to slide the knots together and continue pulling hard until the knot is *tight*. Trim both tag ends and the loop of doubled line very close to the coils.

Shock-Leader Uni-Knot

Another 95–100 percent version of the Uni-knot, this variant is used to join heavy shock leaders (those testing five or more times the pound-test of the line) to your main fishing line when angling for fish that have very sharp teeth, scales, or gill covers, or when fishing around wrecks, rocks, and coral. It may also be used to attach the long shock leaders used to absorb the shock of casting heavy lures or sinkers on long surf rods. This knot may be used in lieu of the Albright special, key loop, half blood knot, and other special shock-leader ties.

1. Double the ends of both line and leader back about 6 to 8 inches each. Slip the loop of line through the leader loop far

enough to permit tying a Uni-knot around both strands of the leader.

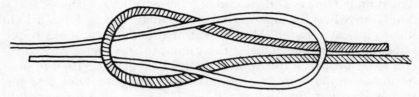

2. Make a Uni-circle *with the doubled line* and tie a *four*-turn Uni-knot around both strands of the leader.

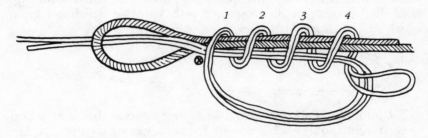

3. Snug the wraps down by pulling on both strands (tag end and standing part) of the line with one hand and the loop of doubled line with the index finger of the other hand.

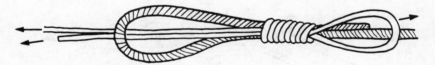

4. Tighten the knot by pulling on the standing part of the leader (not both strands) with one hand and on both strands (tag end and standing part) of the line with the other hand. Pull slowly and steadily, without jerking. Pull too fast and the leader will cut into the line. Once the knot stops slipping and the coils of line have cinched up on the leader loop completely, finish tightening by pulling on both standing parts (line and leader) in opposite directions. Clip both tag ends and the loop of doubled line.

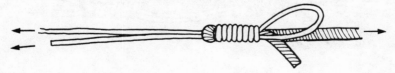

Uni-Knot Double

The doubled line is *de rigueur* in big-game trolling offshore, and is handy anywhere in tapering your terminal rigging from a light line to a heavy leader. This variant of the Uni-knot looks tricky, but consider the alternatives: the Bimini twist, which is very difficult to tie properly; the Spider hitch, which can't be used in lines testing above 30 pounds; and the double surgeon's knot, which is very bulky when tied in heavy lines. The Uni-knot double tie will test at 90 to 100 percent.

1. Clip off the length of line needed to make the double; if you want 15 feet of doubled line, clip off a 30-foot length. Tie the two ends of this piece of line together with a simple overhand knot, which will be clipped off later.

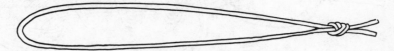

2. Double the end of the standing line (the one that is attached to your reel spool) back on itself for 8 inches or so and overlap this doubled end by 6 inches with the knotted end of the separate doubled piece of line. Form a Uni-circle with the separate double and tie a *four*-turn Uni-knot around both strands of the doubled standing line. Snug up as usual.

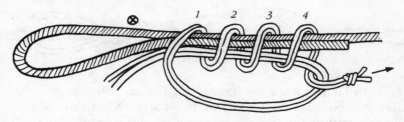

3. With the looped or doubled end of the main line, form another Uni-circle and tie another *four*-turn Uni-knot around the looped double. Snug up the coils.

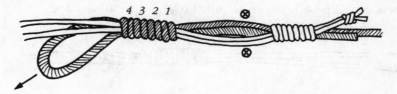

4. Holding both strands of the main line and both strands of the doubled piece, pull in opposite directions until the knots slide together and barely touch. Do *not* tighten at this point!

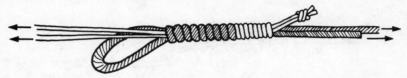

5. Tighten by pulling hard and steadily on both strands of the looped piece and on the *main strand only* of the standing line. (See arrows.) Trim all three of the tag ends close (the *looped and tag* ends of the standing line but only the *knotted* end of the doubled loop).

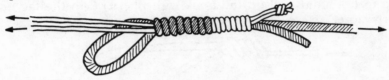

Uni-Knot Snell

Formerly called the whipped snell, the Uni-knot snell is about as strong (85–95 percent) as the standard snell, but a lot easier to tie. It also permits snelling a hook directly to the end of the line that is attached to the reel, something that can't be done with the standard snell.

1. Thread the end of the line through an up- or down-turned hook eye about 6 inches, then hold the line against the shank of the hook and form a Uni-circle. (If you are snelling your line or leader to a hook that has a regular ringed eye, one that isn't turned up or down, do not pass the line through the eye of the hook. Doing so would cause the hook to dangle awkwardly and would interfere with the penetration geometry of the hook.)

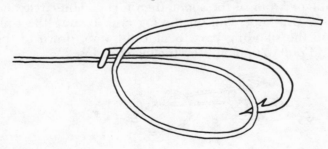

2. Tie a Uni-knot around the hook shank, using no less than three or four turns, certainly, but as many as you like. Close the wraps by pulling on the tag end.

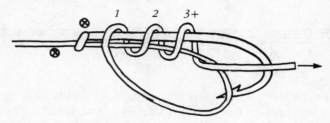

3. Tighten the Uni-snell by pulling the standing line in one direction and the hook in the other. (In brawny saltwater tackle, I like to hold and pull on the hook with pliers.) Clip the tag end fairly close.

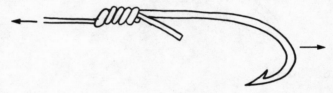

Arbor Uni-Knot

Any number of knots may be used for tying new line onto a reel's spool or arbor. The Uni-knot is just about the easiest of the lot. Strength is inconsequential here, because even the overhand knot is strong enough to let you retrieve a rod that has been dropped overboard, and no knot is going to stop a fish whose run has stripped all the line off the reel.

The procedure varies slightly with the different types of reels.

1. On *fly reels and revolving spool or "conventional" reels* (e.g., trolling, boat, casting, and multiplying reels), pass the end of the line around the hub or arbor of the spool, then form a Uni-circle and tie a three-turn Uni-knot. Pull on the tag end to snug the coils down, then on the standing part to slide the knot down to the spool arbor and pull to tighten. Clip the tag end close.

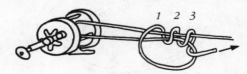

2. On *either spinning or spincast (fixed-spool) reels,* double the end of the line and make a loop by tying a three-turn Uni-knot and snugging it down. (Now proceed to step 3 or 4, depending upon which type of reel it is.)

3. On *open-face spinning reels,* simply open the bail and slip the loop over the spool. Pull on the standing part of the line to tighten the loop and knot. Clip the tag end close.

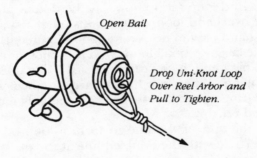

Open Bail

Drop Uni-Knot Loop Over Reel Arbor and Pull to Tighten.

4. On *spincast or closed-face spinning reels,* remove the nose cone from the reel, push the looped end of the line through the opening in the nose cone (from front to rear!), and proceed as in number 3 above.

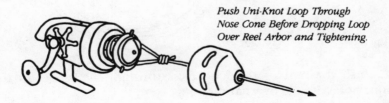

Push Uni-Knot Loop Through Nose Cone Before Dropping Loop Over Reel Arbor and Tightening.

Notice that there are no fixed end-loop knots or dropper loops in the Uni-knot system. You can make them by tying the knots backwards, but the resulting knots are actually variants of the double surgeon's knot and aren't really Uni-knots at all.

END LOOPS, DROPPER LOOPS, AND LINE DOUBLES

Add an end-loop knot and a dropper loop to the Uni-knot system, and you will have all the knots you really need in angling on any waters with any tackle (except that dry-fly fishermen probably wouldn't be comfortable without some sort of Turle knot, and with good reason). I'm including two line-doubling knots in this section (the Bimini twist and the Spider hitch), even though a Uni-knot angler can get by without them, because they are closely related in principle to the end-loop knots.

Surgeon's End Loop

For tying a fixed loop in the end of a line, leader, or hook snell, the surgeon's end loop (also known as the double surgeon's loop knot, double overhand loop, and various other names) is hard to beat. It is fast and easy to tie, strong (90–95 percent), and secure. You can make large or small loops with this knot, and if you make the end loop big enough you can make a 15-foot doubled line for big-game trolling. When my fingers are numbed with cold, or when I'm wearing gloves, the surgeon's is the only loop knot I can tie quickly and reliably.

1. Double the end of the line to form a loop of desired size. Then form a circle with the doubled line at the place you want to tie the knot.

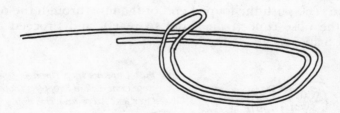

2. Push the end of the loop *twice* through the circle, in the manner of a double overhand knot.

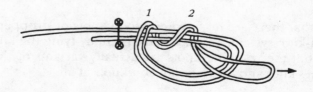

3. To tighten, hold the standing line and tag end in one hand and insert the index finger of the other hand through the loop. Pull in opposite directions. Clip the tag end about ⅛ inch from the knot—closer on thinner, light-test lines.

Surgeon's Dropper Loop

This dropper loop is tied in much the same way as the preceding knot, and it is just as strong. It is the strongest, easiest knot I know for making a dropper loop anywhere along a line or leader from which may be hung dropper flies or jigs, snelled hooks, secondary leaders, sinkers, whatever. Because of its strength and the ease with which it can be tied, this is the dropper loop knot I use most of the time.

1. Gather a doubled section of line or leader at the point you wish to make the dropper loop.

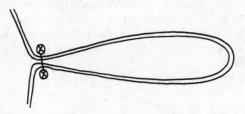

2. With the doubled loop, form a circle of appropriate size (slightly larger than you wish the finished loop to be).

3. With the looped "end," tie a double overhand knot, using both strands. (With surgeon's and double overhand knots, terminology is very confusing. A double overhand is nothing but an overhand knot tied with two passes of the line through the loop; a

surgeon's knot is just an overhand knot tied with double strands; so this is actually a double surgeon's knot.)

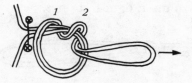

4. Tighten by holding both strands of the standing line in one hand and pulling the loop with the fingers of the other hand. Finish tightening by pulling, in opposite directions, each of the strands of standing line. There are no tag ends to trim.

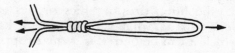

Dropper Loop

This loop knot (also known as the blood dropper or blood-knot dropper) is more difficult to tie than the surgeon's dropper loop, and isn't quite as strong (80–90 percent), but many anglers prefer it because it makes very neat dropper loops that stand out perpendicular to the line.

1. Form a looped circle in the line.

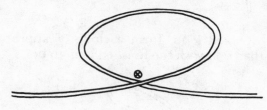

2. Pull one "leg" of the circle down behind the standing line and hold the loose strands where they cross.

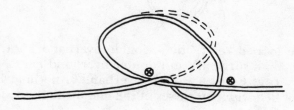

3. Holding the knot together at the two points marked "X," use the fingers of one or both hands to twirl or turn the center loop formed in step 2 over itself at least *four* times. This will create four wraps on one side and five on the other.

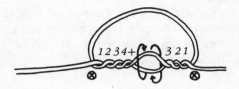

4. Push the middle point of the original circle down through the center loop. You will have to slip a finger into this dropper loop to keep it from springing back out.

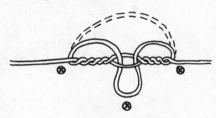

5. Lubricate the whole knot *thoroughly*. I stress this because this knot isn't easy to seat properly, thanks to the double-jointed contortions you have to go through. Now, hold the dropper loop in the mouth *(behind the teeth, being careful not to nick the line)* or, better yet, anchor it over a convenient peg or nail. Pull in opposite directions on both standing parts of the line, causing the wraps to gather neatly on either side of the loop, which is held to the proper size by a modest amount of pressure in its perpendicular direction. Pull as tight as possible, being careful not to make this tightening process anything but a single, steady pull. There is nothing to clip.

Because most anglers tie this dropper by holding the loop between their clenched teeth, and because they tighten it by pulling in a series of unsteady jerks, the dropper loop often tests below its design strength of 80 to 90 percent. Practice this one until the contortions don't feel so awkward, and you will be able to make it quite strong. (There is an advantage to knowing this dropper well, which will become apparent once we get to the blood or barrel knot a little later.)

Either of the two dropper-loop knots just described can be turned into single-strand dropper knots. After either knot is finished, just clip one leg of the loop (which should be large) about ⅛ to ¼ inch from the knot's coils.

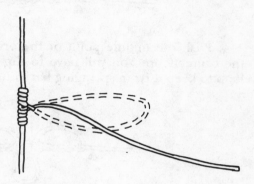

*Dropper Strand Made from
Dropper Loop*

Spider Hitch

In lines testing 30 pounds and under, the Spider hitch is just about the best knot to use for doubling a line, being both very strong and very easy to tie. It isn't a very good candidate for making end loops, however, because you can't make small loops with this knot. Tie the Spider hitch carefully, and it will hold the full strength of the unknotted line. It isn't as resilient under sharp impacts as the more difficult Bimini twist.

1. Double the line back on itself to form a long loop of the desired length. Near the upper end of that loop, form a small circular loop in the doubled line.

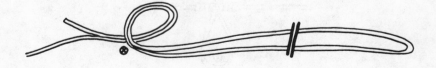

2. Hold the small circle loop between thumb and forefinger as shown. The forefinger must be crooked so that the thumb ex-

tends well beyond the crooked finger, and the circular loop must extend beyond the thumb tip.

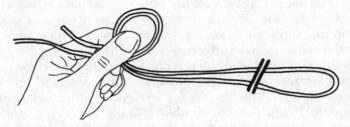

3. Wind the doubled line of the big loop around both the thumb and the small circular loop *five* times. *Important:* Do not let the doubled strands cross over themselves or the finished knot won't hold full strength. Now pass the doubled end of the long loop through the smaller loop, from the top side.

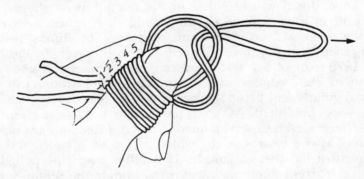

4. Pull slowly and steadily on the long loop to draw the five wrapped turns off the thumb one at a time. To tighten the Spider hitch, pull alternately on the loop and the two strands above the knot. Clip it close.

Bimini Twist

Also known as the rollover knot, twenty-times-around knot, double tie, or 100 percent double, the Bimini twist is a difficult knot to tie. Out on the water, I've heard it called any number of unprintable names. Don't be surprised if your first two or three attempts at tying a Bimini twist end in dismal failure. This is a knot that requires practice, and plenty of it. You have to tie it and tie it until you develop a feel for all the little things that can go wrong. Once you have mastered it at home, you will have to practice some more, until you can tie a Bimini twist dependably well under the actual (usually adverse) conditions of fishing.

Is the Bimini twist really all it is cracked up to be? Is it worth all the trouble? Yes, and maybe. No knot surpasses, and few even come close to, the Bimini twist for strength and impact or shock resistance. Among the line-doubling knots that are considered full-strength ties, the Bimini certainly is the most streamlined; it fairly sails through rod guides. But, is it worth the effort in learning and tying? Frankly, not for most fishermen. Unless you troll with lines that test over 30 pounds, unless you fish for pelagic heavyweights and other supermuscular speedsters that can subject lines to terrible impact stresses, you can skip right on to the next knot. But if you fit either of the categories mentioned, or just want to learn how to tie the strongest, toughest knot ever invented, take a deep breath and read on. The Bimini twist is strong medicine; if you really need it, it's a lifesaver. In the January 1979 issue of *Salt Water Sportsman*, the results of a knot poll among its staff editors and columnists—all of whom fish salt water regularly and battle the big-gamesters more than once in a while—was published. Asked to name their five "most essential" knots, those eleven experts named a total of fifteen knots (including the haywire twist wire tie, which isn't truly a knot), and the Bimini twist led the hit parade. If another magazine polled its light-tackle, freshwater angling experts, I doubt the Bimini would even be mentioned once.

To tie long doubled lines, such as those used in big-game fishing, this is a two-man knot; to tie doubles of 5 to 6 feet you can do it alone, but you will have to sit down to do it. I'll describe the solo version, because it is the more difficult to master. Tying a Bimini twist is tough enough, but describing its tying is even tougher, so don't be too put off by the labyrinthine description that follows.

1. Double the end of the line back on itself to form a double-strand loop that is slightly longer than necessary, but no longer than 6 feet if you are tying it alone. Holding the two strands together, insert your other hand through the loop so formed and rotate the loop twenty times, putting that many twists into the double strands.

2. Spread the loop to force the twists together about 10 inches below the tag end. Step both feet through the loop, trapping the end of the loop under your feet, so that you can put tension on the knot by spreading the knees apart.

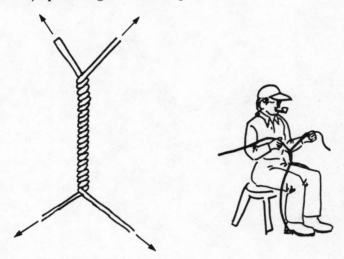

3. Hold the standing line in the left hand and the tag end in the right, each about 45 degrees above the horizontal. Now move the line in the left hand up toward a vertical position, maintaining some tension all the while. Don't go all the way vertical, because you will need some cant in the line to control the necessary tension. With the knees slightly spread against the two strands of the loop so that the twists in the line are being pressured together, drop the tag end in the right hand to just barely above the horizontal position (the angle between the standing line and tag end should be a little more than 90 degrees).

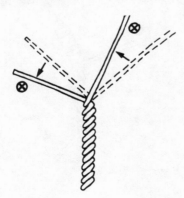

4. *Gradually* ease the tension on the tag end, while maintaining the pressure of the spread knees, causing the tag end to begin rolling over the column of twists, just below the uppermost twist.

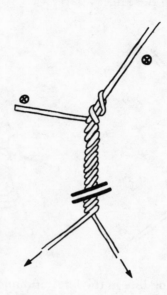

5. Spreading the knees slowly apart, to maintain uniform tension on the knot, allow the tag end to keep feeding slowly from your right hand. The coils being wrapped around the twists should be close and parallel. If you get one (or more) that is too loose or that crosses back over the coil above it, just pull back on the tag end to remove it.

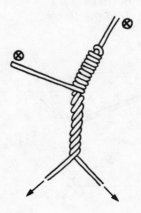

6. Once the spiral coil has reached the bottom of the column of twists, maintain pressure with the knees and tag end, but work the left hand slowly down the standing part of the line and over the knot, pinching the crotch of the loop to prevent the knot from slipping. Now take a half hitch around the nearer leg of the loop with the tag end and pull the hitch tight.

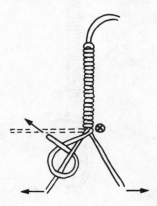

7. Now you can relax tension on the knot, because the half hitch will prevent its coming undone. However, keep the doubled loop fairly well stretched out. With the tag end, take a half hitch around *both* legs of the loop, but do *not* pull it tight. Instead, take two more half hitches around both legs of the loop, above the first half hitch and inside the bend of line that was formed by that hitch.

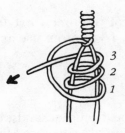

8. Pull the tag end slowly, to gather the three hitches into a spiral. You will probably have to use the fingers of your other hand to help in this gathering, first by keeping the turns away from the bottom of the coil and then by working them up against

the coils. Once the hitches are seated against the bottom of the coils, pull hard on the tag end to lock the knot in place. Trim the tag end to about ¼ inch.

There are several variations on the finishing of the Bimini twist with half hitches. All seem to work reasonably well, so don't be afraid to try another version that uses, say, a half hitch around each leg and then two half hitches around both legs. But beware of those versions which use just a single half hitch around each leg; they will work loose.

TERMINAL KNOTS

I use the Uni-knot most of the time for tying on lures, but for snaps, swivels, and hooks, I will often use another knot, particularly the Palomar.

Palomar Knot

Based on hundreds, maybe even thousands, of tests at their laboratories, Du Pont technicians are convinced that the Palomar knot is the most dependable and consistently the strongest of the terminal knots, testing at 95 to 100 percent. It is also the easiest to tie of all the high-strength terminal knots.

1. Double the line back on itself to form a 4-inch loop. Pass the loop through the eye of a hook (or other terminal hardware).

2. Tie an overhand knot in the doubled line, letting the hook hang loose. *Be sure to avoid twisting the strands or allowing them to cross over themselves;* this is the key to the Palomar's dependable strength. Don't tighten the overhand knot at this point.

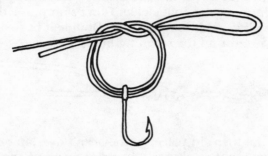

3. Pull the loop of line down over the hook, making sure that it passes completely over and off the hook and back up onto the doubled strands of line as the knot is tightened.

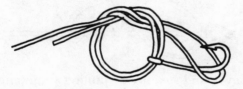

4. Pull both the tag end and standing line to tighten. Clip the tag end within ⅛ inch or less.

Improved Clinch Knot

This old standby was one of the first knots discovered to be reasonably strong and secure in the new nylon monofilaments that were so slippery and so eager to destroy themselves when knotted. As a result, every angler who has come along in the past quarter of a century has been teethed on this knot. Up to lines of 20 pounds, the improved clinch will hold 95 percent or more of a good line's unknotted strength, but its strength falls off as the line gets thicker. In really light-test lines, the improved clinch is strongest when tied in double strands. There are many variants, such as the two-circle improved clinch, but we'll stick to the standard version here.

1. Pass the end of the line 6 inches or more through the eye of the hook, lure, or terminal tackle. Don't skimp, for the key to this knot's reliability is this long tag end. Double it back over itself and take *six* turns around the standing line.

2. Hold the turns in place, so they can't overlap one another (a potential source of weakness), thread the end of the line through the first loop above the eye, then through the big loop.

3. Tighten slowly and steadily by pulling simultaneously on the hook and standing line. *Don't touch the tag end while tightening,* or you will ruin the knot's dependable strength. Clip the tag end close.

Return Knot

This little dandy—also known in the traditional knot books as the Wood knot, safety link, or single Cairnton knot—is a good snell for baitfishing, particularly if you are using small hooks, because it isn't as bulky as the true snells described below. It is also a good one to use for tying flies and streamers onto fairly heavy tippets. I can't tie this one securely on hooks with straight eyes; better restrict its use to those with eyes that are turned up or down.

1. Pass the end of the line or leader down through the eye of the hook, then pass the tag end around behind the shank, coming around so that the tag end, after this first turn, is pointing in the same direction as the hook's eye is turned. Pass the tag end in front of the shank, then make a loose figure eight by passing the end behind the leader just above the eye. Pinch the crossing strands in the middle of the figure eight.

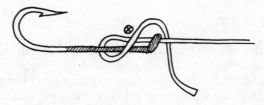

2. Continue by passing the tag end back up in front of the hook eye, then through both of the figure eight's loops. You will have to hold both loops in place now. (It all sounds much more complicated than it is; the drawing explains it better.)

3. Holding the knot together where all the strands cross at the eye, push the uppermost loop back over the hook eye as you begin to draw the knot up tight by pulling slowly and steadily on the standing part of the leader. Once you get the hang of tying the return knot, you won't need to anchor the hook point in a wooden gunwale or other "third hand," but I think you will learn it faster if you do. So, with the hook point thus anchored, and holding the knot together and the tag end in place, pull slowly and steadily on the standing part of the line or leader. Be sure the upper loop gets pushed back down over the hook eye.

4. Finish tightening by pulling the leader in one direction and the tag end (with pliers) in the other. Clip the tag end moderately close (within ⅛ inch).

Offshore Swivel Knot

As good as the above terminal knots are, nothing beats the offshore swivel knot for attaching a heavy-duty swivel or snap-swivel to the Bimini loop at the end of a big-game trolling line. Some saltwater anglers also like to use it for tying on hooks when fishing for such species as bonefish, permit, and jacks. And it has plenty of freshwater applications, too. The great thing about the swivel knot is, if one strand of the double line breaks, the other end won't slip. That is a major asset when fishing for big, strong, hard-fighting fish. It can be tied in braided line, but I think it works better in monofilament, in which it will hold 95 to 100 percent of the line's strength. Sufficiently wetting the line with water or saliva is the key to its tying ease. It looks and sounds tougher to tie than it is, so be sure to try it before shrugging it off.

1. Insert the looped line through the eye of the swivel (or other piece of tackle) for several inches. Pinch the two strands together above the swivel with your right hand. Place the fingers of your left hand inside the end of the loop and rotate your hand a half turn, placing a twist in the line.

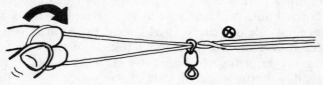

2. Fold the end loop back over the swivel, and pinch it (along with the double strands) between the fingers of your right hand. Take the swivel in your left hand. You now have, in effect, two loops of line between your right and left hands.

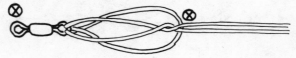

3. Use the fingers of your left hand to push the swivel toward your right hand and through the center of both loops at least six times.

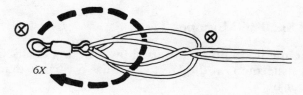

4. This is what the knot will look like after the swivel has been passed through the loops six times:

5. Thoroughly wet the twisted strands to lubricate them. Holding the swivel firmly in your left hand (with pliers, if necessary), pull steadily on both strands of the original (Bimini twist) loop with your right hand, causing the twists to slide down toward the eye of the swivel.

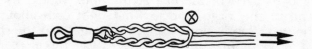

6. Finish by gripping the swivel with pliers and forcing the wraps down tight against the swivel with the thumb and forefinger of the right hand. Be sure not to nick the line with your fingernails. There are no tag ends to trim.

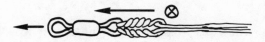

HOOK SNELLING

A hook that is snelled, rather than knotted, to a line or leader is less likely to dangle awry and to move awkwardly when you try to set the hook on a biting fish—provided the hook has been snelled correctly. I use the Uni-knot snell (see page 363) most of the time, but I haven't given up all the other methods of snelling. The quick snell, for example, is about as easy to tie as the Uni-knot snell, and sometimes it is easier to pull up properly on the hook shank. And the bumper tie is great for fishing soft baits.

Standard Snell and Bumper Tie

This is the method known and used by most anglers. Salmon and steelhead fishermen on the West Coast use a variant that is called the bumper tie.

1. Insert one end of a separate length of leader material through the up- or down-turned eye of a hook so that it extends past the bottom of the bend. Pass the other end of the snelling material through the eye in the opposite direction, forming a large loop.

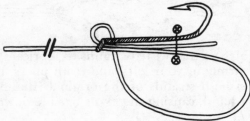

2. Holding both parts of the line at the hook shank, use the forward strand of the large loop to wind tight coils about the shank and the two strands alongside it, working down the shank from the eye. Take as many turns as you wish; five to ten are normal.

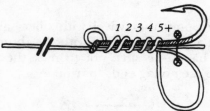

3. Holding the coils in place with the fingertips of one hand, pull with the other on the leader that extends up above the hook eye. Pull steadily until the entire loop has been drawn up under the coils. Pull tight.

4. Holding the hook firmly, pull on the tag end with pliers, to cinch the snell up tight. Clip the tag end and tie a loop knot in the other end of the leader, or tie it directly to the fishing line.

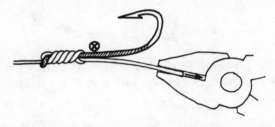

5. To make a **bumper tie,** form and cinch the coils on the shank some distance down from the eye. The loose strand of material extending from the coils to the eye can be used to hold salmon-egg clusters, mussels, other soft baits, colored yarn, and so on.

Quick Snell

This snell, which is actually a variation of the clinch knot, is a good one for baitfishing with lines that test heavier than 10 pounds. In lighter lines it is not reliable.

1. Pass the end of the line or leader through the turned eye from above, and form a six-turn clinch knot around the hook shank. Bringing the tag end back under the hook (on the side of the shank that is opposite the point), pass it back through the first loop at the eye.

2. Holding the hook firmly in one hand, and pulling on the standing part of the leader with the other hand, draw the snell up

slowly and steadily, jamming the coils up against the tag end and hook eye.

3. Clip the tag end fairly close, or—if you want to make a handy little baitholder—snip it off about a quarter of an inch above the coils.

Locked Snell

This one could also be called Izaak Walton's snell, because it is virtually identical to the method Walton outlined in *The Compleat Angler*. At first glance, it might closely resemble the standard snell, but the locked snell needn't be tied in a separate length of leader; it can be tied in the end of the line that comes from the reel.

1. Pass the end of the line or leader twice through an up- or down-turned eye, in opposite directions. Then form a loop above or below the shank (opposite the direction in which the eye is turned), so that a 3-inch-long tag end extends down from the eye. Notice the direction that the tag end must pass through the eye.

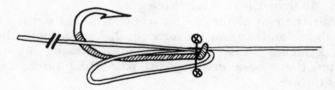

2. Holding the hook and the "inside leg" of the loop with the fingers of one hand, use the tag end to take six tight turns around both strands of the loop and the hook shank. Some anglers find it easier to tie this snell if the hook point is secured in a gunwale or board.

3. Pass the tag end through the loop. Holding the coils together, pull slowly on the leader. Once the coils have been snugged up so that the tag end can't pop loose from the loop, hold the hook firmly in a pair of pliers and pull heavily and steadily on the leader until the loop tucks under the turns. Clip the tag end at ⅛ to ¹/₁₆ inch.

LEADER AND LINE-JOINING KNOTS

The Uni-knot is the simplest, and one of the strongest, knots for joining lines together or attaching leaders to lines, but there are sometimes good reasons for selecting other knots. Blood knots, for example, are less likely than Unis to jam in rod guides, tiptops, and reel levelwind guides, because the tag ends are in the center of the finished knot rather than on each end. If streamlining isn't important, the double surgeon's knot is a very fast knot for attaching a shock leader. And the Albright special is the best knot for attaching a monofilament leader to a braided line (or mono line to braided backing); I can't always get the Uni-knot to pull up properly when it's tied in these two materials, and I've sometimes had the same problem with blood knots.

Blood Knot

The blood or barrel knot is the traditional favorite for joining lines or attaching leaders when the diameters of the two lines aren't too dissimilar. Tied properly, the blood knot will test at 80 to 95 percent strength. After learning to tie a blood knot in lines of roughly equivalent diameter, study the variants that follow.

1. Cross the ends of the lines for about 8 inches.

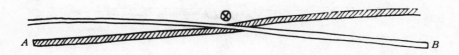

2. With one tag end, take *five to seven* turns around the other line; then double back over the turns, tuck the tag end up through the crossover, and hold in place. Note that so far this looks very much like an unimproved clinch knot, which is known Down Under as a half blood knot.

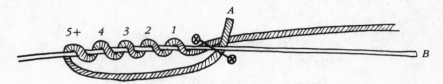

3. With the other tag end—let's call it tag end B—take *five to seven* turns around standing line A. If the lines are of equal diameter or test strength, or very close, take the same number of turns on each side. Otherwise, you can vary by a turn, taking the smaller number in the heavier line (wrapping it around the lighter). As before, tuck the tag end through the crossover, which is now a loop, making sure you pass tag end B through the crossover loop in the opposite direction as tag end A. Use your fingertips or teeth to hold both tag ends in place.

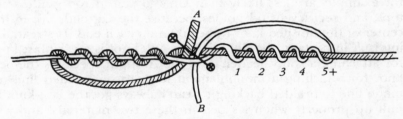

4. Moisten the knot well prior to tightening. Some prestidigitators can tighten blood knots properly by pulling slowly and steadily, but mine usually fall apart. There is some controversy on this point, but I'll go with Mark Sosin and Lefty Kreh in saying that the blood knot is exceptional in that it should be (or at least can be) tightened with a single swift yank. In light-test lines, though, you had better pull it up slowly. Once the knot has been tightened securely, clip the tag ends close, within 1/16 inch.

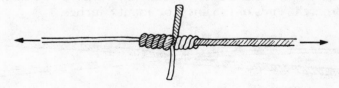

Blood-Knot Variants

There are several tying variations in blood knots. One is used for ease and simplicity, the others to compensate for dissimilar diameters when attaching leaders to fishing lines.

1. Many anglers find it easier to tie blood knots—ones in which the tag ends aren't always popping out during the tightening—if they first tie the two ends of line together and tie it as a **dropper loop** (described earlier.) Tie the dropper loop so that the overhand knot stays in the loop (which gets trimmed off at the end). This variant is theoretically less strong than a regular blood knot, but most of us can't tie knots consistently enough for such small differences to show.

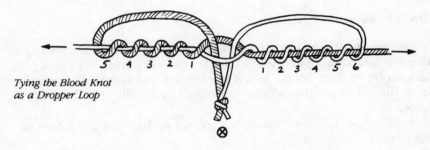

Tying the Blood Knot as a Dropper Loop

2. When the lines to be joined are noticeably dissimilar in diameter or test strength, tie an **offset blood knot** by tying different numbers of turns in the lines, usually *three turns in the heavier line* and *five turns in the lighter line*.

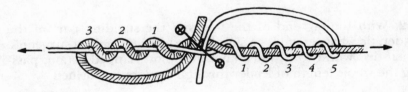

Offset Blood Knot

3. When one of the lines to be joined is *four or more times heavier in diameter or test strength,* the lighter line should first be doubled and an offset blood knot (see step 2 immediately preceding) should be tied, using *five turns in the doubled lighter line* and *three turns in the heavier line* or leader. This is known as the **Stu Apte—improved blood knot,** and is the strongest of all the blood-knot

variations, virtually always testing higher than 90 percent and sometimes at 100 percent.

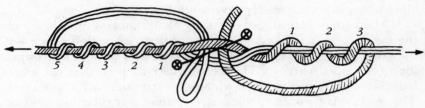

Stu Apte-Improved Blood Knot

Double Surgeon's Knot

When tying on a leader that is *no more than five times heavier* than the line, the double surgeon's knot is very easy and very strong—at least 90 to 95 percent. When the lighter line is doubled first, as in a Bimini twist, the double surgeon is virtually a full-strength knot.

1. Overlap the two strands by several inches, maybe a foot or more in the beginning.

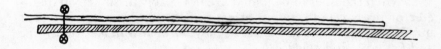

2. With the tag end of the line and the standing part of the leader, tie what resembles a simple overhand (actually a surgeon's, when tied with two strands) knot in the overlapped action, passing the whole length of leader through the loop so formed.

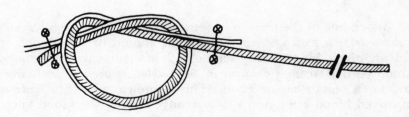

3. Finish forming the knot by passing the whole leader and the tag end of line through the loop once again, as in tying a double overhand knot.

4. To tighten, this knot must be lubricated well, and in heavy lines and leaders you may need to use a rag, handkerchief, or gloves. Pull *all four parts* to tighten, pulling the pairs *steadily* in opposite directions. Trim the two tag ends very close, virtually flush.

Albright Special

The Albright special or Albright knot (sometimes miscalled key loop knot, which is a similar knot that is tied differently) was invented for the purpose of tying very heavy monofilament shock leaders onto much lighter monofilament lines, but it is also the preferred knot (in combination with a haywire twist) for joining monofilament leader or backing to a wire trolling line when swivels are not practical. I find it is also the best knot to use when tying mono leaders onto braided lines. If the lighter-test line is first doubled in a Bimini twist or similar loop knot, the Albright is a 100 percent knot; otherwise it will go about 95 percent or better. (For simplicity's sake, I'm illustrating it in the single-strand version.)

1. Bend a loop in the heavier line that is at least 2 or 3 inches long. Insert at least 6 to 8 inches of the tag end of the lighter line behind the loop just formed. Lay the lighter line along one leg of the loop and bend the lighter line around the loop. (When the Albright is used to join monofilament and wire, the end of the wire should be looped first, using a haywire twist, and the loop should be pinched down so that it is long and fairly narrow.)

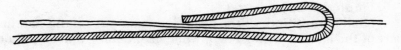

2. Wrapping the tag end of the lighter line around all three strands (both legs of the loop and the parallel strand of lighter line), *wrap at least a dozen* turns (ten will suffice when joining mono to wire), slipping the fingers of the hand that is holding the loop to hold the turns in place.

3. After all the turns are completed, slip the tag end of the lighter line back through the loop. The light mono *must* enter and leave the loop *on the same side*.

4. Maintaining some light tension on the tag end and standing line with the right hand, slide the coils or turns down the loop with the thumb and forefinger of the left hand, stopping short of the loop end by about ⅛ to ¼ inch.

5. Using pliers, pull the tag end of the light mono tight while holding onto both strands of the heavier loop. This is necessary to keep the coils or wraps from slipping off the loop.

6. Finish tightening in stages:
a) Hold both strands of the heavy loop and pull on the standing part of the lighter mono. Then, while maintaining a hold on both

parts of the heavy material, pull first on the tag end of the lighter line, and then on the standing part.

b) Now, holding *just the standing parts* of both lines, pull heavily in opposite directions. If the knot is going to fail it will fail now. Trim both tag ends closely.

When you are tying mono leader onto braided line, the mono leader is doubled over as the loop and the braided line does all the wrapping.

STOPPER KNOTS

From time to time you may want to rig up a sliding float, and that will require the use of some sort of stopper. Almost anything can be used—from a knot tied directly in the fishing line through various sorts of hardware tied into the line as stoppers to patented float stoppers—but the most versatile is a removable and adjustable stopper knot. This is nothing but an extra, short piece of monofilament fishing line or leader material knotted around the main fishing line in such a manner as to permit its being moved to adjust fishing depth. Again, many knots can be used—clinch, nail, overhand, and so on—but the one I like best is a variant of the double overhand knot that Australian angler Dick Lewers (in his excellent little book, *Fishing Knots and Rigs*) simply calls the float stop.

Lewers Float Stop

Like all good stopper knots, the Lewers float stop is easy to tie, permits adjustment of position, is fairly streamlined for smooth sailing through rod guides, and can be tied in monofilament that may be lighter, heavier, or identical to the main fishing line around which it is tied. I like to keep the knot as small as possible by using fairly light-test line to tie the stopper and a small bead sliding on the line between float and stopper. Without the bead you either have to use a very large stopper knot or shop around until you find floats with very tiny eyes or center holes.

1. Wrap a 6-inch length of monofilament around the line, forming one complete wrap or turn.

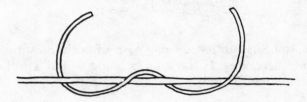

2. Wrap the tag ends around each other twice, making four interlocking turns and forming what is in effect a double overhand knot.

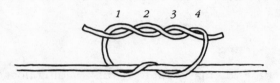

3. Pull the knot fairly tight—but not too tight—and clip the tag ends within 1/16 inch. It will take a little practice to get the feel for the proper tightening of the knot, which must be secure enough to hold the float in place, but capable of being slipped along the line to a new position.

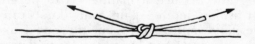

SPLICING BRAIDED LINES

Some braided lines are made with a so-called solid core, which is usually a strand of twisted or braided fibers. Others—including most Dacron and polyester *trolling* lines—are made hollow, particularly those intended for the saltwater market. But some of the same materials are braided into solid-core *casting* lines for freshwater fishing. Among the braided nylon lines, the freshwater casting lines are made with a solid core, but those intended for surfcasting usually are made hollow. Most saltwater nylon braids are called *squidding* lines. While there are several important differences between the solid- and hollow-core braided lines, the one that concerns us here is the spliceability of the hollow braids.

Contrary to widespread opinion, line splices aren't necessarily stronger than knots. Stronger, certainly, than sloppily tied, ill-chosen knots, but probably not quite as strong as knots carefully selected and tied according to the principles already discussed. A braided line that has been spliced will always be a little weaker than one that hasn't. How much weaker is difficult to measure because of the variables: The length of the splice, its tightness, how many times the line was pierced, and how many fibers were broken or damaged in the piercing.

Stronger or not, splices have some distinct advantages over knots. Since they are smoother, slimmer, more tapered, and more streamlined than knots, and don't have those tag ends that often get knots into trouble, line splices cause less friction during casting. They are also much less prone to fouling or picking up weeds and other gunk, and they do not subject the connected line to so many hard knocks. Braided lines are much less abrasion-resistant than monofilament lines, so the smooth, slim, tapered splices help to protect the frayage-prone braids.

Splicing Needles

Some manufacturers of hollow braided lines pack a splicing needle with each spool; others include the needles only with bulk or high-capacity spools. But most tackle shops that sell such lines also sell the needles, which are not expensive. It isn't necessary to use the special splicing needles, and some anglers prefer to use nothing but a bent piece of wire.

Splicing Needle

The special splicing needle—the angler's equivalent of the sailor's rope-splicing fid—is a complicated little instrument, prone to loss, damage, and breakage, so one is never enough. Most are made flat rather than round, with a tiny hook and a hinged jaw on the business end. The hook permits pulling a piece of line through a hollow core and the jaw permits doing so without snagging the hook in the braided "walls" of that hollow-core "tunnel." Some companies make two sizes of splicing needles, one for lines testing above, say, 30 pounds, and the other for lighter lines. It is difficult, if not impossible, to splice lines that test below

20 pounds, so count on having to knot 6- and 12-pound-test braided trolling lines. Naturally, the heavier the line, the bigger the core, and the easier the splicing job.

A simple *sewing needle* (preferably made of stainless steel, to resist corrosion) may be a satisfactory line-splicing tool. It should be fairly long—at least 2½ inches and preferably 3 inches or more. If you use the sewing needle in tailor's fashion, you will have to make many adjustments in the techniques described below. It's better and easier to use it backward—eye first—and follow the same procedures that are used with the splicing needle.

The *bent wire* should be a fairly long (6- to 10-inch) piece of thin, stiff wire leader material, not supple trolling wire. No. 3 (0.012-inch diameter) wire is ideal, but you can get by with no. 5 (0.014). The wire should be bent double in the middle, forming a long, narrow Vee. Use pliers to make a severely sharp bend that forms an actual point. The bent wire is used in the same manner as the splicing needle, so you needn't make any adjustments to the splicing descriptions below.

No matter which sort of splicing tool you use, you will discover that working a tool in braided line is a little like using those "Chinese hand-cuffs" you used to see when you were a kid. You know, the little tubes woven of rush fibers that you put on all ten fingers so you couldn't pull your hands apart. You may recall that pulling your fingers apart caused the tubes to restrict and bind onto your fingers. But if you pushed your fingers toward one another, the tubes actually expanded in diameter. It is the same with braided line. Work the line up over the needle or wire to increase its diameter and make the process of splicing easier. As you pull the line through, it will contract.

Basic Splice

The principles you learn in this basic splice, which is used to join together two separate pieces of braided line, can be applied to the spliced loops described later and to other spliced connections you can "invent" on your own. The first principle is that any splice should be at least 3 inches long, *in toto;* a 6-inch splice will provide just about maximum strength for big-game and other stressful forms of fishing.

1. Insert a splicing needle into the hollow core of one length of line (call it line A) about 6 to 8 inches up from the tag end, aiming the needle down toward that tag end. Push the needle down the

hollow core about 2 inches, then push it back through the line and out. With the hook of the needle, grasp line B about an inch or so from its tag end.

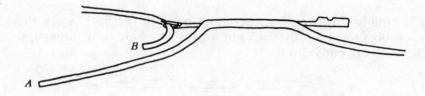

2. Pull line B through line A, exiting at the original point of entry. Pull a couple of inches of line B's tag end through, so you needn't worry about its slipping back inside line A.

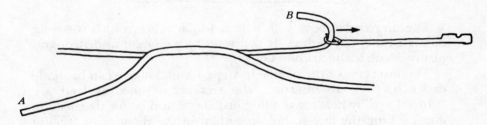

3. Insert the splicing needle into the hollow core of line B, about 3 inches up from its junction with line A, aiming the needle down toward that junction. As in step 1, slide the needle through 2 inches of line B's core, then exit on the side the tag end is pointing, about 1 inch from the junction of the two lines. Grasp the tag end of line A in the hook of the needle.

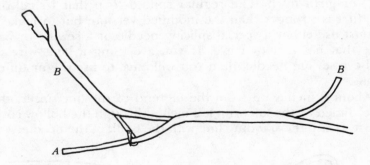

4. Pull line A through line B.

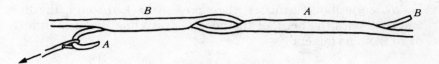

5. Pulling slowly on both standing parts of the lines, work the two splices together. Smooth out any lumps with your fingertips. Clip both tag ends close.

6. By pulling on the lines and massaging the splice, work both of the shortened tag ends inside the lines.

The directions above will form a 4-inch splice, which is strong enough for most angling. If you want to go longer and stronger, just recalculate the arithmetic.

The insertion of the needle in steps 1 and 3 above can be made easier if, prior to insertion, the sections of line involved are "fluffed up" by holding the line just above and below that section and pushing the line so held together, in the manner of freeing one's fingers from those Chinese handcuffs. Keep this point in mind as you read on.

Spliced Loop

Neat end loops can be spliced into braided lines to provide convenient means for attaching snaps or swivels via the lark's-head "knot" or girth hitch. The regular spliced loop that I shall describe first is stronger than the modified version, but to make it you must use either a special splicing needle or a sewing or bait needle that has a slotted eye. If you are using a bent wire or closed-eye sewing needle, then you will have to use the modified version.

1. About 6 inches up from the tag end of the line, insert the needle, aimed *up* the line, run it 2 inches through the hollow core, and exit. Grasp the standing line with the hook of the needle.

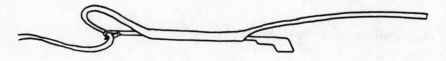

2. Pull the standing line through the core (leaving no loop on the left by the standing line) and form a loop on the right as large or as small as you want. You can make a doubled trolling line for big-game fishing this way, but it won't make quite as strong a double as a Bimini twist.

3. Use the fingertips to work the tag end back up toward the reel, turning the spliced section inside out.

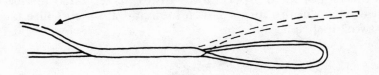

4. Insert the needle, aimed back at the loop, into the hollow core of the standing line about 2½ inches up the line from the splice or junction. Proceed down through the hollow core, exiting *on the same side* as the tag end about ½ inch short of the junction. Take the tag end in the hook of the needle.

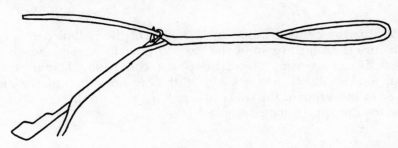

5. Pull the needle and tag end back out of the line, work the two sections of the splice together, clip the tag end, and massage it into the splice.

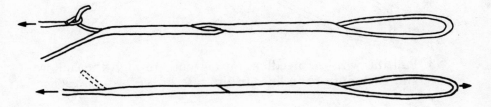

Modified Spliced Loop

This is the version you will have to use to splice an end loop into a Dacron, Micron, or squidding line if you use a bent wire or regular sewing needle for splicing. Some anglers make a simpler splice than the one I shall describe, but it isn't quite as strong. If, however, simplicity tops strength in your value system, then make a triple- or quadruple-length version of the splice in steps 1 through 3, then skip step 4 and get on with the trimming and massaging of the ends in step 5.

1. Insert the bent wire into the hollow core of the line (aimed down at its tag end) at a point determined by the size of the loop and the length of the splice you wish to make. The dimensions shown here will produce a 2-inch loop and a 4-inch splice (actually two 2-inch splices).

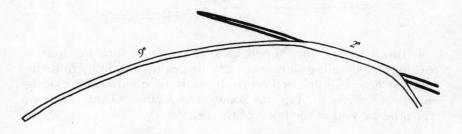

2. Pass the bent wire through 2 inches of the hollow core and out. Insert an inch or so of the tag end into the Vee of the wire. *(Note:* If you are using a sewing needle in conventional tailor fashion, you can insert the tag end into the eye first, then pierce the line at the bottom of the splice and pull the tag end directly *up* the line for the appropriate distance.)

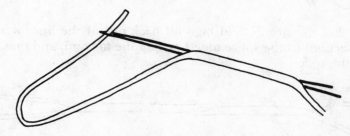

3. Pull the wire (or needle) and tag end through the hollow core and back out of the line. In the case of the two-part splice

being described here, you will need to expose at least 4 inches of tag end. If the loop at this point isn't the desired size, pull the line back out and start again, recalculating your dimensions accordingly.

4. Insert the bent wire, again aimed *down* the line toward the loop, into the hollow core about 2½ inches above the junction from which the tag end protrudes. Work the "needle" through the hollow core for about 2 inches, exiting on the same side as the tag end about ½ inch from the junction of the first splice. Insert the tag end into the Vee.

5. Pull the wire and tag end back out of the line, work the two spliced sections together, clip the tag end, and massage it inside the line.

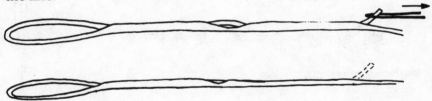

INTERLOCKING LOOPS AND RING HITCHES

At this point, it is probably worthwhile to discuss briefly the interlocking of looped lines and leaders, or the attachment of end loops to ringed pieces of tackle such as snaps and swivels. There are three ways to interlock looped lines and leaders or to attach end loops to terminal tackle.

The two ring hitches (girth hitch and lark's-head) are formed in the same way. Any appropriate knot may be used to form the end loops. In the case of linked loops, obviously one of the loops must be tied after the unknotted line is inserted through the loop-knotted end of the other (or of a swivel's eye).

Popular folklore has it that the girth hitch (which is properly called the reef hitch or reef knot bend when it is used to join two looped lines) is by far the strongest of the three methods. Well, technicians at Du Pont's test labs have tried them all and discovered it doesn't make any difference at all which method you use. All are full-strength connections. In every test case, the lines broke in the knots that were used to make the end loops. Not once did the interlocked loops themselves break.

I can't advise using the girth or reef hitch to attach a looped leader or hook snell to the working end of a snap, though. Under heavy tension, that loop is going to pull the two sides of the snap together, causing it to come open in too many cases. On any snap that opens by pinching, you had better use the lark's-head or the linked-loop method of attachment.

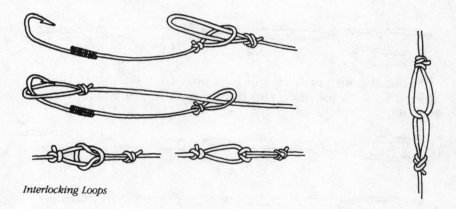

Interlocking Loops

WIRE TIES AND CONNECTIONS

With perhaps one exception (which is described below), wire lines can't be knotted. There are various methods for attaching them, and whether you call them ties or connections or twists or anything else, you must learn to make them correctly if you don't want a weakened line or leader.

Figure-Eight Knot

This is the principal exception to the rule that wire lines can't be knotted successfully. The figure-eight knot can be tied in any material—monofilament or braided, say—but quite frankly, it isn't a very good knot in soft lines. Most anglers who do use it, use it to tie stranded wire lines and leaders, particularly the plastic- or nylon-coated versions. In wire, the figure-eight is a knot that will test 95 to 100 percent, even though it looks considerably less than secure.

1. Run the tag end of the wire through the eye of a hook or lure for 3 inches or so; then bring the tag end back and lay it against the standing part of the line. Try not to make a sharp kink in the wire at this point.

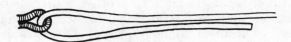

2. Pass the tag end around the standing part and insert it through the loop thus formed at the eye, making a figure eight.

3. Hold the hook or lure in the left hand (you may need to use pliers) and, with the right hand, pull on the standing part of the stranded wire until the knot is properly seated against the eye. The trick here (and it's one I haven't perfectly mastered) is to pull hard enough on the line to seat the knot without putting all sorts of kinks in the wire. Use side-cutting pliers or wire clips to trim the tag end to about 1/16 inch.

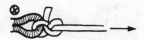

There are a few other knots than can be tied in stranded wire, but they aren't very strong and they are more difficult to tie.

Heated Twist

Also called the fused twist, this is a very simple method of forming a loop in the end of coated wire to attach it to a jig, hook, or lure. If you do it properly, it is a 95- to 100-percent connection. I've talked to those who claim to be able to handle it solo, but I need another pair of hands assisting.

1. Insert the tag end of the coated wire through the eye of the hook or lure for 3 inches or so, and double the tag end back,

twisting it around the standing part of the coated wire *at least four* times.

2. Now, while holding the hook or lure in one hand and the upper end of the twists in another (to prevent untwisting), have a companion hold a match, lighter, or other source of heat to the twists. Hand-warmers and such won't do, because it takes about 500 degrees Fahrenheit to melt plastic. The trick is to apply enough heat to fuse the plastic coating without melting it away or setting it on fire, and that is why I don't consider this a two-handed job. Working solo in the wind—and it always seems to be windy when and where I fish, no matter what—something always gets burned, either the plastic coating on the wire or the skin on my fingers, or both. The safest and best way to heat the plastic with an open flame is from above, which permits you to get close, but it can be done from below as long as you keep the flame an inch or so away. Move the flame back and forth over or under the twists. Remove the flame as soon as the plastic turns milky white —before it begins to drip, blacken, or burn. Let it cool for several seconds, then give it a test yank. Clip the tag end as close as possible to minimize fouling and friction.

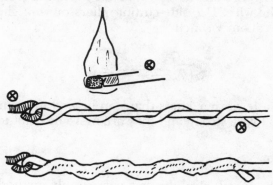

The neatest and safest fused twists are made by stripping the coating off a 2-inch section of the end before beginning. These 2 inches of uncoated end don't count in figuring the number of twists, but they do get twisted. That way, when you hold on to the uncoated end of the twists (an end that doesn't need heating), the flame can fuse the entire coated length of the twists (remember, four or more coated twists). When you clip the uncoated wire off, the tag end will be about as flush and as streamlined as possible.

Crimping Cable

Let's face it: Interesting and useful as the preceding methods are, most of us resort to crimping sleeves when we use stranded wire or cable. They are the easiest things to use when you want to attach hooks, swivels, lures, or other tackle to a stranded-wire leader, and they can be the most secure. "Can be," not "are," because too many people select and crimp sleeves improperly to be really secure. Used properly, however, a crimping sleeve ought not reduce the strength of the wire or cable by much—5 percent at most.

COMMON CRIMPING MISTAKES

Wrong Size Sleeves: Crimping sleeves and wire leader material must be perfectly matched in size; close won't cut it. Alas, once again the tackle industry has not seen fit to standardize its wares so you had best stick to using the same brand wire and sleeves, and follow the size recommendations assiduously.

Improper or Inadequate Crimping Tool: You *can* use ordinary pliers to crimp sleeves, but you won't get a very secure connection unless you are very lucky or very painstaking. Stick with special crimping pliers. I have tried using the inexpensive crimping tools sold in hardware stores for home electrical work, but they are not useful on the heavier, stronger crimping sleeves used in fishing. There seem to be three general types (and price ranges) of crimping tools, and your best bet is to save your pennies until you can afford the best, typified by Sevenstrand's Type C crimping tool and wire cutter. It will cost you close to $30, but it is worth it. It is also the easiest of the crimping tools to use. The middle-of-the-road tools are well represented by Berkley's heavy-duty model and the one sold by Al's Goldfish Lure Company. At $10 to $20 it is a cost-effective instrument, but it isn't as easy to use as the Sevenstrand. It takes me about twice as long to make a crimp. The bottom of the barrel, in price and usefulness, are the crimpers that sell for about $5; avoid them.

Crimping Improperly: Even with a proper tool, you can go awry. Most crimping tools have two or more notches, plainly or obscurely marked according to sleeve sizes, and you must use the proper notch. Having matched sizes of sleeves and wire, and selected the proper crimping notch in a good crimping tool, squeeze those

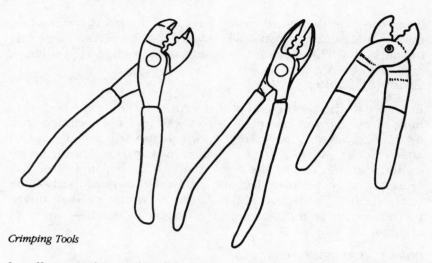

Crimping Tools

handles together as hard as you can. That will give you a secure connection—if you haven't allowed the wire strands to become crossed inside the sleeve or crimped the sleeve only once with a tool that requires double crimping. (Tools with narrow crimping jaws are intended for double crimping of standard-length sleeves.)

Crimping Monofilament: Don't use cable-crimping sleeves on monofilament leaders and terminal rigs. I know—heavy, stiff monofilament is difficult to tie, and the knots are bulky, but crimped connections in mono often fail under pressure. First, it is difficult not to nick, and therefore weaken, the mono leader with the metal sleeves, either in the crimping or the fishing. Second, a cautiously crimped sleeve that won't nick the mono may allow the nylon to slip free; remember, when nylon stretches it gets skinnier as well as longer. Now that Sevenstrand has finally come out with special crimping sleeves for monofilament, you can safely crimp all your leaders and terminal rigs. Just be sure to use the right size sleeves for the diameter of the line or leader, and a good crimping tool.

It doesn't make any difference whether the stranded wire you use is twisted, braided, or cable-laid, or whether it is coated or plain; you have to crimp it properly or it won't hold. The sleeves

Crimping Sleeves   *Monofilament*   *Cable*

themselves are made of various materials—copper, stainless steel, nickel-plated brass tubing, heavy brass tubing, machined brass. The strongest and best sleeves I have seen and used are those sold by Sevenstrand. In the super-heavyweight classes of 49-strand aircraft cable, which commercial longliners and some shark fishermen use, you need to use very heavy-duty sleeves and big, long-handled, compound-action, industrial crimping tools.

CRIMPING CORRECTLY

Now let's take you through the easy steps of making a simple crimped connection with a narrow-jaw crimping tool:

1. Slip the end of the stranded wire through a sleeve (two sleeves, if you are making a heavy-duty connection), then through the eye of the hook, swivel, or other hardware.

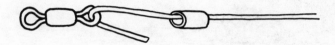

2. Now, double back and slip the end of the cable into the sleeve again. Adjust the size of the loop, keeping the tag end of the wire or cable just barely protruding from the top of the sleeve.

3. Select the proper notch in your crimping tool, and grip the sleeve near the loop end in that notch. Crimp down hard.

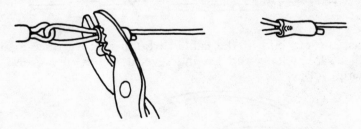

4. Repeat step 3 near the upper end of the sleeve. Be sure that the two strands of wire don't get crossed inside the sleeve, or you will damage the wire when you make your crimp. If it is a real

hassle to keep the strands from crossing, you are using a sleeve that is too large. There shouldn't be any tag end to trim.

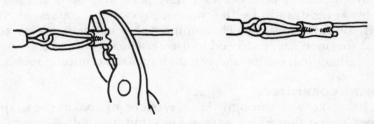

5. For big-game fishing, the double-sleeve crimp is even more secure. Just slip two sleeves onto the wire in step 1 and crimp the sleeves onto the wire no farther than 1 inch apart (to minimize hook fouling, weed pickup, and the creation of strike-misdirecting bubbles).

Big-Game Cable Loop

When fishing 49-strand aircraft-cable leaders for heavyweight oceanic game fish, it is best to use the big-game cable loop. This will minimize the fraying and abrasion that can take place among those tiny strands when they are rubbed so violently against the metal eye of a big hook or swivel.

1. Slip two crimping sleeves of the proper size onto the cable, then slip the end of the cable through the hardware eye.

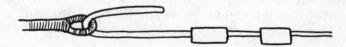

2. Pass the tag end of the cable through the eye once again, forming a closed loop and leaving several inches of tag end to work with.

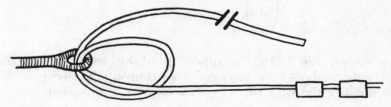

3. Holding the standing part of the cable with the palm and three fingers of one hand, and the hook eye and cable loop in the thumb and forefinger of the same hand, use the other hand to pass the tag end of the cable through the loop three times, as if you were tying a triple overhand knot. Do not tighten.

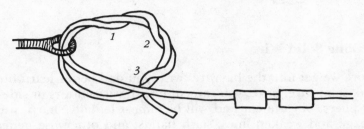

4. Holding the tag end of the cable alongside and parallel to the standing part, work the loop down toward the eye of the hook, so that the loose triple overhand knot becomes small and fairly tight.

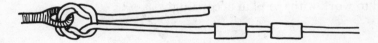

5. Slip the first sleeve down over both parts of the cable—tag end and standing part—until it is seated as close to the loop as possible. Crimp as above. Now do the same with the second sleeve, locating it an inch or less above the first sleeve. Incidentally, some trollers feel that double-sleeve connections are marginally more secure, and less likely to become fouled, if the tag end of the cable is wrapped once or twice around the standing part (as illustrated) after the first sleeve is crimped but before the second is slid into place.

Note: You can rig the same sort of trolling loop in heavy monofilament without crimping. Follow steps 1 through 4 above (omitting the crimping sleeves, of course, and the terminal hardware if you are making a loop in the upper end of a big-game trolling leader). This time, leave a tag end that is 12 to 18 inches long. Finish off by tying a surgeon's end loop in the doubled mono.

Because Della Miller, formerly Mold Craft's ace rigger, taught me this knot, I call it *Della's Loop*.

Della's Loop

Breaking Solid Wire

Before we get into the haywire twist, you had better learn how to break solid wire. Sure, you can cut it with wire cutters or side-cutting pliers, but the cut end will be almost lethally sharp, sure to damage and weaken lines, slash hands, and otherwise generally bollix things up.

1. At the conclusion of any wire connection (haywire twist, barrel turn, wrapped eye, whatever), turn the tag end up so that it stands at a right angle to the standing part of the wire. Until you get this down pat, you probably will want at least 3 inches of tag end to work with, so plan accordingly.

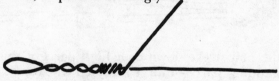

2. Now, bend the upper inch of tag end at a right angle sidewise to the perpendicularly standing tag end just formed.

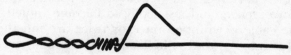

3. Holding the standing part of the wire and wire connection in one hand, take the "crank handle" tag end just formed in steps 1 and 2, and start bending the wire back and forth, immediately above and in line with the standing part of the wire. Don't bend it back and forth across the standing part of the wire. You can, however, turn your crank handle in circular motions.

4. When the wire breaks, the break will occur cleanly at the last wrap or turn of the connection, eliminating those sharp, slashing, tackle-fouling tag ends you get when you cut wire.

Haywire Twist

This is *the* basic connection to use in solid, single-strand wire. You can use it to join two lengths of wire end to end; or to attach hooks, swivels, snaps, and lures, or to form end loops such as those needed when you want to use an Albright special to attach wire to monofilament.

When working with soft trolling wire, you absolutely must use the haywire twist, or some variant, in all connections. With stiffer, harder wire leader material, you might be able to get by with barrel turns alone (see step 3 below), but only if you are using big-game wire in light-tackle applications. For example, you can use a barrel turn when using no. 10 or 12 wire (which test at 124 and 140 pounds, respectively) for making freshwater rigs and spinners that will be fished on 10- or 12-pound-test line. Otherwise, use the haywire twist.

Here is the haywire twist as applied to *joining wire lines together*:

1. Overlap the two ends of wire line by several inches (a foot or more until you get used to it), at an angle to each other—like crossed swords.

2. Twisting both strands of wire around each other, so that the strands become "married," make *at least four to six* complete wraps. This is the haywire or baling twist.

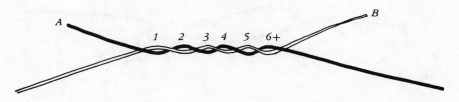

3. With tag end A, make four barrel turns by wrapping tight, neat coils around standing part B. The barrel turns are wrapped at right angles to the standing wire and should be perfectly parallel to and hard up against one another. Break the tag end off as described above.

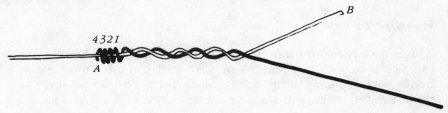

4. Duplicate step 3, using tag end B to wrap four barrel turns around standing wire A. Break off.

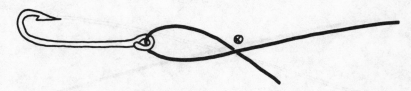

To use the haywire twist *to attach a hook or other piece of terminal hardware, or to make an end loop,* proceed as follows:

1. Pass the tag end of the wire through the hook eye at least 6 inches, doubling back with the tag end in crossed-swords fashion. The crossing point of the tag end and standing wire is determined by the size of the loop you wish to make.

2. Holding the tag end and standing wire in one hand, and making sure that the two parts of wire remain at virtually right angles to one another, twist the hook or loop in the other hand, making four or more married wraps in the two wire parts.

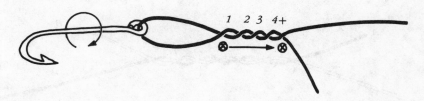

3. As described in step 3 above, wrap four barrel turns around the standing wire with the tag end and break off.

Trolling Spoon Loop

This is the solid-wire equivalent of the big-game cable loop already described. The trolling spoon loop is used, however, by medium-weight-tackle trollers—such as those who troll for bluefish on the East Coast, muskies in the Great Lakes region, and barracuda on the West Coast—and who want to give their metal spoons maximum freedom of action without risking the kinking or nicking of the wire. (This same loop is also used when fishing coated multistrand wire; the wrap is finished off in a heated twist rather than the barrel turns described below for solid wire.)

1. Pass the tag end of the wire through the spoon's ring twice, forming a complete loop of desired size and leaving a foot-long tag end.

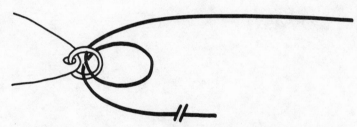

2. Pass the tag end of the wire past and under the standing part of the wire, as if you were going to make another circle, but begin wrapping the tag end in and out of the loop as soon as the tag end has crossed the standing wire. These shouldn't be parallel wraps or coils, but they should be wrapped tightly around the loop.

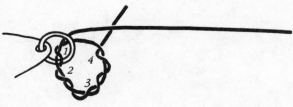

3. Continue wrapping until the tag end has completed the circle, taking at least four wraps around the loop. Finish off by making a short haywire twist and four neat, tight, parallel barrel turns around the standing wire immediately above the loop. Break off.

1234

There are a great many more knots and wire ties you could learn (my knot notebook contains a couple or three hundred knots of varying value, though I certainly haven't mastered them all). But you don't really need to know more than those covered in this chapter. In fact, very few readers will ever need to use all those I have included. Remember, it is how well you can select and tie knots that counts, not how many.

11

C-o-r-r-o-s-i-o-n
Spells
Trouble

CORROSION RUINS EVERYTHING it touches: It weakens metals, dulls hooks, tarnishes bright surfaces, binds moving parts, and stains bucktails, feathers, plastics, and other materials it can't attack directly. Like cancer, corrosion spreads rapidly, accelerates as it grows, and is tougher to cure than to prevent. Unlike cancer, corrosion is contagious, spreading like the plague from one piece of tackle to the next.

WHY METALS CORRODE

"Rustproof" seems to be a favorite word when labeling packages for or writing advertisements about fishing tackle. If you have had much experience with "rustproof" tackle, you know that it corrodes, particularly when exposed to salt water, so you may have wondered whether truth-in-advertising laws apply to fishing tackle. They do, but there is a catch. To be metallurgically precise, rust is a hydrated ferric oxide that is formed by the slow oxidation of iron or iron-containing metals. Even if a piece of brass tackle dissolves into a blue-green mush that resembles the crumbly deposits around automobile battery terminals, it can still be called rustproof. No iron, no rust.

Given enough time and the right conditions, every metal will corrode. Some are much worse than others, of course, and fresh-water anglers won't have nearly as much trouble as saltwater fish-

413

ermen. Seawater is probably the most corrosive medium to which your tackle will normally be exposed, but there are some very corrosive "fresh" waters as well: acidic swamp waters in the South's bass belt, alkaline lakes and reservoirs in the West, and industrially polluted water which, alas, may be found almost anywhere these days.

Corrosion is a chemical, rather than a physical, phenomenon. Common as it is, we still don't understand everything about the electrochemistry that causes, promotes, accelerates, or inhibits corrosion. We do know that the necessary ingredients for a corrosion reaction are very few and very common: metal, moisture, and time.

Only a few of the so-called noble metals—gold and platinum, for example—occur in nature in a metallic state. Most metals occur as oxide or sulfide minerals. The naturally occurring forms of metal are relatively stable, and in those forms and states metals don't react much with their environments. It's too bad we can't use them as is. But we can't; we have to refine and process the metals into usable metallic states. It takes a lot of energy and ingenuity to free the metal ions from the natural bonds of their ores.

The metallic states that are so industrially useful are unnatural and unstable for most metals, and they react with their new environments in an attempt to revert to a more stable condition. Many corrosion products are chemically similar to the mineral forms from which the metals were extracted. Each metal exhibits its own energy potential to react with its environment and to effect this chemical change. Some metals are more able to break their industrial bonds than others, and some environments are more reactive than others.

Most corrosion products are oxides, but not all metal oxides are harmful. In fact, a little corrosion can be a very good thing. Aluminum, for example, is relatively immune to corrosion because it "corrodes" so readily, combining its atoms with the oxygen of our atmosphere and waters to form a thin, tough, protective film. That dingy gray look that aluminum develops is a thin oxide film that is both a corrosion product and the metal's protection against further, harmful corrosion. There is ample oxygen in the atmosphere for most metals to form these protective oxide films. Iron and steel are notable exceptions. Their oxygen demand simply can't be satisfied in nature. Less free oxygen is dissolved in water than in air, so a lot of metals that won't corrode in air will corrode in water. Besides denying oxygen, water also promotes electrical reactions, and corrosion reactions are electrochemical in nature.

By blending metals, metallurgists can produce alloys in which the corrosion potentials of the individual metals are masked, offset, or otherwise "tied up." Add enough chromium and other elements to iron and you come up with stainless steel, not entirely rustproof, but close enough for most angling purposes. Stainless steel doesn't corrode readily because its chromium ions combine with oxygen to form a protective film of very complex chromic oxides. Eventually, though, even stainless steel will rust and corrode.

Tackle companies could use nothing but corrosion-resistant metals, but you wouldn't like the results. Such tackle would be awfully expensive, for one thing. And corrosion isn't the only thing a tackle designer or engineer must consider when selecting a metal. Strength, stiffness, hardness, weight—these are just a few of the factors that contribute to a piece of tackle's overall angling performance. Some highly corrosion-resistant metals just don't measure up in other respects, which may be equally or even more important. The goal—not always achieved by the tackle companies—is to choose a metal that possesses a good mix of metallurgical assets and liabilities. In general, though, most tackle companies do a pretty fair job of metal selection, and if you stick to the well-regarded brands, use the tackle as directed, and take good care of it, it ought to provide good service and reasonable resistance to corrosion. Subject the tackle to conditions other than those for which it was designed, and you can't fairly blame the manufacturer for what happens.

TYPES OF CORROSION

There are several different kinds of corrosion. A few needn't concern you because they aren't likely to attack terminal tackle: stress corrosion, cavitation corrosion, and graphitic corrosion, for example. (However, your boat and motor might be susceptible to them.) There are enough kinds of corrosion that do attack terminal tackle to keep the conscientious angler hopping.

General or Uniform Corrosion

Uniform corrosion is a simple wasting away of the entire surface of a metal. It is the most common kind of corrosion, but it is rarely the most troublesome. The rusting of iron and steel is a particularly odious form of general corrosion, because rust is messy and unsightly, and because the rate of corrosion is relatively high. As a metal corrodes over its entire surface, the metal is getting thinner and weaker all the time, and in some cases the fine details of its shape will be consumed by the corrosion. Most of the metals that are used in fishing tackle have a relatively slow rate of uniform corrosion, which usually shows up as simple tarnish or dinginess. The formation of protective oxide films by metals like aluminum, brass, and stainless steel could be considered beneficial forms of general corrosion.

Lead is subject to uniform corrosion, but it isn't often troublesome. When a sinker or jig comes out of a mold, the lead is bright and shiny. In a few days or weeks the shininess gives way to dinginess, and finally the lead becomes quite dull. Lead corrodes much more rapidly in salt water than in fresh water or air, but the corrosion rate isn't so fast that you will notice much weight loss in a sinker or jig. But a lead-core trolling line used in saltwater will lose enough weight to become relatively ineffective in deep fishing.

How troublesome is lead corrosion? Ignoring its possibly toxic effects on your health (about which I wonder, but really don't know), the corrosion isn't very worrisome. It isn't particularly messy and doesn't generate much new corrosion of other metals in your tackle box. However, you can't paint a jig or sinker and expect the paint to stick unless you first remove the oxide corrosion film with an acidic metal cleaner (a patented product, acetone, or simple vinegar will do).

Pitting

Pitting is the most destructive and insidious form of corrosion. Because the corrosion attack is concentrated in small areas, the reaction is usually very intense. A leaky automobile radiator is often the result of a corrosion pit that has eaten its way entirely through the metal. Most of the corrosion you notice on your chrome-plated tackle is pitting. It may look as if a spinner blade is corroding pretty generally, but look at it through a hand lens and you will see that the corrosion is actually occurring in a very large number of individually small spots.

Metals that are fairly immune to uniform corrosion are susceptible to pitting, because the intensity of the concentrated attack can overpower the metal's inherent corrosion resistance. Pores or breaks in protective platings or finishes, material impurities at the surface of the metal, mechanical defects such as scratches and cavities, and surface deposits of salts and sediments can cause pitting. Ever notice fingerprints etched into a piece of metal tackle? Your skin oils contain various salts and acids, all of which promote corrosion. The oils hold them to the metal and the ridges and grooves of your fingerprint concentrate them in fine lines.

Crevice Corrosion

Also called concentration-cell corrosion, this is a special kind of pitting. Aluminum, nickel, and stainless steel are normally quite corrosion-resistant, even in salt water, but all are prone to crevice corrosion, particularly stainless steel. This kind of corrosion occurs because a small area of metal is "starved" of the oxygen

A BROAD-BRUSH LOOK AT SUSCEPTIBILITY TO CORROSION

METAL	UNIFORM CORROSION	PITTING
Aluminum Alloys	no	YES
Anodized Aluminum	no	YES
Brasses	YES	no
Bronzes	YES	no
Cadmium	YES	Sometimes
Carbon Steel	SEVERE	no
Chrome Plate	no	YES
Copper	YES	no
Gold	no	no
Lead	YES	no
Monel	no	Mild
Nickel	no	YES
Silver	YES	no
Stainless Steel	no	YES
Tin	no	YES
Zinc	YES	Sometimes

NOTES:

1. The above characterizations are general guidelines only, because susceptibility or proneness to corrosion can be affected or altered by numerous factors and conditions.

2. In addition to the types of corrosion listed above, brasses, bronzes, and some copper-nickel alloys are subject to dealloying corrosion.

3. Corrosion by pitting is complicated by salt and sediment deposits, scratched or defective platings, physical design of the metal parts, and galvanic reactions. In salt water, stainless steel is particularly susceptible to crevice corrosion, which occurs in oxygen-deficient crevices, nooks, and crannies. Aluminum and nickel alloys are also subject to crevice corrosion, but less so.

4. Marine-grade aluminum alloys are generally subject only to mild pitting. However, all aluminum alloys in contact with copper, iron, and their alloys may be pitted severely. Nickel, lead, and stainless steel may cause aluminum alloys to pit. Anodized aluminum is normally very resistant to corrosion, but if the anodized coating is broken by scrapes or scratches, the aluminum underneath becomes subject to severe pitting.

necessary to form its protective film. Crevice corrosion is quite common around salt water in such tight, enclosed places as under the heads of nuts and bolts, in the grooves of threaded fasteners, inside unplated ball-bearing swivels, and in the packed coils of wet, stainless-steel trolling wire left on a reel.

Once crevice corrosion gets started, it usually rips right along. It can so affect the electrochemical makeup of the metal that the whole piece may begin corroding. This is not exactly rare in the case of nickel and stainless steel, both of which normally exist in an electrochemically passive state but can be made active once corrosion gets a toehold.

Dealloying

In particularly corrosive environments, certain metal alloys may enter into a reaction in which they give up certain of their metallic ions, usually zinc or aluminum. It is almost as if the metal were being electrochemically leached from the alloy. Once enough of the metal has departed, you wind up with an alloy that isn't anything like the one you started with. Sometimes the alloy even falls apart or crumbles like a burned cookie.

Brasses that contain more then 15 percent zinc are subject to dezincification in seawater and certain other corrosive waters and environments. So-called naval brass is sometimes used in tackle because its name has such a salty ring, but unfortunately it contains about 39 percent zinc and simply won't hold up in salt water. The same goes for admiralty brass. Dealuminification is less common in alloys, but is electrochemically quite similar.

Galvanic Corrosion

Whenever two dissimilar metals are joined or brought into contact in the presence of an *electrolyte,* an electrical current begins flowing between the metal parts and back through the electrolyte, just as it does in an electrical cell or battery. There also occurs between the metals a counterflow of electrons. The metal giving up the electrons is corroded and the other metal is protected against corrosion. This reaction is called galvanic corrosion.

Fresh water is a very poor electrolyte, so galvanic corrosion usually isn't serious unless the water contains certain salts or other dissolved solids (as in the case in many western lakes.) But seawater is an excellent electrolyte, the most abundant naturally occurring one on earth.

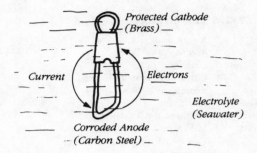

Protected Cathode
(Brass)

Current

Electrons

Electrolyte
(Seawater)

Corroded Anode
(Carbon Steel)

The Galvanic "Battery"

To understand galvanic corrosion you have to know where the involved metals stand in the *galvanic series*. (The galvanic series is a ranking of metals by their electrochemical potential to participate in galvanic reactions.) If they are close together in the series, there will be very little galvanic corrosion. The farther apart they are, the greater the corrosion. In any given pair of metals, the one closer to the *anodic* end of the series will be corroded. The other metal—the one nearer the noble or *cathodic* end—will be protected. The galvanic reaction can take place only when the metals are in electrical contact and in the presence of an electrolyte. Insulate the metals from one another, or remove the electrolyte, and the reaction stops.

Actually, galvanic corrosion is more complicated than that. Some metals, like stainless steel and nickel, occupy two places in the series. Normally both metals are passive, but they can become active if something causes them to begin corroding—crevice corrosion, perhaps. Stainless steel, titanium, and a few other metals also tend to become polarized when they react galvanically with certain other metals. This is much too complicated to explain here in detail. Briefly, though, what happens is that the galvanic reaction itself causes the metals to become electrochemically similar, which stops the reaction. Stainless steel and aluminum, for example, are quite far apart in the galvanic series, yet they become polarized in seawater, *as long as the surface area ratio is at least five or six to one, aluminum over stainless.* Reverse the ratio and it's goodbye, aluminum.

Polarization, galvanic reversals, and other strange things tend to happen during galvanic reactions, making it almost impossible to predict with any accuracy just how the corrosion will turn out.

GALVANIC SERIES (SEAWATER)

ANODIC END	Magnesium
(Corroded)	Magnesium Alloys
	Zinc
	Galvanized Iron and Steel
	Aluminum Alloys (part)
	Cadmium
	Aluminum Alloys (part)
	Mild Steel
	Cast andWrought Irons
	Stainless Steels (active, corroding)
	Lead
	Tin
	Manganese Bronze
	Naval Brass
	Yellow Brass
	Nickel (active, corroding)
	70/30 or Cartridge Brass
	Admiralty Brass
	Aluminum Bronze
	Copper
	Silicon Bronze
	Phosphor Bronze
	Cupronickel and Copper-Nickel
	Nickel-Aluminum Bronze
	Monel and Inconel
	Nickel (passive)
	Silver
	Stainless Steel (passive)
	Titanium
(Protected)	Graphite
CATHODIC OR	Gold
NOBLE END	Platinum

NOTES:

1. This is not a ranking of metals by their resistance to corrosion. This ranking serves only to rank metals by their galvanic potential.

2. Stainless steel and nickel generally exist in the passive state. If, however, something causes either metal to begin corroding, it may become active and assume the more anodic position in the series.

3. The different aluminum alloys exhibit a rather broad range of galvanic potentials, but most will fall within the two positions listed.

4. Because of its tendency to become polarized with respect to other metals, stainless steel will not necessarily take part in a galvanic reaction with a metal listed nearer the anodic end of the series: i.e., it won't automatically cause most other metals to corrode in salt water.

5. Not all of the metals listed are commonly used in the manufacturer of fishing tackle. They are listed to maintain the appropriate distance relationships between the more relevant metals.

6. Once localized corrosion begins—as in the case of pitting or crevice corrosion—some metals can function as their own galvanic pairs, the corroding areas becoming anodic to the noncorrod-

The relative position of metals in the galvanic series is based on equal or nearly equal surface areas. When the sizes of the two metals are greatly dissimilar, the effect is the same as if the metals were moved closer to or farther apart from one another in the series. Let me give you a more concrete example.

In any galvanic pair of metals, one serves as the anode and the other as the cathode. If the cathodic metal—the one nearer the noble end of the series—has a much larger surface area than the anodic metal, the corrosion reaction can be unbelievably swift and severe. This is called large-cathode–small-anode galvanic corrosion. It is the worst kind. This is the kind of corrosion that results when a nickel-or gold-plated steel hook or brass spinner blade starts corroding at pores, nicks, scratches, or other small breaks in the plating.

Nickel and especially gold are quite noble or cathodic, and in the case of a plated hook or spinner, the plating surface area is very large compared to the exposed steel or brass in the vicinity of a plating "holiday" (that's the term metallurgists use). That is why it is so difficult to keep plated-metal tackle shiny in saltwater service.

Carbon-steel hooks will corrode in fresh or salt water, and they usually are plated or otherwise finished to protect them from corrosion and to give them a particular color or brightness. Gold and nickel platings are very protective of steel, but in the sea they can make matters much worse if the platings aren't perfect—and they rarely are. The thicker the plating, the better the corrosion protection, but the duller the point. Sharpen the hook by triangulating the point, and you remove the plating, exposing the point to galvanic corrosion. You have to sharpen hooks anyway, so it is best to use tinned or cadmium-plated hooks in salt water. Even bronzed or blued hooks are better than nickel- or gold-plated ones. Stainless-steel hooks are better still.

HOOKS AND CORROSION

Corrosion, not wear and tear, is the chief cause of dullness in hooks. It is also a source of weakness. What it all boils down to is the relative effectiveness of the metals, platings, and finishes used in protecting hooks from corrosion.

ing areas. This apparently is what makes stainless steel so susceptible to crevice corrosion in the sea.

7. Graphite is listed because it is considered a near-metal or semimetal. It won't corrode by itself in seawater. The graphite fibers used to make fishing rods won't participate in galvanic reactions because the fibers are completely encapsulated in resin.

Nickel Alloys

The most nearly corrosion-proof hooks are not made of steel but of nickel alloys like Duranickel, Inconel, Z-Nickel, M-Nikkel, and the like. Maybe someday we'll see titanium-alloy hooks, but for the moment the nickel alloys are tops in corrosion resistance.

Nickel-alloy hooks are not very popular for several reasons. First, they are much more expensive than plated or stainless-steel hooks. Second, they are much thicker and heavier. Third, they are difficult to make. Nickel alloys can't be hardened by heat treatment after they are formed, so the wire used must be soft enough to permit bending and shaping, but strong enough to resist opening. To get the strength, the wire must be thick—usually about twice as thick as the steel wire used to make a hook of similar strength. Even so, I doubt the nickel-alloy hooks really match steel hooks for strength. Given these problems and the market resistance to price, nickel-alloy hooks aren't exactly setting the world on fire. O. Mustad withdrew its M-Nikkel hooks from the market a few years ago, and the only nickel-alloy hooks still being made that I know about are a small California company's Siwash salmon hooks of Inconel.

Stainless Steel

When stainless-steel hooks first hit the angling market they had some faults. Typically, they were softer and weaker than carbon-steel hooks. Then heat-treatable grades of stainless steel were developed. These were hard but occasionally brittle. Stainless steel is more difficult to work than ordinary steel and is less tolerant of error or variation. A few years ago, many hook manufacturers had trouble turning out stainless hooks of uniformly high quality. Now the top hook producers can handle stainless very well and it isn't uncommon to find stainless hooks that are harder and stronger than carbon-steel ones.

Not all stainless-steel hooks are alike, though, because different alloys are used. Wright & McGill admits that the heat-treatable alloys used to make stainless-steel Eagle Claw hooks are not as corrosion-resistant as the standard marine grades of stainless steel that are used to make boat parts and other pieces of tackle that don't have to be heat-treated. Mustad uses a Swedish stainless alloy that contains a rather high percentage of molybdenum, an alloying metal that preserves the corrosion resistance while increasing the heat-treatability. Are Mustad's stainless-steel hooks superior? In a metallurgical sense, I suppose they are. But I can't say I've ever had any real trouble with corroding Eagle Claws. They are corrosion-resistant enough.

Stainless-steel treble hooks are a special case. Mustad doesn't make them because the high heat that must be used in brazing the third barb to what is essentially a double hook affects the chemical structure of the stainless steel in the vicinity of the brazing. As a result, a stainless treble will rust fairly readily on the shank. The only stainless-steel trebles I've seen are Eagle Claws. Rusting shanks or not, I use them fairly frequently in salt water because I want the *points* to remain rust-free and sharp.

There is a myth afoot that stainless-steel hooks can't be sharpened as well as carbon-steel hooks or that they won't hold a sharp point. Stainless steel may be more difficult to sharpen, but if you spend those few extra seconds you will discover that stainless hooks hold the sharpness of their points better and longer.

The polarization I alluded to in the section on galvanic corrosion is another plus for stainless steel. Nickel-alloy hooks will react galvanically with most other metals—piano-wire leaders, brass plug wires, and so on—causing them to corrode. And many of the platings I'll discuss next also participate in galvanic reactions, either as the corroder or the corrodee. But stainless steel can be joined to most metals without causing an undue amount of corrosion.

In salt water, I use stainless-steel hooks whenever I can. Alas, there are plenty of times when stainless hooks aren't feasible, either because I need to use a pattern or style that isn't available in stainless steel or because Eagle Claw stainless trebles are too heavy to use on delicately balanced plugs like Rapalas and Rebels. And sometimes, when I am fishing under conditions that are going to cause a lot of tackle loss because of snags and breakoffs, I won't bother using the more expensive stainless hooks.

Stainless-steel hooks have a disadvantage. If a hooked fish manages to break your line, or if you release a fish by cutting the leader (the best way to release a fish), a stainless hook's corrosion resistance just might cause the fish to die anyway, because the hook won't rust away and fall out of its mouth soon enough to allow it to resume normal feeding. Some hook designers and manufacturers think this isn't a valid concern, because stainless steel does *eventually* corrode. But eventually may be too late to save a fish's life. If I know I will be releasing the fish I catch, I prefer not to use stainless steel.

Cadmium-Plated Hooks

Because of worker-safety and environmental rules and regulations, which are getting tougher, don't be surprised if cadmium—an extremely toxic metal—disappears from the hook market altogether some time in the future.

Actually, the "cadmium-plated" hooks made by Mustad, Eagle Claw, and the other top hook manufacturers are first cadmium-plated and then tinned. The cadmium plating is anodic to steel and therefore protects it galvanically by sacrificing itself. To protect the soft cadmium from wasting or wearing away too rapidly, a harder, cathodic plating of tin goes on top. The cadmium protects the steel, the tin protects the cadmium. Clever.

Tinned Hooks

Mustad also makes plain tinned hooks, which Mustad (USA) president Klaus Kjelstrup refers to as "our cheap tinned hooks." These are inexpensive, budget-grade saltwater hooks, intended chiefly for commercial fishing or for supplying tackle companies. Many hook-makers produce similar tinned hooks. These budget-grade hooks aren't very corrosion-resistant because the tin plate is never free from small pores—which metallurgists call holidays—and because the tin is somewhat cathodic to steel. It thus tends to promote galvanic corrosion of the steel that is exposed by the pores or by sharpening the point.

Perma Plate

In 1979 the French company, Viellard Migeon et Cie., which makes VMC hooks, introduced a new plating it calls Perma Plate. Christophe Viellard won't divulge the company's secret, but based on a little bench testing and telephonic conferring with metallurgists, my guess is that Perma Plate is a sacrificial or anodic plating of aluminum or magnesium. This means that you can safely sharpen the point by triangulation and the anodic plating will keep the exposed steel from being corroded by seawater. The plating itself will be corroded galvanically, but not very rapidly or massively. And the corrosion product is a fine, inoffensive, grayish-white "dust"—what metallurgists call "white rust."

VMC calls its Perma Plate hooks "2,000-hour hooks" because that is how long the hooks will resist corrosion in salt water, according to their lab tests. VMC's Perma Plate is a real comer, one that is going to give tin, cadmium, and stainless steel a real run for the money.

Nickel-Plated Hooks

Bright, nickel-plated hooks are very popular in some places, and a lot of tackle companies and anglers apparently think that they are effective in salt water. I simply can't agree with that. Nickel-plated hooks are terrible in salt water. Nickel itself is extremely corrosion-resistant, but it is very noble or cathodic relative to steel and most other tackle metals. Therefore it will cause most other metals to corrode galvanically in salt water.

If the nickel plating is thick and heavy, it will be absolutely necessary to sharpen the hook by filing the plating away from the point section. This will expose the point to a very severe, large-cathode—small-anode galvanic corrosion. If the plating isn't very thick, it will be so full of pores it will expose the whole hook to galvanic pitting.

Nickel-plated hooks are very good in fresh water, if you want and need a flashy hook, and I suggest you use them only in sweet waters. Unless, in salt water, you consider them disposable hooks, to be discarded after a single use.

Gold-Plated Hooks

Everything I said about nickel-plated hooks applies to gold-plated hooks, only more so. Gold is one of the most noble of all metals, and it will cause virtually all other metals that are used in terminal tackle to corrode in salt water. Because gold is so expensive, gold platings tend to be very, very thin and full of pores. The best gold-plated hooks have two layers of nickel plate under the gold. The cheap hooks, which apply a single, porous plating of gold directly on the steel, are simply awful.

Gold-plated hooks are very popular, in salt water as well as fresh, because a great many anglers believe that fish are attracted to the flashy gold. In some cases, at least, I believe they are right. If gold finish isn't a major part of the rig's attraction, then don't use gold-plated hooks in the sea. In fresh water they are fine.

Bronzed, Blued, Japanned, and Black-Lacquered Hooks

These can be treated together because in all cases it is the lacquer that provides the corrosion protection. Steel hooks are bronzed or blued by an oxide-conversion process that provides very, very little protection against corrosion. Except in the case of incredibly cheap and inferior hooks, a coat of lacquer—often a colored lacquer—is then applied, to provide corrosion protection and to keep the thin oxide film from being scratched or worn away. Oxidized or not, some hooks these days are being given epoxy coatings to protect them—with varying degrees of success.

Well-made hooks are adequately protected against corrosion by lacquer. Poorly made hooks are not, because the lacquer coat is thin and discontinuous. Lacquering doesn't provide the corrosion protection of a real plating, but it doesn't cause galvanic corrosion, either.

HOOK MATERIALS AND FINISHES RATED ACCORDING TO THEIR RESISTANCE TO CORROSION

GENERALLY	POINTS TRIANGULATED
1. Nickel Alloy	1. Nickel Alloy
2. Stainless Steel	2. Stainless Steel
3. Perma Plate	3. Perma Plate
4. Cadmium-Plated and Tinned	4. Cadmium-Plated and Tinned
5. Epoxy-Coated	5. Epoxy-Coated
6. Nickel-Plated	6. Blued
7. Gold-Plated	7. Bronzed
8. Tinned	8. Lacquered or Japanned
9. Blued	9. Tinned
10. Bronzed	10. Bright (Bare-Finish Steel)
11. Lacquered or Japanned	11. Nickel-Plated
12. Bright (Bare-Finish Steel)	12. Gold-Plated

tie { 6. Blued 7. Bronzed

NOTES:
1. Corrosion resistance in hooks depends very much on quality. The rankings above assume uniform, fairly high quality.
2. The general rankings listed above are for salt water. In fresh water, gold- and nickel-plated hooks would fare much better. In fact, the platings and finishes ranked 3 through 7 above might be tied for third place in fresh water. Also, in fresh water, triangulating the points would not change the rankings because no galvanic corrosion would occur.

CORROSION PREVENTION AND TACKLE MAINTENANCE

Corrosion prevention is so much easier than corrosion cure that I will start there.

Tackle Selection

Choose metals, platings, and finishes that are appropriate to the waters you fish. In fresh water, that simply means using well-made, high-quality tackle. In salt water, you have to choose a little more carefully. The previous section on hook corrosion adequately discusses most of the metals used in tackle, except for copper and the copper-based brasses and bronzes. In fresh water, most brasses, bronzes, and copper will not corrode unacceptably. In salt water, forget copper, and be careful about the brasses and bronzes.

Stainless-steel ball-bearing swivels can be a problem, particularly in salt water, unless the bearings and their raceways are nickel-plated prior to assembly (as they are in Sampo ball-bearing swivels). Cheap ball-bearing swivels, which are not plated, tend to lose most of their swiveling efficiency to crevice corrosion after a few exposures to fresh water and even just a single dunking in salt water.

When choosing a wire trolling line, don't forget to take into consideration the metal or metallic plating of your reel's spool, if the line and reel will be used in salt water. If you use a stainless-steel or Monel line on an aluminum spool, you'll have trouble.

In general, be very careful about joining metals together in a saltwater outfit. Refer to the galvanic series before deciding upon the metal bits and pieces that will be joined together. The same caution applies, but somewhat less urgently, if you fish alkaline lakes or acidic, swamp-fed waters.

Preventive Maintenance

Most tackle corrosion occurs during storage rather than during actual use. So you needn't spend any of your actual fishing time dealing with corrosion and corrosion prevention. A little postangling, prestorage maintenance should keep your metals sparkling. Neglect this maintenance and you will find corrosion eating into your fishing time and fun.

RINSING AND DRYING

Before you store fishing tackle, it should be thoroughly dried. This is especially critical if the tackle in question is going to be stored in a tackle box, drawer, locker, closet, or other dank, enclosed place. Natural drying by fresh air, breezes, and sunshine is probably the best and easiest method.

Even dry tackle can be dampened by rising atmospheric humidity. For this reason, it is a good idea to rinse all terminal tackle thoroughly in fresh water prior to drying and storage. In the case of tackle that has been used in salt water, freshwater rinsing is imperative. Dried salt deposits will cause corrosion every time the humidity rises enough to moisten it. In the case of freshwater tackle the problem isn't usually as severe, but dried bits of dirt, weed, slime, and other muck act like sponges. And some of them can contain corrosion-promoting salts, minerals, or chemicals. Seawater contains dozens of corrosive elements: mineral salts, dissolved sediments, microscopic marine organisms, natural chemicals.

Most saltwater anglers know that rods and reels should be rinsed and dried after use and prior to storage, but not very many give the same attention and treatment to their lures, hooks, snaps, swivels, sinkers, metal leaders, and other terminal gear. As John E. Spriggs, Sampo's president, told me, "We believe that any swivel, ball-bearing or otherwise, should be well rinsed in fresh water after each use."

You can soak or spray your terminal tackle to rinse it. Soaking is easier and frees your hands for other cleaning up or maintenance. Terminal tackle isn't lubricated, so you can use a little alcohol to speed up the drying. Be sure not to use alcohol or other drying agents on reels and other geared and lubricated machinery. If you want to fast-dry a wire line spooled onto a reel, go ahead and soak the whole reel, but remove the spool from the reel before using alcohol. A little elbow grease applied to a fairly stiff-bristled brush, such as an old toothbrush, will help to remove caked deposits.

If you do nothing else to your terminal tackle, rinse and dry it after use and before storage and you will cut out most of your corrosion troubles. It is probably the single most important step in corrosion prevention and metal-tackle maintenance.

OVERCOATS AND TOUCHUPS

Plated metals will corrode if the platings or other finishes become scratched, nicked, worn, abraded, or otherwise broken. Some platings and finishes are so porous they don't need any wear and tear to become corrosion-prone. Touch up the wounds as soon as you spot them, using paint, epoxy cement, rod varnish, a clear plastic spray, clear fingernail polish, decoupage finish coat, or almost anything else that is waterproof and nonporous. Don't delay until you get just the right color and chemistry, because corrosion in plated metals is very difficult to arrest. Sometimes, when I notice a nick or break in a plating and haven't any of the mentioned treatments handy, I'll rub a little reel oil on the perforation. It tends to inhibit corrosion and gives me a better shot at nipping the problem in the bud a little later.

Bare, unplated metals can be protected by coating them with the same stuff. I've been able to get an appreciable amount of saltwater service out of some corrodable freshwater spoons and spinners by giving them the clear-plastic or epoxy treatment. You won't be able to home-finish a metal lure with a perfectly nonporous and permanent protective coat, but it's better than nothing. Some anglers paint all their sinkers, feeling that the color helps to attract fish and that the protective coating insulates them and the watery environment from toxic lead.

POLISHING
The smoother a metal surface, the less likely it is to corrode. That is one reason why corrosion seems to accelerate as it goes. It provides the tiny pits and roughened surfaces that enable new corrosion to get started. So keep your metal spoons, spinners, cowbells, squids, herring dodgers, rotating flashers, and other large, bright pieces of metal polished. It doesn't take much to give corrosion a toehold—a speck of dirt, a greasy fingerprint, a shred of dried weed. Any one of these can cause pitting or crevice corrosion, and a corrosion pit is a perfect matrix for further corrosion.

It probably isn't practical to polish your hooks, snaps, swivels, split rings, and other tiny bits and pieces of terminal tackle. Anyway, they tend to be the least expensive, least long-lasting parts of your terminal gear. Mustad sells one hook—its no. 7691S knife-edge-point Southern & Tuna hook—that is made of stainless steel and then electropolished to smooth the surface, seal most of the intergranular surface pits, and generally increase corrosion resistance. Virtually all hooks are polished to some extent, usually in a tumbler or other mechanical polisher.

Corrosion Cures

Once corrosion has gotten started, things become more difficult. Corrosion seems to beget corrosion, and everything slides downhill. There are concoctions on the market like Naval Jelly that "dissolve" rust and others like Trustan 7 that chemically interact with it, turning the rust into something other than ferric oxide. Frankly, I haven't had much luck with either when it comes to fishing tackle. Trustan 7 creates a blue-black mess that stains and tarnishes everything. Naval Jelly is okay, but it can damage chrome-plated pieces of tackle.

Surgery is called for when corrosion strikes. You must get rid of the corrosion. If the patented rust-removers won't work, use a file. This isn't a very desirable approach on chrome-plated spoons and spinner blades, but it is an excellent way of coping with corroded bare metals. Let me stress again that preventing corrosion is easier and better than curing it.

Hooks, particularly those used in salt water, will corrode, and the only way to contain the problem is to keep filing it away as it occurs. I triangulate all of my hook points, in fresh water and salt, and I manage to keep the rusty-hook situation under control and within manageable proportions by touching up hooks frequently, making sure they are rinsed and dried before being returned to the tackle box, and keeping unused and used hooks segregated.

On lures, metal parts are bound to corrode, usually at different rates, and the best way to keep up with the problem is to touch up nicks and scratches, rinse and dry after each use, polish frequently, and replace rusty hooks and split rings. Those who fish spoons, spinners, and jigs in salt water already know that you can't really stay ahead of the corrosion; you have to work pretty hard to keep just a half step behind. If you don't replace hooks and split rings on saltwater plugs rather frequently, eventually the hook hangers or through-wires will become weakened by corrosion. Prior to that, the hooks and split rings themselves may be weakened enough to cause you to lose a once-in-a-lifetime fish. And rusted hook points are dull hook points, incapable of penetrating readily, rapidly, or securely.

Appendix A:
Some Useful Tables

WITH MOST OF THE WORLD already on the metric system and the United States slowly converting to it, confusion has crept into the American marketplace. Some tackle manufacturers label their wares with metric units, some use the traditional units, and some use both. Until they all standardize their product labeling, it will be difficult to make direct comparisons between different brands. Also, some manufacturers use decimal numbers for very small measurements, while others use fractions. The conversion tables that follow can be useful in finding your way around the tackle shelves.

METRIC CONVERSION TABLES

OUNCES TO GRAMS

$oz \times 28.34952315 = gm$
$gm \times 0.03527396 = oz$

OUNCES	GRAMS	OUNCES	GRAMS	OUNCES	GRAMS
1/64	0.443	1/2	14.175	6	170.097
1/40	.709	5/8	17.718	7	198.447
1/32	.886	3/4	21.262	8	226.796
1/16	1.772	7/8	24.806	9	255.146
1/10	2.835	1	28.350	10	283.495
1/8	3.544	1¼	35.438	11	311.845
1/6	4.725	1½	42.525	12	340.194
3/16	5.316	1¾	49.612	13	368.544
1/5	5.670	2	56.699	14	396.893
1/4	7.088	3	85.049	15	425.243
1/3	9.450	4	113.398	16	453.592
3/8	10.631	5	141.748		

POUNDS TO KILOGRAMS

$lb \times 0.45359237 = kg$
$kg \times 2.204623 = lb$

POUNDS	KILOGRAMS	POUNDS	KILOGRAMS
1	0.454	80	36.287
2	.907	90	40.823
3	1.361	100	45.359
4	1.814	125	56.700
5	2.268	130	58.967
6	2.722	150	68.039
7	3.175	175	79.379
8	3.629	200	90.718
9	4.082	250	113.398
10	4.536	300	136.078
12	5.443	350	158.757
15	6.897	400	181.437
20	9.072	450	204.117
25	11.340	500	226.796
30	13.608	550	249.476
35	15.876	600	272.155
40	18.144	700	317.515
45	20.412	750	340.194
50	22.680	800	362.874
60	27.216	900	408.233
70	31.751	1000	453.592
75	34.019		

INCHES TO CENTIMETERS AND MILLIMETERS

in × 2.54 = cm   *cm × 0.3937008 = in*
in × 25.4 = mm   *mm × 0.03937008 = in*

INCHES	CENTIMETERS	MILLIMETERS	INCHES	CENTIMETERS	MILLIMETERS
1/64	0.040	0.397	11/16	1.746	17.462
1/32	.079	.794	3/4	1.905	19.050
3/64	.119	1.191	13/16	2.064	20.638
1/16	.159	1.588	7/8	2.223	22.225
5/64	.198	1.984	15/16	2.381	23.812
3/32	.238	2.381	1	2.540	25.400
7/64	.278	2.778	1 1/8	2.858	28.575
1/8	.318	3.175	1 1/4	3.175	31.750
9/64	.357	3.572	1 1/2	3.810	38.100
5/32	.397	3.969	1 3/4	4.445	44.450
11/64	.437	4.366	2	5.080	50.800
3/16	.476	4.762	3	7.620	76.200
13/64	.516	5.159	4	10.160	101.600
7/32	.556	5.556	5	12.700	127.000
15/64	.595	5.953	6	15.240	152.400
1/4	.635	6.350	7	17.780	177.800
5/16	.794	7.938	8	20.320	203.200
3/8	.953	9.525	9	22.860	228.600
7/16	1.111	11.112	10	25.400	254.000
1/2	1.270	12.700	11	27.940	279.400
9/16	1.429	14.288	12	30.480	304.800
5/8	1.588	15.875			

FEET TO CENTIMETERS AND METERS

ft × 30.48 = cm   *cm × 0.03280840 = ft*
ft × 0.3048 = m   *m × 3.280840 = ft*

FEET	CENTIMETERS	METERS	FEET	METERS
1	30.48	0.305	50	15.240
2	60.96	.610	60	18.288
3	91.44	.914	75	22.860
4	121.92	1.219	100	30.480
5	152.40	1.524	150	45.720
6	182.88	1.829	200	60.960
7	213.36	2.134	250	76.200
8	243.84	2.438	300	91.440
9	274.32	2.743	350	106.680
10	304.80	3.048	400	121.920
12	365.76	3.658	450	137.160
15	457.20	4.572	500	152.400
20	609.60	6.096	550	167.640
25	762.00	7.620	600	182.880
30	914.40	9.144	750	228.600
40	1219.20	12.192	1000	304.800

YARDS TO METERS

$yd \times 0.9144 = m$
$m \times 1.093613 = yd$

YARDS	METERS	YARDS	METERS	YARDS	METERS
5	4.572	80	73.152	500	457.200
10	9.144	90	82.296	600	548.640
15	13.716	100	91.440	700	640.080
20	18.288	125	114.300	750	685.800
25	22.860	150	137.160	800	731.520
30	27.432	175	160.020	900	822.960
40	36.576	200	182.880	1000	914.400
50	45.720	250	228.600	1200	1097.280
60	54.864	300	274.320	1500	1371.600
70	64.008	350	320.040		
75	68.580	400	365.760		

OTHER METRIC CONVERSION FACTORS AND RELATIONSHIPS

WEIGHT

1 kilogram (kg) = 1000 grams (gm)
1 gram (gm) = 0.001 kilogram (kg)
1 gram (gm) = 15.43236 grains (gr)
1 kilogram (kg) = 35.27396 ounces (oz)

LENGTH, DISTANCE

1 millimeter (mm) = 0.1 centimeter (cm) = 0.001 meter (m)
1 centimeter (cm) = 10 millimeters (mm) = 0.01 meter (m)
1 meter (m) = 1000 millimeters (mm) = 100 centimeters (cm)
1 kilometer (km) = 1000 meters (m) = 0.54 nautical miles (nm) = 0.62137 statute land miles (mi)
1 nautical mile (nm) = 1.1508 statute miles (mi) = 1.852 kilometers (km) = 1852 meters (m)
1 statute mile (mi) = 1.6093 kilometers (km) = 1609.3 meters (m) = 0.869 nautical miles (nm)

SPEED

1 inch per second (ips) = 2.54 centimeters per second (cps or cm/sec)
1 foot per second (fps) = 30.48 centimeters per second (cps or cm/sec) = 0.3048 meters per second (mps or m/sec)
1 mile per hour (mph) = 1.6093 kilometers per hour (kph) = 0.869 knots (kt) = 1.467 feet per second (fps) = 0.447 meters per second (mps or m/sec)
1 knot (kt) = 1.1508 miles per hour (mph) = 1.852 kilometers per hour (kph) = 1.688 feet per second (fps) = 0.5144 meters per second (mps or m/sec)
1 kilometer per hour (kph) = 0.62137 miles per hour (mph) = 0.54 knots (kt) = 0.911 feet per second (fps) = 0.27778 meters per second (mps or m/sec)

PRESSURE, TENSILE STRENGTH, ETC.

1 pound per square inch (psi) = 0.7 grams per square millimeter (gm/mm^2) = 0.07 kilograms per square centimeter (kg/cm^2)
1000 pounds per square inch (1 kpsi or 1 ksi) = 0.7 kilograms per square millimeter (kg/mm^2)

AREA

1 square meter (m²) = 10,000 square centimeters (cm²) = 1,000,000 square millimeters (mm²) = 1550.003 square inches (sq in or in²) = 10.76391 square feet (sq ft or ft²)

10,000 square meters (m²) = 1 hectare (ha) = 2.171 acres

100 square meters (m²) = 1 are (a) = 0.025 acre

1 square inch (sq in or in²) = 6.4516 square centimeters (cm²)

1 square foot (sq ft or ft²) = 929.0304 square centimeters (cm²) = 0.09290304 square meters (m²)

1 square centimeter (cm²) = 0.1550003 square inches (sq in or in²)

1 acre = 0.404686 hectare (ha) = 4046.856 square meters (m²) = 43,560 square feet (sq ft or ft²) = 0.001562 square mile (sq mi or mi²)

VOLUME

1 cubic foot (cu ft or ft³) = 1728 cubic inches (cu in or in³) = 28,316.847 cubic centimeters (cm³ or cc) = 0.028317 cubic meters (m³) = 28.3168 liters (1)

1 liter (1) = 0.001 cubic meter (m³) = 1000 cubic centimeters (cm³ or cc) = 61.024 cubic inches (cu in or in³) = 33.814 fluid ounces (fl oz) = 1.057 liquid quarts (qt) = 0.264 liquid gallon (gal)

1 gallon (gal) = 128 fluid ounces (fl oz) = 231 cubic inches (cu in or in³) = 0.1336806 cubic feet (cu ft or ft³) = 3785.42 cubic centimeters (cm³ or cc) = 0.003785 cubic meter (m³) = 3.785 liters (l)

1 cubic meter (m³) = 1000 liters (l) = 1,000,000 cubic centimeters (cm³ or cc) = 61,023.74 cubic inches (cu in or in³) = 35.31467 cubic feet (cu ft or ft³) = 1.308 cubic yards (cu yd or yd³) = 264.17205 gallons (gal)

AIR AND WATER TEMPERATURE

To convert from degrees Fahrenheit (°F) to degrees Celsius (°C), subtract 32 degrees and multiply the remainder by ⁵⁄₉ or 0.556. ([°F−32] × ⁵⁄₉ = °C)

To convert Celsius to Fahrenheit, multiply the °C by ⁹⁄₅ or 1.8 and add 32 degrees. ([°C × ⁹⁄₅] + 32 = °F)

At sea level, water boils at 100°C or 212°F, and freezes at 0°C or 32°F.

To use the temperature-conversion table below, find the known temperature in the center column: If converting from C to F, the answer will be found in the righthand column; if converting from F to C, the answer will be found in the lefthand column.

CELSIUS	KNOWN	FAHRENHEIT	CELSIUS	KNOWN	FAHRENHEIT
−45.6	−50	−58	10.0	50	122
−40.0	−40	−40	15.6	60	140
−34.4	−30	−22	21.1	70	158
−28.9	−20	− 4	23.9	75	167
−23.3	−10	14	26.7	80	176
−17.8	0	32	29.4	90	194
−12.2	10	50	35.0	95	203
− 6.7	20	68	36.7	98	208.4
− 1.1	30	86	37.8	100	212
4.4	40	104			

TABLE OF DECIMAL EQUIVALENTS OF FRACTIONS

You will find many uses for this table when making various mathematical calculations and particularly when making conversions from customary to metric weights and measures.

n	n/2	n/3	n/4	n/5	n/6	n/8	n/10	n/16	n/32	n/64	DECIMAL EQUIV.
										1	0.0156
									1	2	.0313
										3	.0469
								1	2	4	.0625
										5	.0781
									3	6	.0938
							1				.1000
										7	.1094
						1		2	4	8	.1250
										9	.1406
									5	10	.1563
					1						.1667
										11	.1719
								3	6	12	.1875
				1			2				.2000
										13	.2031
									7	14	.2188
										15	.2344
			1			2		4	8	16	.2500
										17	.2656
									9	18	.2813
										19	.2969
							3				.3000
								5	10	20	.3125
										21	.3281
		1									.3333
						2					.3438
								11	22		.3438
										23	.3594
						3		6	12	24	.3750
										25	.3906
			2				4				.4000
										26	.4063
										27	.4219
								7	14	28	.4375
										29	.4531
									15	30	.4688
										31	.4844
	1		2		3	4	5	8	16	32	.5000

n	n/2	n/3	n/4	n/5	n/6	n/8	n/10	n/16	n/32	n/64	DECIMAL EQUIV.
		1	2		3	4	5	8	16	32	0.5000
										33	.5156
									17	34	.5313
										35	.5469
								9	18	36	.5625
										37	.5781
									19	38	.5938
			3				6				.6000
										39	.6094
					5			10	20	40	.6250
										41	.6406
									21	42	.6563
		2			4						.6667
										43	.6719
								11	22	44	.6875
							7				.7000
										45	.7031
									23	46	.7188
										47	.7344
			3			6		12	24	48	.7500
										49	.7656
									25	50	.7813
										51	.7969
				4			8				.8000
								13	26	52	.8125
										53	.8281
					5						.8333
									27	54	.8438
										55	.8594
						7		14	28	56	.8750
										57	.8906
							9				.9000
									29	58	.9063
										59	.9219
								15	30	60	.9375
										61	.9531
									31	62	.9688
										63	.9844
1	2	3	4	5	6	8	10	16	32	64	1.0000

Appendix B:

Terminal Tackle by Mail

You won't find all of the terminal tackle discussed in this book at your neighborhood tackle shop. In fact, chances are that, wherever you shop, you will find only a sampling of the enormous range of terminal tackle. Some tackle is regional in use, and some is so special-purpose it may be very difficult to find anywhere. Sometimes you have to resort to mail order to get what you want. Besides availability, there's price to consider; you may find that mail-order catalogs offer the bits and pieces you need at prices well below those you are used to paying. I'm all for patronizing local businesses, but I like to save money where I can. If the price differential is great for the same quality merchandise, I'll use the mail-order houses. If the prices are close, or if I don't know how good the quality of the mail-order stuff is, I'll stick by the local tackle shops.

Mail-order sources have been organized into two categories: (1) houses that specialize in selling fishing tackle by mail, and (2) tackle manufacturers, distributors, and jobbers. Neither list pretends to be complete, merely representative. And both are alphabetized, so don't try to make any judgments based on a firm's high or low listing. In the case of companies that use a person's full name—for example, Tony Accetta & Son, Inc.—I have used the last name for alphabetization. A caveat: The fishing-tackle business is a volatile, competitive one, and some of these tackle companies and mail-order houses are working on very thin profit margins. So don't be surprised if some of your catalog requests get returned by the post office. Like most small businesses, tackle companies are constantly being gobbled up by larger companies, moved to bigger (or cheaper) quarters, and liquidated by choice or by bankruptcy. I haven't yet been stung buying tackle by mail. Every house I have dealt with has either delivered the merchandise or returned my money.

MAIL-ORDER TACKLE HOUSES

Most of the mail-order houses listed below carry reasonably full lines of tackle. All carry some terminal tackle. Some of them also sell other outdoor sporting gear. If a company's line is very limited, and it isn't obvious from the name, I have noted what they carry. In some cases, I have also indicated that a catalog is the only mail-order source I know for a particular type of tackle. I have ordered from most, but not all, of these companies, and I have been generally pleased with the prices, promptness, and accuracy.

All of these mail-order houses have catalogs. I haven't tried to indicate which ones are free or how much the others cost, because inflationary paper, printing, and postage costs keep the situation in too much flux. If you ask for a catalog, and it isn't free, most houses will let you know how much to remit.

If you decide to write to one of the mail-order houses or tackle companies, I'd appreciate your mentioning *Hook, Line, and Sinker*. Some of these places routinely send me catalogs and new-product listings, but many don't. Without them, keeping up with all the changes is murder. Maybe your letter will encourage them to put me on their mailing lists permanently.

Angler's Workshop, P.O. Box 1044, Woodland, WA 98674. Fly-fishing tackle.

Augie's Custom Tackle, 450 Fire Island Ave., Babylon, NY 11702. Saltwater tackle.

Dan Bailey's Fly Shop, P.O. Box 1019, Livingston, MT 59047.

Bass Pro Shops, P.O. Box 4046, Springfield, MO 65804.

L. L. Bean, Inc., Freeport, ME 04033. Fly-fishing tackle, mainly.

Boyd Tackle Shop, 508 N. Andrews Ave., Fort Lauderdale, FL 33301. Saltwater tackle.

Breck's, Sherbrooke, Que. J1K 1C1, Canada.

Brielle Bait and Tackle, 800 Ashley Ave., Brielle, NJ 08730. Saltwater tackle.

Cabela's, 812 13th Ave., Sydney, NE 69162.

Capt. Harry's Fishing Supply, 100 N.E. 11th St., Miami, FL 33132.

Casco Saltwater Flies, 19 Spring St., Yarmouth, ME 04096.

Classic & Custom Fly Shop, 477 Pleasant St., Holyoke, MA 01040.

Dale Clemens Custom Tackle, 444 Schantz Spring Rd., Allentown, PA 18104. Fly-tying gear and jig heads, mostly.

Custom Tackle, P.O. Box 38, Seaford, NY 11783.

Eric le Moucheur, Inc., 5314 Belanger Est., Montreal, Que. H1T 1E2, Canada. Fly-fishing tackle.

Euro-Tackle, Box 755, Keyport, NJ 07735. Floats.

Fisherman's Paradise, 3800 N.W. 27th St., Miami, FL 33142. Saltwater tackle.

Fishing Tackle Grab Bag, 5521 N. State Rd., Davison, MI 48423.

Fish'n Shack, P.O. Box 1080, Camdenton, MO 65020.

Flyfisher's Paradise, P.O. Box 448, Lemont, PA 16851.

The Fly Shop, 4140 Churn Creek Rd., Redding, CA 96002.

Gander Mountain, Inc., P.O. Box 248, Wilmot, WI 53192.

Goldberg's Marine, 201 Meadow Rd., Edison, NJ 08818. Saltwater tackle.

Graber Tackle, Box 3223, Hutchinson, KS 67504. Jigs.

Great Rip Tackle, P.O. Box 647, Norfolk, MA 02056. Saltwater tackle.

Hackle & Tackle Co., Central Square, NY 13036. Fly-fishing tackle.

High Creek Anglers, 19 W. Main, Richmond, UT 84333. Flies.

The Hook & Hackle Co., P.O. Box 1003, Plattsburgh, NY 12901. Fly-fishing tackle.

Hunter's Angling Supplies, Central Sq., Box 300, New Boston, NH 03070.

Jack's, 2545 S. Delaware Ave., Milwaukee, WI 53207.

Kaufman's Streamborn, P.O. Box 23032, Portland, OR 97223. Fly-fishing tackle.

Marriott's Flyfishing Store, 2634 W. Orangethorpe, Fullerton, CA 92633.

Midland Tackle Co., 66 Route 17, Sloatsburg, NY 10974.

Mouldy's Tackle Co., Rte. 4, Box 3001, Chippewa Falls, WI 54729. Muskie tackle.

Mountaintop Tackle, Box 66, Eden, VT 05652. Fresh- and saltwater tackle.

Mud Hole Custom Tackle, 126 N. Rte. 9, Forked River, NJ 08731. Saltwater tackle.

The Netcraft Co., 2800 Tremainsville Rd., Toledo, OH 43613.

Okiebug, 3501 S. Sheridan, Tulsa, OK 74145.

Outer Banks Discount Marine Outfitters, P.O. Drawer 500, Beaufort, NC 28516. Saltwater lures, attractors.

Pennsylvania Outdoor Warehouse, 1508 Memorial Ave., Williamsport, PA 17701. Fly-fishing tackle.

Boyd Pfeiffer's Tackle Crafters, 14303 Robcaste Rd., Phoenix, MD 21131.

Reed's, P.O. Box 490, Walker, MN 56484.

The River's Edge, 2012 N. 7th Ave., Bozeman, MT 59715. Fly-fishing tackle.

Rivers Edge Trading Company, Jct. Rtes. 125 & 111A, Brentwood, NH 03833.

Sportsman's Supplies, 2929 South Ave., Toledo, OH 43609. Molds, hooks, line, lure kits, etc.

Streamside Anglers, P.O. Box 2158, Missoula, MT 59801. Fly-fishing tackle.

Stump-Knocker Tackle Distributors, 300 N. 34th St., Decatur, IL 62521. Carbonyte floats, etc.

The Surfcaster, 113 Maywood Rd., Darien, CT 06820.

The Tackle Shop, Box 369, Richardson, TX 75080.

Terminal Tackle Co., Box 427, Kings Park, NY 11754.

Toledo Tackle Factory Outlet, P.O. Box 5, Minden, LA 71058.

Umpqua Feather Merchants, P.O. Box 700, Glide, OR 97443. Flies.

Westbank Anglers, P.O. Box 523, Teton Village, WY 83025. Flies.

West Falmouth Tackle, P.O. Box 873, West Falmouth, MA 02574.

World Wide Outfitters, 425 College Ave., Santa Rosa, CA 95401. Leaders, hooks, etc.

World Wide Sportsman, P.O. Box 787, Islamorada, FL 33036. Saltwater tackle.

Yellowstone Angler, P.O. Box 660, Livingston, MT 59047. Hot Butt fly-fishing leaders.

TACKLE MANUFACTURERS, DISTRIBUTORS, JOBBERS

Sometimes, when you can't find a particular kind of tackle in the shops or mail-order catalogs, you have to go right to the source: the manufacturer, importer, distributor, or jobber. Many of these companies have catalogs, and most of them will sell to you directly, if you can't find a retail outlet; the others should be willing to let you know where you can buy their merchandise. Some of these companies are set up to handle retail mail-order trade, but most aren't. So don't count on fast service, especially not during those seasons when they are shipping dealer orders or preparing for the trade shows. In other words, best go right to the horse's mouth only as a last resort.

If the entry isn't followed by an indication of what the company makes and sells, either it offers a fairly full spectrum of terminal tackle or its name tells you what its business is.

A & S Custom Lures, 14342 Victory Blvd., Van Nuys, CA 91401. Baja Bigeye jet lures.

Abu Garcia, Inc., 21 Law Dr., Fairfield, NJ 07006. Line.

Accardo Tackle Co., 3708 Conrad Dr., Baton Rouge, LA 70805. Lures, line.

Tony Accetta & Son, Inc., 932 Ave. E, Riviera Beach, FL 33404. Lures.

Acme Tackle Co., 69 Bucklin St., Providence, RI 02907. Lures.

Action Lure Co., P.O. Box 10529, Jackson, MS 39209.

Advanced Lure, Inc., 139 N. Eisenhower Lane, Lombard, IL 60148. Phosphorescent plastic worms, Lazerlures.

Aftco Manufacturing Co., 17351 Murphy Ave., Irvine, CA 92714. Roller-Troller line-release clip.

Airlite Plastics Co., 914 N. 18th, Omaha, NE 68102. Floats.

Al's Goldfish Lure Co., P.O. Box 13, Indian Orchard, MA 01151.

Ament Mold Co., 402 Capelle, Grain Valley, MO 64029.

American Cyanamid Co., 1 Cyanamid Pl., Wayne, NJ 07470. Lightsticks, light-emitting lures.

American Fishing Wire, 205 Carter Dr., West Chester, PA 19380.

Ande, Inc., 1310 53rd St., West Palm Beach, FL 33407. Line.

Angler Lure, Inc., 115 E. Illinois Ave., Carterville, IL 62918.

Angler Products, Inc., 210 Spring St., Butler, PA 16001. Stink baits, salmon eggs, etc.

Angler's Pride/Crankbait Co. *See* Luhr Jensen & Sons, Inc.

Aqua-Clear Products, 314 Cherry Rd., Atco, NJ 08004. Rigs.

Araty USA, Inc., 44 Sunset Ave., Old Saybrook, CT 06475. Line.

Fred Arbogast Co., 313 W. North St., Akron, OH 44303. Lures, etc.

Area Rule Engineering, 32232 Azores Rd., Laguna Niguel, CA 92677. Doorknob offshore lures.

Arkie Lures, Inc., P.O. Box 1460, Springdale, AR 72764.

Ashaway Line & Twine Mfg. Co., Laurel St., Ashaway, RI 02804.

Atlas Bait Co., P.O. Box 1, Fort Atkinson, WI 53538. Salmon eggs, bait.

Atom Manufacturing Co., Box 45, South Attleboro, MA 02703. Lures.

Jim Bagley Bait Co., P.O. Drawer 110, Winter Haven, FL 33882. Lures, line.

Barracuda Jigs. See Dura-Pak Corp.

Bass Buster Lures. See Johnson Fishing, Inc.

Bass Hunter Lures, Inc., R.R. 1, Box 193, Yorktown, IN 47396.

Bass Unltd. Lure Co., 620 Monroe St., Beatrice, NE 68310.

Bay de Noc Lure Co., Box 71, Gladstone, MI 49837.

Bead Tackle Co., P.O. Box K, Bridgeport, CT 06605. Bead Chain swivels, Bridgeport diamond jigs, etc.

Bear Paw Tackle Co., Inc., P.O. Box 355, Bellaire, MI 49615. Lures, rigs, knotless connectors, hones, etc.

Berkley, Inc., One Berkley Dr., Spirit Lake, IA 51360. Line, leaders, snaps, swivels, rigs, scents.

Betts Tackle, Ltd., P.O. Box 57, Fuquay-Varina, NC 27526. Lures.

Big Jon, Inc., 14393 Peninsula Dr., Traverse City, MI 49684. Trolling lures, line-release clips.

Bingo Bait Co., P.O. Box 30093, Houston, TX 77249.

Black Marine Products, P.O. Box 1137, Homestead, FL 33090. Line-release clips.

Blakemore Sales Corp., P.O. Box 1149, Branson, MO 65616. Road Runner lures.

Blue Fox Tackle Co., 645 N. Emerson, Cambridge, MN 55008. Lures, scents.

Bomber Bait Co., P.O. Box 1058, Gainesville, TX 76240. Lures.

Boone Co., P.O. Box 4009, Winter Park, FL 32793. Lures, attractors, hooks, floats.

Braid Products, Ltd., P.O. Box 1305, Woodland Hills, CA 91364. Lures.

Brawley Lures, 1450 Carpenter Ln., Suite A, Modesto, CA 95357.

Bremer Mfg. Co., Box 548, Elkhart Lake, WI 53020. Line-release clips.

Charlie Brewer's Slider Co., P.O. Box 130, Lawrenceburg, TN 38464. Crappie lures.

Brothers Bait Co., P.O. Box 24078, Lexington, KY 40524. Lures.

Brown Bear Bait Co., 2100 E. Ohio St., Pittsburgh, PA 15212. Stink baits, salmon eggs, lures.

Buchertail, P.O. Box 276, Boulder Junction, WI 54512. Hooks, lures.

Buck Stop Lure Co., 3600 Grow Rd. N.W., Stanton, MI 48888. Scents.

Bullet Weights, Inc., P.O. Box 187, Alda, NE 68810.

Bumble Bee Bait Co., P.O. Box 1169, Mountain Home, AR 72653. Lures.

Burke Fishing Lures, P.O. Box 72, Traverse City, MI 49684.

C & H Custom Lures, 142 Mill Creek Rd., Jacksonville, FL 32211. Offshore lures, lure-making & rigging tackle.

California Tackle Co., 17100 Keegan Ave., Carson, CA 90746. Sea Strike lures.

Phil Camera, P.O. Box 4031, Woodland Park, CO 80866. Leader lead.

Cannon/S & K Products, Inc., 1732 Glade St., Muskegon, MI 49441. Line-release clips.

Canyon Lures, Inc., 2465 Northern Ave., Kingman, AZ 86401.

Catchit USA, 750 Bryant St., San Francisco, CA 94107. Artificial bait.

Charlie's Wonderworm Co., 7001 Orchard Lake Rd., West Bloomfield, MI 48033.

Jack Chancellor Lure Co., P.O. Box 1608, Phenix City, AL 36867.

Lew Childre & Sons, P.O. Box 535, Foley, AL 36536. Speed Sticker worm hooks.

Chum-It, 12892 Western Ave., Garden Grove, CA 92641. Scents.

Cisco Kid Tackle, Inc., 2630 N.W. First Ave., Boca Raton, FL 33432. Lures.

Citation Tackle Co., P.O. Box 39, Boston, GA 31626. Lures.

Classic Manufacturing Co., P.O. Box 1249, Clermont, FL 32711. Culprit lures.

C-Lite Industries, Inc., 4800 No. 3 Rd., Suite 224, Richmond, B.C. V6X 3A6, Canada. Lures.

The Color Box, Inc., P.O. Box 800036, Houston, TX 77280. Lure paints.

Columbia/Bruin, P.O. Box G, Columbia, AL 36319.

Comet Co., P.O. Box 329, Greentown, OH 44630. Lures.

Allen Comstock's Cable Rigs, 2521½ South Vista Way #85, Oceanside, CA 92054.

H. C. Cook Co., P.O. Box 1886, Venice, FL 34284. Hook hones, tools.

Cotton Cordell Tackle. *See* Plastics Research & Development Corp.

Cortland Line Co., P.O. Box 5588, Cortland, NY 13045. Line, leaders, etc.

Cossack Caviar, Inc., 101 S. Dakota St., Seattle, WA 98134. Salmon eggs, stink baits, etc.

Cottee Industries, 537 E. Oakridge Ave., New Port Richey, FL 33552. Lures, pliers, etc.

Creative Lures, Inc., P.O. Box 391029, Solon, OH 44139.

Creek Chub Bait Co. *See* Dura-Pak Corp.

Creme Lure Co., P.O. Box 87, Tyler, TX 75710.

C. S. & Son Fishing Lure, Inc., P.O. Box 1022, Miami, FL 33156. Offshore lures.

Custom Jigs & Spins, Inc., 1504 Highwood, Pekin, IL 61554.

Custom Mounts International, Inc., P.O. Box 7081, Warwick, RI 02887. Smoker Baits offshore lures.

Les Davis, P.O. Box 297, Hood River, OR 97031. Lures, attractors, planers, line, etc.

Den Manufacturing Co., 1406 16th St., Racine, WI 53403. Lures, snubbers.

Ditto Manufacturing, Inc., Airport Industrial Park, Bay 13-3, Palatka, FL 32077. Gator Tails, plastic worms.

DMT Inc., 85 Hayes Memorial Dr., Marlborough, MA 01752. Hook hones.

Doel-Fin, Inc., 25570 Rye Canyon Rd., Unit L, Valencia, CA 91355. Fish Seeker planer.

Do-It Corp., 501 N. State St., Denver, IA 50622. Jig and sinker molds.

Donnmar Enterprises, 2700 N.W. 185th Ave., Portland, OR 97229. Hook sharpener.

The Dragon Fly Co., P.O. Drawer 1349, Sumter, SC 29150. Lures, rigs, etc.

Dry Dock Tackle Corp., R.R. 1, Wall Lake, IA 51466. Lures, scents.

Du-Bro Products, 480 Bonner Rd., Wauconda, IL 60084. Wire and knot tools.

The Du Pont Co., Wilmington, DE 19898. Stren, Stren Class, and Prime lines.

Dura-Pak Corp., P.O. Box 1173, Sioux City, IA 51102. Lures, etc.

Durafloat Sports Pliers, P.O. Box 6494, Denver, CO 80206.

Eagle Claw Tackle. *See* Wright & McGill Co.

Eatumup Lure Co., 506-D Edwardia Dr., Greensboro, NC 27409. Saltwater lures.

Eppinger Manufacturing, 6340 Schaefer Hwy., Dearborn, MI 48126. Daredevle lures, etc.

Erie Dearie Lure Co., 2252 Greenville Rd., Cortland, OH 44410.

ESA, Inc., P.O. Box CC, Deer Park, NY 11729. Striker brand tackle.

Glen L. Evans. *See* Luhr Jensen & Sons.

Eze-Lap Diamond Sharpeners, 15164 Westate St., Westminster, CA 92683.

Fair Waters Co., Rte. 2, Box 281K, Fairhope, AL 36532. Lures.

Al Feather's Custom-made Fishing Products, 78-05 Springfield Blvd., Bayside, NY 11364. Lures.

Fin Baits. *See* Fred Arbogast Co.

FisHair, Inc., 1484 W. County Rd. C, St. Paul, MN 55113. Lure- and fly-tying nylon fibers.

Fishie Tackle Co., 2540 Morningside Dr., West Columbia, SC 29169.

The Fishin' Worm Co., 5512 S. Florida Ave., Lakeland, FL 33803.

The Fish Monger, P.O. Box 5286, Lake Worth, FL 33466. Hook-disgorger.

Fishtec, Inc., 101 John Roberts Rd. #19, South Portland, ME 04106. Sue Burgess fly lines, leaders, etc.

Fleck Lure Co., P.O. Box 715, Marlboro, MA 01752.

Flitz International, Ltd., 821 Mohr Ave., Waterford, WI 53185. Metal polish.

FMF Tackle, Ltd., 2 Bell Walk, The Brewery Yard, Reigate, Surrey, England RH2 7BF. Flies, hooks.

Bob Folder Lures, R.R. 2, Springfield, IL 62707.

Frontier Distributors, 20880 Raddison Rd., Excelsior, MN 55331. Hide-A-Hook rigging tool.

The Gaines Co., Box 35, Gaines, PA 16921. Lures.

Gapen's World of Fishin', Inc., Big Lake, MN 55309. Lures, Bait-Walker sinkers, etc.

Garland Lures, 502 Topeka St., Kingman, AZ 86401.

Gladding Fishing Line Division, Gladding Cordage Co., P.O. Box 164, South Otselic, NY 13155.

Go-Getter Manufacturing Co., P.O. Box 992, Parksville, B.C. V0R 2S0, Canada. Line-release clips.

Gopher Tackle Mfg. Co., Rte. 3, Box 45B, Aitkin, MN 56431. Lures.

Grand Lake Tackle Co., Box 185, Grand Lake, CO 80447. Super bait hooks.

Grape, Inc., 431 State Ave., Owatonna, MN 55060. Lures.

Green Point Lures, P.O. Box 474, Cortland, OH 44410.

Grizzly Tackle. *See* Dura-Pak Corp.

Gudebrod, Inc., P.O. Box 357, Pottstown, PA 19464. Line, lures.

H & H Lure Co., 10874 N. Duval St., Baton Rouge, LA 70814.

Hankie Lures, 2 Germantown Rd., Danbury, CT 06810.

Harrison-Hoge Industries, Inc., P.O. Box 944, Smithtown, NY 11787. Panther Martin, Super Frog, other lures.

Hart Tackle Co., 300 W. Main, Stratford, OK 74872. Lures, rigs.

James Heddon's Sons. *See* Plastics Research & Development Corp.

Helin Tackle Co., 8824 Shoal Creek Blvd., Austin, TX 78758. (805 Front Rd., Windsor, Ont., N9J 2A4 Canada.) Flatfish lures.

Highland Enterprises, Star Rte. Box 24, Kane, PA 16735. Hooks.

High-Tech Tackle, 3030 Emmons Ave., Brooklyn, NY 11235. Jenkai line.

John J. Hildebrandt Corp., P.O. Box 50, Logansport, IN 46947. Lures.

Hilts Mold & Mfg., Inc., 422 N. Valley St., Burbank, CA 91502.

Hi-Seas Industries, Inc., 325 Spring St., New York, NY 10013. Regal line, swivels, etc.

Hopkins Fishing Lures Co., 1130 Boissevain Ave., Norfolk, VA 23507.

Hubs-Chub, R.R. 2, Box 259A, Sheridan, IN 46069. Lures.

Hudson Tackle Co., P.O. Box 437, Kearney, NJ 07032. Rigs.

L. B. Huntington Co., Luce Creek Dr., Annapolis, MD 21401. Drone lures.

Hunton Offshore Lures, P.O. Box 844, Abingdon, MD 21009.

Industrial Grain Products, Inc., P.O. Box 3520, Lubbock, TX 79452. Chum.

International Hairgoods, 6811 Flying Cloud Dr., Eden Prairie, MN 55344. Hairabou & Flashabou synthetic fibers.

Invader Downriggers/K-Line Industries, 315 Garden Ave., Holland, MI 49424. Gator line-release clips.

ITX Inc., P.O. Box 39A78, Los Angeles, CA 90039. Siglon line.

Izorline International/Sufix USA, Inc., 813 Gardena Blvd., Gardena, CA 90247. Line, lures.

Luhr Jensen & Sons, Inc., P.O. Box 297, Hood River, OR 97031. Lures, attractors, etc.

J & L Tool & Machine, Inc., P.O. Box 367, Shelbyville, IN 46176. Jigs, hook sharpeners.

J & S Lures, 3921 Starwood St., West Valley City, UT 84120.

Jeros Tackle Co., 37 Hayward Ave., Carteret, NJ 07008.

J-Mar Enterprises, P.O. Box 1070, Melbourne, FL 32902. Line-release clips.

Johnson Fishing, Inc., 1531 Madison Avenue, Mankato, MN 56001. Silver Minnow, Bass Buster lures, scents.

Keeper Bait Co., 107 Allen St., Bruceton, TN 38317. Scents, lures.

Knight Manufacturing Co., P.O. Box 6162, Tyler, TX 75711. Tube worms, lures.

KR Spinnerbaits, 126 Ave. Algodon #B, San Clemente, CA 92672.

Kwikfish Lures, Ltd., 3440 Wyandotte St., E., Windsor, Ont. N8Y 1G1, Canada. (Kwikfish Lures, Inc., Ren Cen Sta., P.O. Box 43014, Detroit, MI 48243.)

L & S Bait Co., 1500 E. Bay Dr., Largo, FL 33540. MirrOlures.

Lakes Systems Divn., 315 E. South St., Mt. Vernon, MO 65712. Color-C-Lector, pH monitors, etc.

Gene Larew Tackle, Inc., 11 E. Commercial, Inola, OK 74036. Lures, baits.

Lash Lure, Inc., 3524C Colony Rd., Charlotte, NC 28211.

Lazy Ike Lures. *See* Dura-Pak Corp.

L.C.D. American, Inc., 232 N.E. Lincoln, Suite B-3, Hillsboro, OR 97124. Line Sickle tool.

LC's Lures, P.O. Drawer S, Corbin, KY 40701.

Bill Lewis Lures, P.O. Box 4062, Alexandria, LA 71301.

Lil' Hustler Tackle Co., P.O. Box 19957, Oklahoma City, OK 73144. Lures.

Lindy-Little Joe, Inc., Box C, Brainerd, MN 56401. Lures, rigs, hooks, etc.

Liquid Lure, Inc., 5150 S. Memorial Dr., Suite D, Tulsa, OK 74145. Scents.

Lit'l Buffalo Bait Co., Rte. 1, Box 22, Mineola, TX 75773. Lures.

Little Dixie Flies, 3801 Eminence Ave., Berkeley, MO 63134.

Lobo Tackle, 247 Gardner Rd., Hubbardston, MA 01452. Lures.

Lucky's Bait Mfg. Co., 5641 Grove St. N.E., Louisville, OH 44641. Lures.

LumaLure Manufacturing, Inc., 4403 Russell Rd., Lynnwood, WA 98037. Lures, light-emitting attractors.

Lurco, 2210 Wilshire Blvd. #389, Santa Monica, CA 90403. Tornado offshore lures.

M & M Tackle, Inc., P.O. Box 2154, Hyannis, MA 02601. Spreader-bar trolling rigs.

Mac-Jac Manufacturing Co., P.O. Box 821, Muskegon, MI 49443. Line-release clips.

Mainliner Lures, 4653 Fennessy Dr. S.W., Grand Rapids, MI 49504.

Mako Engineering, 4900 W. Washington Blvd., Los Angeles, CA 90016. Jet lures.

Mann's Bait Co., P.O. Box 604, Eufaula, AL 36027. Lures.

Marathon Tackle. *See* Dura-Pak Corp.

Martin Tackle & Mfg. Co., 3822 Latona Ave N.E., Seattle, WA 98105. Lures, etc.

Mason Tackle Co., P.O. Box 56, Otisville, MS 48463. Line, leaders, etc.

Maxima/Jatra International, 5 Chrysler St., Irvine, CA 92718. Line.

Mepps Lures. *See* Sheldon's, Inc.

Metalcrafts, Inc., 27770 S.W. Parkway Ave., Wilsonville, OR 97070. Li'l Mac sinker molds.

Mister Twister, Inc., P.O. Drawer 996, Minden, LA 71055. Lures, hooks, sinkers, rigs.

Mold Craft, Inc., 501 N.E. 28th St., Pompano Beach, FL 33064. Soft Head offshore lures, attractors, rigs, etc.

Mother of Pearl, 8617 Mayland Dr., Suite 919, Richmond, VA 23229. Offshore lures.

Mowatt Sporting Goods, P.O. Box 158, Brewer, ME 04412. Foggy Mountain scents & lures.

Murray Brothers Sportfishing Supply, 207 E. Blue Heron Blvd., Riviera Beach, FL 33404. Saltwater lures, attractors, line, etc.

O. Mustad & Son (USA) Inc., Box 838, Auburn, NY 13021. Hooks, etc.

F. J. Neil Co., P.O. Box 617, Lindenhurst, NY 11757. Dolphin brand tackle.

Nekton Corp., 21-S Olympia Ave., Woburn, MA 01801. Z-Wing planer.

Carl W. Newell Mfg. Co., 940 Allen Ave., Glendale, CA 91201. Lures, floats, etc.

No-Alibi Corp., P.O. Box 3664, West Palm Beach, FL 33402. Lures.

Bill Norman Lures, P.O. Box 580, Greenwood, AR 72936.

Normark Corp., 1710 E. 78th St., Minneapolis, MN 55423. Rapala lures, etc.

Northland Tackle Co., 3709 Mill St., N.E., Bemidji, MN 56601. Lures.

Oberlin Canteen Co., P.O. Box 208, Oberlin, OH 44074. Rigs, sinkers.

Offshore Lures, 5733 La Jolla Blvd. #7, La Jolla, CA 92037.

Opitz Lures, 285 Hagan Pl., Secaucus, NJ 07094.

The Orvis Company, Manchester Center, VT 05254. Fly-fishing and ultralight spinning tackle.

Outdoor Enterprises, Inc., 347 S. Market, Opelousas, LA 70570. Decalure attractors.

Ozark Mountain Tackle Co., 2231 Missouri Ave., Carthage, MO 64836. Woodchopper lures.

Pacific Atlantic Products, Ltd., 395 S. Pitcher St., Kalamazoo, MI 49007. Lures, Walker line-release clips.

C. Palmer Manufacturing Co., P.O. Box 220, West Newton, PA 15089. Jig, sinker, and lure molds.

Palsa Outdoor Products, P.O. Box 81336, Lincoln, NE 68501. Lures, floats.

Penn Fishing Tackle Mfg. Co., 3028 W. Hunting Park Ave., Philadelphia, PA 19132. Line-release clips.

Perfection Tip/Hank Roberts, 4550 Jackson St., Denver, CO 80216. Flies.

Pflueger Fishing Tackle, P.O. Drawer S, Columbia, SC 29260. Line.

Pharmacist Formula, Inc., 1228 S.E. Harlow St., Troutdale, OR 97060. Scents, lures, baits.

Phillips Fly & Tackle Co. *See* The Gaines Co.

PICO Lures, Inc., P.O. Box 17687, San Antonio, TX 78217.

The Pilot House, P.O. Box 155, Dover, MA 02030. Pointmatic hook sharpener.

Pisces Corp., P.O. Box 610, Lexington, OK 73051. Lures.

Plastics Research & Development Corp., 3601 Jenny Lind Dr., Fort Smith, AR 72901. Cotton Cordell, Heddon, Rebel lures.

Plastilite Corp., P.O. Box 12457, Omaha, NE 68112. Floats.

Pompanette, Inc., 190 Bryan Rd., Dania, FL 33004. Snaps, swivels, teasers, etc.

Prescott Spinner Co. *See* Fred Arbogast Co.

Producto Lure Co., 590 Rinehart Rd., Lake Mary, FL 32746. Lures, scents.

Profi-Blinker GMBH, Artilleriestrasse 15, D-5000, Cologne 90, West Germany. Lures, line, wire line, attractors.

Pro Line Lure Co., 3490 Democrat Rd., Memphis, TN 38118.

PTC, Inc., 1102 E. Michigan, Kalamazoo, MI 49001. Lures.

Quadrum Corp., 333 Cobalt Way, Suite 107, Sunnyvale, CA 94086. Delta-Glo planer, light-emitting attractors.

Queen City Tackle Co./Weezel Bait Co., P.O. Box 44246, Cincinnati, OH 45244. Lures.

Rabble Rouser Lures, 1831 E. High Ave., New Philadelphia, OH 44663.

Rainbow Plastics Co., P.O. Box 1861, Fort Collins, CO 80526. Floats, trolls, lures, sinkers.

Razor Edge Systems, Inc., P.O. Box 150, Ely, MN 55731. Hook sharpeners.

Rebel Lures. *See* Plastics Research & Development Corp.

Red Eye Tackle Co., 6619 Oak Orchard Rd., Elba, NY 14058. Lures.

Riviera Marine and Tackle Co., 3859 Roger B. Chaffee Blvd., Grand Rapids, MI 49508. Line-release clips.

RLM-sales, P.O. Box 69, Tualatin, OR 97062. Sinker molds.

Rodon Manufacturing Co., 123 Sylvan Ave., Newark, NJ 07104. Fly lines.

Walt Rogers, 2803 Homedale Rd., Klamath Falls, OR 97603. Bingo Bug lures.

L. J. Roemer Mfg. Co., 27 Forgham Rd., Rochester, NY 14616. Liberator line-release clip.

Rick Rose Custom Lures of Hawaii, P.O. Box 2384, Orange, CA 92689.

S & G Tackle Co., 1775 E. 48th St., Brooklyn, NY 11234. Lures.

Sampo Division, Rome Specialty Co., Inc., P.O. Box 328, Barneveld, NY 13304. Swivels, snaps.

Bob Schneider, Inc., 1125 Old Dixie Hwy., Lake Park, FL 33403. Lures.

Scientific Anglers/3M Company, 3M Center, Bldg. 223-5, St. Paul, MN 55101. Fly line, leaders.

Scotty Downriggers, P.O. Box 991, Lafayette, CA 94549. Line-release clips.

Scrounger Lures, 417 W. Walnut, Gardena, CA 92048.

Sea Rock Lures, 65 Bethpage Rd., Copiague, NY 11726. Saltwater lures.

Seneca Tackle Co., P.O. Box 2841, Elmwood Sta., Providence, RI 02907. Lures.

Sevenstrand Tackle Corp., 5401 McFadden Ave., Huntington Beach, CA 92649. Lures, wire, lines & leaders, crimping sleeves & tools.

Shadow Lake Lures, Box 757, Marion, IL 62959.

Shakespeare Fishing Tackle Divn., Drawer S, Columbia, SC 29260. Sigma line.

Shamrock Flies/Umpqua Feather Merchants, Inc., P.O. Box 700, Glide, OR 97443. Flies, hooks, leaders, etc.

M. Sharf & Co., Inc., P.O. Box 527, Canton, MA 02021. Line, fly line, hooks, flies, lures.

Sheldon's, Inc., 626 Center St., Antigo, WI 54409. Mepps lures.

Lee Sisson Lures, Inc., Box 666, Auburndale, FL 33823.

Smith & Associates, 321 Enterprise Dr., Ocoee, FL 32761. Triple Fish Perlon line.

Smithwick Lures, P.O. Box 1205, Shreveport, LA 71163. Devil's Horse & Rattlin'Rogue lures.

Snag Proof, 11387 Deerfield Rd., Cincinnati, OH 45242. Lures, scents.

South Bend Tackle. *See* Luhr Jensen & Sons, Inc.

Southern Pro Lures, Highway 49 N, Brookland, AR 72417.

South Port Divn., C & J Manufacturing, P.O. Box 5117, North Muskegon, MI 49445. Lures.

Sports Resources Co., P.O. Box 3730, Kent, WA 98032. Gamakatsu hooks.

Squidco Corp. of America, P.O. Box 13665, San Diego, CA 92113. Saltwater lures.

Stanley Jigs, Inc., P.O. Box 722, Huntington, TX 75949.

Storm Mfg. Co., P.O. Box 265, Norman, OK 73070. Lures.

Streamlife Innovations, P.O. Box 266, Hailey, ID 83333. Climax line and leaders.

Strike King Lure Co., 174 Highway 72 W., Collierville, TN 38017.

Strike Master, Inc., 411 N. Washington Ave., Minneapolis, MN 54401.

Sunrise International, 71 Lake Rd., Calcutta, India 700 029. Flies, etc.

T's Bass Lures, Inc., 7 Timothy Ln., Somerset, KY 42501.

The Testor Corp., Fisherman's Edge Divn., 620 Buckbee St., Rockford, IL 61108. Lure paint pens.

Texas Tackle Products, P.O. Box 834306, Richardson TX 75083. Point Maker hook sharpener.

Thomas & Thomas, P.O. Box 32, Turners Falls, MA 01376. Fly-fishing tackle.

Tomic Lures, Ltd., P.O. Box 550, Sooke, B.C. V0S 1N0, Canada.

Tournament Tackle, Inc., P.O. Box 2820, Satellite Beach, FL 32937. Iland offshore lures.

Trawlite Co., P.O. Box 791, Gloversville, NY 12078.

Tru-Turn, Inc., P.O. Drawer 767, Wetumpka, AL 36092. Hooks.

Uncle Josh Bait Co., P.O. Box 130, Fort Atkinson, WI 53538. Pork rind, stink baits, lures, etc.

Uncle Meek's Co., P.O. Box 323, Collinsville, IL 62234. Lures.

Upper Midwest Marketing, Box 411, Dodge Center, MN 55927. Lures.

U.S. Fly Tiers, c/o Robert Markowski, P.O. Box 4374, Harrisburg, PA 17111.

VMC, Inc., 1901 Oakcrest Ave., Suite 1, St. Paul, MN 55431. Hooks.

Vortex Lures, 640 W. Montana, Kalispell, MT 59901.

Water Gremlin Co., 4370 Otter Lake Rd., White Bear Lake, MN 55110. Sinkers.

The Weller Co., P.O. Box 784, Duluth, MN 55801. Line, leaders, rigs, lures.

Whizkers Fishing System, P.O. Box 837, Minden, LA 71055. Lures, scents.

Whopper Stopper/Fliptail, *See* Plastics Research & Development Corp.

Wille Products Co., P.O. Box 532, Brookfield, WI 53005. Line-release clips.

Williams Sporting Goods Intl., 30 Courtwright St., Fort Erie, Ont. L2A 2R7, Canada. Lures.

Wilson-Allen Corp., Box 64, Windsor, MO 65360. Hooks, snaps, eyelets, etc.

Witchcraft Tape Products, P.O. Box 937, Coloma, MI 49038. Attractors.

Woodstream/Canada, Niagara Falls, Ont. L2E 6T3, Canada. HTM line.

Worden's Lures. *See* Yakima Bait Co.

World Craftsmen, 222 W. Adams St., Suite 725, Chicago, IL 60606. Flies.

The Worth Co., P.O. Box 88, Stevens Point, WI 54481.

Wright & McGill Co., P.O. Box 16011, Denver, CO 80216. Eagle Claw hooks, leaders, rigs.

Joan & Lee Wulff, Inc., Box 14A, Lew Beach, NY 12753. Flies, fly line.

Wye Mountain Wildlife Products, Inc., 1 Trapper Trail, Bigelow, AR 72016. Scents, stinkbaits, etc.

Yakima Bait Co., P.O. Box 310, Granger, WA 98932. Lures, attractors, line.

Zetabait Co., P.O. Box 7985, Jacksonville, FL 32210. Lures.

Zuker's, P.O. Box 1192, Oceanside, CA 92054. Offshore lures.

Appendix C:
Fish Temperature Chart

IN CHAPTERS 5 AND 8, I made much of the importance of fishing at the proper depth, and that translates into fishing in water that's the right temperature. Each species of fish has its own preferences and requirements when it comes to water temperature. Mostly it's a matter of physical comfort, but sometimes fish will venture into water that's a bit warmer or cooler than ordinary because of changes in dissolved oxygen or in pursuit of a favored or abundant forage species. Generally, though, if you know what water temperature a species of fish prefers, you know how deep to fish for it. If you use a thermometer of some sort, you can determine precisely the right depth for a given temperature, and therefore for a given species. Otherwise, you might have to experiment until you come up with the winning combination of water depth and temperature.

Most of the time, bodies of water are stratified into three layers. The upper layer, or epilimnion, is a reasonably broad band of warm water that is heated by the sun. The lowermost layer, or hypolimnion, is right on the bottom or is so deep as to be little affected by the sun's radiation. In very deep lakes, the hypolimnion may extend upward a considerable distance from the bottom. In between these warm and cold layers of fairly uniform temperature is a relatively thin band called the thermocline, which is a transitional zone of rapid temperature change. In the

451

thermocline, water temperature changes at least half a degree per foot of depth. The species anglers care about are usually found patrolling their preferred temperatures in the thermocline.

Currents, springs, stream inflows, and other factors may complicate the picture in any body of water, so that classic thermal stratification may not exist. And, early each spring and late each fall, most ponds and lakes "turn over," producing a brief period when water temperatures are almost uniform from top to bottom. This phenomenon is caused by the changeover from winter to summer conditions. During the winter, surface waters are typically colder than deeper waters, especially in frigid northern climes. Winter water temperatures may range from 32 degrees Fahrenheit just below the ice to about 39.2 degrees at the bottom.

The situation gets even murkier when you consider that ongoing ichthyological research is constantly turning up new information on water-temperature preferences, and that scientists working with different populations of the same fish species don't always come up with the same results. But common sense ought to tell you that largemouth bass in an Alabama lake are probably used to warmer temperatures than the bigmouths that live in the Saint Lawrence River between New York State and Ontario. I don't know of anyone who does a better job of keeping tabs on the situation than *Fishing World* magazine, which publishes an updated chart of preferred water temperatures. Editor Keith Gardner was kind enough to grant permission to reprint his magazine's most current chart:

FISHING WORLD'S FISH TEMPERATURE CHART

SPECIES	LOWER AVOIDANCE	OPTIMUM	UPPER AVOIDANCE
Freshwater Gamefish			
American Shad (*Alosa sapidissima*)	66°	86°	
Atlantic Salmon (*Salmo salar*)		62°	
Atlantic Sturgeon (*Acipenser oxyrhynchus*)	56°	66°	70°
Black Crappie (*Pomoxis nigromaculatus*)	60°	70°	75°
Bloater (*Coregonus hoyi*)	43°		50°

SPECIES	LOWER AVOIDANCE	OPTIMUM	UPPER AVOIDANCE
Bluegill *(Lepomis macrochirus)*	58°	60°–70°	75°
Brook Trout *(Salvelinus fontinalis)*	44°	58°	70°
Brown Bullhead *(Ictalurus nebulosus)*		74°	
Brown Trout *(Salmo trutta)*	44°	56°–65°	75°
Buffalo Species *(Ictiobus spp.)*	81°		94°
Burbot *(Lota lota maculosa)*		52°	
Carp *(Cyprinus carpio)*	75°	84°	88°
Chain Pickerel *(Esox niger)*	60°	66°	74°
Channel Catfish *(Ictalurus punctatus)*	55°	82°–89°	
Chinook Salmon *(Oncorhynchus tshawytscha)*	44°	54°	60°
Chum Salmon *(Oncorhynchus keta)*		57°	
Cisco *(Coregonus artedii)*		52°–55°	
Coho Salmon *(Oncorhynchus kisutch)*	44°	54°	60°
Flathead Catfish *(Pylodictus olivaris)*	81°		90°
Freshwater Drum *(Aplodinotus grunniens)*		74°	
Grass Pickerel *(Esox americanus vermiculatus)*		78°	
Grayling *(Thymallus thymallus)*			64°
Green Sunfish *(Lepomis cyanellus)*	73°	87°	91°
Goldeye *(Hiodon alosoides)*	72°		83°
Kamloops Trout *(Salmo gairdneri)*	46°	47°–54°	
Kokanee *(Oncorhynchus nerka)*		52°–55°	

SPECIES	LOWER AVOIDANCE	OPTIMUM	UPPER AVOIDANCE
Lake Trout *(Salvelinus namaycush)*	42°	46°–52°	
Lake Whitefish *(Coregonus clupeaformis)*	43°	51°	
Landlocked Atlantic Salmon *(Salmo salar sebago)*		50°–55°	65°
Largemouth Bass *(Micropterus salmoides)*	50°	65°–75°	85°
Longnose Gar *(Lepisosteus osseus)*		92°	
Longnose Sucker *(Catostomus catostomus)*		53°	
Mooneye *(Hiodon tergisus)*	72°		81°
Muskellunge *(Esox masquinongy)*	55°	63°	72°
Northern Pike *(Esox lucius)*	56°	63°	74°
Pink Salmon *(Oncorhynchus gorbuscha)*		49°	
Pumpkinseed *(Lepomis gibbosus)*		82°	
Rainbow Trout *(Salmo gairdneri)*	44°	54°	75°
Redhorse Suckers *(Moxostoma spp.)*	72°		79°
Rock Bass *(Ambloplites rupestris)*		70°	
Round Whitefish *(Prosopium cylindraceum)*		63°	
Sauger *(Stizostedion canadense)*	55°	67°	74°
Shortnose Gar *(Lepisosteus platostomus)*	81°		94°
Smallmouth Bass *(Micropterus dolomieui)*	60°	65°–68°	73°
Sockeye Salmon *(Oncorhynchus nerka)*		55°	
Spotted Bass *(Micropterus punctulatus)*	60°	75°	80°
Steelhead Trout *(Salmo gairdneri)*	38°	48°–52°	

SPECIES	LOWER AVOIDANCE	OPTIMUM	UPPER AVOIDANCE
Sunfishes (Centrarchidae)	50°	58°	68°
Tench (*Tinca tinca*)			79°
Walleye (*Stizostedion vitreum*)	50°	67°	76°
White Bass (*Morone chrysops*)	62°	70°	78°
White Crappie (*Pomoxis annularis*)		61°	
White Perch (*Morone americana*)		75°	
White Sucker (*Catostomus commersoni*)		72°	
Yellow Bass (*Morone mississippiensis*)		81°	
Yellow Bullhead (*Ictalurus natalis*)		83°	
Yellow Perch (*Perca flavescens*)	58°	68°	74°

Saltwater Gamefish

SPECIES	LOWER AVOIDANCE	OPTIMUM	UPPER AVOIDANCE
Albacore (*Thunnus alalunga*)	59°	64°	66°
Amberjack (*Seriola dumerili*)	60°	65°	72°
Atlantic Bonito (*Sarda sarda*)	60°	64°	80°
Atlantic Cod (*Gadus morhua*)	31°	44°–49°	59°
Atlantic Croaker (*Micropogon undulatus*)			100°
Atlantic Mackerel (*Scomber scombrus*)		46°	
Barracuda (*Sphyraena barracuda*)	60°	75°	82°
Bigeye Tuna (*Thunnus obesus*)	52°	58°	66°
Blackfin Tuna (*Thunnus atlanticus*)	70°	74°	82°
Black Marlin (*Makaira indica*)	68°	75°–79°	87°

SPECIES	LOWER AVOIDANCE	OPTIMUM	UPPER AVOIDANCE
Bluefin Tuna *(Thunnus thynnus)*	50°	68°	78°
Bluefish *(Pomatomus saltatrix)*	50°	68°	84°
Blue Marlin *(Makaira nigricans)*	70°	78°	88°
Bonefish *(Albula vulpes)*	60°	75°	93°
Crevalle Jack *(Caranx hippos)*	70°		90°
Dolphin *(Coryphaena hippurus)*	70°	75°	82°
Fluke or Summer Flounder *(Paralichthys dentatus)*	56°	66°	72°
Haddock *(Melanogrammus aeglefinus)*	36°	47°	52°
Horn Shark *(Heterodontus francisci)*		75°	
Kelp Bass *(Paralabrax clathratus)*	62°	65°	72°
King Mackerel *(Scomberomorus cavalla)*	70°	75°	88°
Opaleye *(Girella nigricans)*		79°	86°
Permit *(Trachinotus falcatus)*	65°	72°	92°
Pollock *(Pollachius virens)*		45°	60°
Pompano *(Trachinotus carolinus)*		77°	
Red Drum *(Sciaenops ocellata)*	52°	71°	90°+
Red Snapper *(Lutjanus campechanus)*	50°	57°	62°
Sailfish *(Istiophorus platypterus)*	70°	79°	82°
Sand Seatrout *(Cynoscion arenarius)*	90°	95°	104°
Sea Catfish *(Arius felis)*			99°
Skipjack Tuna *(Euthynnus pelamis)*	65°	73°	82°

SPECIES	LOWER AVOIDANCE	OPTIMUM	UPPER AVOIDANCE
Snook *(Centropomus undecimalis)*	60°	70°–75°	90°
Spotted Seatrout *(Cynoscion nebulosus)*	48°	72°	81°
Striped Bass *(Morone saxatilis)*	54°	60°–70°	77°
Striped Marlin *(Tetrapturus audax)*	61°	70°	80°
Swordfish *(Xiphias gladius)*	50°	58°	68°
Tarpon *(Megalops atlantica)*	74°	76°	100°+
Tautog *(Tautoga onitis)*	60°	70°	76°
Wahoo *(Acanthocybium solanderi)*		70°–86°	
Weakfish *(Cynoscion regalis)*		55°–65°	78°
White Marlin *(Tetrapturus albidus)*	65°	70°–80°	
White Seabass *(Cynoscion nobilis)*	58°	68°	74°
Winter Flounder *(Pseudopleuronectes americanus)*	35°	48°–52°	64°
Yellowfin Tuna *(Thunnus albacares)*	64°	72°	80°
Yellowtail *(Seriola dorsalis)*	60°	65°	70°

Freshwater Baitfish

SPECIES	LOWER AVOIDANCE	OPTIMUM	UPPER AVOIDANCE
Alewife *(Alosa pseudoharengus)*	48°	54°	72°
Bitterling *(Rhodeus sericeus)*		77°	
Bluehead Chub *(Nocomis leptocephalus)*	50°	59°	63°
Bluntnose Minnow *(Pimephales notatus)*	70°	84°	88°
Emerald Shiner *(Notropis atherinoides)*	61°		
Fathead Minnow *(Pimephales promelas)*	77°	84°	90°

SPECIES	LOWER AVOIDANCE	OPTIMUM	UPPER AVOIDANCE
Fourhorn Sculpin (*Myoxcephalus quadricornis*)	39°		
Gizzard Shad (*Dorosoma cepedianum*)	69°		
Golden Shiner (*Notemigonus crysoleucas*)		70°	
Goldfish (*Carassius auratus*)		77°	
Guppy (*Poecilia reticulata*)		84°	
Lake Chub (*Couesius plumbeus*)		48°–52°	
Longjaw Mudsucker (*Gillichthys mirabilis*)	48°	72°	
Moapa Dace (*Moapa coriacea*)		85°	
Mosquitofish (*Gambusia affinis*)		81°	85°
Mottled Sculpin (*Cottus bairdi*)		48°–52°	
Mozambique Mouthbrooder (*Tilapia mossambica*)		83°	92°
Nine-Spine Stickleback (*Pungitius pungitius*)		48°–52°	
Quillback (*Carpiodes cyprinus*)		72°	
Rainbow Smelt (*Osmerus mordax*)	43°	50°	57°
River Carpsucker (*Carpiodes carpio*)	79°		94°
Rosyface Shiner (*Notropis rubellus*)	70°	80°	88°
Slimy Sculpin (*Cottus cognatus*)	39°		43°
Spotfin Shiner (*Notropis spilopterus*)	79°	85°	95°
Spottail Shiner (*Notropis hudsonius*)		54°	
Stonecat (*Notorus flavus*)		59°	
Stoneroller (*Campostoma anomalum*)	75°	84°	91°

SPECIES	LOWER AVOIDANCE	OPTIMUM	UPPER AVOIDANCE
Trout-Perch *(Percopsis omiscomaycus)*	50°		61°
White River Killifish *(Crenichthys baileyi)*		85°	
Saltwater Baitfish			
Atlantic Silverside *(Menidia menidia)*			90°
Atlantic Threadfin *(Polydactylus octonemus)*			92°
Bay Anchovy *(Anchoa mitchilli)*		82°	92°
California Grunion *(Leuresthes tenuis)*	68°	77°	93°
Gulf Grunion *(Leuresthes sardina)*	68°	89°	98°
Gulf Menhaden *(Brevoortia patronus)*			86°
Pacific Silversides SUCH AS JACKSMELT AND TOPSMELT *(Atherinopsis spp.)*	72°		84°
Rough Silverside *(Membras martinica)*			91°
Skipjack Herring *(Alosa chrysochloris)*	72°		84°
Spot *(Leiostomus xanthuras)*			99°
Tidewater Silverside *(Menidia beryllina)*			93°

Reprinted by permission. ©1987 *Fishing World*.

Shark fishermen are probably amused that only the horn shark, a West Coast species, is listed in *Fishing World*'s chart. As fish go, sharks aren't very well understood by scientists, who find them difficult and expensive—and sometimes even dangerous—to study. Naturally, each of the two hundred or so species of sharks has its own water-temperature needs and preferences, but only a few dozen shark species are actively sought by sportfishermen. Frank T. Moss, who knows as much about saltwater fishing as almost anyone alive, has written that most sharks prefer temperatures in the range of 50 to 80 degrees Fahrenheit, with 70 or more degrees considered optimum. Among the sharks most often pursued by anglers, whites and porbeagles lean toward cooler waters, while tigers are more likely to be found in warmer waters. Makos, blues, and hammerheads mostly occupy the intermediate temperatures. But, as it is with almost everything else about sharks, exceptions are to be routinely expected.

As water pollution, habitat destruction, and fishing pressure continue to make fishing more difficult, anglers who know temperature preferences and who use thermometers to select their fishing depths will probably experience better fishing than most. And it won't be a matter of luck.

INDEX